Grounds of Judgment

OXFORD STUDIES IN INTERNATIONAL HISTORY

JAMES J. SHEEHAN, SERIES ADVISOR

The Wilsonian Moment
Self-Determination and the International Origins of Anticolonial Nationalism
Erez Manela

In War's Wake
Europe's Displaced Persons in the Postwar Order
Gerard Daniel Cohen

Grounds of Judgment
Extraterritoriality and Imperial Power in Nineteenth-Century China and Japan
Pär Kristoffer Cassel

Grounds of Judgment

*Extraterritoriality and Imperial Power
in Nineteenth-Century China and Japan*

PÄR KRISTOFFER CASSEL

OXFORD
UNIVERSITY PRESS

Oxford University Press, Inc., publishes works that further
Oxford University's objective of excellence
in research, scholarship, and education.

Oxford   New York
Auckland   Cape Town   Dar es Salaam   Hong Kong   Karachi
Kuala Lumpur   Madrid   Melbourne   Mexico City   Nairobi
New Delhi   Shanghai   Taipei   Toronto

With offices in
Argentina   Austria   Brazil   Chile   Czech Republic   France   Greece
Guatemala   Hungary   Italy   Japan   Poland   Portugal   Singapore
South Korea   Switzerland   Thailand   Turkey   Ukraine   Vietnam

Copyright © 2012 by Oxford University Press, Inc.

Published by Oxford University Press, Inc.
198 Madison Avenue, New York, NY 10016

www.oup.com

Oxford is a registered trademark of Oxford University Press

All rights reserved. No part of this publication may be reproduced,
stored in a retrieval system, or transmitted, in any form or by any means,
electronic, mechanical, photocopying, recording, or otherwise,
without the prior permission of Oxford University Press.

Library of Congress Cataloging-in-Publication Data
Cassel, Pär Kristoffer.
Grounds of judgment : extraterritoriality and imperial power
in nineteenth-century China and Japan / Pär Kristoffer Cassel.
p.   cm.—(Oxford studies in international history)
Includes bibliographical references and index.
ISBN 978-0-19-979205-4
1. Capitulations—China—History—19th century.
2. Capitulations—Japan—History—19th century.
3. Exterritoriality—China—History—19th century.
4. Exterritoriality—Japan—History—19th century.
5. Europeans—Legal status, laws, etc.—China—History—19th century.
6. Americans—Legal status, laws, etc.—China—History—19th century.
7. Europeans—Legal status, laws, etc.—Japan—History—19th century.
8. Americans—Legal status, laws, etc.—Japan—History—19th century. I. Title.
KNC127.C37   2011
341.4'2—dc23   2011019517

1 3 5 7 9 8 6 4 2

Printed in the United States of America
on acid-free paper

Den här boken tillägnas min morfar Gustaf Ranhagen, som gav mig mod att studera främmande språk och fick mig att påbörja min långa resa till fjärran länder.

CONTENTS

Acknowledgments ix

Introduction 3

1. Excavating Extraterritoriality: The Legacies of Legal Pluralism, Subjecthood, and State-Building in China and Japan 15

2. Codifying Extraterritoriality: The Chinese "Unequal Treaties" 39

3. Institutionalizing Extraterritoriality: The Mixed Court and the British Supreme Court in Shanghai 63

4. Exporting Extraterritoriality: The Evolution of Jurisdiction over Foreigners in Japan from the "Expulsion Edict" to the Sino-Japanese Treaty of Tianjin 85

5. Executing Extraterritoriality: Sino-Japanese Cases, 1870–95 115

6. Expelling Extraterritoriality: Treaty Revision in Meiji Japan and Qing China, 1860–1912 149

Conclusion 179

Glossary of Chinese and Japanese Terms 187
Notes 197
Bibliography 231
Index 251

ACKNOWLEDGMENTS

Like many other academic works, this book started as a dissertation, but it is the product of a much longer intellectual trajectory. My love of language and history were two of the reasons why I chose to study Chinese, Japanese, and East Asian history in the first place. My interest in law goes back to my days as an undergraduate, when I applied and was admitted to the Law School at the University of Stockholm. However, I was also awarded a Swedish-Chinese government scholarship to study Chinese history at Nanjing University, so I chose to turn down the offer of Law School and go to China instead. During my year in Nanjing, I became fascinated with the history of the city, where the Manchu Qing dynasty, Chinese nationalism, and Japanese imperialism have left indelible traces. After finishing my undergraduate degree, I worked as an assistant sinologist at the Embassy of Sweden in Beijing, and assisting in the visa section of the embassy opened my eyes to the vagaries of citizenship and nationality laws. My brief stint in government service convinced me that I belonged in academe, and I accepted a Japanese government Monbusho scholarship to study Japanese history in Kanazawa in Japan, where I was finally able to improve my Japanese and consider different graduate programs.

It was in graduate school at Harvard University that I was finally able to combine my interests in a dissertation topic. The idea to draw a parallel between the Qing legal order and consular jurisdiction occurred to me in a conversation with Izumi Nakayama at the Harvard-Yenching Library early in 2001. My advisor, Philip Kuhn, encouraged me to write a seminar paper on the topic of extraterritoriality and publish it as an article in *Late Imperial China*. (Part of this article is republished in chapters 1 and 2 in this book with the kind permission of Johns Hopkins University Press.) While I was writing the seminar paper, my Manchu teacher, Mark C. Elliott, generously shared his yet unpublished manuscript with me, which helped me to develop my ideas on ethnic relations in the Qing. Dani Botsman also gave me important feedback on the Japanese aspects of my project.

The Harvard Merit Fellowship and funding from the Reischauer Institute and the Urban China Research Network made it possible for me to explore my ideas on location in China and Japan. When I was a visiting scholar at Tokyo University in 2003, Kishimoto Mio generously welcomed me into her graduate seminar and gave me important feedback on my research. During my stay at Renmin University in 2004, Zhang Shiming was my cicerone into the world of Chinese archives, and Ding Yizhuang at the Chinese Academy of Social Sciences was a source of inspiration and encouragement. During the writing of the dissertation, the Weatherhead Center for International Affairs kindly provided me with an office and resources to complete my project. William Alford and Andrew Gordon read my dissertation in its entirety and provided valuable advice.

My colleagues and friends in the Department of History at the University of Michigan have been of tremendous support. Miranda Brown, Christian de Pee, James Lee, and Leslie Pincus read my manuscript at an early stage and gave valuable comments. Joshua Fogel and Melissa Macauley kindly accepted my invitation to be discussants at my manuscript workshop in April 2009, during which Micah Auerback, C. S Chang, Geoff Eley, Dario Gaggio, Nico Howson, Doug Northrop, Brian Porter-Szűcs, Hitomi Tonomura, Tom Trautmann, Yiching Wu, and many others gave me important feedback. During the workshop, Christian de Pee suggested a new title for the book, *Grounds of Judgment*, which I gratefully adopted for my manuscript. During my stint at Stockholm University, I discussed my work with Joakim Enwall, Fredrik Fällman, Marja Kaikkonen, Johan Lagerkvist, Börje Ljunggren, Torbjörn Lodén, Jan Romgard, and Li Silfverberg. At conferences and many other occasions, I have had the benefit of discussing my book project and sharing ideas with Jennifer Altehenger, Aglaia de Angeli, Cemil Aydin, David Bello, Robert Bickers, Bettine Birge, Jérôme Bourgon, Tom Buoye, Carolyn Cartier, Chen Li, Yung-chen Chiang, Grace Chou, Juan Cole, Frédéric Constant, Pamela Crossley, Evan Dawley, Charles Desnoyers, Kevin Doak, Fabian Drixler, Lane Earns, Cord Eberspächer, Johan Elverskog, Edward Farmer, Douglas Fix, Carol Gluck, Whit Gray, Robert Hellyer, Denise Ho, Richard Horowitz, Doug Howland, Ying Hu, Akira Iriye, Yonglin Jiang, Noriko Kamachi, Jaymin Kim, Loretta Kim, Konrad Lawson, Eugenia Lean, Scott Levi, Adam McKeown, Jonathan Lipman, Y. W. Mah, Victor Mair, Brett McCormick, Erling von Mende, James Millward, Micah Muscolino, Matthew Mosca, Klaus Mühlhahn, Max Oidtman, Peter Perdue, Anne Reinhardt, Jennifer Rudolph, Teemu Ruskola, Andreas Siegl, Shao Dan, Matthew Sommer, Mark Swislocki, Ronald Toby, Shirley Ye, Ernest Young, Madeleine Zelin, Lawrence Zhang, and many, many others.

I am deeply grateful to Jeffrey Wasserstrom, who introduced me to Susan Ferber at Oxford University Press. She has been a terrific editor and gave me crucial feedback that helped me make my manuscript into a publishable book.

My two anonymous readers helped me to think about how to frame my project and gave many important suggestions for improvements. I want to express my gratitude to my parents, Jan and Åsa, and my brother, Carl, for their support and for visiting me in different corners of the world. Finally, I wish to thank my wife, Liang Luo, and our daughter, Ingrid, for their love and their patience with me when I was working on this project all these years.

Grounds of Judgment

Introduction

> Owing to difference of Opinion between the Swedish Consul and myself as to certain Points of Law (Swedish); I now beg to inform the Public of Shanghai that I have withdrawn from the protection and jurisdiction of the SWEDISH CONSULATE, and placed myself voluntarily under the protection and Laws of the Land that we live in.

On 29 October 1877, Swedish businessman Nils Möller placed the above "Public Notice" on the pages of the *North China Daily News*. In the preceding days, Möller had been sued in the Swedish-Norwegian consulate for damage to a cargo of seaweed that had been shipped from Hakodate to the busy port of Shanghai. The ship in question was registered as British, but it was chartered by a Chinese merchant, and its captain was Danish. The buyer of the seaweed and the plaintiff in the case was a German, who claimed that Möller was the agent of the ship and thus liable for the damages to the cargo. The consul trying the case was Frank B. Forbes, an American businessman whom the Swedish foreign ministry had appointed consul general of Sweden and Norway and who thus held jurisdiction over Swedish and Norwegian subjects in the treaty port of Shanghai.

Möller did not accept that the Swedish-Norwegian consul general held jurisdiction over a case that centered on a British-registered ship. Consequently, he refused to appear as a sworn-in defendant in the consular court, but attended the hearings only in order to answer simple questions of a factual nature. When Forbes declared to the courtroom that he accepted jurisdiction over the case, Möller "demanded in language more forcible than polite that his name be erased from the register of Swedish subjects."[1] Having heard all witnesses to the case, Forbes dismissed the case on account of the fact that the damage to the cargo had been caused by inclement weather, but this failed to soothe the feelings of Möller, who published his declaration in *North China Daily News* the following day. In so doing, he had effectively renounced his Swedish citizenship for the purposes of consular jurisdiction and submitted himself to the jurisdiction of the Mixed Court in Shanghai, which tried Chinese residents of the International Settlement as well as foreigners who were not represented by consuls.

To contemporary Western observers, it was ridiculous for a European to voluntarily submit himself to the laws and jurisdiction of the country he happened to live in—the Qing Empire. Möller persisted in refusing the protection of the consulate, and when he made news in the Shanghai press some fourteen years later, one anonymous commentator scorned him for "deliberately lowe[ring] himself to the legal status of a shroff or a coolie."[2] Möller, on the other hand, proudly regarded himself as a "citizen of Shanghai," took exception to the assertion that "all natives of this country" belonged to the class of "shroffs and coolies," and defended his decision to withdraw from the protections of the Swedish consul, as he "considered that neither a man's time nor money were safe under such jurisdiction."[3]

Möller's case speaks volumes about the distance foreign residents in Shanghai were expected to maintain between themselves and the Chinese population of the city, and the peer pressure that faced any foreigner who dared to break the mold by even distantly associating himself with the local legal system. The episode also betrays the acute sense of indeterminacy that surrounded one of the most maligned institutions of nineteenth-century East Asia, an institution that was supposed to give foreigners a privileged status: extraterritoriality.

In the decades preceding the Möller case, gunboats from a number of Western nations had forced Qing China and Tokugawa Japan to open new ports for trade with their merchants. The Qing Empire concluded its first two treaties with the British Empire in 1842–43, followed by the United States and France the next year. In the following two decades, the Qing Empire would conclude a slew of treaties with other nations and colonial empires, eager to avail themselves of the same privileges as the Great Powers. In the 1850s, American gunboats prompted Japan to enter into agreements that were similar to those that the Qing Empire had concluded, and only twenty years later, Japan pioneered the "opening" of Chosŏn Korea by imposing its own commercial treaty on the "Hermit Kingdom," followed by the Qing Empire, the United States, Britain, France, and a number of Western countries in subsequent years.[4] Anyone who wanted to understand the complexities of the new diplomatic order in East Asia had to understand law and had to engage in intricate legal texts, which were sometimes the product of the whim of a diplomat, sometimes the outcome of protracted negotiations and careful deliberations.

The commercial treaties opened a series of coastal ports for trade with Western merchants and laid down regulations for the conduct of trade. They allowed Western consular agents to reside in the new ports, where they could communicate directly with local authorities, and established fixed rates for the tariffs that local authorities could levy on merchandise traded in the ports. Wherever a military conflict had occurred, the commercial treaties regulated the cessation of hostilities and payment of indemnities. Most important, the treaties established a legal régime for foreign sojourners and subjected them to the jurisdiction of their own consuls. This practice soon emerged as one of the most controversial aspects of the "treaty port system." Over time, the arrangement came to be known sometimes as extraterritoriality, sometimes as consular jurisdiction.[5] Most treaties were not symmetric, which meant that East Asian sojourners in Europe or North America could not expect to enjoy the same privileged status Westerners were granted in East Asia. As a result, these "unequal treaties" became a target of rising nationalist propaganda in the late nineteenth and early twentieth centuries.

The original treaty stipulations regarding jurisdiction over aliens were usually rather vague, merely establishing the basic principle that foreigners who committed crimes in the treaty ports, or were involved in criminal and civil suits, were to be tried by officials appointed by their home government. Western diplomats justified this concession on the grounds that East Asian penal and legal practices—such as torture and the practice of corporeal punishment—were not suited to Europeans.[6] Yet over time, consular jurisdiction developed into a practice that granted most foreigners nearly complete immunity from both local laws and jurisdiction. These privileges often went far beyond the legal immunities that diplomatic personnel typically enjoy under international law.

Although most treaties contained very similar clauses on foreign jurisdiction, extraterritoriality would follow very different trajectories in the different East Asian countries where it was practiced. In Japan, the conclusion of the treaties in the 1850s was followed by drastic régime change a decade later, often called the "Meiji restoration"; extraterritoriality, as well as the entire set of "unequal treaties," were abolished in less than fifty years and replaced by reciprocal arrangements that closely followed European standards.[7] In Korea, the extraterritorial privileges of Westerners, Japanese, and Chinese were soon overshadowed by the ascendance of direct Japanese imperialism after 1895, and the Siamese government was finally able to abolish consular jurisdiction in the 1920s.

In China, on the other hand, extraterritoriality endured for exactly one hundred years, and in the 1920s, China stood virtually alone in having a full-fledged extraterritorial legal order. When the treaty port system reached its apogee in the early twentieth century, there were no fewer than ninety-two treaty ports in China, in addition to several leased territories, extensive Christian missionary activities, economic and strategic spheres of influence, foreign-controlled railroads, and mines.[8] Practically any interaction between foreigners and native populations could be "extraterritorialized." The foreigner not only carried his own laws and institutions into the host country, but the nebulous idea of "foreign interests" meant that almost anything a foreigner was involved with had an extraterritorial aspect.[9] Yet extraterritoriality was far from a coherent legal order that was simply implanted from the outside. In the most important treaty port, Shanghai, a large number of different consular courts coexisted, which often competed for jurisdiction and sometimes did not even cooperate with each other.[10] This allowed foreign and native vagrants to evade jurisdiction by claiming different nationalities according to circumstances.[11]

Far from being a *system*, in the sense of a planned and orderly arrangement, extraterritoriality is better regarded as a *practice*, which evolved and took shape in contact with a legally pluralistic environment. Further complicating the problem was the fact that most "unequal treaties" contained most-favored-nation clauses, which in theory meant that any treaty power could claim privileges conceded to any other nation. However, the extent to which extraterritorial privileges were covered by most-favored-nation clauses is a complicated question and depended on the actual wording of the article in the relevant treaty. In the British and American construct, extraterritorial privileges were not covered by the most-favored-nation arrangement, whereas in the French construct they were. Indeed the legal scholar Georges Soulié de Morant identified no fewer than five different constructs of the arrangement, which illustrates that the treaty port system was very far from being a monolith.[12]

By the 1920s, the entire corpus of commercial treaties with China had attained such an extraordinary degree of complexity that even accomplished international lawyers complained that it was difficult to say with certainty exactly what China's treaty obligations were, and scholars still argue over exactly how many unequal treaties China signed during the "Century of Humiliations."[13] The complexity of the treaty port system intruded on everyday life in a variety of ways. The quaint anomalies of the system ranked high among the things first time foreign visitors to the major treaty port of Shanghai had to acquaint themselves with. A guidebook from 1934, for example, pointed out that whereas eastbound traffic on Avenue Edward VII was subject to the traffic rules of the International Settlement, westbound traffic on the very same road were subject to the regulations of the French Concession.[14] Yet this extraordinary development was not originally spelled out in the treaties and could hardly have been foreseen by either of the contracting parties when the first commercial treaty was concluded in 1842.

Given the obviously "foreign" nature of extraterritoriality, it is easy to lose sight of the equally obvious fact that the history of extraterritoriality in East Asia can teach us just as much about the nature of colonial forms of law as it can about indigenous legal systems and the trajectories of state-building in the region. It was one thing to force or intimidate Asian officials into signing a treaty that ceded jurisdiction over foreigners; it was quite another to devise a new legal order that would work for both native and foreign merchants once the gunboats had left the shores of East China Sea for more pressing imperial tasks elsewhere.[15] The British may have been able to enshrine the English versions of the treaties as the legally binding ones,[16] but in actual fact the treaties had to work in more than one language. In the mid-nineteenth century, very few officials in East Asia had even a rudimentary understanding of English or French, and a lot of correspondence between diplomats and officials had to be conducted in the local language, or through an intermediary language such as Dutch. Whereas the Japanese government trained officials who were able to negotiate with the foreign powers in English after the Meiji restoration in 1868, Qing officials insisted on using Chinese in their diplomatic correspondence for most of the nineteenth century.[17] As the Qing Empire and Meiji Japan concluded a treaty in 1871 that granted Chinese and Japanese extraterritorial privileges in each other's countries, this "linguistic hegemony" of the Chinese meant that classical Chinese had to convey the concepts of extraterritorial jurisdiction in correspondence between Chinese and Japanese officials. However, the Japanese had developed their own varieties of classical Chinese over the centuries and also used Chinese characters to assimilate Western legal concepts, so Japanese officials did not always understand the terms of traditional Chinese legal language. Qing officials were equally puzzled by the way their Japanese counterparts used Chinese characters. Getting a better grasp on how extraterritorial jurisdiction was understood by Chinese and Japanese requires attention to how their native legal orders operated, how they used language and terminology, and how this changed over time. Extraterritoriality was not only a product of the encounter between the "East" and the "West" but also the result of a complex and triangular relationship between China, Japan, and the Western powers.

Indeed, the "unequal treaties" were not concluded in a vacuum, but in polities that had their own legal orders with long histories of engagement with the outside world and with conflicts over jurisdiction. When the Manchus established the Qing Empire in the early seventeenth century, they not only inherited the edifice of the Chinese legal tradition from the Ming dynasty, they also brought their own indigenous legal tradition and the Mongol legal tradition. When the Manchu emperors expanded their empire west into Central Asia and established both direct and indirect rule in these regions, they encountered a number of different legal traditions with which they had to establish a new modus vivendi. As the Manchus confronted the expanding Romanov Empire in Siberia, they chose to define their relations in a number of formal treaties beginning in 1689, aided by Jesuit missionaries.[18] Japan's relative geographical isolation created a different trajectory. The Tokugawa state, the dominant polity on the Japanese archipelago from the seventeenth through the nineteenth centuries, had to contend with a number of smaller territorial states, and the legal order was thus considerably fragmented. At the fringes of the Tokugawa order, local lords maintained their own forms of foreign relations with Chosŏn Korea, which carefully avoided any violation of contemporary standards of tributary protocol.[19]

The contentious question of extraterritoriality and foreign jurisdiction needs to be understood within this context of competing institutions and legal orders. Every new legal instrument had to be reconciled within the framework of the existing legal structures, and any attempt to challenge or renegotiate these treaties posed new challenges to the existing legal order. Scholars of premodern Asia and early modern Europe have pointed out that imperial and royal sovereigns usually claimed sovereignty over people rather than over territories, and the shift from sovereignty over people to exclusive sovereignty over territories is intimately connected to projects of state-building and the emergence of the centralized nation-state.[20] In order to fully understand how extraterritoriality operated within the native legal order, it is necessary to look beyond the modern concept of exclusive territorial sovereignty, not only because it is a product of the modern nation-state and thus ill suited to describe the legal realities of nineteenth-century East Asia but also because any narrative that is based on the idea of modern state sovereignty will privilege current nation-states at the expense of other historical state formations in the region.

One of the most fruitful ways of approaching the question of foreign jurisdiction and its relationship to state-building is by employing the concept of legal pluralism. This concept was first developed by legal scholars and judges who were studying the legal order in colonial settings, where European settlers established a dual legal system, one for the native population and one for Europeans.[21] In order to determine what constituted local law, anthropologists and other social scientists were sent to collect and identify local customs in order to set up "native courts" for native populations, a process that inevitably involved the invention of local legal traditions. One of the most prominent examples of these efforts is the compilation of customary law (*adat*) in the Dutch East Indies.[22] Following decolonization after World War II, the concept of legal pluralism widened. Instead of assuming that uniform territorial jurisdiction is the norm for all societies, anthropologists have claimed that almost any social order evinces some degree of legal pluralism.[23] The advantage of this approach is that it moves the focus away from the state as the supreme law-making and law-enforcing agency and toward different forms of law made in local communities. For instance, anthropologists studying Brazilian shantytowns have observed how the *favelados* have "created their own legality" in the absence of effectively administered justice by the state. Those researching the legal order in Papua New Guinea have found that village courts there "replicate state structures."[24]

Although anthropologists studying China have generally not used the term "legal pluralism" explicitly,[25] scholars have pointed out that nongovernmental institutions such as common descent groups did exercise important legal functions, and that local contractual practices created a legality that ran parallel to the formal state apparatus.[26]

While such a wide definition of legal pluralism may be a suitable framework for an anthropologist or sociologist, who collects research data through interviews and surveys, it can be unwieldy and difficult for the historian, who often must use primary sources that are generated through the state. In order to bring about some coherence to an increasingly confusing field of inquiry, some scholars have suggested that a distinction be made between legal pluralism in a "juristic" and a "social" sense.[27] According to anthropologist Sally Merry, a "legal system is pluralistic in the juristic sense when the sovereign commands different bodies of law for different groups of the population varying by ethnicity, religion, nationality, or geography, and when the parallel legal régimes are all dependent on the state legal system."[28]

The concept of "classical" legal pluralism in its juristic sense is a fruitful way to analyze how the legal orders of Qing China and Tokugawa Japan were renegotiated and reshaped by the introduction of extraterritoriality in the nineteenth century. This approach bridges national histories and brings the long nineteenth century back to the core of historical inquiry in East Asia. One corollary of legal pluralism is the inclination of the legal order to rule over persons rather than territories, often called "personal jurisdiction," which is the governing principle of all extraterritorial régimes.[29] Personal jurisdiction has prevailed in many premodern legal orders and often coexisted with forms of territorial jurisdiction. In premodern state formations, which did not claim or were unable to exercise exclusive territorial jurisdiction, personal jurisdiction was most problematic when the plaintiff and the defendant in a given lawsuit belonged to two different jurisdictions, so-called mixed cases. In such cases, the competent authorities had to negotiate rules to decide which agency or agencies should assume jurisdiction and what body of law should determine the outcome of the case. In order to prevent too many mixed cases from occurring, the authorities often implemented systems of residential segregation. By contrast, modern nation-states usually claim jurisdiction in all cases that occur with their territorial boundaries, especially in criminal matters, whereas the law applied can vary in civil and commercial cases. Indeed, the idea that the law follows the person remains an important element in the field of family law. The fact that national authorities in Europe claim jurisdiction in so-called honor killings within immigrant communities is another contemporary example of how the modern nation-state asserts legal sovereignty in cases where a premodern legal régime would not necessarily have insisted on criminal jurisdiction.[30]

While the invocation of unequal power relationships in the nineteenth century might explain why one party managed to force its will on another, it cannot adequately account for the conditions under which cooperation between two governments took place in such a complex legal order as extraterritoriality. Here the use or threat of force might explain *why* extraterritoriality was introduced in China, but not *how* it worked or why it endured for so long. As historian John King Fairbank pointed out in relation to the establishment of the international settlement in Shanghai:

> the British could force their way into the power structure of China's composite ruling class and in time play a part in the government of the empire. But they could do this only with Chinese help, only by making a mutual accommodation with the ruling establishment, and only so long as the Chinese populace was not mobilized against them by modern nationalist sentiment.[31]

It is far too simplistic to reduce the problem of extraterritoriality to a simple power relationship. Indeed, Qing policy-makers sometimes chose to go to war over ostensibly smaller issues, such as the residence of foreign diplomats in Beijing,[32] while they did not challenge extraterritorial institutions, even when there was little risk involved. For instance, when the Japanese government managed to convince British diplomats to prohibit Britons from running Japanese-language newspapers in Japan, the Qing government did not avail itself of the opportunity to do the same to the lively Chinese-language press in Shanghai, even though it was certainly aware of the Japanese precedent.[33]

One of the most puzzling aspects of the Chinese encounter with extraterritoriality is the fact that the topic seems not to have attracted the attention of Chinese writers until the late nineteenth century. The famous drug czar Lin Zexu confronted the British on the question of criminal jurisdiction in 1839–40, but after the defeat of the Qing Empire in the Opium War, there is very little evidence that a debate on foreign jurisdiction took place in China, either in official circles or among private scholars.[34] In a magisterial work on the momentous Treaty of Nanjing, historian Guo Weidong failed to find a single instance of resistance to extraterritoriality prior to 1868, the year when senior Manchu statesman Wenxiang suggested to the British diplomat Sir Rutherford Alcock that the Qing Empire might be willing to allow Britons to reside in the interior of China, if the British government gave up the privilege of extraterritoriality.[35] Even after that date, for most of the nineteenth century, there is little evidence that the Qing government ever made a concerted effort to abolish extraterritoriality.[36] The only evidence of resistance to the practice consists of scattered remarks by astute observers both outside and inside the government, such as the scholar

Wang Tao.[37] Confronted with the alleged Chinese failure to tackle extraterritoriality, most writers have concluded that Qing officials were ignorant of international law in general and extraterritoriality in particular.[38] This is seen as a reflection of the corrupt Qing dynasty and its inept Manchu officials, often symbolized by the affable nobleman Qiying, who negotiated most of the early treaties with the West. However, this simplistic portrayal is belied by the fact that Qing officials—both Manchu and Chinese—spelled out on several occasions the acceptable limits for foreign legal privilege, declarations that are not easily framed by modern concepts such as territorial sovereignty. For instance, while Qing policy-makers generally accepted that foreigners were under the jurisdiction of their own consuls, they consistently resisted any extension of such privileges to Chinese subjects. As early as 1844, the Manchu statesman Qiying agreed to persuade his government to rescind the ban on Christianity, on the condition that this should not be used as an excuse to extend extraterritorial privileges to Chinese.[39]

Needless to say, China's "failure" and Japan's "success" in abolishing extraterritoriality cannot be reduced to a single, monocausal explanation. Using the concept of legal pluralism, however, will shed new light on how and why extraterritoriality penetrated the Chinese legal order far more deeply than its Japanese counterpart. Foreign models certainly mattered in the evolution of extraterritoriality in East Asia, but established practices such as extraterritoritial privileges in the Ottoman capitulations or the piecemeal adoption of international law cannot fully account for the way the practices of extraterritoriality developed in East Asia. Nowhere is this clearer than in the case of Sino-Japanese relations. As the central chapters of this book demonstrate, extraterritoriality was a defining feature in the encounter between the Qing Empire and Meiji Japan. The single largest community that enjoyed extraterritorial privileges in Japan before 1895 was the Chinese one, which was much more influenced by its own native legal order than by Western precedents when it conceptualized extraterritorial privileges. This crucial period in Sino-Japanese relations from 1871—when the first Sino-Japanese treaty was concluded—to 1895 forces a rethinking not only of the nature of extraterritoriality but also of Sino-Japanese history in the latter half of the nineteenth century that has been completely overshadowed by the Japanese victory in the Sino-Japanese war in 1895.[40]

It is a central argument of this book that extraterritoriality and the treaty port system can only be properly understood within a larger framework of international history, which is why I have deliberately avoided some teleological assumptions of postcolonial discourse, which tend to privilege current nation-states at the expense of alternative narratives.[41] In the totality of the interactions between the Qing Empire and the Tokugawa state on one hand and their neighbors on the other, there is no reason why first Western, and later

Japanese, intervention in East Asia should be considered more "imperial" or "colonial" than the actions of other empires in the region. It is true that the treaty port century integrated China into what in retrospect looks like the "discursive hegemony" of national sovereignty and international law, but many of those concepts cut both ways. At the same time that the British Empire and other colonial powers set up extraterritorial enclaves in the Eastern seaboard of China, the imperial powers propped up the Qing Empire for most of the nineteenth century and recognized its claims on its territories in Central Asia right up to the fall of the dynasty. Furthermore, Qing statesmen were discussing and tentatively executing rather ambitious projects of internal colonization in the Western parts of the empire.

The chapters that follow will employ the concept of legal pluralism to explore the question of extraterritoriality in order to trace the trajectories of state-making and modern citizenship in China and Japan. Prior to the Opium Wars in the mid-nineteenth century, both Qing China and Tokugawa Japan were familiar with the principle of personal jurisdiction and the fact that some ethnic and social groups had separate legal existences prior to the Opium War. In the Qing legal order, the Manchu conquest elite enjoyed extensive legal privileges, which placed them outside the criminal jurisdiction of the local Chinese administration. Similarly, the Tokugawa shogunate was accustomed to devolving jurisdiction to local domains and different status groups. The fact that the Tokugawa order collapsed in 1867 whereas the Qing dynasty did not collapse until 1911 would have momentous consequences for the implementation of consular jurisdiction in the two countries. Chapters 2 and 3 chart the evolution of jurisdiction over foreigners in Qing China from the late nineteenth century through the Sino-British "Chefoo Convention" of 1876, which was the last British treaty to deal with extraterritoriality to any large extent before the turn of the century. Prior to the Opium War, the Qing Empire granted foreigners far more legal autonomy than the contemporary Ottoman Empire did under the "Capitulations," a series of treaties between the Sublime Porte and Western nations, which were concluded from the sixteenth through the early nineteenth centuries. Chapter 3 follows the institutionalization of consular jurisdiction after the Opium War, with a special focus on the Mixed Court and British Supreme Court in Shanghai, which were established in the 1860s in order to resolve criminal and civil cases between Britons, Chinese, and other nationalities. Comparing the Chinese version of treaty texts with other legal sources shows that Qing officials borrowed and adapted long-standing Sino-Manchu legal concepts and institutions when they accepted and cooperated in the establishment of these courts.

Chapter 4 explores the evolution of jurisdiction over foreigners in Japan from the promulgation of the "expulsion edict" in 1825 through the conclusion of the Sino-Japanese Treaty of Tianjin in 1871, a neglected chapter in Sino-Japanese relations. I compare the extraterritorial arrangements in the "Ansei Treaties," which Japan concluded with Western powers in 1854–58, with the corresponding arrangements in the Sino-Japanese Treaty of Tianjin. The extraterritorial arrangements in the Treaty of Tianjin were informed by the Chinese experience of legal pluralism, which stood in sharp contrast to the lack of reciprocity in the Qing Empire's relations with the Western treaty powers. Since there were far more Chinese in Japan than there were Japanese in China prior to 1895, the Treaty of Tianjin had a much greater impact in Japan than in China. In effect, the treaty amounted to an extension of the Qing legal order into Japan, which chapter 5 demonstrates by analyzing a series of criminal cases in China and Japan, most of which were prosecuted under the Treaty of Tianjin. Qing statesmen were quite successful in exporting their understanding of consular jurisdiction into Japan; they were not particularly impressed with contemporary Japanese legal reforms, which were designed to convince the Western treaty powers to abolish consular jurisdiction in Japan. Japanese politicians gradually realized that failure to revise the treaty with China might threaten—or even jeopardize—Japan's efforts to revise the treaties with the West. Consequently, the Japanese resolved to circumvent their obligations to China under the Treaty of Tianjin, by skillful use of international law and Western criminal procedure.

Consular jurisdiction and extraterritoriality were abolished in Japan in the late nineteenth century and in China in the mid-twentieth. Following the Meiji restoration, the Japanese government quickly abolished all territorial domains and the "status system," and set out to create a uniform citizenry, a necessary prerequisite for any modern nation-state. Consular jurisdiction remained an alien body in the Meiji state, and Japanese policy-makers were determined to keep it that way in order to prevent it from affecting other institutions. In the 1890s, consular jurisdiction was finally abolished in Japan, after Japan had convinced the Western treaty powers that their legal system was sufficiently "modern." The Treaty of Tianjin was abrogated during the Sino-Japanese war of 1894–95 and replaced by the onerous Treaty of Shimonoseki, which granted unilateral extraterritorial privileges to Japanese in China. In Qing China, serious efforts to abolish Manchu privilege, creating a "modern" constitution and eliminating consular jurisdiction, did not start until after the Sino-Japanese war. When the Qing dynasty and its legally pluralistic order finally collapsed in 1911, extraterritorial jurisdiction had already sunk deep roots in Chinese society, and subsequent efforts to abolish consular jurisdiction through legal reform under the nationalist régime failed. Consular jurisdiction was not abolished until 1943, as part of the Allies' efforts to strengthen their alliance with China against Japan.[42]

Nils Möller would do well without the protection of the consul general of Sweden-Norway and created a fortune through his businesses in Shanghai. The fact that he had "denationalized" himself in 1877 did not prevent him from eventually returning to his native Sweden, where he passed away in 1902.[43] He left behind no fewer than ten children, some of whom would continue to live in Shanghai and leave a certain legacy to this day. Whereas the old Mixed Court, the chancellery of the Shanghai magistrate, and most consular courts have disappeared without a trace,[44] the residence of one of his sons, Eric Möller, survived the end of the treaty port era. After 1949, it served as an office building of the Communist Youth League, and with the advent of the reform era, it was opened as a luxury hotel for foreign visitors, who are once more taking up residence in the old treaty port to make business, albeit this time without any extraterritorial privileges.[45]

1

Excavating Extraterritoriality

The Legacies of Legal Pluralism, Subjecthood, and State-Building in China and Japan

Prior to the arrival of Western gunboats, Qing China and Tokugawa Japan possessed rich legal traditions that could be described as two discrete plural legal orders. Both countries had centuries of experience in handling conflicts between ethnic, professional, and social groups that belonged to different jurisdictions, experiences that had profound consequences for how the nineteenth century's commercial treaties were received by the local legal system. China and Japan were not the only countries in East and Southeast Asia that were forced to sign "unequal treaties" that included unilateral extraterritorial arrangements. In 1858, the kingdom of Siam entered into a commercial treaty with Britain,[1] and Japan concluded a treaty with Korea in 1876, soon followed by a number of countries, including the Qing Empire, which imposed similar unequal treaties on Korea.[2] However, China and Japan constitute comparative counterparts in a number of ways. Both countries share a common cultural heritage and were forced to "open" to the West at roughly the same time. In contrast to Korea, which was first forcibly "opened" by Japan in 1876 and then gradually succumbed to Japanese colonialism, neither Japan nor China ever became colonies in the strict sense of the word. Despite external constraints, the governments of both countries, with different degrees of success, possessed a certain degree of freedom to design their own—sharply divergent—policies on how to deal with the problem of extraterritoriality.

Subjecthood and Legal Pluralism in Qing China

The late imperial Chinese state has often been described as a "highly centralized" and "unitary state."[3] In the Qing dynasty, the territories of China proper were organized into twelve to thirteen hundred districts (*xian*) and one hundred departments (*zhou*).⁴ These were the smallest administrative units in the empire, and they were run by centrally appointed magistrates, who were in charge of the administration of justice, taxation, public welfare, and public works. The magistrates obtained their qualifications through the imperial examination system, which tested their proficiency in the officially sanctioned Neo-Confucian doctrine, and they could rule over as many as hundreds of thousands of households in a single county. Above the district and department, the country was organized into another hierarchy consisting of prefectures, subprefectures, and independent subprefectures, which in turn were grouped into provinces that were directly subject to the central government. Beneath the districts and departments, there was no formal government structure, and the magistrates had to manage local society through lineage associations or village headmen, who had no formal relation to the state as such.⁵

When it came to the services the people were expected to render to the state, the government made a distinction between "loyal ministers" (*zhongchen*) and "obedient subjects" (*shunmin*). Imperial officials were not bound to the people they ruled over by any contractual obligation, and under the law of avoidance, no official was allowed to serve in his home province. Only civil and military officials were expected to be loyal to the emperor and render active service to the state; in this sense, "patriotism" was the realm of officialdom. The imperial subjects, on the other hand, did not stand in any direct ritual relationship to the state or the emperor and usually did not interact with the state as individuals, but through their households, in which they were expected to fulfill their ritual duties according to Confucian precepts. To the extent that the common people had any duties to the state beyond taxation and corvée labor, they were framed negatively in the form of prohibitions against participating in acts of treason and seditious religious sects. Confucius himself had nothing but praise for fathers and sons who covered up for each other's crimes rather than reporting them to the authorities,⁶ and in line with this idea, the Confucianized legal order of late imperial China punished family members for reporting on each other for criminal behavior, with the notable exception of sedition.⁷ The most patriotic service an imperial subject could render was to be a filial son or daughter, and the *Sacred Edict* of the Kangxi emperor did not even mention loyalty to the emperor among the sixteen virtues the emperor expected of his subjects.⁸ Indeed, it was a privilege to be subject to the Qing Code, which the rulers had designed to give legal sanction to the Confucian social hierarchies.

In this political and ritual order, theoretically the same laws were in force in all territories belonging to China proper. The Qing legal order was also pluralistic in the sense that it gave preferential legal treatment for certain groups of "virtuous people," such as members of the royal family and officials, under the paragraph called the "Eight Considerations" (*Bayi*) in the Qing Code. This arrangement, which can be traced back as far as the Wei dynasty (220–265),[9] can only be described as a rather weak case of legal pluralism, since most people enjoying these privileges could not pass them on to their offspring.

Undoubtedly, Qing China was a legally pluralistic society in the sense that the state was not the only source of law or the sole locus of jurisdiction. Below the level of the district, a number of different social entities, such as common descent groups, native place associations, and guilds, carried out important legal functions, sometimes with the explicit sanction of the state.[10] Nonetheless, the idea that the Qing government was a "unitary state" is still very powerful in the field of Chinese history.[11] This is natural, given the overriding importance of the imperial state in Chinese jurisprudence, the long tradition of codified law, and the fact that relatively few substantial holdings of nongovernmental archives antedating the Republican era have survived.[12] Still, many of the "conquest dynasties" did bequeath a considerable legacy of both ethnic and legal pluralism to the Chinese legal order. One of the first recorded instances of ethnic legal pluralism during China's middle period is the Liao dynasty (907–1125).[13] The unapologetically alien Yuan dynasty (1271–1368) practiced personal jurisdiction rather aggressively, and divided the population into different legal categories. The most famous legal division was the descending hierarchy of Mongols, Central Asians (*Semu ren*), northern Chinese, and southern Chinese, but the same principle also applied to many professional groups, such as clergy, physicians, actors, and musicians. On China's southwestern frontier, the Mongols created a flexible system of hereditary officials (*tusi*), who were selected from local tribes and were given a large degree of autonomy to administer their own affairs.[14]

All these different ethnic and social groups were usually subject to different laws and courts of law, and in order to adjudicate legal cases that arose between different ethnic and social groups, the Mongols introduced "joint conferences," in which the competent officials jointly decided on the merits of cases that involved more than one jurisdiction.[15] In full form, these conferences were called *yuehui* in Chinese, which is a contraction of the longer term *xiangyue huitong shenli*, meaning "to meet together and rule,"[16] of obscure origin and quite possibly a direct translation from a lost Mongolian original.[17] The joint conferences were an important institution in Yuan China, and the *Yuan dianzhang* (Institutions of the Yuan dynasty) contains numerous sections that deal with joint conferences and the agency (*gongxie*) that was responsible for these conferences.[18] The Yuan court system can be seen as a precursor to the Mixed Courts in China.[19]

The Yuan dynasty lasted for less than a century in China proper, and the subsequent Ming dynasty (1368–1644) was in many ways a protonationalist restoration of Han Chinese rule, which had important consequences for the way legal order was shaped. The first Ming emperor, Zhu Yuanzhang, defined his dynasty in explicit opposition to the previous dynasty, vowing to eradicate the Mongol past and revive Chinese laws and institutions as they had taken shape under the Tang dynasty.[20] The Ming emperors distanced themselves from the previous plural legal order and tried to use the law as a vehicle for state-building and assimilation of non-Chinese peoples. One of the most famous expressions of this was article 122 in the Ming Code, which laid down that Mongols and Central Asians had to marry Chinese wives and were forbidden from marrying their own kind.[21] The Ming dynasty also endeavored to use the law as a vehicle to assimilate and transform ethnic groups on China's southwestern frontier and initiated a program to replace hereditary tribal chiefs with regular officials (*gaitu guiliu*) whenever the government had determined that local tribes had been transformed (*jiaohua*) by Chinese civilization.[22]

The rulers of the subsequent Qing dynasty (1644–1911) were of Manchu origin, and their dynasty has often been characterized as an example of successful "alien" rule, sometimes even as the best example of "sinicization."[23] Indeed, the Manchus were the most sinicized of all the conquest dynasties, in the sense that the Manchu rulers had adopted a Chinese-influenced style of government prior to their conquest of China proper and adopted Neo-Confucianism as the official creed of their dynasty.[24] In their capacity as outsiders, the Qing rulers succeeded in creating a legally uniform populace in a way that their Chinese predecessors would never have been able to do. In the treatment of its imperial subjects following the conquest of China proper, the Qing régime endeavored to abolish all legal differences among its subjects in order to establish what historian Philip A. Kuhn has called "commoner equality."[25] Beginning in the immediate aftermath of the Qing conquest of China proper, the Manchu régime abolished the "status system" of the Ming dynasty, under which some commoners were forced to work for the government in hereditary occupational groups (*jiangji*).[26] These arguably egalitarian tendencies culminated during the Yongzheng reign (1723–35), when a series of "emancipation edicts" abolished the category of "mean commoners" (*jianmin*) and declared that they were henceforth to be regarded as "good commoners" (*liangmin*).[27]

It is also abundantly clear that a state of legal pluralism in its juristic sense prevailed in the vast territories that were under Qing rule. In China proper, the Manchus inherited the system of hereditary headmen on the southwestern frontier as well as the Ming program to transform these chieftaincies into regular government counties.[28] However, it is usually in respect to the efforts to promulgate separate codes and statutes for different ethnic groups on the periphery that the Qing legal order has been identified as legally pluralistic. The Mongols were the only ethnic group under Qing rule that had their own separate legal code, the *Menggu lüli* (Mongol Code), which was originally a product of negotiations between the Manchus and the Mongols prior to the conquest of the China proper.[29] It later evolved into a Qing instrument of control over the Mongolian tribes, a situation that can be loosely compared to British colonial policies in its overseas colonies in the nineteenth and twentieth centuries. However, the system was difficult to administer, and the Qing emperors made great efforts to unify the legal code of their empire, which meant that originally Chinese legal norms were forced on the Mongols. As a consequence of increased settlement of Han Chinese in the Mongol lands in the mid-Qing era, the number of disputes between Han Chinese and Mongols increased, and it became more difficult to maintain the legal distinctions between the two ethnic groups. As a result, the Qing court tried to lay down rules that established a territorial application of the Mongol Code, but this policy was never executed consistently, and the tension between personal and territorial jurisdiction persisted throughout the dynasty.[30] After 1817, no new laws were added to the *Menggu lüli*.[31]

Local elites in the two regions of Xinjiang and Tibet had considerable room to shape their own legal order under Qing rule. Following the conquest of Zungaria and Altishahr in the 1750s, the Qing Empire incorporated the local Muslim nobility of *begs* (*boke*) into the Qing official hierarchy and gave them ranks and emoluments within the Qing civil service system. Each local Muslim official (*hakim beg/aqimu boke*) was responsible for a number of *begs* with specialized functions and reported to the local Qing imperial agent (*banshi dachen*).[32] Mediators between the local Muslim society and the secular Qing legal order, these *begs* possessed significant autonomy to settle legal cases on their own, which was especially important in the field of family law, where Muslims were allowed to practice Islamic law.[33] The imperial court also promulgated a collection of precedents for the administration of law in these predominantly Muslim regions (*Huijiang zeli*), which regulated the administration of justice in cooperation with local elites.[34] The Qing Empire never incorporated Tibet fully into its legal and administrative structure, and the region possessed its own distinctive legal system, which was steeped in Buddhist cosmology.[35] The imperial resident in Lhasa (*amban*) usually did not interfere with the internal jurisdiction of the Tibetan government, except in some rare cases of treason against the dynasty.[36] Mongol and Manchu officials and soldiers had a near monopoly on defending imperial rule in Xinjiang and Tibet, and the imperial court did not undertake any effort to assimilate the populations of these regions into Han Chinese society until the last decades of the dynasty, with mixed results.[37]

Although the Qing Empire has been recognized as allowing plural jurisdictions in the periphery, the administration of justice in China proper can also be described as a plural legal order. The fact that the Manchu rulers adopted a version of the Ming Code as the basis of the Qing Code has obscured the fact that the new code was a much greater innovation than it initially appears. The Qing rulers modified the Ming Code by inserting substatutes that were based on legal material that often antedated the conquest of China proper.[38] Indeed, the extensive use of substatutes during the Qing dynasty made it possible to create different legal régimes within the framework of an ostensibly uniform legal code that would create the impression of continuity and uniformity. Consequently, the Qing Code included numerous sections devoted to different ethnic and religious groups, such as Miao, Yao, Muslims, and Mongols. For instance, under the statute that regulated "barbarians outside of civilization" (*huawairen*), the *Supplement to the Collected Statutes of the Great Qing Dynasty* (*Da Qing huidian shili*) made several references to special substatutes for Miao, Mongols, and Moslems, and the statute also laid down procedures for mixed trials in cases where different ethnic groups were involved.[39]

The Status of Manchus under Qing Rule

The Eight Banners were the elite army of the Qing Dynasty as well as the major social organization of Manchu, Chinese, and Mongol bannermen and their families. From its inception, the Qing emperors practiced the principle of administering bannermen and Han Chinese commoners separately.[40] The ultimate provenance of the descriptive four-character term *qimin fenzhi* for this policy of segregation is not clear, but the term's two component parts were widely used in Qing administrative language.[41] The most obvious source of this policy of ethnic segregation was the legal order in Manchuria prior to the conquest of China proper. After initially experimenting with integrated administration and cohabitation for both Manchus and Han Chinese, the preconquest Qing régime had already opted for residential and jurisdictional segregation by the 1620s. These changes were not only a reaction to outbreaks of Chinese resistance against incipient Qing supremacy in the early seventeenth century but also a result of pressure from Han Chinese officials, who were eager to protect the integrity of Han Chinese.[42]

Although segregation was observed for many ethnic groups in Qing China, the fact that the régime was a conquest dynasty and that bannermen and Han civilians usually inhabited the same areas in the empire both contributed to making the jurisdictional segregation of the two groups especially conspicuous. The residential segregation in "Manchu cities" (*Mancheng*) was a regular feature wherever banner troops were stationed until the end of the dynasty.[43] This separation had linguistic consequences. Even after the Manchus had stopped using Manchu as their native language, they continued to speak Northern Mandarin centuries later, rather than the language of those in the cities around them.[44]

As an ethnic group, the Manchus did not constitute a uniform legal category under Qing law and were not subject to a separate legal code.[45] Members of the imperial family were under the jurisdiction of the Imperial Clan Court (*Zongrenfu*), which possessed its own legal code and court system. The overwhelming majority of Manchus were enrolled in the Manchu Eight Banners, the main branch of the armed forces of the empire and the social organization of practically all Manchus.[46] In principle, the members of the Manchu, Mongol, and Chinese banners, collectively known as "bannermen" or the "banner people" (*qiren*) were subject to the same laws as Han civilians (*minren*), but they were exempt from certain forms of punishment under an article called "Committing Offenses and Avoiding Banishment" (*fanzui mian faqian*). Instead of being whipped with the regular "heavy bamboo," they were to be whipped by a "light bamboo" with an equal number of strokes. Sentences involving banishment were to be commuted to the wearing of the cangue—a large wooden frame—for a certain time depending on the severity of the crime.[47] Most significantly, bannermen were generally exempt from capital punishment, except in cases of severe crimes against the state and family relations, such as treason, desertion, parricide, and fratricide.[48]

Another important source of the special status of bannermen was the Ming Code, which had inherited the institutions governing the trial of "mixed cases" from the Mongol Yuan dynasty.[49] As the Ming Code incorporated Mongol elements, only one remnant of the joint conferences remained, a statute called "Coordinating Litigation Involving Military Personnel and Civilians" (*junmin yuehui cisong*). It stipulated that when soldiers committed murder, military and civilian authorities were to examine the case jointly. In the case of other crimes, such as theft, illicit sexual relations, and fraud, in which civilians were involved, "the case must be tried by both authorities together" (*yiti yuewen*). If no civilians were involved, the case was to be handled solely by the military authorities.[50] During the Ming dynasty, the armed forces did not constitute a separate ethnic group, so the statute did not reinforce any ethnicized boundaries between ruler and ruled. In a limited sense, this arrangement can be seen as an extension of the Eight Considerations, which provided for special treatment to subjects who had rendered service to the dynasty. However, when the Qing rulers adopted and accommodated the Ming Code to their own needs, this statute took on a new importance, as the Eight Banners were made up of largely non-Han ethnic groups.[51] During the course of the Qing dynasty, several substatutes were added to this statute.

Bannermen in general and Manchu bannermen in particular were also subject to certain restrictions, aimed at reinforcing their separation from the civilian population. Manchu bannermen were not encouraged to take Chinese primary wives, but they often took Chinese banner or civilian women as concubines, who then joined the household as banner women and whose children were considered Manchu. Women from the Manchu banners, on the other hand, were not allowed to marry Han civilian men, and such marriages almost never happened.[52] No bannerman could leave his garrison (*sizi chujing*) further than twenty kilometers (forty *li*) in the capital and ten kilometers in the provinces without special permission from his superiors.[53] The Kangxi emperor regarded desertion as such an heinous crime that he inserted a prohibition against sheltering deserting bannermen in the *Sacred Edict*, which warned the commoners that any household harboring fugitive bannermen would be punished by decapitation and that neighboring households would be charged with complicity.[54] In order to help commoners to avoid such a punishment, one of the commentaries to the *Sacred Edict* even listed ways of identifying bannermen by their looks, Beijing accents, dress, and behavior.[55]

That ethnic identity took precedence over other distinctions is further demonstrated by the fact that many of these privileges and restrictions did not apply to Chinese bannermen. For instance, although Chinese bannermen were technically subject to the same restrictions on marriage as Manchus, marriages between Chinese bannermen and Han civilians became so common that the Qianlong emperor eventually had to concede defeat.[56] In 1726, an official suggested that due to the differences between Manchus and Mongol bannermen and Chinese bannermen, the substatute commuting exile to bamboo should be retained for the former, whereas Chinese bannermen could be punished like Chinese civilians. The emperor approved the change.[57]

Following the scaling down of the Chinese banners and the encouragement of Chinese bannermen to leave the banner system from the Qianlong era (1736–95), the Han Chinese component of the banner system was reduced, whereas Manchu bannermen and their dependents were firmly kept within the system. In contrast to other groups, such as the scholar gentry, who also enjoyed certain legal privileges, all bannermen were born into the system, and their dependents were registered as bannermen and subject to the same jurisdiction and laws. This made the Manchu banner populations a closed group, whether they be defined as an ethnic group or just an "occupational caste."[58] In common parlance, the words "bannerman" and "Manchu" were virtually synonymous by late Qing.[59]

The Establishment of the Judicial Subprefect

From early on, it was abundantly clear that these residential and legal arrangements were not enough to maintain law and order between Chinese and Manchus in the areas brought under Qing rule. At the same time that the Qing rulers were introducing the banner system to China proper and adapting the old Ming state to their needs, they also made important institutional adjustments in order to rule effectively and maintain peace between the mass of Han Chinese and their Manchu overlords. This was especially salient during the tumultuous first decades of Qing rule. In June 1680, the twenty-six-year-old Kangxi emperor discussed these problems with one of his censors, Wei Xiangshu, who was in charge of suppressing anti-Manchu rebellions in the south. The emperor asked if there was any good method whereby bannermen and civilians could be brought to live together in mutual harmony. Wei responded rather technically and said that the best way would be to settle minor disputes locally and only refer bigger problems to the Six Boards, so as to avoid a case overload, a perennial concern for the chronically understaffed Qing bureaucracy. The emperor did not seem to be convinced and responded:

> Previously, when bannermen [zhuangtun] and commoners got into conflicts, their cases were referred to the prefectures and districts, and then it was said that bannermen were wronged. Later, cases were referred to the military adjutant [zhangjing], and then civilians were said to suffer. Thus it is very difficult to build a legal system.[60]

Clearly, there was a need for a separate institution to try mixed cases. The first step in this direction had already been taken in the later part of the Shunzhi reign (1644–61), when a special "judicial subprefect" (lishi tongzhi) was established in Jiangning prefecture in order to try "mixed cases" (qimin jiaoshe anjian) in lieu of the military authorities.[61] The establishment of the judicial subprefect was an ad hoc solution to local problems and initially not imposed in other areas. Indeed, a request to introduce the system was turned down by the Board of Personnel in 1685.[62]

Following the suppression of the Rebellion of the Three Feudatories (Sanfan zhi luan) in 1681 and the subsequent deployment of banner troops to central and southern China, records of conflicts between bannermen and civilians increased. In 1682 shopkeepers in Hangzhou went on strike to protest the alleged failure of the local authorities to intervene against bullying criminal bannermen.[63] The Da Qing lichao shilu (Veritable records of the Qing dynasty) recorded legal battles being fought in 1686 between the civilian and military administrations in Guangzhou, with each side trying to protect its own ethnic constituency.[64] The gazetteer of Guangzhou banner garrison is particularly rich in entries on banner-civilian conflicts in the Kangxi period. Officials were often praised for their ability to mediate disputes between bannermen and civilians. Most of these entries date from the period before the judicial subprefect was introduced in Guangzhou and leave an impression that early Qing rule was especially tumultuous in this region. Even the northern accents of Chinese bannermen were enough to provoke incidents.[65]

Consequently, in the Kangxi period, judicial subprefects were gradually introduced to all regions where banner garrisons were stationed, replacing the "competent superior officer" as the authority trying bannermen involved in legal disputes with civilians.[66] Extant gazetteers of Eight Banner garrisons often contain detailed entries on the introduction of the judicial subprefect,[67] and the section relating to Personnel (*Libu*) in the *Supplement to the Collected Statutes* suggests when and where judicial subprefects were introduced in the Qing Empire. In smaller jurisdictions, "assistant judicial prefects" (*lishi tongpan*) were established.[68] The restrictions and privileges that were imposed on Manchus residing in China proper did not necessarily apply to Manchus in Manchuria, where the Qing government made careful arrangements to make sure that the banner establishment did not have too much say in the civilian administration.[69]

The *Supplement to the Collected Statutes of the Great Qing Dynasty*, specifically its statute "Arranging the Trial of Cases Involving Military Personnel and Civilians," gives the most comprehensive treatment of the legal and institutional development of the judicial subprefect. The formative period of the office appears to have been the Yongzheng reign and the last amendment to this statute dated to the Jiaqing period. According to this section, local officials (*difangguan*) could try lesser offenses committed by bannermen only if the suspect confessed without reservation.[70] If the bannerman did not confess and even started to implicate innocent people (*wugu qianlian ren*), he had to be handed over to the judicial subprefecture for trial, a measure designed to protect bannermen from being tortured by local officials.[71] In the case of murder or suicide involving both civilians and bannermen, the case had to be tried by both local officials and the judicial subprefect in a joint trial (*huitong shenli, huishen*). The judicial subprefect had a limited mandate to sentence bannermen independently, and he had no authority to rule in cases involving bannermen only. Severe crimes punishable by banishment and death (*tuliu yishang*) had to be directly referred to the board of punishments (*songbu*). Once a verdict was reached, the enforcement of punishments had to be left to banner authorities.[72]

Joint trials and joint hearings (*huishen*) served a number of significant purposes in the Qing legal order, the most important being the joint sessions held during the autumn assizes.[73] Within the context of local jurisdiction, joint trials were performed when a case involved more than one personal or territorial jurisdiction, and such joint hearings were held both in the border regions of the empire and in China proper.[74] Theoretically, the discretionary powers of local officials were low in criminal cases. They were merely charged with the duty of ascertaining the facts in the case and determining punishment according to the code.[75] Local officials were usually not allowed to quote precedent in delivering judgment; this remained the prerogative of higher levels of the judicial hierarchy.[76] The function of the joint trial was to ascertain guilt on the basis of the evidence and the depositions that both officials had collected, whereas the official holding jurisdiction over the defendant was charged with the determination of the actual punishment and its execution. The "inquisitorial" procedure in Chinese jurisprudence and the conflation of "law" and "fact" in Chinese law are indeed very similar to the way traditional Islamic jurisprudence focuses on "truth" (*haqq*) in determining the outcome of a given case.[77] Of course, this technical way of approaching criminal procedure did not always work as a check against abuse of authority, and Manchu officials often functioned as advocates of their own "constituencies."[78] The evolution and interpretation of the term *huishen* would come to attain tremendous importance in the institutionalization of extraterritoriality in the treaty ports.

The Qing government's extreme sensitivity to claims that Manchus were given preferential treatment is indicated by the fact that the judicial subprefect was technically not part of the banner hierarchy. The officials thus filled the function of dissociating the trials of bannermen from their superiors in the banner system.[79] As the terms "subprefect" and "assistant prefect" indicate, the office evolved from the civil administration.[80] There have been various officials called *tongzhi* since at least the Song dynasty,[81] and the Qing dynasty inherited the office from the Ming system of government after the conquest of China proper.[82] Nevertheless, the Qing dynasty appears to have been the first régime to charge the subprefect with such a wide variety of duties. Under its administrative system, there were a number of subprefects and assistant prefects with specialized functions, such as water works, naval defense, administration of justice, and the management of various ethnic groups, such as Yao (*li Yao tongzhi, sui Yao tongzhi*), Miao (*li Miao tongzhi*), and "barbarians" in general (*fuyi tongzhi, lifan tongzhi*).[83] In areas where Chinese were new to settle, such as Xinjiang and Mongolia, subprefects often pioneered central imperial jurisdiction.[84] Sometimes a subprefect was charged with a broad range of duties. In the instructions for the subprefect for naval defense (*haifang tongzhi*) in Xiangshan county, the task of managing "Macau barbarians" (Ao *yi*) was also included.[85] This duty had been added in 1743 at the proposal of the garrison general of Guangzhou, Dzereng (Celeng), who suggested that the subprefect be responsible for lawsuits between Chinese and foreigners. In order to justify this move, he drew a direct comparison to the duties of the *Li* Yao *tongzhi*.[86]

The judicial subprefect, too, was originally responsible for a wide range of duties. According to the Guangzhou garrison gazetteer, he was in charge of managing saltpeter, ammunition and granaries.[87] Two books from the early Qing period indicate that the *lishi tongzhi* was responsible for levies and corvée labor (*fuyi*) in Rehe and Bagou in Manchuria.[88] However, the office was gradually transformed into an institution specifically dealing with banner-civilian disputes. The Fuzhou garrison gazetteer records approval of a request to devote the office exclusively to judicial functions in 1741/1742.[89] Thus in contrast to most other local officials in China, the judicial subprefect and the judicial assistant prefect exercised nonterritorial jurisdiction and were not in charge of administrative duties,[90] which set them apart from other officials of the same rank and established an important precedent for the nonterritorial legal duties of the Mixed Court magistrate in Shanghai.

The Chinese term *lishi* does admittedly suggest a wider range of functions, which might have contributed to the relatively scant attention that both Western and Chinese scholarship have given to the office. In casual literary Chinese, the term *lishi* roughly corresponds to the idea of "handling affairs," sometimes with a religious connotation. In Qing administrative Chinese, however, the meaning of administrative terms was much more circumscribed than in ordinary prose.[91] *Lishi* usually denoted the adjudication of legal disputes but occurs infrequently in that sense, whereas the term was almost exclusively used to refer to offices that adjudicated interethnic disputes. Qing officials chose to use this very term when they were looking for terms to describe the judicial duties of Qing consuls in Japan or Mixed Court magistrates in Shanghai.[92]

Among this multitude of subprefects, the *lishi tongzhi* held a unique position. Unlike other subprefects with similar tasks, he was not just in charge of administering an ethnic or social group but was responsible for the delicate task of adjudicating disputes between the ruling Manchu group and the mass of Han Chinese subjects, a fact that was not lost of contemporary foreign observers.[93] Although the position initially was open to both Han Chinese and Manchus, the office was soon turned into an exclusive Manchu slot (*Manque*). This was a gradual process: in Hangzhou, the position was reserved for Manchus by imperial decree in 1695 and then in Jingzhou in 1719. The fact that most bannermen in early Qing were not proficient in Chinese was often cited as one of the reasons for reserving the slot for Manchus. Another reason was that Manchus would supposedly have greater chances of keeping order among bannermen. But as time passed and Manchu bannermen residing in China proper gradually lost their native language, the linguistic factor loses its explanatory power.[94] By mid-Qing, the judicial subprefect had effectively become an agent of vested Manchu interests. Local officials seemed loath to intervene in disputes between bannermen and civilians, which often led to the banner garrisons becoming safe havens for criminal bannermen.[95] The fact that the office of the judicial subprefect often was located within the garrison itself must have strengthened the impression that the judicial subprefect was nothing more than a "yes-man" of the banner administration.[96]

Local civilian authorities took banner status very seriously in legal proceedings, as is illustrated by a case from 1803. In June that year, Shuntian resident Chao Tingzuo was arrested after killing a man in a scuffle. The victim was the husband of a woman Chao had accused of stealing wheat from a field he was employed to guard.⁹⁷ When Chao was arrested, he claimed that he was a Chinese bannerman, forcing the district magistrate to make inquiries to the local banner authorities as to whether these claims were true. Only after Chao admitted his lie to the district magistrate could due legal process for a civilian criminal resume.⁹⁸ Chao was first sentenced to death, but following the autumn assizes, his punishment was commuted to exile in Shaanxi province.⁹⁹ Indeed, the mere mention of "banner status" (*qiji*) seems to have stalled due legal process in the Qing Empire.

Attempts to Reform Manchu Privilege

The Daoguang reign (1821–50) marked a crucial period in the evolution of legal pluralism in Qing China, both in terms of the empire's internal and external administration. In 1825, Associate Grand Secretary Yinghe pointed out to the emperor that bannermen often broke the restrictions on free movement provocatively, causing serious friction between bannermen and civilians.¹⁰⁰ Yinghe's memorial signaled a shift in Qing policy toward the banner population, and subsequent amendments to the code enabled the banner authorities to deprive individual criminal bannermen of their banner status and exile them to Heilongjiang. However, this policy led to new problems, since the loss of banner status for one family member could lead to the anomalous situation where a single household was subject to two jurisdictions (*yi jia liang ji*), and it appears that the policy was not fully implemented.¹⁰¹ One of the most interesting cases of corruption of the Manchu privilege can be found in the recollections of the Qing official Zhang Jixin, who relates a case in Taiyuan in 1838. According to Zhang, the judicial subprefect in Taiyuan did not dare to credit testimony against some bannermen who had been accused of assaulting a watchman. Instead he chose to flog the watchman in order to satisfy the local garrison. Zhang noted that this encouraged the bannermen to behave even more outrageously, concluding that if they "continue to behave like this, disaster is not far away."¹⁰²

The Daoguang period also witnessed the Opium War and the "opening" of China, and in contrast to Japan, where the opening of treaty ports soon led to the overthrow of the legally pluralistic Tokugawa order, the Qing legal order survived. At great human cost and with foreign aid, the Qing dynasty managed to stamp out domestic rebellion, most important the fiercely anti-Manchu Taiping Rebellion. In the 1860s, the former Sino-Manchu "diarchy," in which Chinese and Manchus jointly ran the empire, was replaced by an uneasy "synarchy," in which foreigners became stakeholders in the Qing Empire.¹⁰³ The fundamental tension between Manchus and Chinese in the Qing legal system survived the advent of the treaty port era, and this tension troubled both Han Chinese and Manchu officials. In response to a memorial from Shen Guifen, the imperial court issued an edict on 23 July 1865 that allowed bannermen who so desired to leave the system and register as civilians. The edict also made it clear that bannermen who had registered in the civilian registers would be subject to the same laws and jurisdiction as ordinary civilians.[104] The enforcement of this decree is questionable, especially since the edict made the decision to renounce the privileged position of Manchus voluntary. In 1866, Changshan, deputy lieutenant commander (*fudutong*) in Shanhaiguan, complained that the reforms existed in name only (*you ming wu shi*) and suggested that exiled bannermen be forcibly entered into civilian registers. The court complied with his request.[105]

Notwithstanding these half-hearted attempts to relieve the empire of the burden of providing for the banner population and create uniform jurisdictions, complaints of Manchus using their privileges to avoid punishment can be traced into the treaty port era. As late as 1890, the Shanghai *Dianshizhai Pictorial* refers to bannermen trying to "use their banner status as a protective charm" (*yi qiji wei hushenfu*).[106] This can be compared to contemporary complaints that bad people joined Christian sects in order to use their religious status as a protective charm (*youmin mei jie rujiao wei hufu*).[107]

The Manchu cities also remained a prominent feature of the Chinese urban landscape well into the early twentieth century, as foreign travelogues consistently noted. It is significant that four out of the first five treaty ports were opened in close proximity to Manchu cities. Shanghai, the hub of the treaty port order, and its neglected sibling Ningbo were near the banner garrisons of Zhapu and Hangzhou. Further along the Yangtze River were Jingkou and the powerful Nanjing garrison. The inner cities of Guangzhou and Fuzhou hosted banner garrisons, and the fifth treaty port, Xiamen, was not far south of Fuzhou. The close proximity between the early treaty ports and the Manchu cities provides important context, for the first experiments with extraterritoriality took place within the Manchu order as it existed in China proper. Indeed, when Qing officials looked for terms to describe conflicts of jurisdiction or special legal privileges, they did not need to leave their province to find institutional and terminological precedents.

Notwithstanding the well-established separate existence of the Manchu, their assimilation cannot be dismissed altogether. The fact that Manchus and Chinese had been living together under the same jurisdiction in Manchuria since the Qianlong period eventually paved the way for the eventual "Sinicization" of the "Manchurian Manchus," whereas the same process was much slower in the provinces in China proper.[108] Thus, one observer in the early twentieth century commented:

It is indeed a curious fact that there is far less distinction between Manchus and Chinese in Kirin than exists in the garrison towns throughout China Proper, the reason being that, whereas in other towns the Manchu garrison has always been kept separate from the Chinese by occupying a special quarter, in Kirin, which was originally a town consisting solely of Manchus, there has never been such a quarter. The result is that ... the Manchus in their original home have fused far more with the Chinese than when planted in the midst of China Proper.[109]

Even in Manchuria, complaints arose that bannermen used their real or imagined privileges to harass common people. In Shuangcheng in northern Manchuria, Deng Wei filed a suit against his neighbor bannerman Lianrui in 1882 for not having paid in full for thirty-five ounces (*liang*) of opium. In his petition to the magistrate, Deng says that he suspected that Lianrui was "using his status as a bannerman to bully the people" (*yi qi ya min*) in order to get away with fraudulent behavior.[110] His plea did not fall on deaf ears. Lianrui had to agree to pay more than nine strings and five hundred coins of cash in compensation for Deng's loss.[111] Lianrui may or may not have complied with the magistrate's injunction, but the case demonstrates the extent to which Manchus and Han Chinese commoners were integrated in the judicial system in Manchuria in the late Qing period.

There is some evidence that Manchus in China proper pushed back when they felt that their social standing was being threatened in legal proceedings. In 1898, there were two reported incidents involving violent bannermen from the Jingzhou garrison. They not only harassed the local population but also turned on the judicial subprefect when he dared to investigate a case of theft and manslaughter. When the subprefect refused to relent in the face of their threats and announced his intention to report the matter to their superior, the suspected criminals locked him up in his *yamen* (office) and gave him a thorough beating.[112] Despite all attempts to curtail Manchu privilege, and notwithstanding the protestations of the Qing emperor that he did not discriminate between Manchus and Han Chinese,[113] Manchus were still very much beyond the reach of civilian law enforcement by the turn of the century.

The Legacies of Legal Pluralism and State Building in Tokugawa and Meiji Japan

Unlike the Qing emperors, the Tokugawa rulers of Japan made no pretense of running a unitary sociopolitical and legal system. Instead they made a point of presiding over a territorially fragmented yet hierarchically arranged political order. The shogun himself was not even the head of state, but only the "commander-in-chief who conquers barbarians" (*Sei-i tai shōgun*), formally appointed by the emperor in Kyoto, whose functions were mainly ceremonial.[114] The Tokugawa house, along with its branches and retainers (*hatamoto*), ruled directly over territories that comprised about a third of the territory of the four main islands of Japan.[115] The remainder of the Japanese archipelago was administered by territorial lords (*daimyō*), who were divided into two main groups. Those lords who had submitted to Tokugawa rule before the battle of Sekigahara in 1600 were called "inner lords" (*fudai daimyō*); they controlled 20 percent of Japan, and many of them were directly involved in the policy-making of the shogun's government, also known as the "Bakufu." The lords who had failed to support Tokugawa rule prior to 1600 were called "outer lords" (*tozama daimyō*) and ruled over about 40 percent of Japan. They were concentrated mainly in the south and west of Japan and were not consulted when the Shogunate formulated its policies. The number of domains and their relative status, measured in "putative rice yields,"[116] varied throughout the Tokugawa period, and by 1865 there were 265 domains that were allowed to run their own affairs to a great extent, resulting in a multiplicity of jurisdictions.

In addition to this fractured legal and administrative order, the population was divided into four major status groups, the samurai, the peasantry, craftsmen, and merchants, usually enshrined in the Neo-Confucian *shi-nō-kō-shō* formula. As many scholars have pointed out, this description of the status system is somewhat simplistic, and the main cleavage in the status system was between the warrior samurai and the rest of the commoners.[117] During the first decades of Tokugawa rule, segregation between samurai and peasants (*hei-nō bunri*) was enforced, and samurai were herded into castle towns (*jōkamachi*) around the country.[118] While similar to the Qing policy of *qimin fenzhi* discussed above, the Japanese arrangement was a functional separation between different social groups rather than a policy of de facto ethnic segregation.[119] A certain degree of mobility between the different status groups existed.[120]

The status system was the governing principle of the Tokugawa social and legal order, and the status system in the Tokugawa territories did have local counterparts. During the first decades of the seventeenth century, the shogunate laid down a set of codes and instructions that governed its relationship with the domains, the status groups, and the court nobility. Most prominent among these was the "Laws for the Territorial Lords" (*Buke shohatto*) and the "Laws for the Court and the Court Nobility" (*Kinjū narabini kuge shohatto*), both promulgated in 1615. Although no single body of law governed Japan as a whole, Tokugawa laws exercised a normative influence over the laws in the territorial domains, and the evolution of Tokugawa law culminated in the promulgation of the "Written Decisions for Lawsuits" (*Kujikata osadamegaki*) in 1742.[121] Attempts were made to further codify the laws along Chinese lines, but none of these efforts materialized during the Bakufu itself.¹²² Consequently, at its peak the Tokugawa legal order was highly pluralistic, characterized by a multitude of jurisdictions that sometimes overlapped or competed.¹²³ The legal order evolved along two main vectors, one territorial and one status-centered, and the relations between different territorial domains have sometimes been likened to the relationships between different countries.¹²⁴ Even outcasts exercised a limited autonomy and were authorized to execute their own criminals after the Bakufu had determined punishment.¹²⁵

Under this strictly régimented system, many of the status groups were segregated residentially, and the Tokugawa legal language developed a rich vocabulary to deal with conflicts of jurisdiction. Each group was expected to interact primarily with its own members and in theory, every territorial lord exercised full jurisdiction (*shihai*) within his own domain and over his own subjects (*ichiryō ikkachū*). Put simply, the governing principle was that as long as the two parties in a given suit belonged to the same jurisdiction, the case was adjudicated under their territorial lord, who could execute punishment at his own discretion (*jibun shioki*).¹²⁶ The extraterritorial implications of this arrangement are evident from the fact that the territorial lords exercised full jurisdiction over their own subjects in their residences in Edo, where they were required to stay every second year under the system known as "alternate attendance" (*sankin kōtai*).¹²⁷ However, it is also clear that especially smaller domains were reluctant to exercise their judicial privileges in severe criminal cases without consulting the Bakufu first, thus reinforcing the role of the Bakufu as a national authority in legal affairs.¹²⁸

In the wake of the growing commercialization of Tokugawa society and the increased interdependency of different status groups and domains, it proved impossible to maintain the legal separation of different people and different jurisdictions in practice. This was particularly evident in Edo, where a number of different jurisdictions overlapped. Following the increased interaction between individuals from different status groups and different regions, a category of "mixed cases" (*shihai chigae kakaru deiri*) became more frequently used.¹²⁹ There were two general kinds of mixed cases, those between two persons from different domains and those between two persons of different status.¹³⁰ When the two categories conflicted, affiliation by domain took precedence over status.¹³¹

Given the considerable complexity of the Tokugawa legal order, a large number of conceivable combinations of parties were possible, and the shogunate was forced to lay down detailed regulations to govern these.¹³² A given case could become especially complicated when the two concerned parties belonged to different jurisdictions and the incident itself occurred in a third jurisdiction or involved a third party, such as a witness.[133] These constituted another category of "mixed cases" (*hikiaimono*), which were especially frequent in civil suits of a commercial nature. Although the procedure was more decentralized in civil suits, the most basic practice for all cases involving an outside party (*taryō tashihai no mono*) was that the case had to be deferred to Bakufu agencies, which were dispersed at strategic points outside of the Tokugawa domains.[134] Among the duties of one of these agencies, the Nagasaki Magistrate (*Nagasaki bugyō*), was the supervision of the Chinese and Dutch communities in Nagasaki,[135] which formed a Japanese counterpart to the supervisory duties of the magistrate in Macau. In claiming primary jurisdiction in most "mixed cases," the Bakufu asserted its role as a central government in Japan, and this centralizing impulse also served as an important source of law, as embodied in the *Kujikata Osadamegaki*.[136]

At the eve of the modern era, Japan possessed an extremely complex plural legal order, which failed to survive the first decade of the treaty port system. Since the Tokugawa legal order was organized around categories such as status and regional origin rather than ethnicity, it proved difficult to transplant into the arena of foreign relations as they took shape in the mid-nineteenth century. The raison d'être of Tokugawa foreign policy was to repel foreigners rather than integrate them into the legal order. Even though the Tokugawa legal language had a rich vocabulary for the adjudication of cases between different jurisdictions, the Japanese versions of the treaty texts were not infiltrated by Japanese legal thought to any great extent. When the Bakufu concluded commercial treaties with Western powers in the 1850s, very few terms entered the vocabulary of treaty port Japanese, beyond very generic administrative terms such as "legal inquiry" (*ginmi*) or "official" (*yakunin*). Although there is little evidence that extraterritoriality was opposed as such, the Bakufu seems to have understood consular jurisdiction as a practice that for all intents and purposes was separate from its own administrative and legal system.[137]

The fact that the Bakufu had agreed to conclude treaties with the Western powers galvanized political opposition against it, and it was soon evident that the Tokugawa Bakufu could no longer claim to represent the whole country. Within just a few years, the legal and administrative order was completely overhauled. It was by no means a foregone conclusion that a few rebellious domains from the southwest would be able to overthrow the old régime in a coup d'état that has become known as the "Meiji restoration." A number of different political actors competed in formulating agendas for Japan's "modern revolution," many of which involved the centralization of authority and the abolition of the old plural legal order. When Tokugawa Yoshinobu assumed office as the new shogun in January 1867, he was devising far-reaching plans to reform the government in close collaboration with his new ally Léon Roches, the French minister to

Japan.¹³⁸ However, the thirty-year-old shogun was quickly outmaneuvered by a coalition led by the outer domains of Satsuma, Chōshū, Tosa, and Hizen, which enjoyed the support of the British minister Harry Parkes and were able to defeat the Bakufu in a number of military confrontations in 1867.

In November 1867, representatives from Tosa managed to persuade Yoshinobu to retire as shogun and hand over his authority to the emperor, but he still expected to retain his role as an important territorial lord. However, this move did not satisfy the two radical domains of Satsuma and Chōshū, whose military forces quickly seized the imperial palace in Kyoto. On 3 January 1868, they issued an edict that stripped Yoshinobu of all his powers and proclaimed that power had been restored to the young emperor, who had succeeded his father and would in due course assume the reign title "Meiji." The most immediate consequence of this seizure of power for law and jurisdiction was that the Tokugawa lands (*Tenryō*) were submitted to direct imperial control. In order to consolidate imperial rule over the newly acquired territories, the imperial capital was moved in March to Edo, which was subsequently renamed Tokyo. On 5 March 1869, the lords of the four victorious domains set an example for the whole country when they handed over their land registries to the imperial court (*hanseki hōkan*), thus further consolidating the core area of imperial authority in Japan. The defeat of the northeastern domains, which remained loyal to Tokugawa rule and refused to consent to the coup, significantly expanded territories of the imperial government by the end of 1869.

However, the old order remained powerful at a local level, as the former territorial lords were made governors in the provinces. One of the "three heroes of the Meiji restoration" (*Ishin no san ketsu*), statesman Kido Takayoshi, was deeply worried about the future of the new government, and in his diary he frequently complained about the narrow-mindedness of local rulers, not the least his compatriots in the domain of Chōshū. In his entry for 28 July 1871, he wrote:

> Although the new system has been decided on, the general run of the people in the land do not obey central government orders. We must, therefore, at this juncture issue the Imperial order for unification to the domains, and make reality of the principle of centralization of authority; hence, I have argued for this great objective again and again.¹³⁹

Following Kido's suggestions, the Meiji government set out to incorporate all the feudal domains into the state, replacing them with prefectures that were directly subordinate to the central government (*haihan chiken*) on 29 August 1871.¹⁴⁰ Many of these reforms were foreshadowed in the tentative "Constitution" (*Seitaisho*) of 11 June 1868, but the reforms faced serious resistance from many samurai who felt disenfranchised, and it was mainly due to the maneuvering and persuasive powers of Kido that another civil war was averted.[141] Roughly at the same time, the old status system was replaced with a new status system, which was intended to create categories under the new household registration law. The old territorial lords and the court nobility were merged into the new "peerage" (*kazoku*), and most of the samurai were transformed into the "gentry" (*shizoku*). The lower ranking samurai merged with the other status groups into the new class of "commoners" (*heimin*), and outcastes were incorporated into the category of "new commoners" (*shin heimin*). The novelty of the new system was that all groups were now directly subordinate to the emperor rather than to their respective territorial lords.[142]

Having made a unified citizenry a cornerstone of their state-building enterprise, the Meiji oligarchs proceeded to revamp the Japanese legal system in a series of drastic and far-reaching measures that struck at the very foundations of the earlier "feudal" order.[143] The first step was taken when the new, provisional Criminal Code (*Shinritsu kōryō*) was adopted. The origins of this code can be traced back to incremental national and regional efforts during the old régime to create a unified body of written law on the basis of Chinese codes; its most important source was the Tang Code. The new criminal code was promulgated in February 1871 and was quickly extended to all territories that were under direct imperial rule. The Code did retain some legal distinctions between the different status groups, but none of these privileges approached the extent of Tokugawa privilege, and the Code itself went through a number of revisions over the following years.[144] A further blow to the hard-pressed samurai was dealt on 28 December 1872, when an imperial edict announced the introduction of universal conscription, thus depriving the samurai of their raison d'être. As an indication of exactly how far government policies had moved against samurai privilege, the edict compared the supposedly noble warriors of the past with the present samurai class: "They differed from the soldiers of a later period who carried two swords and called themselves warriors, living presumptuously without working, and in extreme instances cutting down people in cold blood while officials turned their faces."[145] The decree referred to the notorious statute in the *Kujikata Osadamegaki* that allowed members of the samurai class to cut down commoners with impunity (*kirisute gomen*) if they dared to behave insolently. It is not clear to what extent samurai actually exercised this infamous privilege,[146] but references like this ensured that *kirisute gomen* would endure in collective memory.[147]

The coup de grâce to the special status of samurai was dealt in 1876, when the ancient samurai privileges of wearing swords (*haitōrei*) and receiving hereditary rice stipends were abolished (*chitsuroku shobun*). The incremental dismantling of samurai privilege spurred a series of revolts that culminated in 1877 when another member of the "three heroes of the Meiji restoration," Saigō Takamori, turned rebel once again and led an insurrection against the new government from his native province of Satsuma. The rebellion was brutally crushed, reaffirming the authority of the new national government.

The extent to which the institutional, political, and social upheavals of the Meiji era amounted to a transition from feudal subjecthood to modern citizenship remains a controversial question in Japanese historiography. Many scholars have claimed that Japanese subjects (*shinmin*) were subservient to the imperial institution in a way that set Japan apart from other contemporary nation-states.[148] Yet in the late nineteenth century, hardly any European nation conformed to the ideal type of a modern society with civil rights and complete equality before the law—not to mention the complex legal situation in the European colonial possessions overseas. More important, when Meiji Japan is compared to Qing China in the 1870s, it is abundantly clear that Japan was a nation of citizens.[149] Unlike Qing subjects in China proper, who owed their primary duties to their families and whose obligations to the state were mainly framed negatively, Japanese citizens were directly ascribed to the state as individual members of the Japanese polity and were tied to the state through a definite set of rights and duties, which were later framed in the Meiji constitution of 1889.

The Meiji oligarchy pushed forward the momentum of legal reform relentlessly, and in 1882, the Japanese legal system went through a second transformation when a new criminal code, based on contemporary continental European models, was adopted under the auspices of the distinguished French legal scholar Gustave Émile Boissonade de Fontarabie, who had been working for the Japanese Ministry of Justice since the early 1870s.[150] Now Japan was in possession a relatively coherent legal system, which projected state power and state jurisdiction uniformly over the whole Japanese archipelago, whose borders had been determined both by military confrontations and international treaties. Although many attempts have been made to identify a distinct Japanese legal culture that has survived the Meiji restoration, very few formal and clearly identifiable traces of the earlier Tokugawa legal order were left in the new legal system.[151] The American legal scholar John Haley has described the transformation of Japanese law after 1868 as follows:

> Even the language of the law was almost completely rewritten. Japanese translators either invented new compounds of Chinese characters [*jukugo*] or adopted older ones for the terminology of Western law. In definition hardly a single term of Japanese legal language survived the transformation. An entirely new vocabulary was created, with new categories, new concepts.[152]

It is difficult to do full justice to the vicissitudes of the Japanese state in the last decades of the nineteenth century. Having created a nation and a citizenry, the Meiji oligarchs eventually had to respond to mounting demands for popular representation, promising a new constitution and the convention of a national assembly. It is important to point out that Japanese policy-makers never allowed a single Western model of modernity to shape the Japanese polity but were very selective in what elements they chose to adopt from Europe and North America. The Prussian constitution is usually singled out as the blueprint for the authoritarian Meiji constitution, and it is often used metonymically to represent German influences on the transformation of many aspects of imperial Japan.[153] On the other hand, the highly centralized Meiji state looked far more like Republican France or Savoyard Italy than Wilhelmine Germany. If the Tokugawa house had presided over the creation of the Japanese nation-state, the monarchical federal structure of imperial Germany might very well have served as the template for a Japanese federal state. Instead, the Chōshū-Satsuma coalition led a "Sardinian" reunification of Japan rather than a "Prussian" one, eventually sweeping away virtually all remnants of local power holders and satrapies.[154]

The major consequence of the strongly centralized nature of the Meiji unification was that Japan's earlier legally plural order was never allowed to exercise a direct influence on how the Japanese state responded to the treaty port system in general or extraterritoriality in particular. The early Meiji oligarchs were deeply concerned about the fractured character of the Japanese state and defined themselves in opposition to the Tokugawa plural legal order. Over time, this intolerance toward competing jurisdictions manifested itself in a strong opposition to any form of consular jurisdiction on Japanese territory.

The Qing legal order showed a remarkable tenacity throughout the nineteenth century. Although the Opium Wars and other conflicts with foreign powers did shake the empire in its foundations and foreign legal orders did make important inroads in major treaty ports, these events did not prompt any fundamental rethinking of the legal order of empire. Legal documents from the beginning and end of the nineteenth century looked very much the same. Someone taking a steamboat from Shanghai to Chongqing on the Yangtze River in the 1890s would not only pass through several different geographical time zones on his way upstream, he would also traverse different legal "time zones" and linguistic zones. In Shanghai, foreign lawyers and judges were practicing law in the major consular courts, which existed alongside their Chinese counterparts and exerted a major influence on the legal landscape in the area. Alongside Chinese, English, and French, cases were pleaded in a myriad of languages and dialects that were spoken in the port. In the newly opened treaty port of Chongqing, on the other hand, the foreign community was small and isolated, and the consular courts had just started to operate. The regional southwestern Chinese dialect reigned almost supreme, and the local magistrate operated very much the same way his colleagues had done for centuries.[155] If the traveler left the steamboat and followed the stream of the Yangtze tributaries into Tibet and all the way to the regional capital of Lhasa, he would find a legal system that was almost completely different from the Qing legal order. The Qing imperial resident (*amban*) only exerted a minor influence on daily legal matters. The Tibetan language reigned in all matters spiritual and temporal, and Chinese could only be heard in the small banner garrison and among local Chinese traders.

None of this implies that any individual island in the legal archipelago of the Qing Empire represented the future of China's legal system more than any other. But if modernity entails the standardization of administration, law, and language across time and space, then modernity had made but a small dent on China during the nineteenth century. Western law would not transform the Qing Empire as a whole; it added yet another layer to the plural legal order of the empire, and different forms of imperialism shaped the legal order in different parts of the empire. This contrasts sharply with the trajectories of the Japanese Tokugawa and Meiji states during the nineteenth century. The Tokugawa legal system constituted its own plural legal order prior to the arrival of Western gunboats.[156] However, within the space of two decades the highly pluralistic Tokugawa state was replaced by the centralized Meiji state. Indeed, in the intensive state-building program they embarked on in the 1870s, Meiji policy-makers did their utmost to distance themselves from that heritage.

Unlike its Tokugawa counterpart, the Qing legal order lasted well into the first decades of the twentieth century. The overthrow of the old political system in the republican revolution of 1911 did not immediately lead to the inauguration of a new legal order, and even after the Qing Code had been replaced by new criminal and civil codes based on continental European models in the 1920s, British colonial authorities in Malaysia, Singapore, and Hong Kong officially regarded the Qing Code as a source of law for the Chinese communities there.[157] The terminology of the Qing legal order lingered on in the interwar period. Again, in sharp contrast to the fate of the Japanese legal order and its language, the Chinese legal language did not change as quickly as the new legal orders it was called on to represent.[158] While new social contexts gave old words new meanings in the twentieth century,[159] the fact that Chinese legal reformers did not undertake any fundamental revision of legal terminology indicates the tenacity of the old order in the face of drastic change. The Qing legal order moved almost seamlessly into the treaty port era. Despite frequent attempts at reform the legal order, the systemic tension between different ethnic groups in the empire would never be resolved, and the Qing legal order would remain basically unchanged well into the first decades of the twentieth century. As a result, the pluralistic Qing legal order influenced the way consular jurisdiction was implemented in China, and concepts of shared jurisdictions infused the legal language of the new treaties with the West.

2

Codifying Extraterritoriality

The Chinese "Unequal Treaties"

Much of the writing about the treaty ports has assumed that consular jurisdiction and extraterritoriality meant that foreign residents in China were able to commit crimes with impunity, sometimes literally getting away with murder. Indeed, stories abound of how foreigners and Chinese claiming foreign nationality were not only beyond the reach of Chinese laws and authorities but sometimes beyond the pale of law itself.[1] Perhaps the most famous example of how extraterritorial privileges led to the sheltering of criminals was the gangster king Du Yuesheng, who was able to elude local Chinese justice by claiming French nationality. Yet the road from immunity to impunity was by no means a predetermined development, and Western diplomats and Qing statesmen may not have envisioned these developments when the first treaties were concluded. Many nineteenth-century apologists for extraterritoriality, such as the prominent British diplomat Sir Rutherford Alcock,[2] were careful to give assurances to both the Qing government and skeptical domestic audiences that British criminals in China were to be given a speedy and fair trial.[3]

Set against the background of Qing legal assumptions regarding the trial of people belonging to different ethnic groups and different jurisdictions, extraterritoriality was not necessarily incompatible with a Chinese legal sensibility. It is reasonable to assume that when Qing officials signed treaties granting extraterritorial privileges to foreign residents in China, they understood the Chinese wording of those clauses from their own legal perspective. This chapter narrates some of the formative episodes in the evolution of extraterritoriality in eighteenth- and nineteenth-century China, using the concept of legal pluralism to identify continuities and discontinuities in the practice.

The Status of Foreigners Prior to the "Unequal Treaties"

European trade with China increased steadily from the sixteenth century onward, and the number of foreigners residing in the Chinese ports open for trade rose accordingly. In general, Chinese authorities did not object to sojourning foreigners resolving disputes among themselves according to their own laws and procedures, but when Chinese were victims of crime at the hand of foreigners, Chinese authorities did, as a rule, insist that foreigners be subject to Chinese laws. In so doing, they were on solid ground from the perspective of Chinese legal doctrine. The statute on crimes committed by "persons beyond the pale of civilization" (*huawairen*) in the Ming Code, for instance, laid down that foreigners who committed crimes "shall be judged in accordance with the Code."[4] This statute had a long history in Chinese law. Article 48:1 in the Tang Code established the principle that conflicts between foreigners of the same nationality were to be tried according to their own laws, whereas conflicts between people of different nationalities were to be resolved according to the Tang Code.[5] In the Ming Code, this qualification was excised from the statute, which read in its entirety that "in all cases where persons beyond the pale of civilization commit crimes, they shall all be judged in accordance with the code."[6] The Ming Code did not provide any official explanation as to exactly who was to be considered a *huawairen*, but a commentary on the Code stated that the term referred to "foreign barbarians" who submitted to the Ming state and to prisoners of war who were in the custody of the government.[7] Under this explanation of the Code, the status of foreign sojourners was left open to interpretation. Some Western commentators on the Qing Code, which had adopted the statute from the Ming dynasty,[8] held that the statute only applied to foreigners who voluntarily submitted to the imperial government and not to temporary sojourners, such as Western merchants in the port of Guangzhou.[9] These commentators pointed out that none of the substatutes to the aforementioned statute mentioned Westerners and that the substatutes mainly dealt with the jurisdiction over Mongols.[10] On the other hand, at least one commentary on the Qing Code from 1832 did cite the statute in three cases dealing with foreigners.[11] Suffice it to say that the relevant legal texts did leave room open for interpretation and, as we will see, Qing officials tended to apply the Qing Code to foreigners selectively and did so with imperial sanction. From a Qing point of view, it was a privilege to submit to Chinese civilization and the Qing Code, which gave legal sanction to the Confucian family system in a carefully elaborated set of penal laws. The minimalist Qing state discouraged people from resorting to the courts to resolve their conflicts and only insisted on jurisdiction over the most severe crimes in the Code.

In 1557, the Portuguese established a settlement on the Macau peninsula, which would become one of the major theaters of Sino-foreign jurisdictional conflict on China's maritime frontier. Although the Portuguese would later claim that the Ming emperors had ceded sovereignty over Macau to Portugal in a "Golden Charter,"[12] the Portuguese originally paid tribute to the Ming Empire in order to maintain their colony on the peninsula. Given the travails of sending a full tributary mission to the northern capital of the empire, this tribute was later commuted to a sum of silver, to be delivered annually to the subprefect of Xiangshan county. This practice continued after the Portuguese colony finally accepted Qing rule over China proper in 1651.[13] As the Chinese government effectively rented the Macanese peninsula to the Portuguese, it also retained ultimate jurisdiction over both the territory and its inhabitants. As far as the Chinese residents of the colony were concerned, Qing magistrates successfully defended their exclusive jurisdiction, but in principle, they did not object to the colonial authorities exercising jurisdiction over the Portuguese residents, as long as Chinese were not victims of crime at the hands of foreigners. The local implementation of Chinese jurisdiction varied considerably over the years, and the Portuguese were often successful in eluding Qing authorities, often by bribing local officials.[14] Another way of avoiding Qing jurisdiction was the systematic misrepresentation or mistranslation of the decrees of the Chinese authorities.[15] This ambiguous state of affairs endured through the establishment of the Manchu Qing dynasty. For the first hundred years of the dynasty, the Portuguese authorities in Macau never once surrendered a Portuguese to local authorities for the killing of a Chinese.[16]

In the Qianlong period (1736–95), the Qing government set out to clarify the criminal jurisdiction over Portuguese residing in Macau, and here we can find clear evidence that Qing officials drew on their experiences from the pluralistic Qing legal order. In 1743, the garrison general of Guangzhou, Dzereng, memorialized the throne and suggested that a subprefect and assistant subprefect be transferred from Zhaoqing prefecture and Xiangshan district, respectively, to nearby Macau in order to take charge of mixed lawsuits between Chinese and foreigners in the area. He quoted the procedure for mixed suits between Yao tribesmen and Han Chinese as a precedent.[17] Later the same year, when a Portuguese was charged with killing a Chinese, Dzereng also suggested that the defendant be tried together by Qing and Portuguese officials and executed under "joint supervision," if found guilty. The emperor approved these suggestions and cited them as a precedent for subsequent cases in which foreigners were accused of killing Chinese. In the cases of other crimes in which Chinese were victims of Portuguese, the Qing authorities also claimed jurisdiction in principle, but they usually contented themselves with ordering the Portuguese authorities to try and punish the offender according to their own law.[18] Ten years later, when a

Frenchman was accused of killing an Englishman in Guangzhou, local Qing authorities tried to assume jurisdiction, but this was rejected by the Qianlong emperor, who reaffirmed the traditional policy of not interfering in conflicts between foreigners.[19] Thus, by the Qianlong period the emperor had established that the Qing government would only claim jurisdiction in cases where Chinese had been killed by foreigners.[20]

Some scholars have interpreted the Qianlong policy as an affirmation of the territorial jurisdiction of the Qing Empire and an implicit rejection of the concept of extraterritoriality. For instance, in his influential study on extraterritoriality in China, Wellington Koo somewhat anachronistically stated: "The Chinese notion of territorial sovereignty and jurisdiction, as entertained, though at times vaguely, by the officials of the Empire in the early days, was not essentially different from that which is maintained by modern international jurists."[21] There were important differences between mid-Qing policy toward foreigners and the full-fledged treaty port system of the late nineteenth century, when most foreigners in China were able to claim nearly absolute immunity from Qing jurisdiction. But it is clear that already in eighteenth-century China, the Qing government did not claim jurisdiction over all cases occurring on its territory; the fact that the nationality of the plaintiff often determined jurisdiction was a fundamental recognition of personal jurisdiction, the operative principle of extraterritoriality and consular jurisdiction. If we compare Qing policy toward foreigners with that of the contemporary Ottoman Empire, the original Ottoman capitulations in the eighteenth century did not go further than conceding consular jurisdiction in cases in which only foreigners were involved. Indeed, the Ottoman policy was stricter than its Qing counterpart and claimed jurisdiction in *all* criminal cases in which an Ottoman subject was the injured party, and not only in cases of homicide. When foreigners were accused of crime in the Ottoman Empire, foreign consuls often sent a "dragoman" to sit as an assessor at the trial to guard against miscarriage of justice. The dragoman had the right to protest a sentence to higher authorities, if he deemed it unjust, but he had no voice in the sentence as such.[22] Foreign powers were not able to claim unilateral jurisdiction in cases where their citizens were defendants until after the mid-nineteenth century, following the weakening of the Ottoman Empire. Thus, the common approaches of the Qing and Ottoman Empires toward criminal cases involving foreigners made a lot of sense for large territorial empires where many different ethnic and religious were living together, but were very far removed from the nearly absolute claims of territorial jurisdiction in the modern nation-state.

Qing policy toward the Portuguese in Macau would, with some modifications, be extended to all foreigners living in Guangzhou, which by 1757 was the only port open to Western maritime trade. The British East India Company

(EIC), which dominated Sino-British trade in the eighteenth country, was not satisfied with the legal régime in Guangzhou and resisted Qing demands that Britons accused of killing Chinese be handed over to local Chinese authorities. British merchants were suspicious of what they regarded as a tendency in the Qing legal order to impose collective responsibility; they were also resentful of the Qing practice of meting out capital punishment in cases of accidental manslaughter.[23] Consequently, EIC officials only surrendered British subjects whom they were convinced would be found guilty of willful murder. When there were doubts as to the guilt of a Briton accused of killing a Chinese, the British supercargo usually spirited the suspect away before Qing officials had a chance to react, giving vague promises of punishment in Britain. After the controversial *Lady Hughes* case in 1784, when a British gunner was executed for accidentally killing a Chinese, the EIC decided that they would never again surrender British suspects to local Qing authorities.[24] The execution of the gunner became part and parcel of British discourse about the alleged barbarity of the Qing legal system and subsequently became a justification of British demands for full extraterritorial jurisdiction.[25]

Foreign Jurisdiction on the Inner Asian Periphery

The Qing dynasty's border policy on its vast Inner Asian frontier suggests where the fault lines were drawn in conflicts over jurisdiction and also shows how flexible the Manchu empire could be in its dealings with jurisdiction over foreigners.[26] As early as 1689, the Romanov Empire and the Qing Empire had delineated their border in the Treaty of Nerchinsk, a much-needed truce that provided the two empires with time to focus on pacifying other enemies.[27] The treaty also laid down some fundamental rules that regulated caravan trade across the border, and article 4 of the treaty provided for the extradition and subsequent execution of criminals who had absconded across the border.[28] The article established the principle that it was the nationality of the criminal that determined jurisdiction, but it also enjoined authorities of the two empires to mete out summary justice when appropriate.

Neither of the two empires was satisfied with the arrangements of the old treaty, and following a conference in the Russian town of Kiakhta on the border to Outer Mongolia, a new treaty was concluded on October 1727 that allowed Russians to open a new "treaty port" for their caravan trade in the small outpost.[29] Crossborder commerce would in due course increase Sino-Russian interaction and pave the way for a lucrative trade that would enrich trade routes in the hinterland of China for the next hundred years.[30] Anticipating an increase in crossborder crime, the Treaty of Kiakhta contained several articles that dealt with jurisdictional questions.[31] Article 1 enjoined each of the two empires to "rule and control its own subjects" in order to preserve the peace.[32] Article 4, which regulated the Russian triennial caravans to Beijing, established that the head of the Russian merchants would "rule and administer" the members of the caravan and resolve any conflicts that might occur.[33] Article 10 laid down that deserters who crossed the Sino-Russian border should be executed on the spot, as well as people who were caught for plunder and murder. People who crossed the borders accidentally without a passport would also be punished, but the punishment was not specified in the article. Taken together, the articles were very much in line with the arrangements that would be established in Macau two decades later, which devolved authority over criminals to officials of their own nationality in most cases, with the notable exception of violent crime. Article 10 subjected deserters, bandits, and murderers to the summary jurisdiction of the authority that caught them, and the only distinction that was made between Russian and Qing subjects was that the former would be executed by hanging whereas the latter would be beheaded, which was in accordance with the preferred mode of execution in the two empires.[34]

As anticipated, increased interaction across the border led to more frequent crossborder crime, and the general arrangements of the old treaties proved insufficient. In 1743, two intoxicated Russian soldiers beat two Chinese merchants to death on the border of Kiakhta. Even though the Qing government presumably had the authority to execute the two criminals according to the letter of the treaty, the Court of Colonial Affairs reported the matter to the Russian authorities.[35] The Russians responded that while there was no precedent for executing drunken people who committed murder, the empress of Russia wished to see the criminals executed "for the sake of the friendship" between Russia and China. The Court of Colonial Affairs deliberated further on the matter and suggested to the Qianlong emperor that the two Russians be strangled in the presence of Russian officials, and the emperor complied.[36]

In order to clarify questions of jurisdiction, the Qing and Russian empires concluded a supplementary treaty at Kiakhta in 1768 that amended the arrangements for deserters, bandits, and murderers. Perhaps the clearest statement of the fact that Qing and Russian authorities shared jurisdiction over crossborder crime was that article 10 in the supplementary treaty provided that Russian and Qing border officials should try bandits at the place of their arrest jointly and behead them, if found guilty, on which the cases should be reported to the home authorities of the executed criminals.[37] The supplementary treaty of Kiakhta was the last Sino-Russian treaty to define the legal status of the subjects of the two empires prior to the first Opium War, which paved the way for a different legal régime.

Even though these summary arrangements are rather different from the practice of consular courts that would develop a hundred years later, the article does not represent the kind of unequivocal assertion of territorial jurisdiction that Wellington Koo assumed more than 150 years later. Instead, the treaties created a rather ambiguous legal régime for crossborder crime that assumed that criminal cases should be solved through mutual consultation between Qing and Russian officials, keeping with the Qing preference for joint investigations. Even though the Russians were referred to in tributary terms in internal Qing documents and the Qing Empire governed its relations with the Russian Empire through the Court of Colonial Affairs, the Sino-Russian agreements avoided any mention of the tributary order as such, and Russian envoys to Beijing rarely insisted that they be allowed to communicate directly with the Qing emperor or be treated on "equal terms." There was nothing peculiar in this Russian tacit acceptance of Qing diplomatic practices, as no specific act of recognition was required under contemporary standards of international relations.[38]

The Qing Settlement with Khoqand

Only a couple of years before the First Opium War, the Qing Empire was renegotiating its policies on jurisdiction on its Inner Asian frontiers. The peace settlement with the Uzbek khanate of Khoqand in the early 1830s contained extraterritorial privileges and other arrangements that are strikingly similar to the ones the British were granted in the wake of the Opium War. By granting Khoqandi traders extraterritorial privileges, the Qing Empire was essentially acquiescing to "a time-honoured custom among Muslim traders," a custom that in the eastern Mediterranean had given rise to the capitulations of the Ottoman Empire in the sixteenth century.[39] Most of the concessions granted to Khoqand were given in a correspondence between Qing imperial commissioners and a Khoqandi envoy in 1833, and there is at least no Chinese archival evidence supporting the claim that a formal treaty was concluded between Qing and Khoqand in Beijing two years later.[40] The Daoguang emperor and his officials on the spot were well aware of the fact that they were in effect giving privileges of self-government to the Khoqandis. The concessions were granted as gifts from the emperor, and the Khoqandis got what they wanted by allowing themselves to be represented in submissive, tributary terms in their dealings with the image-conscious Qing Empire.[41]

Qing policy-makers hardly dwelled on the granting of legal privileges to Khoqandi merchants. Those involved in the settlement were very eager to give the impression that the emperor was restoring the old order of things,[42] and recurrent references to the costs of the war with Khoqand in the archival record indicate that Qing policy-makers were painfully aware of the dangers the overstretched empire was facing in Inner Asia. For instance, the military governor of

Xinjiang, Songyun, gave very pragmatic fiscal arguments in favor of withdrawing troops from the area and exempting Khoqand traders from taxes in 1831.[43] Indeed, the sources show how far the Qing Empire was prepared to go to in order to appease Khoqand and restore order on its Inner Asian frontiers.[44] In the exchange of notes between the Qing imperial commissioners and the Khoqandi envoy from 1832, the envoy explained Khoqandi policy, stressing the difficulty of controlling Khoqandi traders if they were subject to a legal system other than their own:

> Our Bek is afraid that if we trade without a head trader [*toumu*] in charge of the Muslim merchants who come from outside, they will not go about things properly and will not abide by the laws peacefully [*buneng anjing shoufa*]. Now we request that we are allowed to establish one as in the past.[45]

The statement from the envoy has only survived in a translation into the Chinese vernacular, so we have no way of verifying how accurately it reflected what the envoy originally said.[46] However, the purported argument of the Khoqandi envoy resonates very well with the Qing government's concerns about how to maintain order among its subjects if they were to be subjected to a jurisdiction other than its own. One of the things Qing statesmen would later fear the most in the nineteenth-century treaty ports was "extraterritorial Chinese"—that is, Chinese who could claim extraterritorial protection by virtue of association with foreigners—and this concern would become a recurring theme in the treaty port era.[47] Thus it is noteworthy that the translator of the envoy's message of elected to use the term "restrain" (*guanshu*) when referring to jurisdiction over Khoqandi traders,[48] a term Qing diplomats used when they later referred to consular control over Qing subjects.[49] Just as the Sino-Russian treaties would be set aside after China's defeat in the Opium Wars, the khanate of Khoqand was soon engulfed by the Russian Empire. By 1876, Khoqand was annexed as part of Russian Central Asia, and the Sino-Khoqandi agreements were consequently rendered null and void. Yet the Khoqandi settlement gives us an important indication of how flexible Qing policy-makers were and shows how personal jurisdiction could be framed within the Qing legal order.

At the Verge of a New Era

While the Qing government was deeply concerned with the maintenance of law and order among foreign sojourners in the empire, it would be anachronistic to characterize Qing policy toward foreigners in terms of "territorial sovereignty." Qing officials usually insisted that the Qing Code apply to foreigners as a very general normative guide of what constituted a criminal act, but they were quite content to entrust the punishment of most criminal foreigners to their own authorities, except in cases of homicide. Even in such cases, they were open to different ways of meting out punishment. This suggests that maintaining the Qing legal order was not simply a question of rigidly applying legal codes on both native and foreign criminals; it was also a normative legal order that laid down Confucian ideals to which all members of society were supposed to conform, although certain concessions could be made to foreigners with the aim of ultimately integrating them into this legal order. Indeed, as most foreign sojourners in China did not practice the Confucian family system, it was difficult to enforce the letter of the Qing Code on them, since the entire Code was designed to give penal sanction to violations of idealized Confucian norms.[50]

The fact that the Qing government did not insist that the Qing Code be applied literally when dealing with foreign criminals in no way precluded conflicts between natives and foreigners on how to delineate jurisdiction. If we accept the idea that there was a distinction between the Qing Code as a source of norms and as a source of penal laws, the commercial treaties that were concluded after the first Opium War did indeed represent a shift in Qing policy, but it was not as large as is often asserted, nor was it unilaterally imposed by foreigners. The treaties were more a product of give and take, and some of the privileges that were later decried as imperialist impositions on China were actually offered to the Western powers by Qing officials voluntarily.[51] Given the fact that Qing policy-makers were remarkably flexible in their handling of Sino-foreign disputes elsewhere in the empire, it is not inconceivable that British and Qing officials would have been able to iron out an agreement on the settlement of legal conflicts in the mid-nineteenth century, had it not been for the fact that British merchants traded in contraband with the tacit consent of British officials, who further exacerbated the problem by insisting that the British understanding of foreign relations govern the communication between the two empires.[52]

Until the 1830s, the British EIC had been able to monopolize the China trade, and even though the British government owned the company, it did not have any official authority to represent the British government in Guangzhou. The local Chinese authorities regarded the director of the EIC as the "headman" of the British community, and the ambiguous status of the EIC made it possible for its representatives to present themselves in appropriately submissive terms in the interest of trade. However, the established practice was challenged when the EIC lost its monopoly on British trade with China in 1834. The British government sent a superintendent of trade to represent the Crown and enacted legislation to establish a British court in China. However, the British realized that such a move would need approval from the Qing government to have legal force, and the first superintendent of trade, William Napier (9th Lord Napier), was urged not to provoke the Qing authorities when assuming his powers in Guangzhou. However, due to Lord Napier's heavy-handed tactics and his insistence that he be allowed to communicate directly with local Chinese authorities on nominally equal terms, local Chinese authorities refused to recognize him. Sino-British relations were at a stalemate.[53]

The first Opium War is often narrated as a battle over jurisdiction.[54] Opium had been outlawed by the Yongzheng emperor in 1729, and since the beginning of the nineteenth century, Qing authorities had undertaken a number of unsuccessful campaigns to suppress the trade.[55] By the late 1830s, Qing and British positions had hardened for a number of reasons. Signs that opium addiction was adversely affecting the body politic and the balance of trade made Qing policymakers less predisposed to make concessions. By the 1830s, an increasingly influential group of officials in Beijing were pushing for stern measures against the opium trade and a hard-line stance against the British.[56] The British, for their part, made a clear departure from tributary protocol by insisting that *their* understanding of contemporary diplomatic relations should guide Sino-British relations, a demand to which the Qing emperor obviously could not concede.

Following a brief debate whether the problems surrounding the opium trade could be resolved by legalizing the drug, the Daoguang emperor resolved to reaffirm the existing ban on opium.[57] In 1836, he ordered his officials in Guangdong to take active measures to suppress the trade.[58] Emboldened by the successes of the first campaign, the emperor heeded the controversial suggestions from the hard-line official Huang Juezi that the ban on opium be further extended to include capital punishment for opium addicts.[59] The emperor promulgated a set of thirty-nine new regulations to that effect,[60] and in 1838 he appointed the trusted troubleshooting official Lin Zexu imperial commissioner in order to suppress opium trade in Guangdong province, granting him full powers to implement the full extent of the new policy.[61] Up to this point, the question of what to do with foreign opium smugglers had not been at the top of the agenda, and the new regulations, which contained detailed instructions on how to deal with opium offenders from different social groups, did not contain any specific clause regarding alien offenders against the law. In fact, foreigners mainly figure in the regulations as an external force that is corrupting the morals of the Chinese population, and the actual implementation was left up to local officials. Having taken up his office in Guangzhou, Lin Zexu promptly proceeded to execute a number of Cantonese for dealing in and smoking opium, but in keeping with the traditional policy toward Western barbarians, he was reluctant to push the issue of jurisdiction over foreigners and initially refrained from enforcing the new statutes on foreign opium smugglers. It appears that Lin Zexu felt the need to clarify jurisdiction over foreigners and asked for the authority to enforce the new law on foreigners based on the old Qing statute on "foreigners outside Chinese civilization."⁶² Lin Zexu saw the law as a means to suppress opium, not as an end in itself or as an autonomous force outside of government policy with which foreigners were supposed to comply. If the goal of suppressing the opium trade could be attained without applying the full rigor of the law, possibly provoking a full-scale conflict, Lin was quite satisfied with dealing with foreign smugglers through the British superintendent of trade. He issued a number of well-formulated proclamations in order to convince the British to surrender their opium stock to the local authorities and comply with the new policies. One of the most famous documents is Lin's eloquent appeal to Queen Victoria, which is often cited as an example of a principled Chinese opposition to extraterritoriality: "Suppose a man of another country comes to England to trade, he still has to obey English laws; how much more should he obey in China the laws of the Celestial Dynasty?"⁶³

Since the British and the Chinese had been debating legal issues for a century in Guangzhou, it is noteworthy that Lin felt the need to explain the rationale behind the policy at great length, both to the local superintendent of trade and to British authorities at home, who, he assumed, were unaware of the extent of smuggling. More important, when Lin referred to laws in the Chinese original of the statement, he chose to use the word *fadu*,⁶⁴ whose meaning is closer to "legal order" or "law and order."⁶⁵ This term did not occur once in the Great Qing Code but was quite frequently used in official proclamations and less formal statements, such as the famous proclamation the Cantonese gentry issued in 1839 accusing the British of being "ignorant of laws and rites" (*bu zhi fadu, bu zhi liyi*).⁶⁶ Lin's choice of words is important, because if he had meant that Britons should be subject to the territorial jurisdiction of Qing officials, he would have used *guanxia*, which was the standard term for the jurisdiction of a local official in administrative Chinese at the time.⁶⁷ A couple of decades later, the term *guanxia* would be used frequently when Qing officials argued that Western missionaries residing outside of the treaty ports should be subject to the jurisdiction of local officials.

While Lin's attempt to make the British superintendent of trade enforce Qing laws on British opium smugglers cannot be reduced to a question of terminology, it is a frequently overlooked fact that the most principled objections to extraterritoriality usually appear in Western-language sources and in translations of Chinese documents into Western languages. For instance, the *Chinese Repository* and the published correspondence concerning the revision of the treaties of Tianjin contain many of the most eloquent statements on the deleterious effects of extraterritoriality, often in response to the complaints of unnamed Chinese officials.⁶⁸ By contrast, published collections of internal Chinese government documents from the same time period usually devote one or two paragraphs to the subject,[69] whereas other matters, such as permitting foreigners to travel into the interior of China or allowing a resident minister in the imperial Capital, garner much lengthier discussion.[70] It is almost as if nineteenth-century foreign commentators on Chinese affairs acted as ventriloquists of a perceived Chinese resistance to extraterritoriality, reflecting their own anxieties and doubts about the justifiability of a practice that had little foundation in international law. This pattern persists well into the nineteenth century.[71] There is evidence that Lin's thinking on this matter did change as a consequence of his contacts with foreigners and from reading translations of treatises in international law,[72] but his efforts were cut short by his dismissal in 1840 and did not influence official policy.

Adhering to his policy that the British should be persuaded to comply with the new law on opium and only use force as a last resort, Lin Zexu unsuccessfully tried to make British merchants sign bonds (*ganjie, qiejie*) promising not to trade in opium and to comply with the new law. When this failed, Lin finally demanded that the British merchants surrender all their opium to the local authorities, which the British superintendent of trade, Charles Elliot, did after giving the British opium merchants guarantees that they would be compensated by the government for their lost property. When Lin Zexu started to destroy the confiscated opium in May 1839, he was therefore destroying British government property, which would provide the British with an excuse to demand compensation under the threat of war. By the early summer of 1839, Sino-British relations had all but broken down, and in preparation for British retaliation, Elliot moved the entire British community to Macau awaiting orders from Whitehall.[73] When some drunken English sailors killed the Chinese peasant Lin Weixi in the village of Tsimshatsui just opposite the island of Hong Kong during the summer, Elliot refused to surrender the suspects, which further exacerbated Sino-British tensions.[74] By September 1839, the first battle was fought at Kowloon, and early the next year full hostilities had commenced between the two empires.

Over the full course of the First Opium War, the main theatre of war shifted from south to north China twice. After inflicting a decisive blow to Qing defenses in the Yangtze Valley and threatening to sever southern China from the north by occupying the Grand Canal, the British finally forced the Qing government to the negotiation table in the summer of 1842. Despite the fact that law and jurisdiction had been at the heart of the conflict, the resulting Treaty of Nanjing (*Jiangning tiaoyue*), which was concluded in August 1842, was a very basic instrument to cease hostilities and did not contain any specific stipulations about jurisdiction. As a matter of fact, the British prime minister, Henry John Temple, 3rd Viscount Palmerston, did not mention the question of jurisdiction a single time in his instructions to his plenipotentiary Sir Henry Pottinger.[75] Consequently, the treaty covered mainly the immediate settlement of hostilities between China and the United Kingdom, such as the indemnity that the Qing Empire would pay to the British, demobilization of troops, and exchange of prisoners of war. Instead, the imperial commissioner and Manchu nobleman Qiying readily conceded extraterritorial privileges to the British in an exchange of notes with Pottinger at the time of the conclusion of the treaty.[76] The British also brought up the question of the trial of mixed cases, but for unknown reasons the treaty remained ambiguous on this point.[77] Quite possibly, Qing statesmen did not think it necessary to define any procedure for mixed cases in the treaty, since they intended to stick to the Qing policy of segregating different ethnic groups residing in China proper. Consequently, they did not anticipate that a significant amount of mixed cases would arise.

Qing statesmen tried to give the impression that the opening of four new ports to trade, as well as the legal concessions that were granted to the British, were not to be taken as precedents that other countries could claim.[78] Thus when the American Commodore Lawrence Kearny arrived in Guangzhou in December 1842 to ask for similar concessions from China, the Daoguang emperor instructed his officials to rebuff his request and tell the Americans to trade in Guangzhou just as they had done prior to the war with the British. However, on the advice of two Manchu statesmen, Ilibu (Yilibu) and Qiying, the Daoguang emperor reversed this policy, and the following year he instructed the Qing imperial commissioner to extend equal privileges to all foreign powers. The reason for this reversal was that the Qing court wanted to control the new situation and not induce other foreign powers to rely on the British in order to obtain further concessions from the Chinese.[79] This policy to "extend benefits equally" (*yiti junzhan*) would form the basis of what would later be called "most-favored-nation treatment," which would be included in most of the treaties the Qing Empire subsequently concluded with foreign powers and enable all foreign powers to share each other's benefits.[80] It is noteworthy that the term *yiti junzhan* would remain the conventional Chinese term for most-favored-nation treatment in official documents for most of the Qing dynasty and did not yield to the literal translation of the English term (*zuihuiguo daiyu* or *zuihuiguo tiaokuan*) until the turn of the century.[81]

Most-favored-nation treatment and extraterritoriality would first be formally enshrined in the "General Regulations of Trade," signed by representatives of the British Empire and the Qing Empire in July 1843 at Humen near Guangzhou and subsequently included in the Supplementary Treaty of the Bogue (*Humen Tiaoyue*) of October 8 the same year. Article 8 of the supplementary treaty referred to the fact that all Western nations were allowed to trade in the five ports opened for trade "on the same terms as the British" and stated that if the Qing emperor granted other nations "additional immunities and privileges" (*xi en shi ji ge guo*), British subjects would be able to enjoy the same "immunities and privileges." The article also stated that most-favored-nation treatment should not be used a pretext for new demands being "unnecessarily brought forward." Contrary to the idea that Qing statesmen were ignorant of international law, this demonstrates that they were aware of the inherent dangers of unlimited most-favored-nation treatment and wanted to establish clear limits for foreign privilege. Furthermore, it is noteworthy that the Chinese version of the text used the term "grace" or "kindness" (*en*) where the British text talked about "immunities and privileges." In article 13, the regulations stipulated that disputes between Britons and Chinese were to be resolved through negotiations between the British consul and local Qing authorities, who should strive to resolve the matter "amicably." When such a resolution was not possible, the British consul and the Chinese authorities should "together examine into the merits of the case [*gongtong chaming qi shi*], and decide it amicably." The clause further stated that Britons were to be punished according to English law and Chinese were to be "tried and punished by their own laws."[82]

Article 13 of the Treaty of the Bogue was the first explicit statement of the principle that would later be called "extraterritoriality," but it did not introduce personal jurisdiction to the Qing Empire; foreigners had been allowed to manage their own affairs for a long time. What the article did do was to shift the boundary of personal jurisdiction; it was no longer the nationality of the plaintiff—or the victim—that would determine jurisdiction in criminal cases. The article satisfied long-standing British hopes for Britons not to be subjected to the Qing legal order and seemed to establish once and for all that British subjects would only be subject to the jurisdiction of their own legal system. However, the article did not spell out under the laws of *what* country an act would be considered criminal; it merely stated that crimes should be tried according to the criminal laws of the defendant, which left room for interpretation. This ambiguity could—and in due course would—be interpreted to mean that Chinese and British were subject to the same rules and regulations, but were to be punished according to the laws of their respective countries when they committed an offense.[83] In the case of violent crime, such as murder, this posed no problem, since homicide is an offense that is universally condemned. However, the situation was more complicated for political crimes or crimes against public order, and Qing authorities and British consular officials found it difficult to agree on any general principles. Could a foreigner be charged for violating traffic regulations, even if those regulations did not exist in his native country? Or could, for instance, a Briton be indicted for publicizing disparaging remarks about Qing officials? These questions were not given much thought at the time and would only be settled decades later.[84]

A more serious weakness of the article was that it did not make a clear distinction between criminal and civil jurisdiction, which was important from the point of view of British traders, who were eager to obtain legal remedies against Chinese business partners. On the other hand, the article made some sense from the Qing standpoint, which did not make a formal distinction between criminal and civil laws.[85] The article was not drafted by accomplished lawyers, and little thought seems to have been put into it. A systematic comparison of the two texts was never undertaken by either side prior to the ratification of the treaty.[86]

After the Treaty of the Bogue was concluded in July 1843, most Western countries enjoyed the same privileges as the British, given the imperial edict earlier in the year. But the leading foreign powers, none of which had been directly involved in the war of 1840–42, were not satisfied with these reassurances and wanted written guarantees that their particular nations would enjoy the same treatment as the British. The Tyler administration was in the process of annexing vast territories on the Pacific coast to the United States, and the apparent threat of British domination in the Pacific Ocean prompted the president to send Massachusetts legislator Caleb Cushing to negotiate a treaty with the Qing Empire.[87] The new situation in East Asia also offered the ailing July Monarchy an opportunity to restore France to its former glory as a Great Power, and the French prime minister François Guizot sent the seasoned diplomat Théodore de Lagrené to negotiate a treaty with the Qing Empire.[88] After a long wait in Macau, Cushing was finally able to conclude the Treaty of Wangxia (*Wangxia tiaoyue*) with Qiying on 3 July 1844 in the Kun Iam Temple in Mong-ha (Wangxia), in the outskirts of the Portuguese colony.[89] A lawyer and legislator, Cushing ensured that the American treaty contained what was widely regarded as the most precise statement of the principles of consular jurisdiction:

> Article 21: Subjects of China who may be guilty of any criminal act towards citizens of the United States shall be arrested and punished by the Chinese authorities according to the laws of China, and citizens of the United States who may commit any crime in China shall be subject to be tried and punished only by the Consul or other public functionary of the United States thereto authorized according to the laws of the United States; and in order to secure the prevention of all controversy and disaffection, justice shall be equitably and impartially administered on both sides.[90]

Cushing later claimed that he had secured "absolute and unqualified extraterritoriality" for U.S. citizens in China,[91] but the treaty subjected American ships trading outside the treaty ports to confiscation by the Chinese government (article 3) and withdrew consular protection from U.S. citizens trading in opium (article 33).[92] Clearly, the prohibition against opium was an attempt to distance the U.S. government from the opium trade, but the ban remained largely ineffective. The American prohibition on opium would later be exported to Japan with a greater degree of success and inspire the Japanese authorities to include similar clauses in treaties concluded with other nations. Perhaps the most innovative aspect of the treaty was that it represented an attempt to distinguish between criminal and civil jurisdiction, which provided a model for subsequent treaties.[93]

Lagrené concluded the Sino-French Treaty of Huangpu (*Huangpu tiaoyue*) on 24 October 1844. The French had access to excellent Sinological expertise, and the French treaty has been described as the "most carefully drawn" of all the treaties. In sharp contrast to the British and U.S. treaties, which would undergo several revisions in the following tumultuous decades, the French articles governing extraterritorial jurisdiction remained virtually unchanged for the rest of the century.[94] The treaty was more explicit on what acts were to be considered crimes, and the French also reserved their future freedom of action carefully.[95] The treaty enjoined Chinese authorities to protect Frenchmen and to mete out justice with the full strictness of the law if Chinese attacked French subjects. Like the American treaty, it endeavored to make a distinction between criminal and civil jurisdiction and restricted the extraterritorial privileges of Frenchmen to the five open ports.

The negotiations between the French and Qing representatives went smoothly,[96] probably due to the fact that the French were not seen as a significant threat to the Qing Empire, and their terms for extraterritorial arrangements were readily accepted.[97] Lagréné was a man of moderate religious convictions, and there is little evidence that he had any close relationship with the missionary community in Guangdong. Nevertheless, he wanted France to take credit for rescinding the Kangxi emperor's prohibition of Catholicism. Completely on his own initiative, Lagrené raised the question of legalizing Christianity with the imperial commissioner, which led to lengthy exchanges between the two diplomats. Fully conscious of the inherent risks of extending extraterritorial privileges to the Chinese populace, Qiying only agreed to ask the emperor to repeal the prohibition against the Christian religion after Lagrené had convinced him that Christian Chinese would not use the religion as a cover for committing crimes with impunity.[98] To Qiying, the question of granting numerically few foreigners legal privileges was a problem of an entirely different scale from the question of risking loss of control over the native population, which is why it is unfair to criticize Qiying for having agreed to extraterritorial privileges out of ignorance.[99] On 28 December 1844, the Daoguang emperor issued an edict that repealed the ban on Christianity, and on 18 March 1846 yet another edict was promulgated that restored confiscated church property to Chinese Catholics.[100] This would stand out as the most significant contribution of the French to the treaty port system.

Eagerly supported by France, the newly independent kingdom of Belgium also tried to conclude a treaty with China, but the Belgians were told to trade on the same conditions as other European nations.[101] The subsequent success of the Swedish envoy and businessman Carl Fredrik Liljevalch in securing an "unequal treaty" in 1847 can likely be attributed to the stubbornness of Liljevalch, who reportedly refused to leave before a treaty had been signed.[102] The resulting Treaty of Guangzhou (*Guangzhou Tiaoyue*), signed by Liljevalch and Qiying in March 1847, was in effect a copy of the American treaty. However, the volume of the trade between Sweden-Norway and China did not justify any professional permanent representation in the treaty ports.[103] In sharp contrast to the great treaty powers, the Scandinavian kingdom would be represented by American commercial consuls for most of the nineteenth century, much to the chagrin of some Swedish businessmen, who were suspicious of the double roles of commercial consuls.[104] Unlike the previous four treaties, the Swedish-Norwegian one was never formally ratified by the imperial throne, which threw a shadow of ambiguity over Sino-Swedish relations for over half a century.[105] The last power to conclude a treaty in the wake of the first Opium War was the Russian Empire, which concluded the Treaty of Kuldja (Ili) on 6 August 1851. The Russians were still focusing on their inland trade with Qing Empire, and the treaty secured the opening of two new inland "treaty ports," Tarbagatai and Ili. The Treaty of Kuldja gave Russia the right to send consuls to the Chinese treaty ports and provided for mutual extraterritorial rights for both Russians and Qing subjects along the Russo-Chinese border.[106]

The Tianjin Treaties, 1858–60

Qing statesmen involved in the peace negotiations hoped that the Treaty of Nanjing would help prevent future hostilities with the British and called it "a peace treaty of ten thousand years" (*wannian heyue*).[107] The explicit motive behind giving foreigners extraterritorial rights was to define the legal status of foreigners once and for all and to avoid future conflicts.[108] The opening of treaty ports went relatively smoothly in Shanghai, Ningbo, Xiamen, and Fuzhou, where foreign consuls were able to obtain separate areas outside the cities where they created "concessions," nominally Chinese territories where foreign powers exercised varying degrees of control. However, Sino-foreign frictions remained over a number of issues. Sticking to the traditional policy of ethnic segregation, a key element in preserving social stability in the plural legal order of Qing China, both local officials and residents refused foreigners entry into the city of Guangzhou. Most recorded incidents of antiforeign violence in the period immediately following the conclusion of the treaties took place in the city and its vicinity,[109] but not all encounters between local inhabitants and foreigners who happened to stray beyond the invisible dividing line deteriorated into violence.

The Swedish envoy Carl Fredrik Liljevalch, who had arrived in the southern treaty port in 1847, gave a vivid description of what happened when he and a number of other foreigners tried to enter the city gates of Guangzhou. They were quickly surrounded by a group of elderly men who, in the most polite manner possible, "blocked the way, while others were patting our shoulders, uttering sweet words, and pushed us outside of the gate before we had noticed it."[110] While it is true that local officials were channeling both popular and official xenophobia in Guangzhou, the refusal to admit foreigners into the city actually stemmed from the Treaty of Nanjing, the Chinese version of which only permitted foreigners to sojourn in the "harbors" (*gangkou*), not in the cities, where only consuls were permitted to reside.[111] The ascension of the notoriously antiforeign Xianfeng emperor in March 1850 further exacerbated tensions between foreigners and Chinese. He dismissed the two architects of the appeasement policy, Mujangga and Qiying, and appointed the hard-line official Ye Mingchen as viceroy and imperial commissioner for trade in Guangzhou as a reward for his success in keeping foreigners out of the treaty port.[112] The British, on their part, appointed as the new consul to Guangzhou in 1856 the Chinese-speaking hard-line diplomat Sir Harry Parkes, who was determined to force the supposedly recalcitrant local authorities to respect the "treaty rights" of the British Empire.[113]

Both the American and French treaties with the Qing Empire opened the possibility that the treaties could be revised after twelve years, a clause that could be invoked by any country that enjoyed most-favored-nation status, and by 1854 Britain, France, and the United States had agreed to act in concert in order to secure a beneficial revision of the treaties.[114] In 1856, two incidents with strong extraterritorial aspects provided Britain and France with a pretext to start yet another war with the Qing Empire, which was engulfed in the destructive Taiping Rebellion and had lost control of several central provinces of the empire. The first incident was the trial and execution of the French Catholic missionary Auguste Chapdelaine in a remote district of northwest Guangxi province in February 1856.[115] When news of the execution reached Guangzhou five months later, the French consul took stern measures to get redress from the Qing authorities. As gruesome as the details of Chapdelaine's fate were, the facts of the case were not as clear-cut as they first appeared. While the Qing Empire had reluctantly agreed to tolerate Christianity a decade earlier, the interior provinces of China remained closed to foreign visitors, whether merchants or missionaries, and the treaties stipulated that foreigners were to be delivered to their consuls when caught in the interior.[116] Between 1842 and 1856, Qing authorities caught and expelled fifteen French missionaries,[117] the most famous of whom was the eccentric Lazarist missionary Évariste Huc, who became known through his travelogues on China and Inner Asia.[118] In 1846, Huc and his colleague Joseph Gabet had ventured as far as to the Tibetan capital of Lhasa, where they were discovered by the Manchu imperial resident Qishan, who promptly arrested the two "French lamas" and expelled them after a brief trial at the viceroy's *yamen* in Sichuan. By all accounts, Qing officials made sure that both missionaries were well fed and courteously treated during their journey of several months back to Guangzhou.[119]

By 1856, the domestic situation in China was more complex than a decade earlier. Following the outbreak of the Taiping Rebellion in 1851, Guangxi province was in turmoil, and normal criminal procedure in capital cases was suspended in favor of summary executions of rebels.[120] Many Catholic missionaries were proficient in the Chinese language and did their best to blend into Chinese society by wearing local dress, and it cannot be ruled out that the unfortunate Chapdelaine was mixed up with Taiping rebels, who professed a religion that must have appeared almost identical to Catholicism from an official Chinese point of view. At least this was the version of the event that the governor-general Ye Mingchen later told an incredulous British journalist, George Wingrove Cooke:

> Yeh gave us his version of the murder of the French missionary. He says the man was dressed as a Chinaman and spoke Chinese, and no one suspected him of being a Frenchman; that the people accused him of having stolen women, and also of being a rebel; so his head was cut off. "If," said Yeh, "anyone had had a notion that he was a Frenchman he would have been sent to the French consul."[121]

Cooke assumed that "there [was] probably not a word of truth in this,"[122] and public opinion both in the treaty ports and the colonial metropoles were similarly disinclined to give Qing authorities the benefit of the doubt. As the details of the case reached France, the government of Napoleon III immediately seized on the alleged atrocity as an excuse to proclaim war against the Qing Empire, which enabled him to expand French influence in the Far East.[123]

Before the French government was able to finalize its plans for an expedition to China, a second incident occurred. In October 1856, Chinese policemen in Guangzhou boarded the lorcha *Arrow*, which had reportedly been engaged in smuggling in the Pearl River delta. The ship had been registered in the British colony of Hong Kong and was thus nominally under British jurisdiction, but the ship's British captain had let its registration expire. However, the militant Parkes chose to believe the claims that the British flag had been insulted by the Chinese authorities, which gave him a pretext to take military action against the Qing Empire. Without waiting for authorization from London, he shelled Guangzhou and captured Ye Mingchen. The French, who had fought alongside with Britain in the Crimean War, saw this as an opportunity to cement their alliance with Britain and joined the hostilities to avenge the killing of Chapdelaine and demand reparations. The United States and Russia did not take part in the war but watched the developments closely and made sure that they would get their share of the spoils. The "Arrow War" of 1856–60, which would become one of the most humiliating episodes for the Qing Empire, ended in a three-year occupation of Guangzhou, the invasion of Beijing, and the flight and eventual demise of the Xianfeng emperor.

Like the First Opium War, the Second Opium War started in the south but was decided in the north. The northward shift of the theater of war gave Parkes an opportunity to set up his own "puppet government" together with the French in occupied Guangzhou. Parkes commanded a military force consisting of one hundred British and thirty French soldiers, as well as a Chinese police force of more than one thousand men. The allies realized that they would not be able to run the city by themselves, so they enlisted the reluctant participation of the Mongol official Bogui, the acting governor of Guangdong, who was supposed to lend some legitimacy to the occupied government.[124] In a memorial to the throne, the governor-general of Liangguang, Huang Zonghan, rather colorfully described the way justice was administered under Parkes's régime:

> Whenever there is a dispute between commoners and foreigners, the suit has to be brought to their military office, where their judge [*lishiguan*] carries out the trial by himself. All cases are settled by fines and in some suits the fine may be as high as a thousand taels of silver. Sometimes they send a note to Bogui and order him to send an official to sit in a joint trial [*huishen*]. When the official arrives he sits beneath the English and French judges, and although he is present, he is not allowed to talk, to spit or smoke; it is just as if he were held in invisible shackles [*wuxing zhi zhigu*]. If the case is not settled in one day, he has to return the following day.[125]

In Huang's eyes, Parkes's "mixed court" no doubt looked very much like a military tribunal, where the Qing official felt that he was little more than window dressing. However, it is not so much the participation of foreigners in mixed cases that seems to have bothered the governor as the fact that the local official did not have a say in the rulings and was merely there to legitimize the proceedings. The military tribunal in Guangzhou was only a first attempt to establish hybrid institutions, which would provide Parkes with important experience in Chinese administration, impressing on him the necessity of enlisting Chinese support in order to run local government.[126] When Parkes participated in setting up a Mixed Court in Shanghai the following decade, Qing officials willingly took part in the proceedings of the court, while trying to make sure that they had a proper voice in settling cases involving Chinese subjects.

The failure to create a workable legal régime in the treaty ports had convinced the British that the extraterritorial stipulations of the Treaty of the Bogue were unsatisfactory. Following the example of the 1844 American treaty, they created a separate article for civil jurisdiction and virtually copied he clause on criminal jurisdiction from the American Treaty of Wangxia. In the English text of the Sino-British Treaty of Tianjin, concluded on 26 June 1858, the last sentence of article 16 seems to be a general statement on how justice is to be administered, just like the American treaty from which it originated: "Justice shall be equitably and impartially administered on both sides." However, the Chinese wording of the article gives a very different idea, and a literal translation of the sentence would read: "In the interests of justice, all mixed cases between the two countries should be tried jointly and equitably" (*liangguo jiaoshe shijian bici jun xu huitong gongping shenduan yi zhao yundang*).[127]

It is not entirely clear how and why this change was introduced into an article that already existed in a neat Chinese translation in the American treaty. Both British and Qing accounts of the event agree that the British held sway in the negotiations of the treaty,[128] and Thomas Wade, who was present as a junior interpreter, later claimed that he was ultimately responsible for the wording of the article.[129] Nationalist Chinese historiography has interpreted the change in the Chinese wording of the article as part of a British plot to claim mixed jurisdiction in China.[130] Be that as it may, the article is strikingly similar to provisions in the Qing Code regulating mixed cases, which makes it hard to dispel the notion that the Qing negotiators subjected the extraterritorial clause on criminal jurisdiction to subtle manipulation. Given the fact that the British had fought hard to exempt British subjects from Qing criminal jurisdiction for several decades, it is difficult to understand why British representatives would knowingly agree to an arrangement that appeared to give Qing officials an equal part in the sentencing of British criminals. On the other hand, the Chinese wording of the article could possibly soothe some Chinese resentment against British consular jurisdiction and recover some lost ground by granting them a share in judging cases where foreigners stood accused of crimes against Chinese.[131]

Another paragraph pertaining to civil cases was inserted into the treaty that put the settlement of disputes between British and Qing subjects into the hands of the British consul. Only when the consul failed to settle the dispute "amicably" would the Qing authorities be involved.[132] It may seem inexplicable that the Qing authorities agreed to give foreign consuls so much influence over civil jurisdiction, but civil and private law were not recognized as a distinct branches of the Qing legal system. The overburdened magistrates were as a rule reluctant to hear what we would call "civil suits" and endeavored to have them settled out of court as much as possible. When magistrates settled civil cases, they were often settled as criminal cases, involving some kind of penal aspect. Only cases that could not be settled amicably by the foreign consuls would be decided by the consul and the local authorities together, and in the event that the case had to be settled criminally, the treaty ensured that Qing subjects would be punished according to Qing law.

During the negotiations of the treaty, the British representatives raised the long-standing question of allowing British traders to travel and reside in the interior, much desired by the British merchant communities. However, the Qing representatives, Guiliang, Huashana, and Qiying, were clearly aware of the dangers of marrying freedom of movement with unlimited extraterritorial privileges. They expressed serious concern about British traveling to the interior on passports, if they were to be protected by consuls as they were in the treaty ports.[133] The resulting treaty permitted Britons to travel to the interior with passports but did not provide for unrestricted residence in the interior of China. As a precaution against the linguistic confusion that plagued Sino-British relations under the Treaty of Nanjing, article 50 of the Treaty of Tianjin stipulated that English would be the language used in "all official communications" from the British, "accompanied by a Chinese version," but "in the event of there being any difference of meaning between the English and Chinese text, the English Government will hold the sense as expressed in the English text to be the correct sense." However, this clause did not prevent Chinese officials from basing their interpretations of the treaties on the Chinese version,[134] especially in cases of mixed jurisdiction.

In the Sino-French Treaty of Tianjin, which was concluded on 27 June 1858, the French maintained their extraterritorial arrangements largely unaltered but also managed to extract further concessions from the Qing government with regard to the rights of missionaries and the practice of Christianity in China.[135] The nonbelligerent Americans were able to secure more specific clauses on extraterritoriality that put Americans under more exclusive consular jurisdiction than before.[136] Russia, which had maintained its own set of "equal treaties" with the Qing Empire since the seventeenth century, now abandoned these in favor of a new "unequal treaty" based on the British model. The old arrangement, which provided for mutual extraterritoriality for Russian and Qing subjects, was replaced with a new one that granted only Russian subjects extraterritorial rights. Here Russia can be said to have made the transition from a continental power to a maritime one in its relations with Qing China, thus replacing mutual extraterritoriality with unilateral extraterritoriality. Incidentally, the 1858 Treaty of Tianjin between the Qing and Romanov empires was the last to have a Manchu-language version.[137]

The treaties of 1858–60 provided the framework for the early treaty port system, whose essential elements were the opening of coastal ports for foreign trade, extraterritorial rights to Westerners residing in the treaty ports, and fixed tariffs in the Sino-foreign trade. All treaties included a "most-favored-nation" clause, which meant that privileges the Qing Empire had granted to one power would automatically be granted to all others. This made it necessary for all treaty parties to be updated on the other treaties in order to safeguard their "rights," as many foreigners preferred to call their privileges. As regards extraterritoriality and consular jurisdiction, very few innovations were introduced into the Sino-Western treaties after 1860, which remained more or less unchanged for the rest of the century, at least in the formal sense of the term. In the years following the conclusion of the Convention of Peking, a number of European countries, such as Germany, Austro-Hungary, the Netherlands, and Denmark, would follow suit and conclude treaties after the British model. The treaty ports had come to stay.

Attempts at Revision

The Treaties of Tianjin left a number of questions unresolved, such as the question of foreign residence in the interior of China. When treaties came up for revision in 1868, the British merchant community clamored for the right of unrestricted travel and residence in the interior of China, but the Qing government, led by the prominent Manchu statesman Wenxiang, was adamantly opposed to this unless extraterritoriality was also abolished.[138] In opposition to both the British merchant community and the U.S. minister Ross Browne, the British minister Sir Rutherford Alcock was sympathetic to the Qing position. He stated:

> If foreign Powers stipulate that their subjects shall freely reside, trade, and travel in the interior exempt from the jurisdiction of Chinese authorities and laws, and do not mean by that to introduce a state of license and immunity from any legal obligations and with it universal wrong and disorder, the obligation is clear themselves to provide the necessary machinery for governing their own subjects wherever resident or scattered throughout the Chinese Empire. Which of the Treaty Powers has ever thought of undertaking such a task?[139]

Alcock was not willing to trade the abolition of extraterritoriality for the right of residence in the interior, so foreigners remained restricted to the treaty ports. Consequently, the issue of extraterritoriality was not covered by the abortive Alcock Convention of 1869.[140]

If Qing statesmen had been successful in preventing foreigners from settling in the interior of China and bringing their extraterritorial privileges with them, the Qing government was less successful in dealing with missionaries. French diplomats and missionaries did not feel bound by Lagrené's promise in 1844 that the freedom to practice the Christian religion would not interfere with the Chinese legal system. By skillful manipulation of the Chinese text of the 1860 Convention of Beijing, which was a supplementary treaty to the Sino-French Treaty of Tianjin, the French managed to establish the right of Catholic missionaries to buy land and take up residence in the interior,[141] which in turn paved the way for missionaries belonging to other Christian congregations to do the same. However, Qing authorities were not prepared to accept such an arrogation of privileges and tried to convince the treaty powers to withdraw consular protection from missionaries in the interior. Qing authorities claimed that the missionaries interfered in local administration and that they tried to withdraw Chinese Christian converts from local jurisdiction. The Qing government regarded the missionaries (*jiaoshi*) as nothing more than erudite scholars who were preaching a doctrine of benevolence.[142] In a statement dispatched to Alcock in the wake of the Tianjin Massacre in 1871, the Qing government stated that just as Hanlin scholars and other holders of the highest academic degree (*jinshi*) were subject to the jurisdiction of local officials when they lived in the interior, so too were missionaries expected to subject themselves to the local authorities (*gui difangguan guanxia*) in the provinces. The missionaries dressed like Chinese and spoke Chinese dialects, yet they did not adapt themselves to Qing rule and Chinese customs.[143] Indeed, by virtue of having taken up residence in the interior of China, the missionaries had submitted themselves to Qing rule just as the Qing Code prescribed in the statute on people "beyond the pale of Chinese civilization." The treaty powers dismissed these protests,[144] but Qing attempts to regulate missionaries speaks volumes about how consistently Qing officials understood extraterritoriality as a privilege limited to the treaty ports only.

A thorny question that had been left open by the treaties of Tianjin was the question how to deal with mixed cases, and the treaties remained contradictory on this point. Whereas the British and Russian treaties did give some hints, none of the treaties envisaged any permanent institutions for adjudicating mixed cases involving foreigners and Qing subjects. The lack of a fixed procedure was not a big problem in most of the treaty ports, where the number of foreigners was small, and controversial mixed cases could be tried in consular and local Chinese courts on an ad hoc basis. However, by the mid-1860s, the bustling treaty port of Shanghai had outgrown the limitations of the treaties, and local actors would step in to create institutions that would push the interpretation of the treaties in new and novel directions.

3

Institutionalizing Extraterritoriality

The Mixed Court and the British Supreme Court in Shanghai

In the mid-nineteenth century, Shanghai had developed into the hub of the treaty port system in East Asia, where consular courts from a variety of different countries coexisted with a number of local Chinese courts, creating a very complex legal order. In 1908, two British writers traveling along the China coast made the following remark on the state of law and order in Shanghai:

> The administration of justice of the law in Shanghai, considering the volume of business transacted at the port and the amount of property, the ownership of which depends upon the decision of the Courts, would be a hopeless anomaly to a practiced lawyer. If the state of things that prevails here were to be described to a learned theoretic professor in the West, he would probably say that no civilised existence could be led by men under such conditions, and yet the cosmopolitan community live together in surprising peace and good order.[1]

Evidently, early twentieth-century Western observers did not seem to think that the lack of any coherent legal system in Shanghai meant that "peace and good order" could not be maintained in the city. Given the propensity of historians to regard Shanghai as the cradle of modern China, or as the battleground of anticolonial struggles in China's short twentieth century, it is easy to forget that the fragile legal order of Shanghai rested as much on gunboats as on the cooperation between different legal spheres in the bustling treaty port. This chapter explores two of the most important legal institutions in late nineteenth century Shanghai: the Mixed Court in the International Settlement and the British Supreme Court. They were not simple implants of Western legal institutions, or laboratories of "rule of law," but products of a peculiar institutional environment that owed much to Chinese concepts of law and legal institutions.

The Emergence of Shanghai

The treaty port system attained its most sophisticated form in the prosperous Shanghai area, where Britain, the United States, and France established settlements in the 1840s. The treaties that followed the Opium Wars only gave foreigners the right to reside in the newly opened ports and said nothing about any separate foreign settlements as such. Anticipating the opening of Shanghai to foreign residents, Grand Councilor Mujangga (Muzhang'a) memorialized the throne in May 1843 and suggested that the subprefect for supervising granaries (*duliang tongzhi*) in nearby Suzhou be transferred to Shanghai in order to deal with foreign trade, Sino-foreign affairs (*huayi jiaoshe shijian*), and suppressing vagrants from Fujian and Guangdong.[2] When Shanghai was opened to foreign trade in 1843, Britons did not meet the same resistance as they had in Guangzhou in the aftermath of the Opium War, and they were allowed to lease houses both in the city of Shanghai and outside the city walls. However, after two violent incidents involving foreigners,[3] the Shanghai circuit intendant Gong Mujiu grew weary of too intimate Sino-foreign contact. In 1845, he decided to formalize the establishment of a separate British settlement in Shanghai, north of Yangjingbang, a creek that ran north of the Chinese city and whose name would become synonymous with the settlement itself.[4] The same year, Gong Mujiu and the British consul, Captain George Balfour, concluded an agreement called the "Land Regulations" (*Shanghai zudi zhangcheng*), which provided the institutional basis for the British settlement.[5] The circuit intendant played an important part in the drafting of the regulations, and they were first promulgated in the Chinese city of Shanghai and only then submitted to the British consulate.[6]

The Land Regulations determined the conditions under which Britons could lease land in the area allotted to them, and Chinese were in principle not allowed to rent property in the settlement. Article 23 of the regulations authorized the British consul to punish people who were in breach of the regulations, something that many foreigners interpreted as the first precedent for foreign territorial jurisdiction in Shanghai.[7] The regulations also confirmed the establishment of a subprefect for maritime defense (*haifang tongzhi*) in Shanghai, who was put in charge of Sino-foreign affairs, just as Mujangga had suggested. The subprefect was usually called "haifang" by foreigners,[8] and the *Chinese Repository* gave the following account of the officer's duties.

> Shánghái being an important post, and much exposed on account of its position to attacks from robbers and pirates, and withal at the long distance of thirty miles from the seat of the prefect at "Pine River" [Songjiang], this assistant has been placed here for the better defense and control of the people. His authority is both civil and military,

extending alike to the common people and the soldiery. In rank and jurisdiction, he is superior to the Chí-hién [*zhixian*] or proper magistrate, and matters of importance must be reported up through him to the high provincial officers.[9]

Following the British example, the French consul Charles de Montigny and the Manchu circuit intendant Lin'gui agreed in 1849 that a French settlement be set up on the strip of land between the Chinese City and the British settlement.[10] The American consul expressed his dissatisfaction that the British and French had been able to monopolize two of the best plots of land in the area, and after lengthy deliberations, the Americans eventually established their own settlement northeast of Shanghai.[11] Despite subsequent claims to the contrary, the foreign settlements formally remained under Qing sovereignty. Chinese who committed crimes in the British settlement were initially sent to the Chinese City to be tried and punished by the Shanghai district magistrate, an arrangement foreign residents complained was "unsatisfactory."[12] In the French Concession, the powerful French consul developed a different arrangement; the consul tried Chinese criminals alone, and in severe criminal cases he invited the circuit intendant to the bench to rule together with him.[13]

The turbulent 1850s would turn what were originally intended to be predominantly foreign settlements into a diverse, cosmopolitan area, with all the legal problems that would entail. In the wake of the occupation of the Chinese City by the Fukienese Small Sword Society (*Xiaodaohui*) in 1853 and the much more destructive Taiping Rebellion, Qing rule in Shanghai effectively collapsed. A large number of Chinese took refuge in the foreign settlements, and the circuit intendant became increasingly dependent on foreign protection. The new situation necessitated new arrangements, and in 1854 the three foreign settlements took steps to protect their integrity by promulgating new land regulations and founding the "Shanghai Municipal Council," whose Chinese name (*Gongbuju*) meant "Bureau of Works." The French, who wished to turn their settlement into a colony in the proper sense of the word, withdrew from the agreement in 1856 and founded their own French Concession.[14] The British and American settlements eventually merged into the International Settlement.[15] One of the first products of this local co-optation of foreigners into the Qing polity was the Imperial Maritime Customs Service, which was established by the British, French, and American consuls in cooperation with the circuit intendant Wu Jianzhang in July 1854.

The numerous Chinese inhabitants of Shanghai were still subject to Qing law, and the same held for the increasing numbers of foreigners in Shanghai whose status was not defined by treaty and who were not represented by consuls. In the absence of any effective local administration, Chinese and "unrepresented foreigners" were in effect administered by the consuls of the treaty powers.[16] As Qing rule was restored in the Yangtze Valley and things returned to normal in Shanghai in the early 1860s, a group of prominent Shanghai residents argued for turning the International Settlement into a "free city," with its own laws and exclusive jurisdiction, implying that foreign jurisdiction over the Chinese residents would be retained, even after Qing rule was restored in the region. This was resisted in particular by the British diplomats, who did not want to undermine the treaties.[17] The British minister, Sir Frederick Bruce, made the case in the following way:

> I think our policy ought to be based on two principles: Respect for Chinese authority, and efforts to make their authorities do their duty towards us as by Treaty. We ought therefore to insist on their punishing Chinese offenders, and force them, if possible to deal with unrepresented foreigners. We ought to make no arrangements with local authorities in contradiction to these principles, for they are not entitled to abandon their people to our jurisdiction nor are they competent to hand over foreigners to our tribunals. . . . The Chinese inhabiting the settlement must not be taught to believe they are not under Chinese authority. If they are to be emancipated, how is the Chinese Government to be held responsible for the security of British property in Chinese ports? I look forward to increased confusion and difficulty if we cannot make the Chinese exert themselves to do their duty, and if we cannot keep our own blackguards in order. We must work with the Chinese officials, and not be perpetually in antagonism, if we wish to found anything permanent.[18]

Clearly the legal system in Shanghai faced an institutional crisis, and new arrangements were badly needed to create stability in the city. Being the dominant treaty power, the British took the initiative to restore law and order, and in 1864, Harry Parkes, now the British consul, moved to establish a "Mixed Court" in the International Settlement.[19] Parkes's experience administering his puppet government in Guangzhou during the Second Opium War had taught him the importance of working closely with Chinese authorities in times of peace. According to Parkes's plan, a Qing official would be invited to the International Settlement to try mixed cases in which Chinese were defendants and cases involving foreigners of unrepresented countries.[20] The practice of having an assessor present in cases in which foreigners were parties was similar to the practice of sending the dragoman to sit as an assessor in mixed cases tried in the Ottoman Empire, and the assessor was often a vice-consul or an interpreter. In his deliberations with Qing officials on the matter, Parkes accepted the official Qing position that articles 16 and 22 in the British Treaty of Tianjin and article 11 in the American Treaty of Tianjin were to be considered the treaty basis of the Mixed Court, whereas articles 17 and 24 of the British and American treaties, respectively, were not to be applicable to the Mixed Court. The articles that Parkes accepted dealt with the trial of criminal cases and the enforcement of debts, whereas the articles that he rejected vaguely dealt with the settlement of disputes and civil cases. In accepting the Qing view, Parkes implicitly sanctioned the traditional Chinese idea that "law" meant "criminal law," and he was widely criticized for his lack of zeal in reforming the Chinese legal system.[21]

The Mixed Court, initially called *Yangjingbang lishi gongxie*, started holding sessions in the British Consulate on 1 May 1864.[22] As a rule, the subprefect for maritime defense sat as the deputy (*weiyuan*) of the circuit intendant, whereas a translator, or vice-consul, officiated as a foreign assessor. In the absence of any fixed sets of rules and procedure, the nature of the court depended largely on the personal qualities of the subprefect and the assessors. The first British assessor was Chaloner Alabaster, one of the early "enthusiasts" in the Mixed Court,[23] who would compile his observations into one of the most authoritative English-language accounts of the nineteenth-century Qing legal order.[24] Among the early subprefects were the scholar Shen Bingyuan and the famed "millionaire-mandarin" Wu Xu.[25] When the Chinese official and the foreign assessor could not agree on a verdict, the circuit intendant and the relevant consul constituted a "Mixed Court of Appeal," which was supposed to resolve the matter. No fixed set of rules of the early Mixed Court has survived, and the Court only had authority to rule in minor criminal matters and civil suits.[26] The proceedings of the court were followed with great interest by both the foreign and Chinese residents of Shanghai, and *Shenbao* and the *North China Daily News* carried columns on the court.

It is evident that Qing officials drew on their experience of managing interethnic disputes when they agreed to set up the court together with the foreign consuls. While British actors such as Parkes could claim paternity of the Mixed Court,[27] the maritime subprefect was not established because foreigners had asked for him but in *anticipation* of the arrival of foreigners. The Mixed Court subprefect had evolved from the subprefect for maritime defense (*haifang tongzhi*), and it was not unusual for subprefects for maritime defense to be put in charge of managing interethnic relations and mixed cases. For instance, the subprefect for maritime defense in Macau was also responsible for "mixed cases," and his colleague in Zhapu in Zhejiang province had been made into a judicial subprefect when Manchu banner troops were garrisoned there in the Yongzheng period (1723–35).[28] Qing officials elected to use the unusual term *gongxie* for the Mixed Court, a term that was used for the agency that managed joint conferences during the Yuan dynasty. In theory, the assessor had no voice in the judgment as such but was only present to guard the interests of the foreign community. However, in Shanghai the assessors would in practice be able to claim the status of a cojudge, and they were helped by the fact that Qing legal procedure allowed for joint conferences in cases of mixed jurisdiction. At the same time that the foreign assessors believed they were defending "foreign interests" in the International Settlement, they were also being integrated into the Qing legal order.

At the same time that the Mixed Court was established, the British took measures to consolidate their consular courts in China proper. Up to that point, the Supreme Court in Hong Kong had been the highest British court in China, but the development of the Yangtze Valley as the center of British interests in China made it untenable to run the consular court from the Crown Colony, which was entirely under British jurisdiction. The rulings of the Hong Kong court were widely resented by British residents in China, who found the court out of touch with realities on the ground.[29] For instance, in 1863, the London *Times* carried an article that hyperbolically claimed that the "Supreme Court of Hong Kong is the greatest nuisance in the East."[30] In 1865, the British judge Sir Edmund Hornby was dispatched to establish a British Supreme Court in Shanghai.[31] Hornby had served as a consular judge in Constantinople, where he had reorganized the British consular court service, which had fallen into disrepair.[32] The establishment of the Supreme Court was not challenged from any official quarters in China, and there are good reasons to believe that this court was tacitly welcomed.[33] Its establishment made it possible to try British criminals close to the crime scene and for Qing officials to exert direct pressure on British authorities when they were not satisfied with a sentence. The risk of sending British suspects to Britain for punishment was one of the reasons why the Qing emperor had objected to British jurisdiction in China in the first place.[34]

While the British were taking these initiatives, Qing authorities were taking measures to strengthen the position of the Mixed Court, putting an end to the practice of constantly changing subprefects. In 1867, Chen Fuxun was appointed Mixed Court subprefect, a position he would hold for twenty-six years, with only short interruptions.[35] By the end of his tenure, he enjoyed a certain degree of respect in both the Chinese and foreign communities.[36] The following year, the Mixed Court asserted its independence by moving out of the British Consulate into permanent premises on Nanking Road, where it would remain for more than thirty years.[37] In just a couple of years, the Mixed Court grew into the most important court of law in the International Settlement, and in 1868 the British vice-consul and assessor R. J. Forrest said that "ten times more cases come before the Mixed Court in the course of a year than before our Supreme Court in all its branches."[38]

The International Mixed Court on Nanking Road in the 1870s, with a crowd of onlookers watching the proceedings. The site was used for this purpose until 1899, when the Mixed Court was moved to a new location in Zhabei. Today this location has the address 720 Nanjing Donglu and houses the Shanghai No 1 Food Store. Courtesy of Shanghai Municipal Archives.

The Mixed Court Rules, 1869

The local authorities in Shanghai were reportedly not satisfied with the operation of the court, and in the late 1860s the circuit intendant in Shanghai, Ying Baoshi, took the initiative to negotiate a permanent set of rules.[39] The Qing démarche led to a lively discussion in the foreign community, and the negotiations were eventually moved to the capital. The French were also invited to take part in the discussions on the Mixed Court. France had long experience of running commercial mixed courts (*tidjaret*) in Constantinople, and French diplomats were initially favorably disposed to taking part in a Mixed Court in Shanghai. However, once the French realized that the projected rules would permit local Qing authorities to arrest Chinese offenders in the foreign settlements without permission from the French consular authorities, France withdrew from the negotiations,[40] for this arrangement ran contrary to French ambitions to exercise full colonial jurisdiction over the French Concession. The French went on to establish their own Mixed Court, which made use of the Mixed Court rules only to the extent that they did not conflict with the overall aims of French policy in Shanghai.[41]

In December 1866 Rutherford Alcock, the British minister to China, formally suggested that a special official be established in Yangjingbang in order to assume jurisdiction over the Chinese community in the international settlement.[42] The initial response from Prince Gong and the Zongli Yamen was reserved. The Yamen wanted know more details of the local discussions between Harry Parkes and the minister superintendent of trade (*Tongshang dachen*) before any further steps were taken.[43] In May of the following year, Prince Gong was fully apprised of the situation and wrote a longer response to Alcock, in which he stated that according to established practice, it was not possible to establish a new official whose mandate would compete with the existing officials in Yangjingbang. However, the already existing maritime subprefect could be formally appointed to the Mixed Court.[44]

It was not a foregone conclusion that the Mixed Court would remain an assymetric institution, where foreign assessors would take part in the sentencing of Chinese defendants, whereas no similar privilege would be accorded to Qing officials in the consular courts. Indeed, the early successes of the Mixed Court raised Chinese expectations that the court would extend its jurisdiction to foreigners as well. These aspirations were shared by some foreigners, and in a memorandum on the legal system in Shanghai, Vice-Consul Forrest expressed his cautious approval of "amalgamation" of the British Supreme Court and the Shanghai Mixed Court.[45] Alcock shared this view and was also concerned that it would be difficult to obtain Chinese acquiescence to the court unless some degree of reciprocity was attained. To that end, he asked Hornby to draw up a memorandum on how the experience with mixed courts for civil suits in the Ottoman Empire could be used to the benefit of the mixed court in Shanghai. In his report, Hornby responded that the Ottoman legal system was much more "developed" than its Chinese counterpart, and that European and Chinese notions of justice were essentially incompatible.[46] Alcock was not convinced by Hornby's uncompromising stand and retorted:

> Practical difficulties there will be, no doubt, in any attempt to secure justice and a working tribunal of a mixed nationality. But very similar difficulties from precisely similar causes must have been encountered and overcome in Turkey long before there was any knowledge of French or a Code Napoléon....
>
> Without entirely accepting an opinion which has been brought forward by the late foreign co-judge, or assessor, Mr Alabaster, that the principles of European and Chinese justice are at bottom the same, I conclude there must be some principles in common that can be appealed to as a basis for any judicial system that may be proposed. And the special adaptation, which the circumstances may require can be

matter for consideration, and subject from time to time to the modifications experience and precedent will suggest.[47]

Alcock's statement, which was in line with the "co-operative policy" the British government tried to implement in China after the Second Opium War, also demonstrates that the encounter between European and Chinese legal orders in the nineteenth century cannot be reduced to a simple "clash of cultures" or conflicting "discourses" on law.[48] There was considerable latitude of opinion within the British community, and at least some diplomats, such as Alcock and Alabaster, had a certain degree of respect for the Qing legal order and were prepared to allow the Mixed Court to develop gradually through trial and error.

The discussions between the British, Americans, and Chinese continued uninterrupted, and on 20 October 1868, Prince Gong submitted a proposal to the foreign ministers in Beijing. The new regulations confirmed the establishment of the Shanghai subprefect and further stated that he would have the authority to decide cases jointly with a foreign assessor (*pai yangguan huishen*) in commercial, civil, and criminal cases according to Chinese law in mixed cases where Chinese or unrepresented foreigners were defendants. In cases involving only Chinese, the subprefect would decide cases by himself without interference from the foreign consuls (*geguo lingshiguan wuyong ganyu*). The Mixed Court subprefect only had authority to sentence criminals to minor punishments independently, and criminal cases punishable by "death and the various degrees of banishment" (*junliu tuzui yishang*) had to be referred to the surveillance commissioner (*niesi*) by way of the district magistrate's *yamen*. The draft rules also seemed to pave the way for an amalgamation of the Mixed Court with the consular courts in Shanghai. The English text of rule 2 stated: "whenever a foreigner is involved before this court, his national consul, either in person or by deputy, and the subprefect, shall jointly try him according to the facts." But the rules remained ambiguous on this point, because rule 7 also established that foreigners "shall be tried and punished by their own consuls."[49]

The American minister, Ross Browne, was initially not concerned with the possible expansion of the Mixed Court's jurisdiction. His only concern was that direct references to Chinese corporal punishments, such as the cangue and the bamboo, be taken out of the rules. He feared that "if these clauses are retained, they might be misconstrued, and it be inferred that they are approved and that foreigners are thus to be punished."[50] When Browne reported his correspondence to the U.S. State Department, the Bureau of Claims immediately seized on the ambiguity in his position and argued that allowing the Mixed Court to rule in cases in which U.S. citizens were defendants was inconsistent with the U.S. Treaty of Tianjin.[51] The ambiguous wording was subsequently excised from the English version of the rules, but not from the Chinese version, and on 20 April

1869, the new Provisional Rules for the Mixed Court (*Shanghai Yangjingbang sheguan huishen zhangcheng*) were promulgated by the new British Consul, Walter Henry Medhurst.[52]

The rules were initially intended to be valid for only one year, but they remained in force until the rendition of the court to Chinese jurisdiction in 1927. In the words of the Russian émigré author Anatol Kotenev, the rules had been "drafted in Chinese and approved in English,"[53] and a number of striking similarities between the procedures and terms defining the Mixed Court and the judicial subprefect remained. To begin with, the official name of the new Mixed Court was *Huishen gongxie*, literally "Court of Joint Trials,"[54] placing the court within the Qing plural legal order rather than among other mixed courts in the world that may have informed Western perceptions of this one.[55] Indeed, the Chinese version of the rules read very much like the Qing Code stipulations on mixed cases and the jurisdiction of the judicial subprefect. Consequently, the very definition of what constituted a "mixed case" (*jiaoshe anjian*) was different in the English and Chinese texts of the rules. For instance, according to the English version of rule 3, a consul could attend hearings in which the defendant "is a native Chinese servant in foreign employ," but "he shall not interfere if no foreign interest is involved." The Chinese version said nothing about "foreign interest" but simply stated that the consul could not interfere in cases where no foreigners were involved (*ru anzhong bing bu qianshe yangren zhe, bude ganyu*).[56] The Qing legal system did recognize personal jurisdiction to a certain extent, but not the nebulous concept of "foreign interests," which could—and would—expand indefinitely to benefit the treaty powers.

Furthermore, the Mixed Court subprefect had the same nominal rank and roughly the same jurisdiction as the judicial subprefect. Like the judicial subprefect—but unlike regular district magistrates—the Mixed Court subprefect was not charged with administrative duties, nor was he charged with the maintenance of law and order within his area of responsibility, which were undertaken by the police authorities in the foreign settlements or by the Shanghai district magistrate's *yamen*.[57] There was a great deal of variety in the appellations of this subprefect. In official documents, such as court summons and arrest warrants, he was often referred to as *huishen fenfu* or *haifang fenfu*, *fenfu* being an epistolary appellation of the subprefect.[58] In a number of nonofficial sources on the Mixed Court, he is referred to as *huayang tongzhi* or *huishen tongzhi*.[59] Most revealingly, in a gazetteer for Shanghai county from 1918, relating the early history of the Mixed Court and listing the incumbent officials since the Tongzhi period (1862–74), the subprefect is called *huayang lishi tongzhi*, and in another book on the International Settlement from the Republican Era, the subprefect is simply referred to as *lishi tongzhi*.[60] The use of these terms indicates that contemporary Chinese made a direct connection between the Mixed Court subprefect and the judicial subprefect, who took part in trying mixed cases between Manchus and Chinese. It also harkened back to judicial subprefect being called *qimin lishi tongzhi* in the gazetteer of Guangzhou banner garrison, published during the Guangxu period (1875–1908). Earlier documents do not show that *qimin* was ever prefixed to *lishi tongzhi* in this way, so by late Qing there was a need to make a distinction, which indicates that there was a conceptual connection between the two subprefects. Indeed, not far from Shanghai, there were no fewer than four banner garrisons—Jiangning, Jingkou, Hangzhou, and Zhapu—all of which had judicial subprefects who were retained until the end of the Qing dynasty.

A number of additional features set the Mixed Court subprefect apart from other subprefects. He was not listed in the *Supplement to the Collected Statutes of the Great Qing Dynasty*. Although his office was nominally a subprefecture, the actual rank of the incumbent was roughly equal to a district magistrate. The Mixed Court subprefect was a deputy of the circuit intendant; he held a wooden seal instead of a brass seal and could only mete out certain punishments.[61] This had been the practice from the very beginning of the court, and it appears that local authorities were eager not to allow foreign influence to assert itself through the Mixed Court subprefect.[62] Qing officials were well aware of the fact that foreigners regarded Chinese punishments as barbarous,[63] and they had good reason to suspect that too much foreign involvement might lead to undue interference. As things stood after the approval of the Mixed Court rules in 1869, it may seem that the foreign ministers had gotten the better of the Qing authorities on the question of jurisdiction over foreigners in mixed cases. But the exact jurisdiction and construction of the court was still not entirely clear, as was demonstrated by a case of homicide that occurred a couple of months after the Mixed Court rules were adopted.

"Regina vs. George" 1869

Around noon on 23 June 1869, an English watchman, Robert Willis George, shot and killed a Chinese carpenter, Wang Aran, and seriously wounded a colleague of Wang. Both the perpetrator and his two victims were employed by S. C. Farnham & Co. at Collier's Dock. They had been involved in intermittent fights for some time, and the killing of Wang followed an altercation early in the morning between George and a group of carpenters. The fight came to a climax when Wang Aran "broke wind" in front of George, which led to a violent scuffle. The crowd was promptly dispersed, but later George insulted a carpenter and yelled: "I'll have my revenge before 6 o'clock to night." Having delivered on his promise, George made no attempt to escape, and F. N. Prebble, an employee of the company, brought him to the police in the International Settlement later that day. On the way to the police station, George reportedly told Prebble that "he was not sorry for the Chinaman."[64]

Both British and Qing authorities started work on the case promptly. The following day, the Shanghai district magistrate arrived at the crime scene to carry out his own inquest into the murder. On his return to Shanghai City in the afternoon, he was mobbed by a crowd that clamored for revenge. The crowd eventually became so unruly that he had to seek refuge in the French police station.[65] The following day, George was brought to the Police Court, which heard witnesses and evidence for the following two weeks.[66] In the hearings, George reportedly showed no repentance for his act, and the Police Court indicted him on the charge of "wilful murder."

In mid-July, George was brought to trial in the Supreme Court before Sir Edmund Hornby and a five-man jury; the Shanghai district magistrate was also on the bench. Both foreign and Chinese witnesses were called to testify. The trial reached a bizarre climax when George's defense counsel, Nicholas John Hannen, moved to dismiss the Chinese witnesses on account of their lack of Christian faith, which supposedly disqualified them to testify under oath. The perplexed supreme judge then cross-examined one of the Chinese witnesses on his religious faith and established to his satisfaction that the witness did indeed believe that the thunder-god would strike him down if he lied, which was deemed sufficient substitute for a Christian confession.[67] All the witnesses testified to George's callousness, and the jury returned a "guilty" verdict. Hornby—who claimed to agonize over every capital case—had no other choice than to sentence the defendant to death by hanging.[68] Appeals on George's behalf were denied, and the British minister confirmed the capital sentence. George was hanged in the early morning of 31 August 1869, in the presence of the British consul, the Mixed Court magistrate, and the district magistrate, as well as other British representatives.[69]

George was a character of low social standing whom the British authorities had no interest in defending, and no articles plead his case in the pages of the *North China Daily News*. Nevertheless, the defendant was tried as a British subject and was given the same legal counsel as other British defendants who were tried in criminal cases before the Supreme Court. Despite procedural objections from George's counsel, several Chinese witnesses who had been summoned by the magistrate were heard by the court and their testimonies were accepted. Thus, in sharp contrast to the unwillingness of the British to involve Qing authorities in the Lin Weixi case thirty years earlier, it is obvious that the British were eager to make a show of British justice and accepted a certain degree of Chinese involvement. Indeed, it seems that the execution of George was part of an Anglo-American effort in the 1860s to reassure local Qing officials that consular jurisdiction would not be used as a shield to protect criminals.[70]

In English-language accounts of the case, there are no indications that the Qing authorities took any active part in the actual trial beyond the fact that the district magistrate was on the bench and helped summon witnesses. The role of the magistrate appeared to be roughly analogous to the official British idea of an assessor, who sat in the trial to guard the interests of the foreign community, mutatis mutandis. A handbook for Qing diplomats, however, gives a somewhat different account of the trial. Although the facts of the case in the handbook conform to the English sources, it differs in that it indicates that Qing officials understood that they were participating in a joint trial (*huishen*) of George. For instance, the Qing authorities initially made representations to the British that they wanted George decapitated instead of hanged, in conformity with Qing law for premeditated murder, but they were eventually satisfied with the outcome of the case since it upheld the principle of a life for a life. They were especially satisfied with the fact that George was tried and punished in China instead of being sent to England. The handbook stated that the "George Case" should be quoted as a precedent, and it impressed on the readers the necessity of accepting different punishment for the same crime.⁷¹ Here Qing statesmen instinctively reversed the most-favored-nation principle to imply that whatever was granted to the Qing Empire by one treaty power could be expected from all treaty powers.⁷² The authors of the official Chinese account may have exaggerated the extent to which Qing officials took part in the sentencing, but the Chinese narrative helps explain the larger context in which the Qing government agreed to establish the Mixed Court in the first place, and both local Qing officials and the Chinese residents of Shanghai continued to regard it as an essentially Chinese court. Rather than just sitting on the bench to "guard the interests of the foreign community," the foreign assessors were accepted by Qing officials as participants in cases where foreigners had been victims of Chinese crime. The Chinese based their understanding on the Chinese rendering of article 16 in the Sino-British Treaty of Tianjin, and by the same token, they expected to take part in the sentencing of foreigners in mixed cases before the consular courts in Shanghai.⁷³ The Qing authorities did not articulate this assumption in any written agreement paralleling the Mixed Court rules, but Sir Thomas Wade later pointed out:

> It is no exaggeration to say that, while in no instance to my knowledge has a British Consular officer assumed to act as a co-Judge in proceedings against a Chinese defendant, that function has been very frequently claimed by Chinese officials where the defendant was a British subject. And when especially in cases of murder, manslaughter or violent assault, the defendant has been acquitted by a jury, or punished less severely than he would have been, had the charge as a Chinese been proved against him, the word representing "together" in the Chinese

version of Article XVI (for which I am myself responsible) has been quoted to prove that in both trial and sentence the officials of both nationalities should equally bear part.[74]

While Wade was wrong in claming that consular officers never acted as cojudges, he correctly observed that Qing officials thought that they had a treaty right to sit in trials in which foreigners were accused of crimes against Chinese. These expectations were not thwarted by the British government itself but by local actors, such as Hornby. Probably as a reaction against the participation of the Qing officials in *Regina vs. George,* in late July 1869, Hornby decided to go behind the back of Alcock and address the foreign secretary, George Villiers (4th Earl of Clarendon), directly, in order to ensure that no Chinese influence would be allowed to assert itself in the Supreme Court in the future. In his letter, he made no attempt to hide his ignorance and his contempt for the Chinese legal system and for Alcock's gradualist approach:

> I urgently entreat Your Lordship to spare me from being compelled to sit on the bench with a Chinese mandarin whose language I do not know, as he is ignorant of mine—who cannot by any possible amount of interpretation be made to understand the principles of law and the forms of procedure which I am bound to follow—who is, from want of training and education to fit him for the duties of a judge, scarcely competent to undertake or assist in the performance of such duties—and who can only import into the consideration of each case such an amount of personal bias arising from pecuniary inducements, as must seriously prejudice, if it do not wholly sacrifice the interests of justice. The presence of such an official on the bench of an English court must either be an empty form and a farce, or—if it be supposed to give a guarantee for truth being vindicated and right being done—it is an insult to English justice.[75]

It is not clear when the practice of allowing Qing officials on the bench in the British Supreme Court was discontinued, but it seems that Hornby's implicit threat to resign from his position at the Supreme Court did have an effect. Qing officials gradually realized that the foreign consuls were not willing to allow any active Qing participation in the trials of foreigners beyond the possible presence of a magistrate.[76] As early as in 1872, the newly founded Chinese-language daily *Shenbao* carried an article complaining about the lack of reciprocity in the treaty port legal order. The anonymous author pointed out that he had observed numerous cases in the Mixed Court where the consul had acted without consulting the Chinese magistrate, and yet when Chinese file a lawsuit against a Westerner, the case is always brought to the British Supreme Court [*Ying niesi yamen*], where the British judge rules alone. Chinese officials have never been allowed to rule together on the bench [*huitong banli*] and there are numerous cases where Chinese have been wronged.[77]

Chinese dissatisfaction with the Mixed Court was not lost on the British staff of the court, and in a report on the Mixed Court the same year, the British vice-consul, Arthur Davenport, observed that "it seems to them most hard and unjust that only those classes of cases should be dealt with in which foreigners are plaintiffs and Chinese defendants."[78] Despite these defects, ordinary Chinese residents of Shanghai sought the protection of the court when they deemed it expedient,[79] and the Qing authorities continued to regard the court as a legitimate institution. Throughout the nineteenth century, the circuit intendant continued to depute officials to the Mixed Court, who were duly recorded in the official gazetteers for Shanghai, side by side with other Qing officials.[80]

Attempts at Reform and the Chefoo Convention, 1876

The foreign community in Shanghai, as represented by the Municipal Council, treated the Mixed Court as a police court in which the foreign assessor had a right not only to sit on the bench in mixed cases but also to rule in all cases that were of some concern to the foreign community of the International Settlement. Both Qing legal practices and the Chinese text of the Mixed Court rules did allow foreign participation in cases in which foreigners were directly involved, but did not provide for foreign participation when "foreign interests" were concerned. Another source of contention was Chinese penal practices, such as corporal punishments, and many foreigners wanted to treat the Mixed Court as a laboratory for the reform of the Chinese system of justice.[81] To some degree, these ambitions were shared by the diplomats who had taken part in the founding of the court. Foreign critics also felt that "the rank of the sub-prefect was too low" and feared that his prestige did not ensure the maintenance of law and order in the Settlement. They wanted his rank in the Qing official hierarchy to be raised, so that he could pronounce penal sentences using the whole range of the Qing Code.[82] Pending such a promotion, foreigners desired that a prima facie case be established in the Mixed Court in all grave criminal cases before the suspects were sent to the Chinese City for trial and punishment. In so doing, they felt that they could bypass the circuitous routes of criminal procedure in the appellate Qing legal system, from which they felt they were excluded.[83]

The foreign critics of the Mixed Court were not, however, willing to trade anything in return for these suggested improvements, and needless to say, many of these suggestions were mutually contradictory. On the one hand, foreign critics wanted to give the Mixed Court subprefect the authority to impose punishments according to the Qing Code in order to ensure law and order in the International Settlement. On the other hand, they regarded the exact same punishments as barbarous and were committed to making the Chinese reform them. In other words, nothing short of a revolution in the Qing legal order would be needed to address these concerns, and there were as yet no indications of any significant support for such moves, either in Qing officialdom or among the Chinese population.[84] The diplomatic community was similarly disinclined to accept radical views of reform but remained committed to what it regarded as strict adherence to the letter of the treaties. They were acutely aware of the fact that many of the established practices in Shanghai had little or no foundation in the treaties as such, and they feared that forcing the Qing authorities to conform to Western norms would be counterproductive. They were also wary of giving too much power to foreign assessors, because that could lead to counterclaims from the Chinese side.

These widely divergent views soon produced a new institutional crisis. When local tribesmen attacked a British exploratory expedition near the Sino-Burmese border in Yunnan province in February 1875, killing the young British vice-consul Augustus Raymond Margary, many greeted the incident as an opportunity to settle their differences with the Qing Empire. The British minister, Thomas Wade, took a hard-line stand and demanded that the culprits be tried in the presence of a British official, that an indemnity be paid, and that the Chinese concede a number of things that had no direct connection with the "Margary Affair," such as tariff reform, the right of audience to the emperor, and a mission of apology.[85] The Qing government expressed its willingness to punish the offenders and to pay an indemnity but was unwilling to grant the British the right to attend the trial (*pangzuo guanshen*) in Yunnan.[86] This, it feared, might set a dangerous precedent for a general right to observe proceedings in the trial of mixed cases in the interior.[87]

Through Wade's brinkmanship the Qing government was eventually brought to the negotiation table, and on 13 September 1876, Wade and Li Hongzhang met at the sea resort Yantai (Chefoo) and signed the Chefoo Convention (*Yantai tiaoyue*) to settle the affair.[88] The Convention, which met most of Wade's demands, was divided into three sections, dealing with the "Yünnan Case" (*Dian'an*), "official intercourse," and "trade." In the section on "official intercourse," the Convention made a number of consequential statements on extraterritoriality and the trial of mixed cases. To begin with, it quoted article 16 in the Sino-British Treaty of Tianjin and noted: "in order to [*sic*] the fulfillment of its Treaty obligations, the British government has established a Supreme Court in Shanghai" and that the Qing government had similarly "established in Shanghai a Mixed Court." The Chinese text of the Convention states that the British government has sent a "surveillance commissioner [*anchasi*] and other officials to officiate in court."[89] In the Qing state structure, the surveillance commissioner was a provincial judge who was independent from the rest of the provincial administration and could memorialize directly to the throne. Unlike the magistrate, who had no specific training in law, the surveillance commissioner was a legal expert who examined all serious criminal cases before they were passed on to the capital for final decision. In other words, the British Supreme Court was presented almost like an agency of the Qing state that was staffed by foreigners, just like the Imperial Maritime Customs. That this was not an improvised translation of the word is corroborated by the fact that *Shenbao* referred to the Supreme Court as the "office of the English surveillance commissioner" (*Ying niesi yamen*) four years earlier.[90]

The Chefoo Convention further noted that the Mixed Court subprefect "either from lack of power, or dread of unpopularity, constantly fails to enforce his judgments" and promised that in order to remedy to the situation, the Zongli Yamen would invite the foreign ministers to discuss "the measures needed for more effective administration of justice at the Ports open to trade."[91] The article then continued:

> It is farther understood that so long as the laws of the two countries differ from each other there can be but one principle to guide judicial proceedings in mixed cases in China, namely, that the case is tried by the official of the defendant's nationality; the official of the plaintiff's nationality merely attending to watch the proceedings in the interests of justice. If the officer so attending be dissatisfied with the proceedings, it will be his power to protest against them in detail. The law administered will be the law of the nationality of the officer trying the case. This is the meaning of the words *hui t'ung*, indicating combined action in judicial proceedings in Article XVI of the Treaty of Tientsin [Treaty of Tianjin], and this is the course to be respectively followed by the officers of either nationality.[92]

It is quite possible to see this paragraph as an expression of the fact that the British, having induced the Chinese into the hegemonic discourse of international law through a series of treaties, were now expanding their hegemony by trying to dictate the meaning of the Chinese terms in the treaty.[93] But a different reading is also possible: forty-fours years after the first Sino-British treaty had been concluded, and eighteen years after article 50 of the Sino-British Treaty of Tianjin had seemingly established the supremacy of the English language,

British diplomats still had difficulties enforcing their linguistic hegemony and had to venture into the Chinese discursive sphere in order to make themselves understood. Qing officials were relatively uninterested in learning English, and when they complained that mixed trials were not being held in accordance with article 16, they quoted the Chinese text, not the English.[94] The British were self-invited guests in the Qing Empire, and as long as the British government was not prepared to run China as a colony, they had to make necessary accommodations to the local legal and institutional order in order to make the treaty ports run smoothly. Indeed, Whitehall frequently enjoined British merchants that the relatively small volume of trade with China could not justify any ambitious attempts to extend British imperial rule to China.[95] Furthermore, the article shows that Wade realized the inherent dangers of getting entangled in Qing legal procedure and the need to set limits beyond which extraterritoriality should not be allowed to extend itself. To be sure, it was expedient for the assessors in the Mixed Court to act as cojudges and thereby claim an equal part in adjudicating mixed cases. But doing so would legitimize Qing claims for an equal share in criminal cases where foreigners were the defendants, which would effectively frustrate any attempts to reform the Chinese legal system. The only way out was to reaffirm the original idea that the assessors were only present to "watch the proceedings in the interest of justice."[96]

Repercussions of the Chefoo Convention

The stipulations in the Chefoo Convention did not satisfy anyone. From the foreign point of view—as represented by the Shanghailander community—it did not go far enough.[97] The Convention curtailed the right of the foreign assessors to participate in the judgment of mixed cases, and it preserved the Qing Code as the body of law governing the punishment of Qing subjects. This was acceptable when it came to criminal cases, but not in civil cases, because foreigners felt that "in actual practice the settlement of a claim against a Chinese debtor by resorting to a Chinese court was next to impossible."[98] From the Qing point of view, the Convention obviously went too far. Qing legal procedure did not make any meaningful distinction between the role of cojudges and assessors in mixed cases, and Wade's assurances that the foreign official was only present "in the interest of justice" did not, in all likelihood, convince Qing officials that a foreign assessor would not claim the role of a cojudge in practice. On the contrary, the stipulations set a dangerous precedent for foreign intervention in mixed cases in the interior, since they were applicable not just in the treaty ports but in the whole of China.

Nevertheless, the Chefoo Convention prompted the Qing government to articulate its position on the treaty port system, consular jurisdiction, and other pressing issues. In anticipation of the conference with the foreign ministers that was written into the Convention, the Zongli Yamen issued a statement to the Qing ministers overseas on the government's position on treaty revision in March 1878. This statement touches on almost every element of the treaty port system, especially the tariff régime and the most-favored-nation arrangement, and it is one of the most lucid official statements on the question of extraterritoriality prior to the legal reforms of the turn of the century. In the paragraph on "extraterritoriality," the Zongli Yamen reaffirmed Qing acceptance of consular jurisdiction but then proceeded to criticize foreign abuse of the privilege:

> But foreigners claim much more than this; they interpret this exterritorial privilege as meaning not only that Chinese officials are not to control them, but that they may disregard and violate Chinese regulations [*zhangcheng*] with impunity. To this we cannot assent. China has not by any treaty given foreigners permission to disregard or violate the laws of China; while residing in China they are as much bound to observe them as Chinese are. What has been conceded in the Treaties in this connection is merely that offenders shall be punished by their own national officials, in accordance with their own laws.[99]

This statement ingeniously separated consular jurisdiction from the question of extraterritorial legislation. According to this construct, foreigners—just like Manchus and other ethnic groups—were in principle obliged to follow the same laws and regulations as Chinese, but they were to be punished by their own officials when they committed an offense. The Qing government had merely delegated the authority to punish aliens to the foreign consuls.[100] The use of terms indicates this clearly: whereas the English term "extraterritoriality" emphasized the nonterritorial application of laws, the Chinese term used for the arrangement (*bugui guanxia*) focused on *what authority* was to impose the punishment for a given offense.[101] In other words, the Qing Empire reluctantly accepted consular jurisdiction, but was wary of admitting unqualified extraterritoriality. This reconciles the concession of consular jurisdiction in the early nineteenth century with the consistent Qing insistence that foreigners be subject to the norms laid down in the Qing Code. In fact, it demonstrates that the official Qing position had changed very little in the three decades following the First Opium War.

The following year, the foreign ministers in Beijing met to discuss extraterritoriality and jurisdiction in mixed cases. The American minister, George F. Seward, submitted two reports on the matter, which were adopted by the ministers. While paying lip service to Qing concerns about lawless foreigners, Seward rejected the Qing construct as naïve and having little to do with reality in the treaty ports.[102] The main concern of the foreign ministers was jurisdiction in mixed civil cases, as they felt that the Qing Code made it almost impossible to obtain sufficient remedies in a Qing court. The two reports suggested a number of improvements in Qing legal procedure, including giving the Mixed Court subprefect more independence,[103] but the Zongli Yamen remained evasive, and the whole matter was allowed to lapse.[104] Thus ended the last official attempt in the nineteenth century to make Qing and foreign legal systems conform.

In the century's last decades, the International Mixed Court evolved into one of the most important theaters of jurisdictional conflicts in Shanghai. Having failed to come to any permanent settlement over the Mixed Court and Chinese legal reform, the Zongli Yamen and the foreign ministers left the local parties to struggle over the fate of the court.[105] The diplomatic community was attentive to the fact that the legal foundations of the International Settlement were as shaky as the mud the city was built on, and they were not prepared to push the issue too far. The Municipal Council had revised the Land Regulations substantially in the late 1860s and had never been officially sanctioned by the Qing government.[106] If, for some reason, the Qing government decided to withdraw its implicit sanction of the Regulations, the Settlement could fall like a house of cards and with it the Mixed Court.

For the time being, however, both Qing officials and the Chinese community in the International Settlement still regarded the Mixed Court as a legitimate court in the Qing legal order. The Mixed Court was an instrument of Qing rule in the International Settlement, one that Qing officials could ill afford to lose, even if they had reservations about the lack of reciprocity. In a manner of speaking, it asserted the "extraterritorial rights" of Chinese in a territory that was under de facto foreign jurisdiction and where Chinese were treated as temporary sojourners. The last line of defense was jurisdiction over the Chinese community, and Qing officials were loath to admit too much influence of the foreign assessors in cases involving Chinese only. They were on solid ground from a Qing point of view, which recognized personal jurisdiction but rejected the ever-expanding concept of "foreign interests." The "Shanghailander" community had been gravely disappointed by the failure of the Chefoo Convention and the Beijing Conference to come to terms with the problems of mixed cases. By establishing precedents, the Municipal Council set out curtail Qing rule in the settlement in almost every area, even when it was in contravention of the original Mixed Court rules. For instance, by the time the Chefoo Convention was concluded, it had already been the practice that all arrest warrants and official proclamations had to be signed by both the Shanghai district magistrate and the senior consul before they could be executed. In 1883, a precedent was set that a prima facie case had to be established before serious criminals were sent to the district magistrate for trial in the Chinese City.[107]

To a certain extent, these measures were taken in opposition to official policy on the part of the treaty powers. In an exchange of views in the *North-China*

Herald in 1882, an anonymous spokesman for the ministers in Beijing insisted that the assessor should not have the role of a cojudge, which was increasingly the practice in the Mixed Court. Because of the intransigent attitude of both the assessor and the subprefect, they soon developed into advocates for each other's sides.[108] This tug-of-war was peaceful for most of the 1870s and in the early 1880s, but when veteran Mixed Court subprefect Chen Fuxun retired in 1884 and was replaced by the less experienced Huang Chengyi, tensions came to a peak. On 16 June the following year, Huang assaulted the British assessor Herbert A. Giles in a dispute over a ruling, and the Mixed Court was temporarily closed afterward. Underscoring the fact that the Mixed Court was ultimately dependent on their approval, Qing officials made absolutely clear that they would not cooperate if Giles continued as assessor. The court resumed operation after both Huang and Giles had been dismissed from the court, but the struggle over the Mixed Court would continue for the rest of the century.[109]

Whereas the foreigners felt that extraterritoriality had given them a "Midas touch,"[110] making everything they touched exempt from Chinese law, the Qing authorities were increasingly inclined to think of foreign privilege as gangrene in the Qing body politic. The implementation of extraterritoriality in China was not a discrete event but developed incrementally through a series of crises in which the treaty powers would eventually prevail. The institutional genealogy of the implementation of the treaty port system in its first four decades demonstrates the conditions under which extraterritoriality was accepted by Qing statesmen. As the case of Shanghai shows, local contestation and negotiation mattered as much as the treaty texts themselves, and by working against foreign concepts of extraterritoriality and consular jurisdiction, Qing officials were able to mobilize their own assumptions about personal jurisdiction and how the code should be applied to foreigners that were firmly rooted in Qing legal thought. First of all, they felt that extraterritorial privileges should be limited to the treaty ports. Mixed cases between Chinese and foreigners should be tried jointly, or at least through mutual consultation to secure just punishment for offenders. Foreign participation in legal suits in which "foreign interests" were involved should be limited to cases in which foreigners were directly involved. Finally, Qing officials felt that foreigners should be subject to the same laws and regulations as Chinese, but that they could be punished by officials of their own nationality.

Qing statesmen were far from ignorant of the dangers of extraterritoriality, but rather than seriously dealing with the threat, they chose to trivialize the problem. The flexibility of the Qing legal order, and the propensity of Qing statesmen to manage consular jurisdiction as part of the Qing legal order, effectively preempted any efforts to introduce "modern" legal norms into China.

Nowhere was this more evident than in the case of the Mixed Court in Shanghai. Given this background, it is intriguing that between 1871 and 1895 both Chinese and Japanese enjoyed extraterritorial privileges in each other's countries under the Sino-Japanese Treaty of Tianjin, which was concluded on 13 September 1871. The treaty was more than a decade older than the Qing Empire's "unequal treaty" with Chosŏn Korea, and it was not an outcome of Western-style "gunboat diplomacy," which is why it provides us with a unique test case for exploring both Chinese and Japanese attitudes and policies toward extraterritoriality.

4

Exporting Extraterritoriality

The Evolution of Jurisdiction over Foreigners in Japan from the "Expulsion Edict" to the Sino-Japanese Treaty of Tianjin

The Japanese greeted the advent of the treaty port era first as alarmed spectators and then as reluctant participants. As they anxiously observed the Opium War and subsequent events on the Chinese mainland, many of them started to question the tenability of the "policy of national seclusion" that had been in force since the early seventeenth century. The original exclusionary edicts did not reflect a conscious intention on the part of the Bakufu to shut Japan completely off from the outside world; rather, they were a response to specific political circumstances at the time, such as the perceived threat from Christianity.[1] For instance, the original exclusionary edicts only banned Iberians from residing in Japan, and they did not specify what nationalities were allowed to stay. While only Dutch and Chinese were permitted to reside temporarily in Nagasaki, this was not an intended consequence of the seclusion policy. Rather, most other seafaring nations were only moderately interested in trading with Japan, and the Dutch protected their privileges in Japan jealously.[2] Indeed, the Japanese term usually employed to describe the policy—*Sakoku*—was not even of Japanese provenance but derived from a nineteenth-century mistranslation of a passage from Engelbert Kaempfer's famous book *Geschichte und Beschreibung von Japan*.[3] Notwithstanding these ambiguities, the Bakufu guarded its monopoly on foreign policy–making aggressively, and by the early nineteenth century the policy had been elevated to almost constitutional status. The policy attained its most extreme expression in 1825, when the Bakufu promulgated the infamous "expulsion edict" (*Ikokusen uchiharai rei*), which ordered all the domains to expel all foreign ships that appeared outside Nagasaki "without thinking twice" (*ninen mo naku*).[4]

One direct outcome of the policy was that it effectively reduced opportunities for contacts and conflicts between Dutch and Japanese. Thus there is no Japanese counterpart to the string of Sino-foreign incidents that the Canadian diplomat-historian Hosea Ballou Morse chronicled in his classic work on Sino-foreign relations.[5] The Dutch were sojourning in Nagasaki purely at the sufferance of the Bakufu, and there appears to have been no need for a separate system of dealing with Dutch criminals. Before the "seclusion edicts" were promulgated, the Bakufu took quite a pragmatic stance on how foreign criminals should be punished. For instance, in the early seventeenth century, the head of the English trading station was given the privilege of trying and punishing English offenders, but according to Japanese law. One authority on this period of Japanese foreign relations has asserted that "this vaguely worded concession was not extraterritoriality according to nineteenth-century practice. There was no question of immunity from the law of Japan."[6] There is a great deal of truth in this statement, but the scope of extraterritoriality in the nineteenth century should not be exaggerated either. In the case of Qing China, and of Tokugawa Japan, neither régime understood that they had granted Westerners complete immunity from local law by allowing them to exercise consular jurisdiction.

The "Siebold incident" illustrates how the Bakufu dealt with serious offenses committed by foreign sojourners when the policy of seclusion was given its most rigid interpretation. Philipp Franz von Siebold was a Bavarian doctor who had been working at the Dutch trading station in Dejima since 1823 and had even been allowed to set up a small clinic in Narutaki, in the outskirts of Nagasaki, where he trained Japanese students in medicine and biology.[7] He cultivated an extensive network among Japanese scholars and officials and was given access to an unprecedented amount of information on Japanese natural, geographical, and ethnographical conditions. When he was about to leave Nagasaki in September 1828, the ship he was supposed to board was overtaken by a storm and destroyed. Bakufu officials searching the wreckage discovered that Siebold had concealed a couple of illegally obtained maps of Japan in his luggage. The Bakufu ordered Siebold to stay in Japan to face trial for espionage, and the investigation soon implicated almost everyone he had been in contact with during his stay in Japan. The Bakufu was never able to prove that Siebold had been engaged in espionage, so he was released after a year and forbidden from ever coming back to Japan. It is true that Siebold had powerful friends who could intercede on his behalf; even the king of Bavaria reportedly made representations to the Bakufu when he learned about the case. Siebold got away lightly compared to his Japanese associates, many of whom were given heavy sentences, but he was never able to use his foreign nationality to claim immunity from local Japanese law, and there was no question that the Bakufu had jurisdiction in the case.[8]

The Dutch maintained de facto tributary relations with the shogunate, but the Japanese never expected the Chinese to follow the Dutch example; nor were the Japanese willing to submit to China as a tributary. Japan had had no official relations with China since the shogun Ashikaga Yoshimitsu (tenure 1368–94) was invested as the "King of Japan" by the Yongle emperor, a move that would stigmatize him in the annals of Japanese history.[9] Instead, Sino-Japanese intercourse was restricted to the realm of trade, which was dominated by Chinese merchants as a consequence of the self-imposed limitations of the Bakufu. China was far more important than any other trading partner, and the most prominent authority on this epoch, Ōba Osamu, maintains that "Nagasaki trade was China trade."[10] But Japan's trade with China was not only an extension of Chinese merchant networks to Japanese soil; it was also a valuable window onto the outside world. One of the major import products from China was books, a trade that increased in importance from the eighteenth century.[11] Classical Chinese was far more widely read than Dutch, which was the realm of a small group of tightly monitored specialists. It was mainly through classical Chinese that literate Japanese would learn about the dramatic upheaval that took place on the mainland from the mid-nineteenth century onward, and later about such novelties as international law.

In contrast to the tight controls on emigration and trade in Japan, the Qing Empire was never able to enforce its own ban on emigration effectively.[12] Following the growth of Chinese communities in the Pacific region, a small Chinese community developed in Nagasaki as well, whose most prominent members could trace their roots back to Ming loyalist refugees. Whereas the movements of the Dutch were restricted to the artificial island of Dejima, the Chinese were allowed more freedom of movement and were able to move beyond the "Chinese enclosure" (*Tōjin yashiki*) into Nagasaki proper.[13] The Chinese community was under the jurisdiction of the "Chinese commissioners" (*Tōtsūji*), which was a hereditary position. These officers were ultimately accountable to the Nagasaki magistrate (*Nagasaki bugyō*) and did not hold any official position in the Qing civil service. Indeed many of the prominent Chinese families in Nagasaki were descended from Ming loyalist refugees.[14]

As some Japanese patriots proudly pointed out in the mid-nineteenth century, Japan was in much better control of its foreign community than the Chinese.[15] Japan's limited participation in world trade shielded Japan from the kind of pressures the Chinese were facing, and there appeared to be no real threat of a Japanese counterpart of the Lin Weixi incident in Guangdong, which was one contributing factor to the outbreak of the Opium War. Even so, patriot intellectuals like Watanabe Kazan and Koga Tōan realized that more efficient means of transportation and modern military technology would pose a significant potential threat to Japan, and the outbreak of hostilities confirmed their grimmest forebodings.[16]

The news that Britain was able to seal off the Yangtze River in the Opium War with a single warship must have sent shock waves through policy-making circles in Edo: the shogunal metropolis was almost entirely dependent on seaborne rice transports.[17] The Bakufu could no longer count on Japan's geographical isolation shielding it from invasion indefinitely, and Japan watchers in Europe now felt that the time was ripe to ask Japan to "open its doors." Acting on the advice of Siebold, who served as a royal advisor, the Dutch king, William II, sent a letter to the Bakufu in 1844 politely asking it to readdress its policy of seclusion in the light of recent events. The letter was delivered to Edo with much pomp and circumstance, but the shogun Tokugawa Ieyoshi demurred courteously, referring to the allegedly immutable policy of seclusion, which he claimed to have inherited from the founding fathers of the shogunate.[18] The only immediate effect on Bakufu foreign policy was that the "expulsion edict" was rescinded and replaced with instructions to expel illegal aliens peacefully after having provided them with provisions and fuel. No other adjustments were made at the time.[19]

Instead, the discussion on the lessons of the Sino-British War was left to a number of intellectuals both inside and outside policy-making circles, all of whom took great personal risks by discussing foreign policy. By the time hostilities had ceased in 1842, the Japanese had access to enough information to be able to discuss the treaty and the peace settlement in an informed way.[20] The Japanese were not only privy to Dutch and Chinese reports (*fūsetsugaki*) on overseas events that were routinely submitted by foreign ships as they landed in Nagasaki, they also had access to Chinese memorials, diplomatic correspondence from the war, and even poetry. In the following years, a number of political tracts, as well as fictional and semifictional works based on these sources, were written and circulated widely in Japan.[21] Most books focused on the British invasion of China and the opium question, not on the knotty question of jurisdiction over foreigners—indeed it is not even clear that the Japanese were aware of the fact that the Qing Empire had conceded consular jurisdiction to the British in the wake of the war. For instance, the Confucian scholar Saitō Chikudō wrote one of the most popular tracts on the Opium War, but only in passing did he list the major concessions of the peace settlement such as the opening of five ports for foreign trade, the cession of Hong Kong, the hefty indemnity, and consular jurisdiction.[22] For contemporary Japanese, the real disgrace was that China had been humiliated and forced to enter into treaty relations with a "barbarian" country, and there is no evidence that the Japanese were concerned with jurisdiction in particular. This attitude would carry through the first years of the Meiji period.

The Ansei Treaties

The arrival of Commodore Matthew Perry's squadron at Uraga Bay in July 1853 broke the deadlock in Japanese foreign policy. Confused as to how to respond to this unparalleled challenge, the leading policy-maker of the Bakufu, the councilor of state (*rōjū*) Abe Masahiro, took the unprecedented step of inviting not only the inner circle of lords (*fudai daimyō*) to discuss the treaty but also the outer lords (*tozama daimyō*), who traditionally had been left out of Bakufu policy-making. The decision to consult with all of the domanial lords on the treaty set a momentous precedent and opened the door for a national discussion on foreign policy, which in turn seriously undermined the authority of the Bakufu.[23]

Despite some powerful voices in favor of "expelling the barbarians"—most eloquently articulated by Tokugawa Nariaki, the lord of Mito domain—the Bakufu resolved to sign a treaty with the United States. When Commodore Perry concluded the treaty on 31 March 1854, no specific provisions for consular jurisdiction were included, since the treaty did not concern itself with the residence of Americans as such. Japan was divided on the wisdom of entering into such a treaty with the United States, but both proponents and opponents agreed that a momentous step had been taken. Almost as an incantation against a new chaotic period, the imperial court in Kyoto proclaimed a new era on 27 November the same year: Ansei, or "Pacifying Rule."

The American initiative attracted a number of new attempts to widen the scope of treaty relations with Japan. The Russians, who had unsuccessfully tried to open relations with Japan several times, were among the first to take advantage of the opportunity. On 7 February 1855, Russian envoy Evfemii Vasilevich Putiatin and Bakufu officials Tsutsui Masanori and Kawaji Toshiaki concluded the Treaty of Shimoda, which was the first commercial treaty to deal directly with the question of jurisdiction over foreigners. It stipulated that "both . . . a Russian in Japan as well as a Japanese in Russia" were to be punished according to their own laws.[24] The article did not specify any legal procedure for the trial of extraterritorial cases, nor did it determine what authority would be entrusted with the punishment of expatriate Russian and Japanese criminals. A literal reading indicates that Japanese authorities arguably had the right to try Russian criminals with due consideration of Russian criminal law, but there is no record of any Japanese official making that argument, and Russia would soon send consuls to Japan in order to take up jurisdiction. The Bakufu never sent consuls to Russia, and the reciprocity of the extraterritorial arrangements was voided by the fact that Russia had been granted unilateral most-favored-nation treatment by Japan, which supposedly enabled Russia to share all the benefits that other countries might enjoy under subsequent treaties.[25]

As Bob Wakabayashi has pointed out, the "Perry Treaty" was little more than a bilateral sanction of the adjustments in the exclusion policy the Bakufu had introduced in the wake of the Opium War.[26] Article 11 of the treaty did, however, add a new element to Japan's foreign relations, as it gave the United States the right to station a consul in Shimoda, and the U.S. government promptly dispatched Townsend Harris as U.S. consul general with authority to negotiate a more comprehensive treaty with Japan. Harris's arrival in 1856 coincided with the start of hostilities in the "Arrow War," which the hard-line British diplomat Harry Parkes had provoked in order to settle a number of outstanding issues with the Qing Empire.[27] The U.S. consul general did not have ready access to warships as his British colleagues did, but he purposefully used the Arrow War to intimidate the two representatives of the Bakufu, Inoue Kiyonao and Iwase Tadanari. Harris told them that if the Bakufu did not agree to his suggested treaty, the British would soon force the Bakufu to sign a treaty that would be even less favorable to Japan.[28] The extraterritorial provisions of the resulting treaty, which was signed on 29 July 1858, were very similar to those of the Sino-American treaty of 1844: "Americans, committing offenses against Japanese, shall be tried in American Consular Courts, and when found guilty, shall be punished according to American law. Japanese, committing offenses against Americans, shall be tried by the Japanese authorities, and punished according to Japanese law."[29]

Virtually every treaty that Japan would conclude with the Great Powers—including France—would emulate the extraterritorial provisions in the "Harris Treaty." In contrast to the vaguely worded Russian treaty, the American treaty explicitly established the U.S. consul as the competent authority in charge of punishing his compatriots. On the other hand, the American treaty was equally vague in terms of defining what constituted an "offense": strictly speaking, the treaty did not grant Americans immunity from Japanese laws but merely charged U.S. consuls with punishing American offenders according to U.S. laws. The treaty did not lay down the right of Americans to be tried by a jury, nor did it extend safeguards to protect the rights of suspects. Needless to say, Western jurists assumed that these elements of Western law and procedure were implicit in the article. When Caleb Cushing had concluded the treaty with China in 1844, which included a similar article on consular jurisdiction, he had believed that he had "obtained the concession of absolute and unqualified extraterritoriality."[30] But it is not hard to see that in Japan or China, where the legal environment was less conducive to the protection of the individual rights of suspects, the extension of these safeguards could be regarded as an obstruction to the due prosecution of crime. For instance, in Shanghai, one British consul reported that local officials regarded the jury system "as a cunningly devised system to deprive them of their Treaty rights."[31]

After defeating the Qing Empire in the Arrow War in 1858, Britain and France sent warships to support their ambitions to negotiate a treaty with Japan. The extraterritorial arrangements in the British treaty, which was concluded on 26 August 1858, were very similar to the ones in the Harris treaty and virtually copied those in the Sino-British Treaty of Tianjin, including the phrase "Justice shall be equitably and impartially administered on both sides" (*saidan wa sōhō ni oite hempa nakaru beshi*). Whereas the Chinese rendering of this phrase had momentous consequences for the implementation of extraterritoriality in China and formed the legal basis of the Mixed Court in Shanghai, the corresponding Japanese passage was a rather faithful translation of the English original version.[32]

Although Chinese treaties were available in Japan at the time, the Japanese did not yet import the standard Chinese term for consul—*lingshi/ryōji*—nor did they bother to invent a new term; "consuls" were simply translated into *kana* syllabary, and "consular courts" were usually referred to as *Konshuru saidanjo* in the treaties. More significantly, in contrast to the way Qing officials rendered treaty texts and other legal instruments into readily recognizable Qing legal concepts and institutions, the Japanese versions of the Ansei treaties evince very little terminological or institutional influence from the Tokugawa legal order.

The conclusion of the Harris treaty and its European sister-treaties brought the constitutional crisis in the Tokugawa state to a new climax. In 1860, Bakufu councilor of state Ii Naosuke was slain outside the shogun's palace by a group of rebel samurai in retaliation for his purge of the opponents of the new treaty and for his failure to secure imperial sanction for the Harris treaty. The treaties that had been concluded during the turbulent Ansei era (1854–60) formed the core of the Japanese unequal treaties and would be collectively referred to as the "Ansei Treaties." Notwithstanding the upheavals the treaties brought to the domestic political scene in Japan, many scholars have argued that the Japanese treaties were more beneficial to Japan than the Chinese treaties were to China.[33] There is a great deal of truth in that, and even Qing officials were aware of these differences. None of the treaties Japan concluded with foreign countries contained territorial concessions or indemnities, and the right of foreigners to travel in the interior was more circumscribed than in China. Furthermore, Harris made a special point of outlawing opium in the U.S. treaty.[34] However, this was of little comfort to the Bakufu or the increasing number of dissidents who were ready to take matters into their own hands in order to keep foreigners out of Japan. The treaties were concluded in the immediate context of the First and Second Opium Wars, and both the Bakufu and its opponents knew that if the Great Powers resolved to launch a full-scale military campaign against Japan, they might have to concede to even less favorable treaty arrangements.

As regards consular jurisdiction, the Bakufu policy had much in common with the Qing approach. Plural jurisdictions and special legal privileges were nothing new under the Tokugawa legal order, which was arguably even more fragmented than its Qing counterpart. When three drunken samurai from Kōchi domain (Tosa) killed two sailors from the British man-of-war H.M.S. *Icarus* in the entertainment district of Nagasaki in 1867, the Nagasaki magistrate claimed to have no jurisdiction in the case. Instead he deferred the case to representatives of Kōchi domain, who tried and punished the suspects in the presence of representatives from the Bakufu and the British government. The British diplomat and linguist Ernest Satow, who took part in the process, interpreted the Bakufu's approach to handling the case as a recognition of personal jurisdiction, one of the underlying principles of extraterritoriality.[35] Although the crime had been committed in Nagasaki, which was under Bakufu jurisdiction, the punishment of the offenders was deferred to their own domain.[36]

This event and similar occurrences made it possible for Harry Parkes to confidently claim "that there was no surprise on the one hand nor concession on the other when extraterritoriality was established by the treaties of 1858" several years later.[37] While there is no reason to doubt the veracity of Parkes's statement, it does not mean that the Bakufu willingly granted foreigners complete immunity from Japanese law. When Bakufu officials read the treaty clauses on consular jurisdiction, they did not understand them the same way as their Western interlocutors. The Bakufu believed that they had granted Westerners the right to be punished by their own countrymen and nothing else; their standpoint was thus not very different from that articulated by the Zongli yamen in its circular to the ministers abroad several years later.[38] What set the Bakufu officials apart from their mainland contemporaries was that they were somewhat more successful in persuading Western envoys that their compatriots were still obliged to obey Japanese laws.

In November 1860, a Briton called Michael Moss went on a duck hunting expedition outside Edo. Under Bakufu law, it was a capital crime to discharge firearms within a distance of ten *ri* (about forty kilometers) from the shogun's castle, and when Moss was on his way back to Yokohama, the governor of Kanagawa sent some officers to apprehend him. As the officers tried to perform their duty, Moss fired his gun and wounded one of them seriously. Moss was finally arrested after a scuffle with the officers and was subsequently extradited to the British consul. Against the objections of two assessors, who were sympathetic to Moss, the British consul declared Moss guilty of "maliciously wounding" the Bakufu officer and sentenced him to deportation from Japan and a fine of $1,000. On reviewing the verdict, Alcock, the British minister, decided to increase the sentence to three months' imprisonment and also gave instructions that the fine be paid as compensation to the injured Bakufu officer. However, when Moss arrived in the British Crown Colony of Hong Kong to serve his sentence, he was promptly released by the colonial authorities because Alcock had supposedly exceeded his authority by imposing both a fine and a prison sentence. Not only that, the Hong Kong Supreme Court awarded $2,000 as compensation to Moss for his wrongful imprisonment.[39]

The Moss episode has been rightly cited as an example of how foreigners literally got away with murder (or attempted murder) under the protective shield of extraterritoriality. However, it is less known that in response to the mishandling of the Moss case, Alcock promulgated a set of regulations in November 1861 called "Rules and Regulations for the Peace, Order, and Good Government of

British Subjects within the Dominions of the Tycoon of Japan." The regulations gave Bakufu officers with proper consular authorization the right to arrest Britons who committed infractions against a number of local laws, including hunting, the "discharge of firearms," and riding horses in "a furious and careless manner."[40] If the regulations had been fully implemented, they would have given effective sanction to the Bakufu position that consular jurisdiction did not exempt foreigners from local laws and regulations. However, a number of circumstances conspired to thwart Alcock's initiative. Alcock himself left Japan for Britain early in 1862, before he had been able to convince the other consuls to follow his example. Negotiations on the rules were scheduled to resume later in the year, but in September, C. L. Richardson, a British merchant visiting from Shanghai, was slain by samurai from Satsuma for having refused to yield to the entourage of their lord, Shimazu Hisamitsu, who was on his way home from Edo.[41] The "Namamugi incident" produced another diplomatic crisis, and all other initiatives were put on hold for the time being.[42] The Bakufu had demonstrated its inability to impose its will and its laws on the outer domains, and a British flotilla punished Satsuma by bombarding Kagoshima the following year, producing yet another political crisis, which would pave the way for the eventual downfall of the Bakufu itself.

The political realignments of the late 1860s would drastically change the political landscape of Japan and the preconditions for revising the Ansei treaties. What at first looked like an anachronistic return to imperial rule triggered the establishment of a centralized nation-state. The new Meiji government quickly set out to revise the treaties but adopted a gradualist approach. One of the first things the new government did was to reassure the Great Powers that the Ansei Treaties would remain in force for the time being, which was necessary to obtain their support for the new régime.[43] Indeed, the Meiji government even concluded new treaties with Prussia and Sweden-Norway on the old pattern.[44]

Even though Japan had been spared the kind of extraterritorial incidents that frequently occurred in China,[45] an increasing number of statesmen harbored misgivings about consular jurisdiction. Indeed, they seemed to be even more sensitive to the question than their Qing contemporaries, who often objected to the Western implementation of extraterritoriality but had yet to launch any systematic policy to get rid of the practice. The leading court noble Iwakura Tomomi was one of the first to single out consular jurisdiction as a disgrace to Japan as a nation (*waga Kōkoku no chijoku*) in a letter to another prominent court noble, Sanjō Sanetomi, in April 1869. Clearly envisioning Japan as a nation among nations, Iwakura held that only by assuming full territorial jurisdiction within its borders could Japan assert its rightful position in the world, a statement indicating that Iwakura was approaching an understanding of national sovereignty informed by international law.[46] W. A. P. Martin's Chinese translation of Henry Wheaton's *Elements of International Law*, which had been commissioned by the

Zongli Yamen in the early 1860s, was even more popular in Japan than in China, and it had been published in several official Japanese editions by the late 1860s.[47]

Iwakura's criticism put a stop to the conclusion of more treaties modeled on the Ansei Treaties for the time being. Instead he drew up plans for a high-profile embassy, which would visit the most important Western countries in order to learn more about the world and broach the issue of treaty revision with the relevant countries. The time was seen as propitious for such a move, as the U.S. treaty was up for revision in July 1872, and Meiji statesmen held out great hope that they would be able to persuade Western governments to agree to more equal treaty arrangements. The Iwakura embassy is often symbolized by a famous photograph of the five ranking members in San Francisco on 23 January 1872, with all but one dressed up in Western suits. As it turned out, the members of the embassy returned to Japan without new and equal treaties but wearing new Western clothes and having gained a new understanding of world affairs.[48]

It was now eminently clear that the Meiji government would have to embark on extensive administrative and legal reforms in order to be able to convince the treaty powers to revise the unequal treaties and abolish consular jurisdiction. But this did not mean that Japan's new rulers discarded the old policy entirely. The Meiji government endorsed the Bakufu position that Japanese laws were in principle applicable to foreigners, and they made skillful use of all the authorities they could find on international law. Japanese statesmen started to draw clear limits beyond which they did not want consular jurisdiction to assert itself. The government also called off experiments with mixed courts, which had been carried out intermittently in Yokohama since 1865.[49]

Even though the foreign community in Japan was much smaller and less important than its counterpart in China, consular jurisdiction became a symbol of foreign incursion into Japanese national sovereignty. Abolishing consular jurisdiction became a central concern of Japanese politics, and no Meiji politician could afford to ignore his performance in this area. Thus, in contrast to the case of the Chinese treaties, which were constantly being revised and clarified throughout the nineteenth century—which in turn led to new problems that called for clarification—the Japanese government was wary of concluding any new treaties and chose to enforce the existing treaties rigidly.[50] The Ansei Treaties more or less stood until they were finally replaced by "equal" treaties in the late 1890s.

Sino-Japanese Relations prior to 1871

Although events in China had loomed large in Japan, the Qing Empire had not asserted itself in relation to Japan, nor had the Japanese approached the Chinese outside the old framework of informal relations. When the first treaty ports were opened in Japan in the late 1850s, there was already a small Chinese community in Nagasaki, and in the wake of the opening of Kobe and Yokohama, Chinese communities started to grow there as well. In 1864, 100 Chinese lived in Yokohama; by 1870 that figure had risen to 1002.[51] Following the influx of new groups of Chinese into Nagasaki, the old "Chinese enclosure" in Nagasaki lost its purpose and was eventually dissolved. Despite Nagasaki's diminishing role as a center for foreign trade, the Chinese community grew steadily, from 145 in 1864 to 338 in 1870.[52] The Japanese, on the other hand, were slow to move into the Chinese treaty ports after the restrictions on overseas travel were officially rescinded by 1866. Complete statistics do not exist for the number of Japanese living in China during the Bakumatsu period, but in 1870 only seven Japanese were officially registered as living in the International Settlement of Shanghai.[53] However, many Chinese and Japanese took up residence in the treaty ports without reporting to the authorities. Nevertheless, the statistics do show that during the transition from the Bakumatsu to the early Meiji, far more Chinese were moving into Japan than the other way around.

Following the breakdown of the old system of trade, the legal status of Chinese in Japan and Japanese in China became increasingly ambiguous, in the absence of official treaty relations between the two countries. When Japan concluded the Ansei Treaties with the Western powers, the Chinese communities found themselves in a legal vacuum. Their presence in Japan was not regulated by treaty, and the dissolution of the "Chinese enclosure" in Nagasaki, as well as the establishment of a centralized nation-state in the Meiji period, undermined their existence as a self-ruling community. In the new legal environment, the Chinese became "unrepresented foreigners" or, as the Japanese authorities preferred to put it, "foreigners without treaties" (*jōyaku misai no gaikokujin*). Many of the new Chinese immigrants were working for Westerners who had taken up residence in the treaty ports. The Chinese often acted as middlemen, and their know-how in foreign trade enabled them to play a pivotal role in Japan's foreign trade. Many of them became "native managers"—compradors—for Western mercantile houses.[54] However, the absence of any official treaty relations between Japan and China meant that it was difficult for Chinese to take up residence in Japan legally. Consequently, some Chinese even paid Western merchants to register them as their employees, thereby legalizing their residence in Japan and providing them with some form of consular protection.[55] The increase in the number of Chinese in the Japanese treaty ports also meant intensified interaction and a growing number of legal cases involving Chinese. When Chinese fell foul of the law, the problem thus arose to what extent they should be treated as Westerners—enjoying extraterritorial privileges—or as unrepresented foreigners, who were subject to local jurisdiction according to international law.

Japanese and Qing authorities were initially quite reluctant to assume any responsibility over nonrepresented foreigners, so many of the first initiatives to eliminate this ambiguity came from the foreign consuls, both in Japan and China. The Nagasaki Land Regulations, adopted in 1860, placed unrepresented foreigners under the joint authority of Japanese local authorities and the consuls but fell short of laying down any rules for criminal and civil jurisdiction.[56] As shown in chapter 3, the British consul, Harry Parkes and the Qing circuit intendant agreed in 1864 that the newly established Mixed Court in Shanghai would assume jurisdiction over nonrepresented foreigners in the Shanghai area.[57] Three years later, when Parkes was the British minister to Japan, he obtained an agreement from the Bakufu that "the Governor of Kanagawa, acting with . . . such advice as he may obtain from Foreign Consuls will exercise jurisdiction—both criminal and civil—over the subjects of China."[58]

One of the first things the Meiji régime did in relation to jurisdiction was to assume territorial jurisdiction over the Chinese community through "alien registration," which was introduced in 1868. The new policy proclaimed that a new era of international trade and intercourse had begun and that Japan now assumed jurisdiction over Qing households (*Qingguo jimin/Shinkoku sekimin*) in Japan in accordance with international law (*wanguo gongfa/bankoku kokuhō*). It instructed Qing subjects to register with the Japanese authorities and hang a household plate (*jipai/sekihai*) outside their doors. A proclamation from the local authorities in Yokohama instructing the Chinese to obey Japanese laws is still extant.[59]

Chinese communities in Japan were, however, no passive victims of these policy changes. For instance, the different Chinese communities in Nagasaki had formed unofficial regional groups in the 1860s, which initially identified themselves as dialect groups (*bang*), as was common in Annam, Malaya, the East Indies, and elsewhere in Southeast Asia.[60] In response to the new policy, these groups now established associations (*gongsuo*) and petitioned local Japanese authorities for self-rule. Around 1868, the Guangdong community petitioned the Nagasaki prefect for self-rule under the auspices of their association (*Lingnan huisuo*).[61] The Fujian community soon followed suit and formed their own association (*Bamin huisuo*), citing the precedent set by the Cantonese.[62] The ranks of the Chinese associations in Nagasaki were soon joined by the powerful Sanjiang association (*Sanjiang*), which organized Chinese residents from Zhejiang, Jiangsu, and Anhui provinces, the ancestral homes of much of the Chinese business community. In the late 1860s, the Cantonese community in Yokohama also established a "Chinese Chamber" (*Chūka kaigisho*), which soon changed its name to "Chinese Association" (*Chūka kaikan*).[63]

The Chinese associations obtained a kind of semiofficial status; they could petition Japanese authorities directly, and they were put in charge of managing household plates that were required by the Japanese authorities. The associations also seem to have had a limited mandate to prosecute crimes committed by their members. Whenever appropriate, Japanese authorities sent instructions (*yu/yu*) to the Chinese community. For instance on 9 January 1871, the foreign affairs bureau sent instructions to the Fujian and Guangdong associations to clamp down on malpractice in money-changing shops (*duijindian*).[64] The fact that the authorities gave the associations some kind of official status is indicated by the fact that an official instruction to the two associations, prohibiting Chinese peddlers from the streets of Nagasaki, bore the seal of the Fujian and Guangdong associations.[65]

The lack of any official relations with the Qing Empire became a cause of concern in government circles very early. During the first years of the 1860s, Japanese officials lobbied the Bakufu to repeal the ban on overseas travel and to investigate direct links with China in the interest of trade.[66] The first attempt to open negotiations was made in 1862, when the Nagasaki magistrate, Ōkubo Tadahiro, sent the newly purchased ship *Senzaimaru* to Shanghai, carrying Japanese businessmen and officials. The journey is mostly known for the fact that the patriotic samurai Takasugi Shinsaku joined the trip and left a diary in which he recorded his impressions of Shanghai.[67] The ship also represented the first Japanese attempt to establish official relations with the Qing Empire. The representatives of the shogunate, Nedachi Sukeshichirō and Numa Heirokurō, met the Shanghai circuit intendant (*Susongtai dao*) Wu Xu and asked that Japanese be allowed to trade in Shanghai. Wu Xu was initially reluctant to grant this request, erroneously believing that the lack of a commercial treaty meant that trade with Japan was not permitted. The Japanese representatives persisted and asked that Japan be allowed to send a consul like other unrepresented countries. Realizing that a number of countries such as the Netherlands, Italy, and Spain, which had not yet concluded treaties with China, had been allowed to trade in Shanghai, Wu Xu changed his mind and tried to convince his superiors, the minister superintendent of trade, Xue Huan, and Li Hongzhang, who then served as acting governor of Jiangsu. Xue and Li were more suspicious of the Japanese and did not recommend that the request be granted, which is probably why the Zongli Yamen failed to give a conclusive answer to the request.[68]

The Nagasaki magistrate approached Shanghai authorities once more in March 1864. This time Bakufu officials Yamaguchi Shakujirō and Moriyama Takichirō acted through the good offices of Harry Parkes and William Frederick Mayers, who asked the Shanghai circuit intendant and acting customs superintendent Ying Baoshi if the Japanese could file a customs declaration for some seaweed. Ying applied a customs regulation from the Board of Revenue (*Hubu*) dating back to 1781 and was thus able to comply with the Japanese request without initiating a new policy. To the relief of Ying Baoshi, the Japanese returned without making any further requests.[69]

The final attempt to open relations was made in February 1868, shortly after the Meiji restoration, which had not yet fully reached this corner of Japan. This time, the Nagasaki magistrate, Kawazu Sukekuni, sent a letter to Ying Baoshi through the good offices of the British consul, Charles A. Winchester, asking for permission for Japanese to reside in China for the purpose of trade and "study" (*chuanxi xueshu*).[70] Having consulted with Zeng Guofan, Ying Baoshi informed Kawazu that there was nothing that prevented Japanese from coming to China to sell merchandise, just like Yamaguchi had done four years before. However, Ying was not sure what the Japanese meant by "study" and asked for a clarification whether they meant that they would come to study in China or that they would spread their teachings in China. In any case, Ying informed the Japanese that he had no authority to initiate any new policy in his capacity as a local official, but that Japanese would be allowed to visit China as long as they respected Chinese customs and the Chinese legal order (*Zhongguo fadu*) and did not get into conflict with the population.[71]

At the heart of the issue was under what status Japanese could stay in China, if they were to be allowed to stay in China at all. As Ying had pointed out, local officials were not able to initiate new policy, and the old strategy of trying to open diplomatic relations by negotiations at the local level was hampered by the limited mandate of local officials to devise new policies.[72] In the absence of officially accredited consuls, one may assume that the Japanese living in Shanghai would submit to the jurisdiction of the Mixed Court in their capacity as unrepresented foreigners. However, the literature on the Mixed Court in Shanghai does not chronicle any incidents involving Japanese during the 1860s.[73]

The Yanagihara Mission

The establishment of the Meiji régime provided an opportunity to address the problem at a national level. In September 1870, the Japanese government dispatched the twenty-year-old court noble and deputy foreign minister Yanagihara Sakimitsu to China to broach the idea of formal treaty relations with the government in Beijing. The Japanese delegation also included the junior diplomat Hanabusa Yoshimoto, who would become known for his contributions to Korean relations, and the interpreter-diplomat Tei Einei (Zheng Yongning), who was of ethnic Chinese descent. Tei was a transitional figure in Japanese foreign policy who represented continuity with the old Nagasaki system of Sino-Japanese relations. He hailed from a prominent Fujian family in Nagasaki who had fled China with the fall of the Ming dynasty and had served as "Chinese commissioners" for generations. He would play a key role in the first decade of treaty relations between China and Japan.[74]

Yanagihara first arrived in Shanghai on 4 September, where he met with the mixed court subprefect, Chen Fuxun, and the circuit intendant, Tu Zongying, whom he asked for permission to proceed to the capital to negotiate a treaty. Tu tried to dissuade the delegation from proceeding north, but Yanagihara prevailed over his objections and arrived in Tianjin on 27 September. In Tianjin, the northern superintendent of trade, Chenglin, took charge of negotiating with the Japanese delegation, which intended to continue to the capital of Beijing to negotiate a treaty directly with the Zongli Yamen. Chenglin, who was favorably disposed to the Japanese, managed to persuade Yanagihara not to proceed to Beijing but to wait for the answer of the Zongli Yamen. He suggested that the Japanese discuss a treaty with Zeng Guofan and Li Hongzhang instead, who now held the positions of governor-general of Jiangsu-Anhui and Zhili, respectively.[75]

The prevailing mood in Qing official circles was clearly not conducive to any new initiatives in foreign policy. The discussion on the treaty with Japan took place against the backdrop of two events that had occurred only two months prior to Yanagihara's arrival to Tianjin. On 21 June 1870, twenty-one foreigners, most of whom were French, and around forty Chinese Christian converts were killed in what has become known as the Tientsin Massacre, and French diplomats were using all their leverage to obtain a favorable settlement with the Qing government.[76] The following month, the British government refused to ratify the "Alcock Convention," partially in response to the Tientsin Massacre, but also influenced by British merchants' opposition. The Zongli Yamen had taken great pride in their success in negotiating the Alcock Convention, which would have made it possible for the Qing authorities to increase tariffs on certain goods and placed a number of qualifications on most-favored-nation treatment of Western nations. The British failure to ratify the treaty embittered many Qing statesmen, especially the prominent Manchu statesman Wenxiang, one of the Qing signatories to the treaty.[77] It was thus hardly surprising that the Yamen rebuffed Yanagihara's request to negotiate a treaty under the pretext that there was "no precedent" for such a move. Yanagihara insisted on opening negotiations, and Li Hongzhang and Zeng Guofan, who had been impressed with the young envoy's determination, managed to persuade the Yamen that it was in the best interest of both China and Japan to conclude a treaty without Western involvement. Yanagihara eventually reached an agreement with the Zongli Yamen that a Japanese mission would be allowed to arrive the following year with full powers to negotiate a treaty of amity and commerce. Completely on his own initiative, he also left a draft treaty, which was modeled on treaties Japan and China had concluded with the United States, Britain, France, Russia, and Prussia.[78]

Pending the arrival of the next Japanese embassy, leading Qing statesmen started to memorialize the throne, debating the wisdom of concluding a treaty with Japan. The governor of Anhui, Yinghan, led the charge against a treaty:

> The foreign countries have the nature of dogs and sheep; the only thing they look for is profit and the only thing they fear is authority. They are

only observing the strength of China [*Zhongguo*] in order to take advantage of it. Thus when we happen to have problems, they will succeed in running wild and bullying us. That is the origin of the Tianjin Affair. Now Japan is asking to open trade; Japan used to be a tributary state and is not like Britain and France, which have clearly written treaties that can be consulted. Now they are taking advantage of our plight and are suddenly coming to have a try; we do not know what they have in mind. What China grants is of great consequence and shall not be taken lightly. Japan is the country of dwarves, during the Ming dynasty they invaded our ports for hundreds of years. Once they have been able to establish themselves in our country, they will add another disaster on top of Britain and France. We cannot worry too much about this!⁷⁹

Yinghan feared that concluding a treaty with Japan would threaten the hierarchy in East Asia and upset China's relations with its tributary allies, who would swarm to ask for treaties as well.⁸⁰ As conservative and prejudiced as Yinghan may have been, he was apparently right in fearing that a treaty with Japan might weaken the prestige of China; when Korean officials learned about China having concluded a treaty with Japan, they did indeed interpret it as a sign of weakness.⁸¹

Zeng Guofan and Li Hongzhang, who came to decisively favor opening relations with Japan, responded forcefully to Yinghan's objections. In his memorial to the throne, Li pointed out that in contrast to Ryukyu, Annam, and Korea, Japan had not maintained tributary relations with China for centuries. In his view, it would be futile to postpone a treaty until the Japanese would demand one with force or in alliance with the Western powers.⁸² For his part, Zeng pointed out that in contrast to the small number of Chinese going to the West (*Taixi*), Japan had a large Chinese community. Therefore, he had no objections to following Western precedent and sending consuls to Japan, where they would "restrain" (*yueshu*) the Chinese community and set up mixed courts (*huixunju*) to adjudicate mixed cases.⁸³ In the literature on the treaty, *huixunju* has been routinely translated as "consular court," instead of "mixed court."⁸⁴ If consular courts were what Zeng had in mind, he would have most likely used the well-established terms *lingshi yamen* or *lingshi gongtang*.

Confident that Chinese punishments were the only adequate way of maintaining order in the Chinese community and well aware that those very punishments were the target of foreign criticism, Li suggested that serious offenders be repatriated to China for punishment in order to avoid foreign ridicule (*mianzhi shou bi jifeng*).⁸⁵ This shows not only how sensitive Qing policy-makers were to foreign criticism of the Qing penal system but also how determined they were to maintain the Chinese system intact. For example, the Shanghai Mixed Court was given a limited mandate to sentence and punish criminals in order to prevent excessive foreign influence over the court.

Zeng Guofan also favored a fixed tariff, but he strongly suggested that a treaty should not contain any most-favored-nation arrangement (*yiti junzhan*), which would allow Japan to share the same privileges as the other treaty powers.[86] By advocating a treaty without a most-favored-nation clause, Zeng clearly intended to disentangle the Sino-Japanese treaty from the cobweb of treaties that both China and Japan had concluded with the Western powers. More important, the lack of a most-favored-nation arrangement would also mean that the Japanese would not be able to claim unilateral extraterritorially by invoking that principle.[87] That is what happened to mutual consular jurisdiction in the 1855 treaty with Russia. The aging Zeng Guofan's memorial was perhaps his last contribution of any importance to Qing foreign policy. He died the following year and would never see his ideas on the treaty realized.

It is obvious that most Qing statesmen recognized consular jurisdiction as accepted practice (*tongli*) by the early 1870s.[88] The Qing government had no consuls in Europe and America. Most of the treaties did not anticipate that possibility, so the question of Chinese enjoying extraterritorial rights overseas was never seriously considered. The Qing approach to consular jurisdiction was purely pragmatic, and just as Zeng pointed out, the fact that China and Japan had a long history of both formal and informal contacts set Japan apart from all other countries. It was one thing to give numerically small Western communities in the treaty ports some form of legal autonomy. It was quite another to grant the geographically closer Japanese the same and to give them freedom to travel in the interior.[89] To grant the Japanese privileges without getting anything in return was simply to strike a bad bargain.

Moreover, both Qing officials and Japanese observers considered the Chinese community in the Japanese treaty ports unruly. Qing officials feared that granting unilateral extraterritorial privileges to Japanese nationals might provide overseas Chinese with an opportunity to use Japanese nationality as a protective shield in China. To allow the existence of a Chinese enclave beyond the reach of Qing rule yet so close to the Chinese mainland could be dangerous. This is exactly what Qing officials worried would happen in Hong Kong, and they had unsuccessfully tried to assert jurisdiction over the Chinese residents in the Crown Colony in the 1840s.[90]

The Qing Draft

Li and Zeng's suggestions were approved by the throne, and two of Li's lieutenants, Ying Baoshi and Chen Qin, were commissioned to carry out preparations for a formal treaty with Japan. Ying researched the treaties Japan had concluded with the United States, Britain, France, and the Netherlands. Among other things, he noted that the Japanese treaties were stricter than the Chinese ones regarding the right (or privilege) to travel to the interior of the country. Thus it was concluded that on the basis of reciprocity, China should not grant the Japanese this right.[91]

Meanwhile, Chen started to work on the suggestions that the treaty be reciprocal, provide Chinese subjects with extraterritorial privileges in Japan, and not contain any most-favored-nation clause. The Yanagihara draft had clearly provided for extraterritorial privileges for Japanese citizens, whereas the legal privileges of Chinese in Japan were more vaguely defined.[92] There was a distinct possibility that Chinese would not enjoy consular protection at all in Japan, something that was not acceptable for the Qing government. Chen changed this to make the treaty conform to the Qing understanding of extraterritorial jurisdiction: extraterritoriality should be granted mutually, and mixed cases were to be tried jointly by the consul and the local official. Crimes committed in the interior could in certain cases be dealt with by local authorities alone, without the interference of the consul. In other words, the extraterritorial privileges granted under the 1871 treaty had a *territorial* dimension: it was not only the nationality of the person committing a crime that determined jurisdiction but also *where* a crime was committed. This set the 1871 treaty apart from most other treaties that both China and Japan had concluded with Western countries. Some of the first treaties, such as the Sino-American and Sino-French treaties from 1844, appeared to restrict consular jurisdiction to the five treaty ports, but to the extent that such arrangements had not already been voided by most-favored-nation arrangements, they were carefully excised from the treaties that were concluded after the Second Opium War of 1856–60.

Chen also suggested that the consuls not be called *lingshi/ryōji*, as they were in the Japanese drafts, but *lishiguan*, or simply *lishi*. The reason for this was twofold. First of all, Chen noted that the local Japanese official (*difangguan*) who would be the counterpart of the consul had the rank not of "circuit intendant" (*daotai*) but of "prefect" (*zhifu*) or lower. In China, the local counterpart of a foreign consul was usually a circuit intendant. The failure of the Japanese to comply with this norm would be demeaning for the Qing consul, which is why Chen suggested that the consuls be given the rank of prefect. Second, by giving the Qing consul a different name, Chen wanted to make a clear departure from the treaties that had been concluded with the West and break new ground (*biekai shengmian*).[93] Firmly placing them within the Qing institutional order, the Qing consulates would be called *lishi fu* in official communications from the consulates.[94]

It is evident that some of Chen's suggestions were based on a superficial understanding of the new administrative system that the Japanese government was introducing in 1871. The administrative units that went under the Sino-Japanese terms for "prefecture" (*fu*) or "district" (*ken*) in Japan contained much larger populations than their Chinese equivalents. Nevertheless, his suggestions show how inclined Qing officials were to think in terms of parallel terminology.⁹⁵ By advocating the term *lishiguan* for the Qing consul, Chen also established a direct link to other Qing institutions for the adjudication of interethnic disputes such as the Mixed Court in Shanghai, which was initially called *lishi yamen*, and the judicial subprefect (*lishi tongzhi*), which was often referred to as *lishi ting* or *lishi fenfu*.

On the other hand, the fact that Chen tried to disassociate the Qing draft from Western precedents is noteworthy, considering the fact that Chen himself had proofread W. A. P. Martin's Chinese translation of Henry Wheaton's *Elements of International Law* some five years earlier.⁹⁶ Yet his revised draft uses very little of the terminology suggested by Martin's translations, which demonstrates that Qing policy-makers were able to conceive of forms of personal jurisdiction without drawing on international precedents. Ying Baoshi and Zeng Guofan further improved on Chen's draft, and in April 1871, Ying was able to present a draft treaty to the Zongli yamen.⁹⁷

The Envoy's Old Clothes

The Japanese move to establish official treaty relations with China coincided with increased misgivings about consular jurisdiction. Unbeknownst to the Chinese, who had taken the junior court noble's draft as an expression of official Japanese policy, Yanagihara had acted on his own initiative and had no authority to present any draft.⁹⁸ The Japanese government did not feel bound by Yanagihara's initiative and commissioned the Dutch-trained jurist Tsuda Mamichi to draw up an official draft treaty in preparation for the fully accredited mission to China. In many ways, Tsuda embodied Japan's effort to revise the treaties. He was a prominent advocate of treaty revision and legal reform in Japan and was personally committed to both Japanese domestic legal reform and treaty revision with the West, but he harbored no moral qualms about drafting an unequal treaty with the Qing government. Treaty revision was a matter of national prestige; Japan was aspiring to join the ranks of the civilized nations. Nothing less than an "unequal treaty" would do in Japan's relations with the Qing Empire, which many Western-educated reformists like Tsuda regarded as beyond the pale of modern civilization. Consequently, Tsuda drew up a draft treaty based on the Chinese treaty with the Kingdom of Prussia, which in some respects was less equal than the apocryphal draft of Yanagihara that the Chinese had spent a year revising. Tsuda's draft would have put Japan on a par with other Western nations in its relations with China, not the least since it granted unilateral most-favored-nation treatment to Japan. This draft defined the extraterritorial privileges for Japanese in specific terms, whereas the corresponding clauses relating to Chinese extraterritorial privileges were much more vague. Taken together, the draft would have put Japanese on the same footing as Westerners in China and paved the way for unilateral consular jurisdiction for Japanese.[99]

This was the version the former lord of Uwajima, Date Munenari, presented when he arrived in Tianjin in September 1871 to negotiate a treaty as a fully accredited Japanese envoy, together with a delegation, including Yanagihara, Tsuda, and Tei. Not surprisingly, the Qing negotiators were very disturbed when they learned about the new Japanese draft. Ying and Chen wrote to Yanagihara, Date's deputy:

> When you sent your draft to us last year, we found several clauses unsatisfactory, but the rest of it was acceptable. Now your side has come forward with an entirely different draft and wants to discard the earlier one. Your conduct amounts to a breach of faith even before signing a treaty![100]

Much to the dismay of the Japanese delegation, Ying and Chen now produced their own draft, and the Japanese were in effect given an ultimatum: either they accept the Qing draft as the basis for negotiations or there would be no treaty at all. The Japanese were used to regarding Chinese diplomacy as purely reactive and were not prepared for the Chinese to be taking the initiative and drafting their own treaty.[101] The document's lack of most-favored-nation treatment for Japan and the lack of rights to travel to the interior of China were seen as its biggest flaws.[102] However, the inexperienced Japanese delegation was no match to this group of seasoned Qing statesmen, and Date felt that he had no other choice than to give in to the Chinese demands.[103] On 13 September 1871, Date Munenari and Li Hongzhang signed what is usually called the "Treaty of Peace, Commerce and Navigation," or simply the "Treaty of Tianjin" in English. The document was not called a "treaty" in either Chinese or Japanese, but was officially called "regulations of amity" (*Xiuhao tiaogui/shūkō jōki*). This was yet another indication that the Qing Empire wanted to distinguish this instrument from the treaties signed with the West.[104] The official text of the treaty was in Chinese and Japanese, and it did not have an official English text. The supremacy of the Chinese language was enshrined in article 6, which established that China would use Chinese only in official correspondence from China, whereas Japan would use Japanese in conjunction with Chinese.[105] This adds an interesting dimension to recent scholarship on the role of translation of international law in East Asia.[106] Qing officials were far from being passive recipients of Japanese and Western incursions into the Chinese language sphere; instead they confidently asserted their linguistic hegemony in China's relations with Japan and carefully avoided using Sino-Japanese neologisms.

The Sino-Japanese Treaty of Tianjin codified consular jurisdiction in a number of rather lengthy articles, in contrast to the Western treaties, which defined extraterritoriality and consular jurisdiction in brief articles, thus leaving a lot of room for interpretation, extrapolation, and occasional misrepresentation.

Article 8 of the treaty laid down that China and Japan each had the right to send consuls (*lishiguan/rijikan*) to the open ports "for the control of its own merchant community." The article also established the exclusive authority of the consul to rule in certain civil cases in which only his compatriots were implicated. In mixed cases, the consul should endeavor "to prevent litigation by friendly counsel," but when such a solution was not feasible, he should try the case "in concert" with the local authorities (*difangguan/chihōkan*).[107] The following clause anticipated a situation without consular authority in the treaty ports and established that local authorities could claim jurisdiction in cases involving expatriate Chinese or Japanese in the absence of a duly appointed consul.[108]

Article 11 forbade expatriate subjects of the two countries from bearing arms in the treaty ports and imposed a fine on those who violated the ban. It further enjoined Chinese and Japanese to "attend peacefully their own vocations" and provided that "they shall submit to the authority of the consul." Clearly the paragraph reflected both Chinese and Japanese concerns that consular jurisdiction was frequently used as a pretext for violating local laws and customs with impunity, as in the Moss case in 1860. Interestingly, the article laid down a rule that expatriate Chinese and Japanese "shall not be allowed to adopt the costume of the country in which they reside, nor to obtain local registration and compete at the literary examinations." The reference to literary examinations betrays Chinese influence, and the emphasis on dress code demonstrates that jurisdiction was determined not only by one's race or national origin but also by one's acts and appearance. For example, in draft regulations for missionaries from the late 1860s, the Qing government cited the fact that Christian missionaries "dressed like Chinese" as one argument for why Western missionaries living in the interior of China should be subject to Chinese jurisdiction.[109] The British consular authorities seemed to share some of these assumptions, and in a notification of October 1868, the British minister, Alcock, restricted consular protection to British subjects of Chinese descent to those who abandoned traditional Chinese dress.[110]

Article 13 focused on criminal jurisdiction and procedure at great length and laid down limits for the exercise of consular and mixed jurisdiction. In contrast to the arrangements in the treaties with the Western treaty powers, local authorities were given far-reaching authority to arrest and even kill violent foreign criminals who ventured outside the treaty ports. Criminals who were arrested in the treaty ports were to "be tried by the local authority and the consul together," whereas local authorities alone were put in charge of prosecuting and punishing criminals who were arrested in the interior. Whenever a Chinese or Japanese had been arrested and punished in the interior, the national consul was to be duly informed. Finally, the article ruled that the execution of death sentences was to take place at the location of the crime.[111] This is reminiscent of the verdict in the mixed criminal case two years earlier, when the British Supreme Court in Shanghai sentenced the British subject Willis George to death by hanging for having killed a Chinese carpenter. The fact that George had been executed in Shanghai—where the crime had been committed—was quoted by the Zongli Yamen as an important legal precedent in a handbook for diplomats.[112]

Put briefly, the treaty set clear limitations on consular jurisdiction at the same time that it expanded the scope for mixed jurisdiction. The consul only exercised his jurisdictional privileges in the treaty ports, where he and the local authorities were given far-reaching authority to rule in mixed cases together. Both the Chinese and Japanese text made it absolutely clear that the consul was actually involved in the trial of mixed cases.[113] This differed from the official British conception of mixed jurisdiction, according to which an assessor of the plaintiff's nationality was to be present in mixed trials but had no authority to rule in mixed cases.[114]

This was the treaty the former domanial lord felt he had no other choice than to accept. A unique photograph depicts Date with his delegation posing outside the foreign ministry in Tokyo, just before they set out to conclude the treaty with China. All wear traditional Japanese clothes, and Date is seated in the middle, proudly holding his sword, with Tsuda Mamichi and Yanagihara Sakimitsu on each side.[115] In a sense, the picture is a counterpart to the famous photograph of

The Japanese delegation to the Qing Empire, September 1871. Beginning from the second from left are Tsuda Mamichi, Date Munenari, and Yanagihara Sakimitsu. Seated on the front far left is possibly Tei Einei. In contrast to the famous Iwakura mission, which was sent to Europe and North America the same year, the entire delegation is wearing traditional Japanese dress. Courtesy of Nagasaki Prefectural Library.

the leading members of the Iwakura mission posing in Western dress. But in contrast to the Iwakura mission, which would be praised despite its failure to realize its immediate objectives of treaty revision, the Date delegation returned to Japan dressed in their old clothes and with a new treaty, which the Japanese government would disavow immediately.

Repercussions

News of the treaty produced a minor diplomatic scandal when the delegation returned to Japan. Date Munenari was purged from his position in the foreign ministry and was threatened with impeachment for having exceeded his authority (*ekken*).[116] However, after the scandal receded, the Japanese would call the treaty "a temporary treaty" (*kari jōyaku*) in order to show that they intended to revise it, just as they intended to revise the treaties with the West.[117] The Japanese government had high hopes that the Iwakura mission, which had left Japan in December 1871, would secure better treaty terms with the West, impressing on the Chinese the need to revise the Sino-Japanese Treaty of Tianjin. In the meantime, foreign minister Soejima Taneomi and the diplomat Terajima Munenori sent a joint note to Li Hongzhang outlining the Japanese objections to the Treaty of Tianjin. As regards consular jurisdiction, they wrote:

> In virtue of the relations existing between our country and European countries their merchants come here, while our merchants do not go there; but we now intend to propose to them that our merchants may also go there if they wish to do so. As far as we are concerned we intend to observe towards these countries the same course as they observe amongst themselves in virtue of the Treaties which exist among them. As for the Treaty with China certain changes will no doubt become necessary hereafter when we shall have revised our Treaties with European countries. This cannot be looked upon as a treaty which is to endure perpetually, and we therefore expect to propose its revision.[118]

Clearly the Japanese were getting cold feet; the new treaty ran completely counter to their drive to revise the unequal treaties. The Treaty of Tianjin was especially dangerous to the Japanese since the Qing government was lukewarm, at best, when it came to legal reform. Indeed, many Qing officials objected to many of the reforms that were seen as preconditions for treaty revision in Japan.[119] As astute politicians would discover when they were negotiating new commercial treaties, the Sino-Japanese treaty might throw a spanner into the carefully engineered machinery of treaty revision. If the Japanese government succeeded in negotiating new "equal" treaties with Western countries, finally abolishing consular jurisdiction, but failed to do the same in relation to China, it would find itself in a very awkward situation.[120] Moreover, although the Sino-Japanese Treaty of Tianjin lacked a most-favored-nation clause, anything that had been granted to the Qing Empire under this treaty could be invoked by nations enjoying most-favored-nation treatment. In March 1872, Yanagihara and Tei were sent to China one more time to renegotiate the treaty, including the articles that regulated consular jurisdiction. Their efforts were rebuffed by an annoyed Li Hongzhang, and Yanagihara and Tei had to return without having accomplished their mission.[121]

The Sino-Japanese Treaty of Tianjin shows not only that Qing statesmen accepted the principle of joint jurisdiction but also that they actively tried to export it to Japan. Against this background, it is clear that the input of the Qing authorities into the Shanghai Mixed Court rules was based on a coherent set of assumptions about joint jurisdiction that was not just restricted to Shanghai.[122] The Chefoo Convention, sometimes credited with being the instrument that decisively legalized mixed tribunals in China, was not concluded until five years *after* the Treaty of Tianjin of 1871.[123] It is, however, important to keep in mind that the arrangements for mixed trials in the Treaty of Tianjin were unambiguously mutual, thus realizing Qing ambitions for a completely reciprocal Mixed Court, which Qing officials had been unable to fulfill in Shanghai. A couple of years later, the U.S. minister to China, Seward, would smugly quote the treaty as a proof that "the principle of extraterritoriality appears, indeed, to receive spontaneous acceptance among Asiatic peoples."[124] Although the Japanese resistance to the Treaty of Tianjin seems to have eluded Seward, there is a grain of truth in that statement. But the fact that the "principle of extraterritoriality" had been accepted by no means implied that "Asiatic peoples" accepted the Western construct of that principle.

The Japanese government soon realized that it was not in a sufficiently strong position to renegotiate the treaty, and it sent Soejima to China in order to exchange ratifications in 1873. Thus the Soejima mission is usually described as a diplomatic triumph of Japan, in which the modernizing Meiji government asserted its equality with the Qing Empire with a "modern" commercial treaty, secured an audience with the emperor through subtle manipulation of diplomatic protocol, and pushed Qing officials on the matter of sovereignty over Taiwan.[125] Yet the "equal" treaty that Soejima had arrived to ratify was widely resented in Japan, and the Japanese government effectively disavowed it internally once its contents were known. The fact that the treaty granted extraterritorial privileges to Chinese residents in Japan is often overlooked or not mentioned at all.[126]

After the Japanese government ratified the treaty, it was quick to establish regular diplomatic relations with China. In November 1873, the foreign ministry appointed Yamada Akiyoshi minister to Beijing, a post he held concurrently with his position as commander of the Tokyo division of the Japanese army. However, he never took up his post in Beijing and was quickly assigned to more pressing military duties, such as suppressing samurai rebellions in southeast Japan. Instead his deputy, Yanagihara Sakimitsu, and Tei Einei, who was the legation's first secretary, held the position as chargés d'affaires until a more senior appointment could be made.[127] Concurrently, Japan opened a number of consulates in China in swift succession; in 1873, it opened a consulate general in Shanghai, followed by ones in Fuzhou (1872), Xiamen (1875), Tianjin (1875), Niuzhuang (1876), and Yantai (1876).[128] The consulates were established in strict accordance with diplomatic protocol, manifesting official Japanese intentions to build a foreign service based on Western models.

Consul and Community

In contrast to the speedy Japanese dispatch of ministers and consuls, a number of events distracted the Qing government from sending envoys and consuls abroad: the Taiwan incident in 1874, the demise of the Tongzhi emperor, and the accession of the Guangxu emperor.[129] However, since the treaty anticipated a situation without consuls and stipulated that local authorities were entitled to exercise jurisdiction over Chinese or Japanese in the absence of consuls, the conclusion of the treaty initially brought about few substantive changes, and the Japanese government was more than happy to comply with this state of affairs. In the meantime, the Qing government used local officials to solve problems in its relations with Japan. For instance, the ubiquitous Mixed Court subprefect Chen Fuxun was sent to Japan in 1872 to repatriate Chinese "coolie" laborers who had been stranded in Japan.[130]

However, the Chinese communities in Japan were apparently not satisfied with the lack of a permanent presence of Qing diplomats. In 1875, Li Hongzhang received an anonymous appeal from the Chinese community in Japan urging the Qing government to send an official to Japan in order to protect the Chinese there.[131] The settlement of the Margary incident in 1876 necessitated a mission of apology to Britain, which in turn prompted the Qing government to send envoys and consuls abroad, including Japan.[132] Learning about these plans, the Japanese government repeatedly tried to persuade the Qing government to further delay the dispatch of consuls, but when they were eventually sent, Japanese authorities accepted their credentials.[133]

In late 1877, the Qing minister He Ruzhang and his deputy Zhang Sigui set off for Japan. Both of them belonged to Li Hongzhang's vast network of self-strengthening bureaucrats, and Zhang had written a preface to the Chinese translation of Wheaton's *Elements of International Law*.[134] In January the following year, they informed the Japanese foreign minister, Terajima Munenori, in a *note verbale* that they had assumed their office. They thanked the Japanese government for administering Chinese merchants and announced that Fan Ximing would be sent to Yokohama shortly to assume jurisdiction (*guanshu*) over Qing subjects in his capacity as consul. Pending the appointment of Qing officials to Kobe, Nagasaki, Hakodate, and Osaka, Qing merchants residing in these ports would still be subject to Japanese authorities, in conformity with the treaty.[135]

Cantonese official Yu Qiong arrived in Nagasaki in late November 1877 to take up residence and to set up the new Qing consulate.[136] In September the following year, he hoisted the yellow dragon flag of the Qing Empire to announce the opening of the consulate, and the local English newspaper grudgingly reported that "the occasion was taken advantage of to make the day one of festivity and rejoicing among the Chinese."[137] Yu would become a respected member of the Chinese community and was asked to contribute calligraphy and inscriptions for the Chinese associations, many of which can still be admired in the temples of Nagasaki.[138] He also entertained lively exchanges with local Japanese Sinologists.[139]

The reception on the part of the Japanese authorities was considerably colder, perhaps echoing the reluctance of the national government to accept Qing diplomatic representatives. Only half a year after taking up his position in Nagasaki, Yu Qiong was stopped by a group of policemen in Maruyama ward. Even though an English passerby told the policemen that Yu was the Qing consul in the city, the policemen still refused to let him go. An infuriated Yu filed a protest with the Nagasaki prefect, charging that his treatment was extremely impolite and full of contempt (*shi shu wuli, qingmie zhi zhi*) and demanding an investigation.[140] This was Yu's first encounter with the Nagasaki police department, which would soon gain a particularly bad reputation among the city's Chinese and Western communities.

In subsequent years, Qing consuls were dispatched to the other treaty ports to assume their duties, and Qing consular jurisdiction in Japan started to work in earnest. Still operating under Chinese linguistic hegemony, both Chinese and Japanese officials used Chinese as the official language; no evidence has been found of Qing officials using Japanese or English in their contacts with Japanese authorities prior to the first Sino-Japanese war.[141] Japanese neologisms had yet to be adopted by the Chinese, and the Chinese and Japanese often differed in their use of specific terms and concepts. The Japanese, who were very wary of calling the Chinese "Chūgokujin" ("people from the central country") had been calling them "Shinajin" ("people from Shina") for most of the early treaty port era. As Qing consuls started to assume their duties in the late 1870s, Japanese authorities instead started to call the Chinese "Shinkokujin" ("people from the Qing Empire") in an apparent attempt to create terminological consistency. Indeed, the official name of China was the "Great Qing Empire," and the Chinese consuls invariably identified themselves as "consuls of the Great Qing Empire" (*Da Qing-guo lishifu*). However, just as the yellow dragon banner was a political flag, representing the ruling dynasty, in Chinese official usage, the term "Qing" was reserved for official contexts exclusively. There is no evidence that either Qing consuls or members of the Chinese community ever called themselves "Qingguoren," although Chinese merchants occasionally slipped and called themselves "Qing merchants" (*Qingshang/Shinshō*) when they petitioned local Japanese authorities under the early Japanese régime.[142] The Qing consul preferred to call his compatriots "Huaren," and Chinese residents referred to themselves as either "Huaren" or "Tangren." The divergence in terminology used by the Chinese and Japanese is more significant than appears at first sight. While it is a moot point whether Meiji Japanese were "citizens" or "subjects" in the Western sense of the term, it is clear that Japanese authorities considered the Chinese members of the Qing polity in one sense or another. In China, however, the concept of citizenship had yet to develop; the population of the Qing Empire belonged to many different ethnic and subethnic groups, which in turn often belonged to different jurisdictions, and the Chinese were truly "subjects" of the emperor in the strictest meaning of the term. In a sense, Japanese authorities were anticipating the creation of a modern citizenship for the Chinese community.[143]

The contrast between the two polities manifested itself at a number of different levels. As China and Japan were sending consuls to take up office, the Japanese legal system was going through a complete transformation, rendering the terms of the treaty increasingly obsolete from a Japanese point of view. In 1882, the Chinese-inspired *Shinritsu kōryō* was replaced by the new criminal code, based on continental European models. At the same time, the Ministry of Justice was busy reforming the administration of justice, and the different branches of the judicial system were separated in a series of proclamations in the 1880s.[144]

In 1885, the Niigata public prosecutor for minor offenses wrote the foreign ministry in Tokyo to ask for guidance in this matter. He indicated that the term "local authority" (*difangguan/chihōkan*) was meaningless in a Japanese context. Presumably thinking about himself, he asked for clarification as to when this so-called local authority referred to a judge (*saibankan*) and when it referred to the public prosecutor (*kenji*).[145] The terminological confusion clearly reflects of the fact that the Qing judicial system lacked the Western-style division of different branches in the judicial system, but this point should not be exaggerated. Western consuls—who justified their jurisdiction on the basis of the allegedly underdeveloped Asiatic judicial systems—seldom observed these distinctions and would sometimes act as judge, prosecutor, or even legal advisor of compatriot defendants as it suited them. This was especially true for smaller nations that could not afford an elaborate consular court system on the British model. What was different was that Japan and most Western countries were moving in the same direction on judicial reform and could resolve differences quite amicably. Qing officials, on the other hand, did not aim to change their judicial system in the near future, and their sympathy for Japanese judicial reforms could not be taken for granted.

The fact that the Qing consul called himself *lishiguan* also caused some uncertainty among local Japanese authorities. The title was especially confusing for the Japanese, who had created the new title "commissioner" (*rijikan*) at the time of the Iwakura embassy.[146] Thus, when consuls were dispatched to the treaty ports, the foreign ministry in Tokyo felt compelled to issue a circular clarifying that the Qing "commissioner" (*lishiguan/rijikan*) was to be considered a "consul" (*lingshi/ryōji*) for all practical purposes.[147] Henceforth, the Japanese authorities would insist on using the term *lingshi/ryōji* in all official communications to the Qing consul, who continued calling himself *lishi* or *lishifu* according to the letter of the treaty. Even though both the Chinese and Japanese versions used the term *lishiguan/rijikan*, Chinese and Japanese authorities never appear to have challenged each other on this question. Not being under any pressure to use "correct terms," the Chinese and Japanese press did not observe these distinctions consistently. In *Shenbao*, the Qing consul was often called *lingshi*, and the Japanese press occasionally used the Chinese term.[148]

At the heart of the matter were not the terms as such but the status of Chinese in Japan. The Japanese authorities consistently stressed that the Chinese community enjoyed the same privileges as other foreigners in Japan and went to great lengths to make that point.[149] However, as both Japanese authorities and foreigners gradually realized in the 1880s, the Sino-Japanese Treaty of Tianjin gave Chinese a different status from that of other foreigners in Japan, and the actual wording of the treaty became a source of contention. The difference was most saliently manifested in the relationship between the Chinese community and the Qing consul. In contrast to other foreign consuls, who usually interacted directly with their citizens or subjects on an individual level, the Qing consul was just one figure in a multilayered and sometimes overlapping system of governance in a plural legal order. The Qing consul was both a magistrate and a community leader who mediated between different groups and associations, and he represented the Chinese community in its relations with local Japanese authorities. Just like a district magistrate in China, who often ruled over hundreds of thousands of people, the Qing consul preferred that the people under his jurisdiction solve their own problems through their own community organizations.[150] Purely Chinese cases, as defined by treaty, might also fall under different jurisdictions *within* the Chinese community. If the two concerned parties were from the same region in China, the case would in all likelihood be heard and settled within their association. If a conflict arose between two persons of different regional origin, the case would be settled through arbitration between their respective associations. The Qing consul seems to have only exercised his consular authority in purely Chinese cases when they could not be settled out of court.[151] Mixed cases, which under most extraterritorial régimes constituted a minority of reported consular court cases, were subject to the jurisdiction of both the local Japanese authorities and the Qing consul, who would consult the Chinese associations whenever appropriate.

Qing consular jurisdiction developed incrementally. The first step was informal dialect-group organizations (*bang*), which later evolved into associations (*gongsuo*), which were recognized by local Japanese authorities and reported to them. In the late 1870s, the Qing consuls (*lishi*) were dispatched to Japan and replaced the Japanese authorities as the supreme authority over the associations. The Qing approach to extraterritoriality was not just an adoption of Western practices or a mere extension of the Chinese associations, as is sometimes argued.[152] Instead, the establishment of consular authority was part of an institutional continuum of which Western precedents and Chinese community participation formed two distinct ends.[153] The Qing officials, who drafted the treaty with Japan, worked in a legal environment with well-established institutions for the adjudication of interethnic disputes, and the development of Qing consulates took place in dialogue with Qing institutions like the Shanghai Mixed Court. A further extension of the Qing order into Japan is evidenced by the fact that many headmen of the Chinese associations were given nominal civil service ranks.[154] The last step in this evolution of Qing consular rule was taken when an all-Chinese association (*Zhonghua huiguan*) was formed in Kobe in 1890 under the auspices of the incumbent Qing consul, Zheng Xiaoxu.[155]

The Qing consuls' exercise of extraterritorial jurisdiction is significant not only within their Chinese institutional context, given the numerical strength of the Chinese community in Japan. From 1874 to 1893, the Chinese constituted between 50.7 and 72.4 percent of the foreign community in Yokohama; in Nagasaki the Chinese portion of the foreign population was on average 69 percent between 1876 and 1893. Statistics for the Japanese community in China are incomplete, but the contrast between the absolute numbers of Japanese living in Shanghai and the number of Chinese in Yokohama is nevertheless striking. By 1876, only 45 Japanese lived in the International Settlement in Shanghai, compared to 1,231 Chinese residents in Yokohama and 616 in Nagasaki. There was also a marked spike in the Chinese community in Yokohama after 1878, the year when a consul was sent to Yokohama. Though figures for Nagasaki are incomplete for the Chinese community throughout the 1870s, the number of officially registered Chinese increased from 338 to 810 between 1870 and 1878.[156] There was a sharp drop in the Chinese population around 1894, the year hostilities commenced between Japan and China, and the population did not recover until around the turn of the century. The Japanese residents of Shanghai increased sharply and steadily after 1895, the year the Sino-Japanese Treaty of Tianjin was replaced by the notorious Treaty of Shimonoseki, which abolished Qing consular jurisdiction in Japan and extended to Japanese residents in China the same privileges as Westerners, including unilateral extraterritorial privileges.

While some have pointed out that Japanese did not migrate into the Chinese treaty ports until after the conclusion of the Treaty of Shimonoseki,[157] there seems to be a similar correlation between the implementation of the Sino-Japanese Treaty of Tianjin and the increase in the size of the Chinese community in the late 1870s. Increased competition in the shipping industry, with the entrance of several new operators in the 1870s,[158] may have provided a significant "pull" for Chinese migrants to Japan, but that does not explain why there was no similar pull for Japanese into China. These numbers suggest that the implementation of extraterritorial régimes contributed to migration across the East China Sea. Although the extraterritorial privileges of Westerners had a greater significance in national Japanese political debates than those of the Chinese, the extraterritorial privileges of the Chinese community arguably meant more in the everyday life in the treaty ports, given that the Chinese constituted roughly half of the population.[159] The 1871 Treaty of Tianjin had a significant impact on Japan's relations with its western neighbor, and the implementation of the treaty became source of conflict between the two countries, which were moving in very different directions in the late nineteenth century with respect to legal concepts and legal institutions.

5

Executing Extraterritoriality

Sino-Japanese Cases, 1870–95

On a Nagasaki street in November 1881, following a drunken brawl over a woman and an unsettled debt, Wu A'er, a thirty-four-year-old Chinese barber, cut down Furukawa Yoshimasa with a knife. Wu quickly fled the scene but soon came to his senses and realized he had committed a serious crime. Hoping to get a more lenient punishment, he decided to give himself up to the competent authority for Chinese living in Nagasaki—the Qing consul, Yu Qiong.[1] Having obtained a deposition from the repentant offender, Yu contacted the public prosecutor of the Nagasaki district court, Kawano Michitomo, and the two of them started to hear witnesses and collect evidence.[2]

When Yu Qiong started to investigate the Wu A'er case, he had lived in the ancient port city for four years and had served as the consul of the Qing Empire for more than three years, but this appears have been the first homicide case that fell under his jurisdiction.[3] While the Chinese community in Nagasaki had a reputation for being chaotic and disorderly,[4] judging from the correspondence between the local Japanese authorities and the consular body, there were relatively few cases of violent crime involving both Chinese and Japanese for most of the 1870s and the early 1880s. Browsing the files, one is struck by the fact that the local diplomatic correspondence was dominated by communications between the governor of Nagasaki and the Qing consul, reflecting the fact that the numerically significant Chinese played no small part in everyday life in the treaty ports. Indeed, most of the recorded cases deal with quotidian infractions and disputes such as petty theft, substance abuse, noise, land transactions, and illegal adoptions. Westerners, such as Russians and Americans, were involved in violent crime to a far larger extent than Chinese, and most violent incidents involved foreigners of different nations and did not implicate Japanese at all.[5] This chapter will explore the implementation of jurisdiction over Chinese in Japan and Japanese in China before and after the Sino-Japanese Treaty of Tianjin by analyzing a series of consular cases in Yokohama, Nagasaki, and Shanghai, three sites where legal conflicts between the relatively conservative Qing Empire and the insecure Meiji Japan were contested and negotiated.

Japanese Jurisdiction over Chinese

In the 1860s, the Chinese dialect groups (*bang*) in the Japanese treaty ports formed associations and assumed jurisdiction over the different Chinese communities with the permission of the Japanese authorities. This transition from informal to more formal forms of organization followed well-established patterns that had existed in mainland China long before the arrival of Western gunboats.[6] When the Cantonese community (*Lingnan huisuo*) petitioned the authorities for self-rule around 1869, they justified their initiative by referring to the Japanese policy of assuming jurisdiction over all unrepresented nationalities. The Cantonese petitioners also advanced purely practical arguments in favor of their association assuming jurisdiction; they emphasized that they would not dare to disobey the orders of the Japanese sovereign (*zhuanzhu*) and affirmed that they had no doubt that Japanese laws and decrees were "strict and impartial." They also warned that Chinese and Japanese were used to different social mores and to punishments that differed in severity, so conflicts between Chinese and Japanese would inevitably take place.[7] Thus in contrast to Western merchants and consuls, who routinely justified consular jurisdiction on the grounds that local punishments were too severe, the Cantonese association expressed doubts whether Japanese punishments would be effective enough to maintain law and order in the Chinese community.

At the end of the petition, the Cantonese association presented a preliminary set of rules for the trial of Chinese offenders, according to which Japanese authorities were to notify the association whenever a Cantonese criminal was arrested. According to the rules, Japanese authorities should try and punish the criminal acting in conjunction with the Cantonese association. The association was put in charge of the registration of Cantonese households in Nagasaki.[8] The petition that the Fukienese association submitted to the Japanese authorities shortly after the Cantonese was very similar in form and content.[9] This indicates that these initiatives were part of a concerted move from the Chinese community to assert self-rule, initiatives that may have enjoyed tacit support from the Qing government, which clearly was aware of them and sometimes received petitions from the Chinese in Japan.[10]

The Chinese communities established a subordinate relationship to the Japanese authorities, hoping that the Japanese would reciprocate by giving them some degree of autonomy. In their correspondence with the Japanese authorities, the Chinese associations followed Japanese practice, using only Japanese era names and elevating any references to Japanese authorities. As a rule, they addressed local officials as "great lord" (*tai laoye*), which was a popular respectful term for local officials in China at the time. Thus when a Chinese resident of Nagasaki addressed the Foreign Affairs Bureau in a child custody case, he used the term "the great lord, the [foreign] headman of the criminal prefecturate of the foreign affairs bureau" (*Waiguo shiwu xingming fu da toumu tai laoye*). Nevertheless, despite the respectful form of address, it was the Japanese official who was considered the "foreign official" (*toumu*), not the directors of the association.[11] The available archival records do not reveal exactly to what extent local authorities respected the legal autonomy of Chinese communities, but the Japanese authorities in Nagasaki received and filed communications from the associations and sometimes issued joint instructions with them. In ideal cases, it seems that local administration was exercised by consensus and mutual cooperation. For instance, in August 1869, the two directors of the Fujian association (*Bamin huisuo zongli*), Zheng Renrui and Niu Chunbin, wrote to the Nagasaki authorities asking them to take prompt action against a corrupt Japanese merchant.[12]

Notwithstanding this seemingly cooperative relationship between the Chinese communities and the Japanese authorities, the latter reserved their right to take decisive action when needed. This is illustrated by a well-documented criminal case from Yokohama that not only set a precedent for the treatment of Chinese under Japanese law but also quite possibly had consequences for the implementation of the newly adopted Japanese criminal code. In mid-June 1870, Zhu Xi, a thirty-year-old Chinese, and Yafu, also Chinese, and two Japanese accomplices were arrested in Yokohama on the charge of counterfeiting Japanese paper money (*kinsatsu*), a monetary instrument in early Meiji Japan that was very prone to forgery. Zhu Xi, who had come from Xiangshan district in Guangdong province five years earlier and had been employed by a British merchant, had spent months trying to forge paper money. Two impoverished Japanese craftsmen had at first aided in him in the hope of making some ready cash, but they left the venture because they were disappointed with the quality of the product and feared discovery. Then Yafu, who was a fellow villager of Zhu Xi and was working at the British legation, let him use the premises to print some money in the absence of the British minister, Harry Parkes. A Japanese servant working at the legation informed the authorities, and all who had been involved were arrested.[13]

Under the municipal regulations for the foreign settlement in Yokohama that had been promulgated three years earlier, Japanese authorities were obliged to consult with the consular body whenever they took legal action against a Chinese.[14] Consequently, Zhu, Yafu, and their two Japanese accomplices were tried in the seat of the Kanagawa prefectural government in the presence of the

British, American, Belgian, and Italian consuls, and were quickly found guilty. When the U.S. consul inquired what punishment the prisoners would be given, the Kanagawa prefectural government declared that Zhu Xi and his two Japanese associates were to be sentenced to death by decapitation followed by public display of the severed heads (*kyōshu*), and Yafu would serve three years in prison. The punishments were determined in accordance with the new provisional criminal code (*Shinritsu kōryō*), which had been adopted that year.[15]

As the case involved nonrepresented foreigners and capital punishment, the verdict was referred to the ministries of justice and foreign affairs for review. Being apprised of the declared intention of the Japanese government to execute Zhu Xi, both the consular body and the Chinese association in Yokohama asked the central government in Tokyo for leniency. However, the Ministry of Justice was determined to make an example of the case. The consular body realized that a precedent was about to be set on the implementation of the municipal regulations that might have repercussions on the way law and order were to be administered in the foreign settlements. Consequently, the Belgian consul in Yokohama, F. Geisenheimer, wrote a démarche in awkward English asking the Japanese central government to declare what law would be applied in the case:

> In the case before us, the punishment of death may be inflicted upon Chinese, with an apparent reason, as the same fate would be reserved to him in his own country, for similar offense, while taking a Greek or Peruvian, ruled in their own countries by more lenient laws, I feel most strenuously convinced that the Ministers of the Treaty powers, and public opinion amongst foreigners, should earnestly interfere with execution of a like determination, taken on their behalf by the High Board of Justices of Japan.[16]

Behind Geisenheimer's inquiry was not only the concern that unrepresented foreigners might be subjected to harsher punishments than they were used to at home but also the fear that the prestige of the entire foreign community might be put at jeopardy if the Japanese authorities were allowed to execute Westerners. In response, the Foreign Ministry reaffirmed that Chinese and other unrepresented foreigners were subject to the laws of Japan and that they would be punished according to the Japanese criminal code. All the concerned parties having made their positions completely clear to each other, the matter was all but settled, and the Japanese government could proceed to punish the offenders as it saw fit. However, the Japanese envoy Yanagihara Sakimitsu had just arrived in Tianjin to broach the idea of a treaty with the Qing government, and the Foreign Ministry deemed it prudent to ask him to sound out the Qing government on the matter. Yanagihara's interlocutor in the Qing government, Chenglin, responded on behalf of the Zongli Yamen that he had no objections to the Japanese government executing the Chinese, since forgery was a capital crime in China as well. To shore up his position, he quoted a communication from the Shanghai circuit intendant Ying Baoshi to the governor of Nagasaki two years earlier in which Ying had expressed himself in favor of trying Chinese criminals according to local law in the absence of consular representation.[17]

Having obtained official sanction from the Qing government, the Ministry of Justice encountered opposition from an unexpected quarter. The foreign minister, Terajima Munenori, had just returned to Tokyo from a trip to Osaka, where he had learned that forgery of *kinsatsu* was rampant. The minister expressed fear that if the judicial authorities were to follow the example set in Yokohama, perhaps hundreds of people would be executed, which might reflect negatively on the Japanese government. Presumably, Terajima was concerned that this would interfere with the Japanese government's efforts to convince the treaty powers to abolish extraterritoriality. However, the Ministry of Justice was determined to set an example. On 24 December 1870, Zhu Xi and his two Japanese accessories were decapitated in Yokohama and their severed heads displayed to the public. Zhu left behind a Japanese mistress and their two-year-old son, and while he was in prison he expressed his wish that his son be sent to his home village when he had grown up.[18]

The Yokohama forgery case is the only recorded case where a Chinese was lawfully executed under Japanese jurisdiction prior to 1895. Judging by a list the Tokyo district court prepared in anticipation of the arrival of the first Qing consuls, when Chinese were prosecuted for felonies, they were sentenced to varying lengths of imprisonment and hard labor. The early Meiji Japanese government apparently regarded forgery as a more severe crime than homicide, because one Chinese was sentenced to life imprisonment for murder, which was later commuted to ten to fifteen years' imprisonment.[19] Terajima's reservations against the extreme punishment of Zhu Xi and his two accomplices did, however, have an impact on the way Japanese criminal justice was administered in the future. The year after the three forgers were decapitated, the clause on counterfeiting money in the *Shinritsu kōryō* was suspended because it was regarded as excessively severe.[20]

Despite the fact that the punishment of Zhu Xi had been discussed in a principled way in Tianjin, Chinese and Japanese diplomats soon had occasion to return to the question of administering justice to Chinese under Japanese jurisdiction. In 1875, a delegation led by Mori Arinori came to Beijing to discuss a number of unresolved problems in Sino-Japanese relations, such as the Japanese military expedition to Taiwan the previous year, the enforcement of the Japanese opium ban, and the adjudication of Chinese in Japan. The Zongli Yamen suggested that local Japanese authorities should try Chinese criminals together with the directors of the Chinese associations (*huabang sishi*) in the absence of duly appointed consuls.[21] Representing the Japanese delegation, Tei Einei rejected this idea out of hand and quoted the punishment of Zhu Xi as a precedent. With ill-disguised sarcasm, Tei stated that accepting the suggestions of the Zongli Yamen would be like "searching for an ox while riding one" (*qi niu xun niu*).[22] The Zongli Yamen flatly replied that if the Japanese authorities did not want to hold mixed trials (*huishen*) with the Chinese associations, they could allow a representative from the Chinese associations to sit in on the trial (*guanshen*), just as Western consuls did in mixed cases.[23]

This frank and characteristically inconclusive exchange of opinions is interesting for a number of reasons. First of all, it shows that Japanese authorities were still intent on exercising full jurisdiction over the Chinese community in Japan. It also demonstrates that the Zongli Yamen was aware of the fact that Chinese associations were trying to exercise some degree of legal autonomy in Japan and may even had been tacitly supporting these moves. Finally, in contrast to principled Japanese opposition to any form of consular jurisdiction, the communication shows that the Zongli Yamen clearly was of the opinion that mixed cases could be adjudicated in different, but not necessarily mutually exclusive, ways. The Yamen certainly preferred joint trials (*huishen*), which had strong precedents in the Qing legal system, but Qing statesmen understood that consular jurisdiction could be realized in an institutional continuum, where a range of options were available, including allowing representative nationals to sit in on trials with assessors (*guanshen*).

Local Japanese authorities did reserve their right to take unilateral action, especially when it came to opium. Ever since the war between the Qing and British empires, they had kept a watchful eye on the spread of the drug in Japan. To the Japanese, opium symbolized both the incursions of imperialism into East Asia and the perceived backwardness of the Chinese, who were unable to shake this habit.[24] Consequently, when the Ansei Treaties were negotiated in the late 1850s, the Bakufu was more than happy to accept Western offers to include an explicit ban on opium. Harris's famous ban on opium in the U.S.-Japanese treaty of 1858 was not unprecedented; both the Russian treaty of 1855 and the Dutch treaty of 1856 explicitly prohibited the importation of opium to Japan. The Russian treaty was the most specific, prohibiting Russian ships from importing more than three catties of opium, roughly equivalent to 4 pounds. Any Russian violating this restriction was to pay 20 rubles in fines to the Japanese authorities for each catty in excess of the ban, upon which he would be punished by Russian authorities according to the laws of Russia.[25] This, in effect, set an important precedent that Russian subjects were bound to obey Japanese laws. None of the treaty powers had any great stake in the virtually nonexistent opium trade with Japan, and most countries followed suit and included clauses banning opium in their treaties. The

British did not include any ban on opium in the text of their treaty but listed it among prohibited items in the regulations appended to the treaty. The regulations imposed a fine of $15 on each catty in excess of the ban, but only the Japanese text of the treaty clearly stated that the fine was payable to Japanese authorities (*Nihon yakusho e toritatsu beshi*).[26]

The opium ban made no distinction between opium for smoking and opium for medical use, which potentially put the operation of foreign pharmacies in jeopardy. Initially, this had no practical consequences for pharmacists, since the Bakufu did not restrict the importation of opium for medical purposes and foreigners even paid duty on opium as medicine. The Meiji government followed the Bakufu's precedent but in 1872 it tightened up its policy on the drug and started to seize opium imported for medical purposes as well. When faced with protests from the consular body, the Japanese worked out a set of regulations that would be enforced for both Japanese and foreigners—setting another precedent for Japanese jurisdiction over foreigners. The Japanese position gained some support from the U.S. government, and many British officials were favorably predisposed as well, but the Japanese initiative eventually foundered on the objections of Parkes, who defended British treaty privileges more vigorously than his colleague Alcock had done the previous decade. Consequently, the consular body and the Japanese authorities would never reach a conclusive agreement as to how the opium regulations were to be applied to foreigners under consular jurisdiction.[27]

The Chinese communities, on the other hand, were still formally under Japanese jurisdiction, and Japanese authorities exercised their sovereign rights to enforce the ban on opium in the Chinese community on a number of occasions, which elicited rather courteous complaints from the associations. In March 1875, the directors of the Fukienese and Cantonese associations filed a joint petition with the Japanese authorities, occasioned by the arrest of three Chinese opium smokers, which had led to a small disturbance between Chinese and the police. While the petitioners did not object to the ban on opium in principle, or to the need to prevent the habit from spreading to the Japanese population, they emphasized that many opium smokers could not shake the habit and simply were beyond hope. They further cautioned Japanese authorities against carrying out searches in private homes without the cooperation of the associations. To do so alone would be asking for trouble, as residents would resist and disturbances would ensue.[28]

The enforcement of the opium ban does not seem to have led to similar disturbances in Yokohama, but the Japanese policy led to a disagreement within the Chinese community that was aired in the local press later the same year. In June 1875, an anonymous Chinese sojourner in Yokohama wrote a letter to the editor in which he imparted his view that self-rule under the Chinese associations was an absolute necessity. Making an oblique reference to the widespread habit of opium smoking among the Chinese, he stressed that certain things were criminal in Japan but not in China, and he deplored the fact that the association directors and their assistants failed to discharge their duties and assist those Chinese who were so unfortunate as to be jailed for breaking Japanese laws.[29] The letter elicited spirited but courteous responses from two other anonymous Chinese, who claimed that the complainant was ill informed about the real state of affairs in Yokohama and regretted the fact that internal Chinese community affairs were being discussed in the Japanese press.[30] One of the respondents stated that the associations had been established in order to make it possible for expatriate Chinese to meet people from their home region, and there was no license to act brashly when it came to major legal problems: Chinese had to respect local customs and laws, just like everybody else.[31] The whole correspondence was published in its original Chinese with Japanese guiding marks (*kunten*) added, showing that educated Japanese readers were still expected to be able to read literary Chinese (*kanbun*), very much as the readership of the English-language press in the treaty ports were expected to read untranslated French contributions.[32]

Even though Japanese authorities endeavored to exercise full jurisdiction over the Chinese communities in the treaty ports, the Chinese associations were able to play a crucial role in the management of their constituents prior to the dispatch of consuls to Japan in the late 1870s. Both the central government in Beijing and the Chinese associations in the Japanese treaty ports shared a consistent set of assumptions about self-government and consular jurisdiction, assumptions that placed a great emphasis on joint procedures in mixed cases. This is another indication that the clauses defining consular jurisdiction in the Sino-Japanese Treaty of Tianjin were not a mere product of historical contingency but rested in part on legal and social traditions that antedated both the establishment of the treaty ports and the exchange of consuls between China and Japan.

Enter the Envoys

In 1878, the Qing government had finally prevailed over its own institutional inertia as well as Japanese objections to the dispatch of Qing diplomatic personnel to Japan. One of the first things that the Qing minister, He Ruzhang, and his deputy, Zhang Sigui, did when they took up their duties at the Qing legation in Tokyo was to send a proclamation to Chinese merchants in Japan in which they announced that the Qing consuls were now taking jurisdiction over the Chinese and taking over the duty of supervising and managing household placards (*jipai*) from the associations.[33] Now an additional layer of jurisdiction was

He Ruzhang and his Qing embassy arrive in Yokohama, followed by Chinese sailors and a boisterous crowd. The Chinese are portrayed in traditional Qing garments, whereas the minuscule Japanese police officer wears a Western-style uniform. Cartoon by Charles Wirgman, *The Japan Punch,* December 1877. Reproduced from Charles Wirgman, *Japan Punch* (Tokyo: Yūshōdō shoten, 1975).

imposed on the Chinese communities, and the Chinese associations transferred their official allegiance to the Qing consul, who was addressed in terms similar to those that had been used for the governor of Nagasaki.

In response to the complex legal and social situation in the Japanese treaty ports, detailed regulations were worked out in early 1881 for how criminal procedures were to be administered. An undated and anonymous preface to one draft of the regulations reveals the attitude of Qing diplomats toward their constituents in the treaty ports:

> In the four commercial ports of Japan, Yokohama, Kobe, Nagasaki, and Hakodate, there are approximately three thousand sojourners from China [*Zhongtu*]. Among them, merchants are few and vagrants numerous; good people are rare, and bad elements numerous. Many of them stay idly at home and have no livelihood to support themselves on; they are alone and have no families. Some of them may even be criminal elements that have escaped here [from the mainland.] So they are fierce and stubborn, and often stir up trouble. Japanese social mores esteem manliness and take life lightly. [They] often pull their swords

and kill people, and suicides are frequent. Recently, [the Japanese government] has adopted Western laws, which are exceedingly lenient. Ordinary [Chinese] people are ignorant and have grown used to seeing people being killed, and the punishment not being more than imprisonment. They foolishly believe that they do not have to follow local law. Japanese law does not prohibit weapons, which can be procured everywhere, so cases involving the loss of life are frequent.[34]

It is probably true that the Chinese community was mainly composed of young unmarried men of low social standing, typical for immigrant communities in the late nineteenth century. But this official's expression of the characteristically pessimistic view of the magistrate toward the common people and emigrants should not be taken at face value. The Chinese community also had a prominent position in the business community in the treaty ports and reportedly dominated Japan's trade with China almost totally.[35] The anonymous draftsman placed a heavy emphasis on the need to control the Chinese and how to protect them from the insidious influences of brutal customs of Japan and lenient Western laws. From the point of view of Qing policy-makers, the major problem of consular jurisdiction was not primarily how to manage multinational communities but how to maintain control over Chinese, whether they were residing abroad or staying in China.[36] The draft regulations proceeded to lay down rules for trying capital cases, which followed closely the late Zeng Guofan's suggestions of ten years earlier. Minor crimes could be tried in situ, but some cases had to be referred to authorities on the mainland, presumably to avoid the "derision of foreigners" and the pernicious influences of the Japanese legal system. On the whole, the regulations were in the vein of traditional Chinese law and were reminiscent of mixed court procedure, which embraced both the tradition of joint trials in China and the need to prevent excessive foreign interference in Chinese criminal procedure and punishments. What the drafters did not seem to realize, however, was that this set of rules might conflict with article 13 in the Sino-Japanese Treaty of Tianjin, which established that "capital punishment shall be inflicted at the scene of the commission of the crime."

Meanwhile, the Japanese government was working out its own consular regulations and procedures for trying Japanese criminals in China. Unlike the British, who had established a new supreme court in Shanghai in 1869, the Japanese government made a domestic court, the Nagasaki district court, the ultimate authority for trying crimes committed in China.[37] Given that the Japanese criminal justice system underwent two full cycles of reform during the two decades following the Meiji restoration, the very content of Japanese consular jurisdiction was a moving target.

The terms of the Treaty of Tianjin were riddled with contradictions, not so much because the treaty text itself was vague, as some Japanese officials claimed—indeed it was crystal clear from a Qing point of view—but because the social, institutional, and political environment surrounding the treaty was in a state of constant flux, both in China and Japan. In contrast to the Japanese government, which was trying to update its own legal and political order to be more in tune with the new environment, the Qing government remained uncommitted to fundamental institutional reform and was potentially hostile to Japanese legal reforms. Thus the application of the treaty gradually became a source of contention between the countries, as is illustrated by a number of inconclusive cases in the 1880s and 1890s.

There were several areas of conflict in which these contradictions were manifested. For instance, Qing consuls and Japanese local officials seemed to have different levels of tolerance for everyday nuisances such as noise. On 15 January 1889, the Qing consul responded to a note from the governor of Nagasaki accusing the Chinese of "carelessly creating noise or disturbance" by letting off firecrackers in violation of the regulations of the foreign settlement. The consul noted that Chinese merchants had celebrated with firecrackers at festive occasions for many years without Japanese authorities intervening. To ban firecrackers now would be "tantamount to preventing us [Chinese] from practicing our teaching" (*yu zu wo xingjiao wu yi*).[38] Another area of conflict was the fact that wealthy Chinese adopted—or "bought"—children from poorer Japanese families.[39]

Not surprisingly, the area where Chinese and Japanese understandings of consular jurisdiction would clash most violently was where the loss of human life was involved. The irreversible nature of the crime makes it difficult to adjudicate a homicide through negotiations, and it is extremely difficult to cover up a murder case when different social and ethnic groups are involved.[40] The emergence of modern mass media in the treaty ports and the introduction of the telegraph also meant that news and rumors could travel faster and inflame emotions more intensely than before.[41] The first such test of the Sino-Japanese extraterritorial régime came in November 1881 when Wu A'er was charged with the murder of Furukawa Yoshimasa, who was a young Tokyoite of samurai stock. The wife of the newly married victim, Komine Suzu, had been Wu's mistress (*qie*) for some time before having an affair with and then marrying Furukawa. When Wu had learned of her affair with Furukawa, he had dismissed her in the summer of that year. In mid-October, Komine had told Wu that she was no longer seeing Furukawa and asked him to lend her some money to support her sick mother, which Wu had readily done. Then, on 4 November Wu learned that Furukawa and Komine were holding a wedding party in Nagasaki. Feeling humiliated, Wu decided to take Komine to task for her behavior and ended up killing Furukawa in the ensuing brawl.[42]

Needless to say, reports diverge as to exactly what happened when Wu arrived at Furukawa's house, but since Wu admitted to the murder, the punishment of the accused hinged on the extent to which this was a premeditated act. Supported by relatives of the victim, the Japanese prosecutor tried to make the case that the perpetrator should be charged with willful murder, since he had brought the lethal weapon—a knife—to the crime scene.[43] The Qing consul, on the other hand, put weight on the fact that Wu had given himself up voluntarily (*zishou/ jishu*) and had confessed without making any excuses. Voluntary surrender was cause for leniency under both Chinese and Japanese law at the time, though neither allowed for leniency in the case of "personal injury."[44] Nevertheless, Qing law did provide for suspended death sentences in the case of manslaughter, and the Qing consul, in his writ to the authorities on the Chinese mainland, recommended that Wu be given a suspended death sentence, which would be converted to one hundred strokes with the cane followed by exile from his native village.[45] On 11 August 1883, Wu was reportedly sent to the Chinese mainland to serve his sentence.[46] The case was colorfully narrated in the local Nagasaki daily *Saikai Shimbun*, which described the event as the unfortunate result of a love triangle.[47] Quite surprisingly, the case seems to have disappeared from public view during the two years it took to work out Wu's sentence, and his expulsion from Japan two years later does not seem to have elicited any reaction in the Nagasaki press. Although the Japanese authorities had tried to indict Wu for intentional homicide, there are no records of official Japanese protests against the ultimate verdict.

The major concern of Japanese authorities in relation to the Chinese community remained the illegal importation and smoking of opium, a problem compounded by the arrival of the Qing consuls. As far as local law enforcement was concerned, the establishment of Qing jurisdiction was a step backward in the efforts to stem the spread of the drug in Japan. In contrast to the Western treaties, neither the Sino-Japanese Treaty of Tianjin nor the Sino-Japanese regulations on trade mentioned opium, but the Japanese tariff regulations for trade with China listed opium among prohibited items. In the sense of strict legality, there was nothing that prevented the Qing government from taking a rigid stance, arguing that the ban on opium did not apply to Chinese. However, the Qing government apparently did share the Japanese position that Japanese laws were in principle binding on Chinese as well. When Mori Arinori's delegation visited China in November 1875, Qing officials discussed tentatively with Japanese diplomats how the opium regulations were to be properly applied to the Chinese community in Japan.[48]

Consequently, one of the first things that the Japanese foreign minister Terajima Munenori brought up with the new Qing minister and his deputy was the opium regulations. In brief, the Japanese draft regulations established that

Japanese police officers could search homes and turn over offenders to the Qing consul, who would fine and deport them permanently from Japan.⁴⁹ He Ruzhang expressed his understanding that this vile habit had to be prevented from spreading to the Japanese but argued that the Japanese police should petition the Qing consul when they wanted to search homes. Allowing the police "to enter private homes at will" would run against the political order of the Qing dynasty (*woguo conglai wu ci zhengti*) and violate Chinese custom. He warned that the consequences of such an action could be serious, since the police could use it as a pretext for entering homes, and Chinese could in turn use it as an excuse to stir up trouble.⁵⁰ In his response, Terajima reassured the Qing envoys that the Japanese did not intend to enter Chinese homes at will. The police force needed to respond quickly to reports of infractions, and offenders could not be allowed to get the upper hand by destroying evidence. The foreign minister held that it would be more practical to let Japanese police take care of the problem of policing and arresting, whereas the Qing consul could oversee punishment and repatriation.⁵¹ Clearly, the Japanese government wanted to maintain its monopoly on the use of force and assert territorial jurisdiction to the furthest possible extent. The Qing diplomats were more worried about containing the habit of opium smoking than eradicating it altogether, and their reluctance to allow Japanese to search Chinese homes is very consistent with the position taken by the Chinese associations in Nagasaki. The disagreement was apparently never resolved, and the Japanese authorities approved of a diluted set of regulations without waiting for explicit approval from the Qing government. The alleged fact that the Qing minister in Tokyo never protested the move was later interpreted as acquiescence by the Japanese authorities.⁵²

The "Nagasaki Affair" of 1883

A number of circumstances conspired to make Nagasaki the scene of a violent confrontation over opium. Since the late 1870s, the Nagasaki police had had the habit of entering the homes of foreigners with the excuse of "registering the servants."⁵³ The British community in Nagasaki especially resented these visits, and they held that the Japanese police had no right under the treaties to violate the sanctity of a British home. However, the Nagasaki authorities found an ally in the acting British consul, who in June 1883 indicted and fined an Englishman for obstructing a Japanese police officer "in the due execution of his duties."⁵⁴ The offender in question was none other than Arthur Norman, the manager of the local English-language newspaper, the *Rising Sun & Nagasaki Express,* which ensured that this incident would be exhaustively debated in the foreign-language press in Japan.⁵⁵

On 1 September 1883, the tensions between the foreign community and Japanese authorities further escalated when the Nagasaki police department started to furnish their police officers with swords. Exactly two weeks later, plainclothes special agent Mine Susumu and four police constables entered the home of Chinese resident Chen Dezhui in Shinchi ward to search for opium. They indeed found two men and some opium smoking utensils, but when they tried to confiscate the opium smoking set, the two men resisted on the ground that Japanese police had no warrant from the Qing consul and thus had no legal right to enter a private Chinese residence.[56] Multiple stories emerged about what actually happened after that point.

In his deposition, Wei Pengcheng, a forty-four-year-old man from Fuzhou, told the directors of the Fukienese association that on the night of 15 September he had sent his eighteen-year-old nephew Wei Yi'ao to Chen's home to return some money he owed, which was customary during the Mid-Autumn Festival. Chen had a stomachache because he had drunk some alcohol on this festive occasion, so he decided to relieve the pain by having a pipe of opium, which he was smoking when Wei Yi'ao arrived at seven o'clock in the evening. Chen told the young man to sit down and put the money on the opium plate. As they were chatting, "more than ten policemen" barged into the house with their swords pulled, trying to grab the smoking set. Wei Yi'ao wanted to rescue the money from the hands of the intruders but could not understand what the policemen were saying and got involved in a fight with them. At this point, Wei Pengcheng learned about the police raid and rushed to Chen's house, where he found an enraged crowd and his nephew bleeding to death from sword cuts.[57] Wei's lively account of the event was corroborated by the much shorter deposition of Chen Dezhui.[58]

In his letter of explanation (*shimatsusho*) to the Nagasaki police department, Mine Susumu declared that he had brought four of his colleagues to a house in Shinchi ward in the foreign settlement in response to reports that opium was smoked there. When the policemen entered the house, they found Chen Dezhui and another man of unclear identity smoking opium. They confiscated the smoking set and arrested Chen and the unnamed man, but once they had left the house, a crowd of "more than ten people" attacked them at a given sign, armed with sticks and cudgels. Mine and his colleagues were hit several times and knocked over by the crowd. Fearing for his life, Mine grabbed the sword of one of his colleagues and fought back.[59] Wei Yi'ao was found outside the house by Dr. William Renwick and later died in the international hospital.[60]

From the point of view of the Chinese community and the Qing consul, the whole incident was the result of legitimate resistance to an illegal arrest. As they saw it, the treaty placed Chinese under the joint jurisdiction of both Chinese and Japanese authorities, and the police officers had not possessed a search warrant, which had to be duly signed by the Qing consul.[61] The Chinese community was infuriated by this act of police brutality, and the Fukienese association called a meeting to discuss the matter. The two directors of the Fukienese association (*Bamin dongshi*) petitioned the acting consul in Nagasaki, Guo Wanjun, to prosecute the case. Wei had not even smoked opium, they claimed, but had only been at the wrong place at the wrong time.[62] Under strong pressure from the Chinese community, Guo showed remarkable zeal in making his own inquest into the case. He presented a full coroner's report and witnesses, which were forwarded to the Nagasaki authorities.[63] True to the Qing preference for joint procedures, the consul requested the cooperation of the local law enforcement in the inquest, and the incumbent Qing minister in Tokyo, Li Shuchang, sent a letter of protest to the foreign ministry, arguing that the Nagasaki police department had overstepped its authority.[64]

From the official Japanese point of view, the case rested on the enforcement of law and order. Only two decades earlier, the fragmented jurisdictions under Tokugawa rule had imposed limitations on the ability of the authorities to arrest criminals, and the fundamental principles had not been very different from those in operation under Qing rule: arrest were usually made in public, and only severe infractions would be cause for entering a private home.[65] By the early 1880s, Japanese authorities had already gone a long way toward eliminating all competing authorities in their quest for a centralized nation-state and were eager to exercise full and exclusive jurisdiction within the national territory of Japan, which included the confines of a private home.[66] Since smoking opium was illegal under Japanese law, from the official Japanese standpoint, Mine had acted in legitimate self-defense when carrying out his duties. Consequently, the Japanese authorities were not particularly interested in cooperating with the Qing consul in the inquest.[67] On the other hand, they promptly asked foreign experts for legal help. The French legal expert Gustave Émile Boissonade, who was employed as a consultant by the foreign ministry, wrote in his brief analyzing the case:

> to be sure, foreigners in Japan who enjoy the privilege of extraterritoriality cannot claim to be more privileged than foreign ministers; for it is recognized by all authors on international law that the privileges which protect the residence of a foreign minister do not go as far as to permit him to commit acts that are contrary to public security.[68]

Boissonade's counterpart in the Foreign Ministry, the young American jurist Henry Willard Denison, wrote two detailed reports in which he, too, endorsed the actions of the Nagasaki police. In a first memorandum, he outlined a strategy to explode the Chinese claims. Focusing on whether the Japanese police had the right to arrest Chinese offenders in their homes, he pointed out: "It undoubtedly strengthens the Chinese position to regard the question of the right of the Police to enter the private houses of Chinese residents and the killing of the Chinese youth as inseparable, and equally it is of importance to the Japanese Gov't to consider them apart."[69] In his second memorandum, he further developed this line of reasoning:

> If the extraterritorial privileges secured to foreigners by treaties do not exempt them while in the public streets from liability to arrest by Japanese police, it is illogical to claim that they may enjoy such exemption by the simple expedient of leaving the highways and entering compounds which are surrounded by those highways. If, however, this claim is admitted to be well founded it at once results, that those privileges which both Japan and China have contended are personal only, are in fact territorial also.[70]

Denison proceeded to quote the 1878 circular on treaty revision from the Zongli Yamen to prove that the Qing authorities accepted the idea that local laws applied to foreigners under consular jurisdiction. He warned that if Chinese claimed wider extraterritorial privileges, other nations might claim the same by virtue of most-favored-nation treatment.[71] Judged from contemporary standards of international law, their opinions clearly made a lot of sense. The two prominent jurists were not hired to defend the Chinese position, and it is apparent that neither read the Sino-Japanese Treaty of Tianjin in the original Chinese and Japanese versions, nor had they made any serious efforts to understand the contexts in which they had been written. For instance, when Denison quoted the Zongli Yamen's statement on extraterritoriality against the Qing consul, he disregarded the fact that the example quoted in the circular concerned obvious breaches of public order, such as traffic violations, not what happened in the confines of a private home.[72] When the Qing consul contested the right of Japanese police to enter private Chinese homes at will, he did so not only to defend Chinese "treaty rights" but also in the interest of public order as it was understood by Qing officials. District magistrates in China were reluctant to barge into a private home to prosecute offenses of a nonviolent nature; to do so would be asking for trouble. Qing officials had politely tried to make this point to the Japanese when the rules on opium were being negotiated.

The Chinese documents, consequently, contain few references to international law. Personal jurisdiction was firmly rooted in the Qing legal order, and as a rule, Qing authorities did not claim jurisdiction in cases where only foreigners were involved. To Qing officials, the execution of consular jurisdiction chiefly entailed the maintenance of public order and the adjudication of mixed cases.

Consequently, Qing officials seldom talked about "consular courts" as such, but of "mixed courts"—taking personal jurisdiction in nonmixed cases for granted.[73] From the Chinese point of view, there had not been any Japanese party to the Nagasaki opium case until the moment five Japanese police officers entered the home of Chen Dezhui to search for opium. At the moment Mine killed Wei, what could have been construed as a "purely Chinese" consular court case turned into a mixed case, in which Qing and Japanese authorities both held jurisdiction.

Neither the Japanese nor Chinese needed a Western lawyer to tell them that the extraterritorial privileges granted under the Sino-Japanese Treaty of Tianjin had a territorial dimension.[74] Article 13 of the treaty made it clear that consular jurisdiction only applied in the treaty ports and that criminals venturing outside of the treaty ports risked summary punishment by local authorities. Finally, no one reading the 1878 circular would fail to note that one of the main arguments in the circular was that Qing policy-makers did *not* accept the wide interpretation of the most-favored-nation principle that Denison espoused in his memorandum. They only accepted it as a concession granted with certain conditions; any treaty power wanting to claim certain privileges was also "bound by the conditions attached to them."[75] This position can be traced back to article 8 of the Treaty of the Bogue of 1843, which provided that most-favored-nation treatment should not be used a pretext for new demands being "unnecessarily brought forward."

Both the local and national press devoted a lot of attention to the "Nagasaki Affair" and vied with each other to take the most well-informed and principled stand. The Nagasaki daily *Chinsai Nippō* called the actions of the police officers "justifiable self-defense" (*seitō no bōei*) and published lengthy articles defending the official Japanese point of view.[76] The Chinese version of the event was supported by *Rising Sun & Nagasaki Express,* which was not known for supporting the interests of the Chinese community but had its own axe to grind on the issue of how extraterritorial privileges were administered in the treaty port. The editors of *Chinsai Nippō* reacted angrily to this and engaged in a lengthy polemic against their English-language counterparts, who they felt gave too much weight to the Chinese version of the event and printed grave "inaccuracies."[77] The editors of the *Rising Sun* retorted that they had been stonewalled by the governor of Nagasaki: "the Chinese version was the only one obtainable by us, as the Governor at once strictly forbade all officials to give the slightest particle of information on the subject."[78]

The Yokohama-based *Japan Weekly Mail* was far less sympathetic to the Chinese position than its counterpart in Nagasaki and gave more credence to the official Japanese version of the event.[79] But even the editors of this newspaper gradually learned more of the complexities of the Sino-Japanese Treaty of

Tianjin and realized that it gave Chinese a status different from that of other foreigners in Japan. In an editorial on the Nagasaki affair, the *Mail* observed:

> it has been openly stated, indeed the public generally appears to be persuaded, that the status of Chinese subjects living in Japan is exactly the same as that of all other foreigners. The treaty between China and Japan does not justify any such hypothesis. . . . Plainly this treaty places the Chinese in a position very different from that occupied by other nationals in Japan. The jurisdiction of the high contracting parties is concurrent, and in certain contingencies that of Japan alone is competent.[80]

It is noteworthy how successful the Chinese community was in getting its version known in the English-language press, which was shielded from Japanese censorship and appears to have been widely read by both Japanese and Chinese.[81] For instance, a member of the Chinese community in Nagasaki was disappointed with the way the Chinese coroner's inquest had been portrayed in the *Japan Weekly Mail* and tried to make the point that the procedures laid down in the treaty were essentially Chinese:

> The inquest was held purely "à la Chinoise." There was neither "conception" nor desire to hold it after the fashions of a European Coroner. If our proceedings appeared to you in that light, then it must have been an accidental coincidence. I suppose the duties of Coroners, whether Chinese or European, are mainly and essentially the same, but customs and forms, however, must be necessarily different according to the various usages of different nations. It is only right for all Coroners to follow the principles of their own country.[82]

Here we are clearly not dealing with a uniform representation of the limits of consular jurisdiction and extraterritoriality. Faced with a complicated legal case, no one could actually come up with a good definition of exactly what consular jurisdiction meant, and a foreign jurist was as legitimate an expert as a long-term resident. Not only were these points of view informed by different legal traditions and customs but self-interest sometimes created coalitions that cut across national lines. Judged by *Rising Sun & Nagasaki Express*, the Chinese point of view in this particular case was thus very much in line with the rest of the foreign community in Nagasaki. No matter what the treaties or legal experts were saying, treaty port custom dictated that police searches of foreigners be approved by the consul.[83] When the unpopular British minister Alcock had tried to devolve consular authority to local Japanese authorities twenty years earlier, the British merchant community reacted with scorn and stubborn resistance.[84]

As the debate was raging in the press, the Qing minister and Japanese foreign minister were voicing disagreements on how the Nagasaki Affair should be properly addressed. Faced with mounting pressure from both the Western and Chinese community in Nagasaki, the Japanese authorities had no other choice but to allow Mine Susumu to be brought to trial. In his representations to the Japanese foreign ministry on the case, Li Shuchang flatly denied that his predecessors had agreed to impose the Japanese opium regulations on Chinese and argued that the ban on opium should not be applied to Chinese, since the habit had not spread to Japanese anyway. Coming from a legal environment where analogies played an important role in legal reasoning,[85] Li drew a parallel to the early Meiji ban on Christianity and opium: since Japanese authorities had realized that the Christian religion did not do any harm to the Japanese people and consequently relaxed the ban on it, by analogy, the ban on opium should be relaxed as well.[86] Not surprisingly, the Japanese foreign minister, Inoue Kaoru, had no difficulty dismissing Li Shuchang's arguments,[87] which must have appeared far-fetched to him.

More significantly, in a separate démarche two days later, Li also asked why the acting consul, Guo Wanjun, had been excluded from the examination of witnesses in the case. According to Li's sources, Guo had been told not to interfere with the investigation but that he was welcome to attend the main hearing (*dashen/daishin*) instead.[88] The acting consul's difficulties in participating in the inquest into the Nagasaki Affair were in part related to the fact that Japan had adopted a new criminal code under the auspices of Boissonade the previous year. The code introduced a new element into the ever-changing Japanese criminal procedure, stipulating that a "preliminary investigation" (*yoshin*) be held before a criminal case was heard in a trial. The investigation was modeled on the *enquête préliminaire* in the French criminal system, and all preliminary hearings in a criminal suit were held behind closed doors; only the final trial was open to the public, provided that a case had been established against the defendant prima facie.[89]

However, the secretiveness of Meiji criminal procedure cannot be attributed entirely to continental European influences. Japanese legal reformers were by no means passive recipients of foreign models; they certainly knew how to pick the parts of foreign legal systems that addressed their special needs and resonated with the legal traditions of Japan. Criminal procedure under Tokugawa rule had been highly secretive; commoners did not have access to the laws, and trials were not open to the public. Before the magistrate could hear a criminal case, his functionaries were to carry out an initial investigation in order to determine the culpability of the accused,[90] a course of action that bears striking similarities to the preliminary investigation. In the 1870s, Japanese authorities departed from secretive Tokugawa practices by allowing the public and the press to attend trials,[91] but they clearly intended to maintain a veil of secrecy by keeping the preliminary inquest secret. A notorious part of Japanese criminal procedure,[92] the preliminary inquest was not abolished until 1947.

In China, district magistrates also relied on their staff to hold preliminary inquiries, but the magistrate held ultimate responsibility for the whole inquest of a criminal case, and trials were usually held in public.[93] The Qing Code and legal handbooks were accessible to anyone who could read, and information about ongoing legal cases was published in the *Beijing Gazette* (*Jingbao*), which was circulated and read in the empire. In fact, the Qing court was so anxious to maintain the appearance of openness that it promulgated an edict in 1876 stipulating that the *Gazette* had to have at least ten pages, lest the public suspect that important state matters were being covered up.[94] The contrast between the relative openness of the Chinese and the Japanese penchant for secrecy should not be exaggerated; the Qing state had recourse to its own extralegal procedures to punish political crimes, and it did not encourage the development of any independent legal profession.[95] Indeed, the Qing state prohibited anyone from drawing up legal briefs on the behalf of others, thus effectively forestalling the development of any professional corps of jurists outside of the government.[96] Nevertheless, it is clear that the conflict between Chinese and Japanese officials was a clash not just between "modernity" and "tradition" but between two different legal cultures.

It was difficult for Inoue to allow the complete exclusion of the Qing consul from the preliminary proceedings, which would have curtailed Chinese treaty rights significantly, and Guo Wanjun was eventually given access to them.[97] On 24 January 1884, Mine Susumu was sentenced to five years in prison, and an indemnity of $4,000 was paid to the relatives of the deceased.[98] For a moment, the Japanese government considered bringing countercharges against Chen Dezhu but was dissuaded from doing so by its own legal counsel.[99] The Qing minister in Tokyo played no small part in the process and reportedly approved of the verdict.[100] Indeed, joint jurisdiction enabled Qing diplomats to influence the Japanese criminal justice system, and when the regular Qing consul, Yu Qiong, returned to his post in Nagasaki early the following year after a leave of absence, "he expressed his satisfaction with what had been done so far" to the press.[101] Another immediate consequence of the Nagasaki Affair was that the Nagasaki police were prohibited from carrying swords.[102]

However, the Chinese victory in the case was short-lived. Two years later, Mine was released on parole because of his exemplary conduct in prison.[103] The new Qing minister in Tokyo, Xu Chengzu, protested his early release and said that the matter should have been reported directly to the legation before any action was taken.[104] The Japanese authorities, however, could confidently dismiss the protest by referring to the fact that the Japanese legal system now practiced division of powers. The foreign minister, Inoue Kaoru, only responded that he had nothing to do with the matter and that the prison authorities had acted according to law.¹⁰⁵

The Nagasaki Incident of 1886

In the immediate wake of the Nagasaki Affair and the release of Mine Susumu, relations between the Japanese authorities and the Chinese community soured even further. The question of house searches of Chinese would never be fully resolved at a national level.¹⁰⁶ However, in the history of Sino-Japanese relations, these contestations over the implementation of the Sino-Japanese Treaty of Tianjin in the 1880s have been largely overshadowed by the intensifying rivalry between the Qing Empire and Japan over Korea. In 1884, pro-Japanese elements in Seoul made an unsuccessful attempt to drive out the Qing presence in Korea in what became known as the Kapshin Incident.¹⁰⁷ A number of violent clashes between Chinese sailors and Japanese residents occurred in the Korean treaty ports.¹⁰⁸ Only five months after Mine was released on parole, these tensions spilled over to Japan and produced a lethal incident in which both high politics and treaty port conflicts were acted out.

In August 1886, a Qing squadron under the command of Admiral Ding Ruchang made a stop in Nagasaki harbor. The squadron consisted of three German-built ships *Dingyuan*, *Zhenyuan*, and *Jiyuan*, and one Chinese-built man-of-war, *Weiyuan*, all of which anchored in the Kyushu port on their way home from a visit to Vladivostok.¹⁰⁹ On 13 August, several hundred Chinese sailors were allowed to land in Nagasaki, the first time Chinese sailors had visited a Japanese harbor in such large numbers.¹¹⁰ That evening, the proprietor of a licensed brothel in the ward of Yoriai-machi called the police after an altercation with five inebriated Chinese sailors, who had reportedly vandalized some furniture in the brothel. A police officer from the Maruyama police station, Kurokawa Koshirō, soon arrived at the brothel, and the disturbance quieted down after he tried to arrest the sailors. The sailors managed to escape but soon appeared at the police station to harass Kurokawa. Wang Fa, a sailor from the *Dingyuan*, attacked Kurokawa with a sword and was arrested after a scuffle and handed over to Cai Xuan, the incumbent Qing consul in Nagasaki. The following day, the consul met with the governor of Nagasaki, Kusaka Yoshio, to resolve the situation.¹¹¹

The fracas on Friday the thirteenth would probably have receded, like any other street brawl in a red-light district, had Admiral Ding not allowed approximately four hundred sailors to go ashore two days later. According to Japanese reports, a group of sailors brutally ambushed and killed a police officer in Hirobaba, upon which the disturbance quickly spread to other parts of town as Japanese policemen were called onto the scene and clashed with the sailors. The

Chinese naval officer from Ding Ruchang's squadron, which was involved in the Nagasaki Riots of August 1886. Courtesy of Nagasaki Prefectural Library.

confrontation further escalated as Japanese and Chinese residents of Nagasaki entered the fray, aiding their compatriots. The local Chinese communities reportedly provided weapons to the Chinese sailors, who had come ashore unarmed on the advice of the Qing consul. The Chinese sailors outnumbered the Nagasaki police force two to one, so it took the police several hours to get control of the situation. By the end of the weekend, two Japanese policemen and five Chinese sailors were dead, and forty-five Chinese and twenty-nine Japanese were seriously injured.[112]

The Japanese and Qing authorities were quick to blame one another for the incident. In an initial dispatch from the Qing legation in Tokyo, the minister, Xu Chengzu, claimed that the Chinese sailors had been attacked by local police and thousands of Japanese.[113] Japanese accounts of the incident claimed that the clashes were the result of a premeditated attack on the Japanese police. In response to these reports, Xu told the foreign ministry that he was troubled by the fact that the Chinese and Japanese accounts of the event were diametrically opposed, so he ordered his councilor Yang Shu to go to Nagasaki to assist Cai Xuan and Kusaka Yoshio in their inquest to the case. He also reported that the Qing government sent in William Venn Drummond, a British lawyer from Shanghai, in order to ensure that the case would be settled "in accordance with international law" (*yi fu gong fa*).[114] The Japanese government responded by sending a foreign office official, Hatoyama Kazuo, and a British lawyer, Montague Kirkwood, to Nagasaki. The lawyers and Chinese and Japanese officials in due course formed a joint investigatory commission (*huishen weiyuanhui/kaishin iinkai*), which started to meet in early September in order to hear witnesses, identify evidence, and prepare for the eventual prosecution of the guilty.[115]

On 1 September, undersecretary Aoki Shūzō met with Xu Chengzu to discuss the Nagasaki incident face to face. Aoki told the Qing minister that he did not think it was necessary to send a foreign lawyer and more Qing officials to Nagasaki in order to settle the case. The incident could be investigated jointly but should be dealt with strictly as a legal problem, and the culprits should be punished by their own authorities. Aoki stressed that this could all be done according to international law and that he did not think that there was any need to create "a different Asian version of international law" (*Ajia-fū no besshu naru kokusaihō*).[116] Here the use of "Asian" as an unmistakably derogatory term echoes the famous editorial of the journalist Fukuzawa Yukichi, who had called on Japan to "leave Asia" and part company with China and Korea, countries he regarded as hopelessly backward and behind the times.[117]

Meanwhile, the proceedings of the joint investigatory commission in Nagasaki dragged on with no end in sight. One factor behind the protracted negotiations was the fact that Beijing reportedly rewarded its legal counsel, Drummond, with a handsome salary of 100 taels a day,[118] so he had little incentive to bring the inquest to a conclusion. Since negotiations in Nagasaki were so slow, the foreign minister, Inoue Kaoru, finally returned to Tokyo from a trip to Hokkaido and was able to talk directly with the Qing minister on 26 September. Inoue told Xu that under international law, no country had any inherent right to let armed men land in another country; any time it actually happened, it was on the sufferance of the host country. It had been the responsibility of the commanding officer not to land six hundred sailors, allowing incidents like this to happen. In response, Xu Chengzu said he was not very familiar with international law, but according to the few works on the subject that he had perused, there was nothing that banned men-of-war from anchoring in foreign harbors; he could not see what international custom or law had been violated. He also told the foreign minister that the number of sailors had never amounted to as many as six hundred. In a disingenuous attempt to shift blame, he said that Ding initially had resolved not to allow any sailor to land after the incident on 13 August, but his British deputy and consultant, William Lang, had persuaded Ding that it would not be in the interest of the sailors' health to keep them on board and that doing so would show weakness to the Japanese after the 13 August incident. Xu said that Lang bore a heavy responsibility for what had happened and expressed his regret that Lang had injured the dignity of his government.[119]

While the Chinese and Japanese officials were trying to solve the matter in Tokyo and Nagasaki, the press was actively debating the events. Quite predictably, the Chinese- and Japanese-language press sided with their respective governments and drew parallels with the opium affair of three years earlier.[120] *Shenbao* gave prominent coverage to the events in Nagasaki and claimed that the early release of Mine had encouraged local policemen to act even more outrageously.[121] One Japanese newspaper urged the Japanese government not to try to control the reporting of the incident, because tight press controls had allowed the Chinese community to sell their version of the Nagasaki Affair.[122] Xu Chengzu felt that the Japanese press coverage had turned so anti-Chinese that he complained to Aoki, who promptly set up a press censorate with instructions to excise all insulting Sinophobic comments.[123]

The young French artist Georges Ferdinand Bigot made a lithograph of the incident for a Japanese newspaper and published cartoons in his own journal, *Tôbaé*, depicting Japanese and Chinese in the stereotypical way in vogue in the West.[124] The response of the English-language press to the incident was relatively detached, but it clearly tilted toward the Japanese version of the event.[125] The *Rising Sun & Nagasaki Express* expressed no sympathy for the Chinese sailors or the way the Qing officials were handling the matter but, ever mindful of what had happened in the port three years earlier, reported with some apprehension that the superintendent of police had petitioned the governor of Nagasaki to withdraw the ban on swords that had been instituted in response to the Nagasaki Affair:

> to arm a body of young and comparatively inexperienced men with swords, in a thickly-populated town, would, we maintain, be worse than disarming them altogether. . . . had the policeman who was murdered in

Hirobaba recently been armed with a sword instead of a baton, his fate would assuredly [have] been the same, and besides supplying an additional weapon to the rioters, there would afterwards probably have been a doubt whether he had not made use it before there was any occasion.[126]

According to Japanese transcripts of the conversations, the Qing minister was not doing a very good job of building a case for his government. When the punishment of the offenders was discussed again on 12 October, Xu Chengzu came out in favor of solving the issue by singling out officials who could be blamed for the incident and providing compensation in proportion to the number of deceased and wounded rather than in proportion to culpability, which would clearly benefit the Chinese. Not surprisingly, Inoue rejected this solution and said that no compensation would be paid to the relatives of those who had been killed in the pursuit of just self-defense (*seitō bōgyo*). It was the Chinese sailors who had started the fight by killing a Japanese policeman, not the other way around.[127]

Clearly the Qing and Japanese government were far apart, and the negotiations were going nowhere.[128] On 4 December, Xu Chengzu reported to the Japanese government that he had been ordered to withdraw the Qing delegates from the joint commission and to entrust the solution of the affair to Li Hongzhang. Inoue

The first phase of the Nagasaki Affair: two Western lawyers are struggling to keep the Chinese and Japanese apart in the aftermath of the riots, urging them to keep calm. Cartoon by Georges Ferdinand Bigot, *Tôbaé*, 1 March 1887. http://dewey.sfc.keio.ac.jp, accessed 17 January 2004.

told the Qing minister that he did not think the Qing government had any right to dissolve the joint commission unilaterally, but as he did not see any need for the commission any more, he agreed that it could be disbanded.[129] With the two parties unable to settle the affair by themselves, the German minister to Japan, Max von Brandt, mediated a settlement. On 8 February 1887, both governments issued a joint declaration deploring the death of the Chinese sailors and the Japanese policemen, vaguely promising the punishment of their assailants. Compensation was negotiated in secret and paid to the relatives. Only the Japanese authorities seem to have actually punished some of the Japanese rioters; there is no record of the Qing government meting out any punishment to Chinese participants in the riot.[130]

The case revealed tensions between the Qing Empire and Japan on several different levels. At the local level, the incident was a direct result of the long-standing and unresolved problem of how to maintain law and order in the Chinese community, and there is no doubt that the people involved held grudges left over from the Nagasaki Affair. It is also clear that Qing officials were not well equipped to deal with incidents of this order. It was one thing to plead for sympathy when a teenager was killed during a police raid of dubious legality, quite another to deal with an incident involving hundreds of unruly sailors from four warships in a foreign port. Blaming the incident on police brutality or referring to the number of casualties would not suffice this time, and the reluctance of Qing officials to take international law seriously further harmed their international prestige. That said, the Qing government was evidently unhappy with how Xu Chengzu had managed the incident, and when he was later impeached for graft, his handling of the crisis was cited as further evidence of his incompetence.[131] The Nagasaki police force had not come out in the best light either, and Japanese officials privately admitted that many police officers had been too zealous in the execution of their duties.[132]

It is important not to make facile assumptions concerning the power relations between the two countries in 1886. It is true that the Japanese had witnessed the treaty powers thoroughly humiliating the Qing Empire. The Second Opium War was a profound shock to the Japanese, who were alarmed by reports that the British and French had invaded and sacked Beijing and that the emperor died after fleeing the invaders. The Japanese also saw how quickly things could change in this new era of "Warring States."[133] As the Iwakura embassy learned when they visited Europe ten years later, France had just been defeated by Prussia in a short war that had led to the overthrow of the French emperor and the announcement of a new German Reich in the heart of French monarchical power, the Hall of Mirrors in Versailles. Clearly, this débâcle did not prevent the bruised French from expanding their empire overseas and availing themselves of the advantages of imperial status in East Asia. The humbled position of the Qing Empire could not be taken for granted within the ever-changing geopolitics of the late nineteenth century.

Japanese contempt for China was tempered by a keenly felt sense of vulnerability. The Qing Empire had performed reasonably well in the Sino-French war of 1884–85, and when Ding Ruchang's flotilla visited Nagasaki, Japan did not yet possess any comparable warships.[134] When the Nagasaki incident occurred, one Japanese newspaper reported rumors that the four warships had arrived to settle the dispute over Ryukyu.[135] Even though their worst fears were never realized, many Japanese felt that the Chinese had behaved like an invading force, supported by state-of-the-art gunboats. When the Japanese liberal politician Yoshino Sakuzō wrote a book about Sino-Japanese relations many years later, he used the Nagasaki incident to remind his readers of how much the Japanese feared the Qing Empire in the Meiji era.[136] Indeed, if the Qing Empire had not been defeated in 1894–95, the Nagasaki incident would be remembered very differently today.[137]

One immediate consequence of the incident was that the negotiations over the abolition of extraterritoriality, which had been ongoing between the Zongli yamen and the Japanese minister in Tokyo, stalled and never recovered.[138] Another consequence was that no Chinese sailor was allowed to land when Ding Ruchang's naval force visited Kobe in 1891, so as to avoid any recurrence of the Nagasaki incident.[139] In Nagasaki, the memory of the incident was kept alive in ways that included an 1892 memorial service held in the temple of Kōtaiji to commemorate the deaths of the two policemen.[140]

Murder in the City

Compared to the large and assertive Chinese community in Japan, the Japanese community in China remained small and, judging by the scanty records, quiet. No comparable incidents of mass violence involving Japanese occurred in China before 1895. Yet only a couple of months after the Nagasaki riot, a homicide case in Shanghai showed that the Chinese and Japanese stood as far apart as ever in interpreting how the boundaries between consular, local, and mixed jurisdiction were to be properly delineated under the terms of the Sino-Japanese Treaty of Tianjin.

In April 1887, Fukumoto Makoto was indicted for having killed a Chinese who had broken into his house, which he shared with another Japanese, Inoue Masashi. According to Inoue's deposition, he had been awakened at four o'clock on the morning of 7 April by Fukumoto's call and rushed down to the first floor, where Fukumoto lived. There he had found Fukumoto involved in a scuffle with a burglar, who was later identified as Xu Chunfu. Inoue first intended to help

Fukumoto overpower Xu, but when he noticed two suspicious persons at the back entrance, he decided to pursue them instead. The two intruders quickly left the place, followed by Xu, who had managed to disentangle himself from Fukumoto, who in turn proceeded to chase the burglars, while Inoue stayed in the apartment.[141] Fukumoto armed himself with a sword and pursued Xu, who had a wooden cudgel. After a short fight, he cut down Xu, took the cudgel, and returned home, where he and Inoue tried to find out what the thieves had stolen.[142]

This incident soon turned into a battle over jurisdiction and interpretation of the term "joint trial" (*huishen*), the prescribed procedure for mixed criminal cases according to the Treaty of Tianjin. The Shanghai district magistrate Mo Xiangzhi intended to hold a joint trial in Shanghai in accordance with the treaty and summoned the Japanese consul, Kawakami Kin'ichi, to start holding joint hearings in the case.[143] According to the Chinese interpretation of article 13 of the Treaty of Tianjin, offenders in mixed suits had to be tried and punished in the country of the crime. However, the Japanese legal system had evolved since the conclusion of the 1871 treaty, and Japanese consuls had no authority to rule in cases of homicide. Consequently, Kawakami told Mo that he had no jurisdiction in the case and Fukumoto had to be tried in the Nagasaki district court. All the consul could do was to hold a preliminary investigation (*yoshin*) in Shanghai and then forward the evidence together with the defendant to the Nagasaki district court, where the Qing consul could observe the proceedings (*kanshin/guanshen*).[144]

It is evident that the Japanese authorities were trying to avoid their treaty obligation to carry out joint investigation and trial (*huishen*) of mixed criminal cases, which prevented them from exercising full and exclusive jurisdiction over Japanese nationals in China. Instead of using the term *huishen*, which was used for "joint trial" in the treaty, they used the much weaker term *kanshin/guanshen*, which was used to denote Western consuls when they "observed the proceedings" in mixed cases. Needless to say, Mo was not particularly impressed with Kawakami's line of reasoning. Mo pointed out that in 1869, the British Supreme Court in Shanghai had sentenced British subject Willis George to hang for having murdered a Chinese carpenter in the harbor district of Shanghai. George had been tried and executed in Shanghai in the presence of both local Chinese authorities and the British consul. Why could the Japanese not follow this example?[145] If the consul did not have authority to pronounce sentences in severe criminal cases, why did he not forward the depositions (*gongci*) and his recommendation for punishment (*niban*) to the Nagasaki court for approval (*heding*)?[146] Both the Chinese community and local authorities in Shanghai resented the fact that local magistrates were denied full participation in mixed criminal suits in a manner analogous to foreign participation in the Mixed Court. By insisting that Fukumoto be tried and punished in Shanghai, the district magistrate was trying to assert a degree of jurisdiction that the Mixed Court had lost to most Western consular courts in Shanghai.

Learning that the district magistrate was digging up precedents to deal with this case, the Japanese foreign minister, Inoue Kaoru, decided to summon the ghost of Furukawa Yoshimasa, who had been slain by Wu A'er in Nagasaki six years earlier. The foreign ministry forwarded a copy of the dossier on the Wu A'er case to Kawakami and told him that the fact that the Qing consul had sent the offender to the Chinese mainland for punishment had set a precedent.[147] There are no remaining records that tell us whether Mo responded to Inoue's quite plausible argument, but it is clear that article 13 only established that capital punishment be executed at the place of the crime. Wu, on the other hand, had been banished and sent to the mainland with the implicit or explicit consent of the Japanese authorities. In the Fukumoto case, the Shanghai magistrate wanted to pursue a capital sentence for Fukumoto, which made the procedure in article 13 applicable. In contrast to most Western systems of justice, which Japan tried to emulate, it was not necessarily the nature of the crime that determined jurisdiction in the Qing hierarchy of courts but the projected punishment.[148] By determining the punishment to be a commuted death sentence followed by banishment, the Qing consul in Nagasaki had effectively circumvented the treaty stipulation that executions be carried out at the place of the crime.

Mo's reasoning indicates that his understanding of criminal procedure was based on the Qing "appellate system" of justice.[149] In this system, officials of lower rank obtained depositions and recommended punishments, which were carried out at the place of the crime after they had been confirmed by higher authorities, except in cases of rebellion. This was how the Qing consul must have understood the adjudication of the Wu A'er case, save for the fact that Wu had been sent to the mainland for punishment. Furthermore, in the Qing legal order, it was not uncommon for sentenced criminals to be referred to higher authorities for further questioning, so the removal of Wu from Japan was not unusual.

From the official Qing point of view, it was just a question of sticking to the letter of the treaty, whose extraterritorial provisions happened to conform quite well to Qing criminal procedure. If the Japanese government had changed its legal system and was no longer able to fulfill its treaty obligations to the Qing Empire, that was of no concern to Qing authorities; they felt that they had international law on their side and argued that treaty obligations should take precedence over national law.[150] However, given the fact that Fukumoto was in the custody of the Japanese consul, there was very little Mo could do, and after the preliminary hearings had been completed, Fukumoto was quickly spirited away to Japan. The Nagasaki district court was apparently in a hurry to handle the case, because the Qing consul never had a chance to attend the hearing, probably because he was given very short notice. The court noted the consul's absence, and on 30 June it acquitted Fukumoto of murder on grounds of self-defense.[151]

The whole conflict between Qing and Japanese jurisdiction was reenacted when a group of Japanese students killed a Chinese peddler on the evening of 3 July 1891 on Shipi Lane, close to the Western gate of the Chinese city. The students lived in the Guangfu Temple in the Chinese city, where they received instruction in Mandarin Chinese, and every time they returned home, a dog in the neighborhood would bark at them. This time, they decided that they had had enough of it and brought the dog to the owner, a street peddler called Shen Guanfu, who reportedly refused to listen to their complaints. The Japanese left in a huff and decided to procure some weapons in order to intimidate Shen. When they returned, a violent scuffle with Shen ensued, which was witnessed by a number of people who were too afraid to intervene. When the students left the scene, Shen was lying on the ground dying from several stab wounds.[152]

The Shanghai district magistrate, Yuan Shuxun, quickly learned of the incident and managed to arrest three of the students, including two of the main suspects, Fukuwara Hanjūrō and Omoto Jūtarō. Given the violent incidents of just a couple of years earlier, it is noteworthy that Yuan did not ask permission from the Japanese consul to arrest the suspects in their home. Instead he sent his *yamen* runners, who apprehended the three suspects in an ambush after they left their home.[153] The fact that the students lived in a temple may have contributed to the reluctance of the authorities to enter their home to make an arrest, but their course of action also betrays a certain consistency in Chinese attitudes toward the arrest of criminals.

The Japanese consul general, Tsuruhara Sadayoshi, was quickly summoned, and witnesses were heard. This case could not possibly be construed as legitimate self-defense, and Yuan Shuxun was determined to secure a fitting verdict through a joint trial. However, the Japanese consul declared that he had no authority to rule in the case; all he could do was to conduct a preliminary hearing in Shanghai and then send the suspects to Nagasaki for trial.[154] The debate between the consul and the magistrate was publicized in both the Chinese- and the English-language press,[155] and the *Dianshizhai Pictorial* published a dramatic drawing of the five uniformed Japanese students killing the helpless peddler. Soon the English-language press in Shanghai discovered what their colleagues in Yokohama had discovered eight years earlier: the criminal procedure defined in the Treaty of Tianjin differed substantially from that in most other treaties. The *North China Daily News* published a comment on the murder case; the correspondent, having quoted article 13 of the treaty, concluded:

> The whole tenour [sic] of the article points to the recognition of a very modified form of extraterritoriality: an offender is not to be tried by his

Consul in the presence of the local authority, nor, as in the case of British subject committing a crime in China, is he to "be tried and punished by the Consul, or the other public functionaries authorised hereto" according to the laws of his own country; but he is to be tried by the local authority and the Consul together.[156]

Nevertheless, the two defendants were sent to Japan, under protest from the Qing authorities. When they arrived in Japan, the Qing minister in Tokyo tried to involve the consul in Nagasaki, but Japanese authorities did their best to keep the Qing consul away from the trial, and the trial's outcome came as no surprise. In early November, Fukuwara and Omoto were each sentenced to three years' imprisonment.[157] Needless to say, the Qing authorities were infuriated by the verdict, and a foreign newspaper noted: "We now know that the penalty in Japan for premeditated murder, if it is committed by Japanese on a Chinaman, is three years' imprisonment with hard labour. The Chief Judge of the Nagasaki Local Court does not attempt to disguise the fact that it was a premeditated murder."[158]

Japanese and Qing authorities' differences over the Treaty of Tianjin reflected their substantially divergent understandings of how consular jurisdiction should be applied in the treaty ports. Whenever a crisis occurred, both sides found themselves debating once again the fundamentals of the treaty. Qing officials were of the opinion that they interpreted the treaty literally and defended the extraterritorial privileges of the Chinese community jealously, as well as their right to participate in joint trials. As shown in the two Nagasaki incidents, Qing envoys sometimes made quite ludicrous claims when faced with conflicts over jurisdiction, but beyond their rhetoric lay a quite consistent approach to consular jurisdiction. Qing statesmen were by no means ignorant of international law, but they did not necessarily think that treatises of international law were the most useful guides on how to assist Chinese abroad; consequently they made coherent arguments about extraterritoriality with only occasional reference to international law.[159]

The Sino-Japanese Treaty of Tianjin was innovative in form, but it did not revolutionize Qing foreign relations.[160] It did not represent a repudiation of any tributary relationship between the Qing Empire and Japan, because such a relationship had not existed under the current dynasty, and the Qing Empire continued to maintain tributary relations with other neighbors in the region. Nor was the treaty a negation of the treaty port system as such. Instead, the Sino-Japanese Treaty of Tianjin merely represented a limited extension of Qing rule into Japan, and it constitutes further evidence that Qing officials drew on their own legal system when accommodating foreign demands for consular jurisdiction. Thus, unwittingly, the Qing legal system mediated the perpetuation of a system that

A group of Japanese students, dressed in modern school uniforms, kill the street peddler Shen Guanfu on Shipi Lane in Shanghai, July 1891. Shipi Lane was located in the center of the Old City of Shanghai and disappeared in the urban developments of the early twenty-first century.

Chinese nationalists would later claim was detrimental to Chinese sovereignty and Chinese national interests.

The contrast with Japan is very instructive. The Japanese government had set out early to revise all "unequal treaties" and refused to accord any special status to Chinese under the Treaty of Tianjin, no matter what the treaty text actually said. The Japanese government never accepted the Treaty of Tianjin of 1871 as a permanent basis of intercourse with the Qing Empire, and it is clear that it did its utmost to push the interpretation in its favor and to exclude what was regarded as undue Chinese interference. Japanese officials quickly learned to outflank Qing claims of joint jurisdiction and exploit real and perceived inconsistencies in Qing law; whenever serious problems occurred, they made skillful use of expertise in international law. On the other hand, the mutability of the Japanese legal system often frustrated Qing officials, who were only moderately interested in legal reform, and harbored quite justified suspicions about Japanese duplicity.

The Treaty of Tianjin did pose a serious challenge to Japanese law enforcement as regards the Chinese in the treaty ports, but it is nevertheless striking that for all the talk of "unruly Chinese," it was Japanese—both in China and their own country—who had a tendency to find themselves involved in lethal incidents in which Chinese were killed, usually with swords.[161] It is also ironic that the Qing government often had deep reservations about the innovations that the Japanese had introduced to convince the Western treaty powers to abolish extraterritoriality, such as supposedly more lenient punishments and judicial independence. This presented Japanese policy-makers with a dilemma: failure to revise the treaty with China could potentially upset the revision of the "unequal treaties" with the West. If all other countries agreed to revise the treaties and China refused, that could lead to a domino effect in terms of jurisdiction.[162] The crisis in the wake of the Nagasaki incident convinced Japanese policy-makers that revision of the treaty could all too easily be derailed by incidents that quickly blew out of proportion, and the presence of superior Chinese naval power alerted them to the fact that China potentially possessed the means to force its will on Japan, which was not yet ready to engage in a major conflict.

6

Expelling Extraterritoriality

Treaty Revision in Meiji Japan and Qing China, 1860–1912

What the Japanese had not been able to achieve by peaceful means they would conquer by force in the First Sino-Japanese War of 1894–95. Having obtained assurances that their new legal system satisfied the preconditions for treaty revision, the Meiji oligarchs provoked a war with the Qing Empire over Korea.[1] Although the Qing armed forces were numerically superior to the Japanese, the Japanese deployed their limited forces more efficiently and dealt a devastating blow to the Qing Empire that shook the entire polity to its foundations. All the ships in Admiral Ding Ruchang's proud flotilla, which had earlier been implicated in the "Nagasaki Incident," were either sunk or captured by the victorious Japanese navy in February 1895.[2] Rather than surrendering to the enemy, the defeated admiral committed suicide, which earned him the admiration of some Japanese, who seemed to have forgiven his role in the Nagasaki Incident.[3]

In the onerous Treaty of Shimonoseki, which representatives from the Qing Empire and Japan concluded on 17 April 1895, China not only sustained territorial losses by ceding Taiwan to Japan but also suffered an "extraterritorial" setback: the Chinese communities in Japan lost their extraterritorial privileges, whereas the same privileges for Japanese in China were retained and even expanded. As some jurists would subsequently point out, one of the distinctive features of the extraterritorial arrangements in the new Sino-Japanese Treaty of Tianjin was that it ruled out any mixed procedures whatsoever in cases where Japanese were defendants.[4] On the other hand, the Japanese were now able to participate in the International Mixed Court in Shanghai on an equal footing with the other treaty powers, sending assessors to watch and interfere in cases where Japanese brought charges against Chinese or when "Japanese interests" were at stake.

In the decades running up to the First Sino-Japanese War, the legally pluralistic Qing Empire clashed with the increasingly centralistic Japanese state, which had abolished most remnants of government-sanctioned legal pluralism and tolerated little or no foreign interference in its legal system, even when only foreigners were concerned. This chapter examines how legal pluralism and extraterritoriality contributed to shaping the public debate in China and Japan in the last decades of the nineteenth century.

The Emergence of a Public Debate

The conclusion of the Ansei Treaties provoked the intense hostility of the samurai elites throughout Japan, and some shogunal policy-makers paid with their lives for having signed commercial treaties with the West. However, it was not the contents of the treaties as such but the indignity of having concluded a treaty with a foreign nation that fanned the passions of these warrior-activists. Neither the Bakufu nor the rebellious domains cared much about extraterritoriality itself, and there is little evidence that there was any serious discussion on the subject during the last years of the shogunate.[5] All this changed shortly after the two-hundred-fifty-year-old shogunate was overthrown and replaced by nominally direct imperial rule in 1868. Under the new government, treaty revision (*jōyaku kaisei*) rapidly became the chief foreign policy objective, and the success of any important maker of foreign policy was gauged by his performance in this area.

Despite the relatively small number of foreigners in the country, the Japanese government, and later the general public, pursued treaty revision and the abolition of extraterritoriality single-mindedly in the early Meiji era. As Harry Parkes pointed out, only 2,389 foreigners (except the Chinese) resided in Japan in 1887, and they were subject to strict limitations on their freedom of movement.[6] Furthermore, consular jurisdiction did not invariably mean that foreigners in Japan were able to commit crime with impunity.[7] This contrasted with China, where foreigners could travel to the interior with passports and missionaries claimed they even had a right to reside anywhere in the country, both of which had serious consequences for the maintenance of law and order in China. In Japan, the push to revise the unequal treaties and abolish extraterritoriality accompanied the drive to centralize the state and eliminate all competing jurisdictions. Having abolished the legally pluralistic status system and created a Japanese citizenry, the government also created a political constituency for treaty revision, almost in spite of itself. In the 1870s, disenfranchised samurai and other disaffected groups were channeling their political frustrations into the "Movement for People's Freedom and Rights" (*Jiyū minken undō*), campaigning for a more representative form of government. Once the old legal distinctions had been abolished almost completely, it was now possible to argue that not only

Japanese but also foreigners should be equal before the law, and failure to achieve treaty revision became an arena where the government could be legitimately challenged. Indeed, the "unequal treaties" played no small part in the emergence of mass popular politics in the early Meiji era.[8]

While agreeing on the objective, reform-minded and conservative Japanese used treaty revision to promote sharply divergent agendas. For example, Tsuda Mamichi, a reform-minded jurist and one of the authors of the abortive Sino-Japanese draft treaty, used the campaign for treaty revision as an opportunity to agitate against torture, capital punishment, and other forms of cruel punishments. In a series of articles on torture in *Meiroku zasshi* in May 1874, he wrote:

> If we do not abolish torture, we cannot eventually ride forth side by side with the various countries of Europe and America. If we do not abolish torture, we cannot conclude equal treaties with them. If we do not abolish torture, we cannot place under our laws the Europeans and Americans settled in our country.[9]

Other overseas-educated Japanese political activists took the campaign for treaty revision to the reading public in the European colonial metropoles. One of them was Baba Tatsui, who studied law in the United Kingdom, the Netherlands, and France in the 1870s. While he was in Britain in 1876, he published a tract called *The Treaty between Japan and England,* in which he appealed to British public opinion to convince their government to abolish extraterritoriality in Japan.[10] Responding to the recurrent claim that the imperfect state of laws in Japan justified extraterritoriality, he retorted that the English legal system was far from perfect and so complex that no single jurist could claim to understand it completely. It is quite possible that the Judicature Acts, which simplified the complicated English legal system by amalgamating the competing courts of equity and common law, had left a deep impression on Baba.[11] Having admitted that Japanese law might present English visitors with some inconveniencies, he launched a head-on attack on extraterritoriality:

> I still maintain that English people ought to obey the laws of our country as soon as they set their feet on our shore, simply because it is the English who come to our country and reside within the realm of the Japanese empire, and because I do not see the reason why the criminal who committed crime against a Japanese subject in our country should not be tried in the Japanese courts, and punished according to the Japanese laws. In short, I claim that it is an indisputable right of an independent nation to have sole jurisdiction over all those who reside within the territory either in criminal or civil matters.[12]

Baba's pamphlet had a strong impact on public opinion and provided a framework for the case against consular jurisdiction.[13] The combative Baba Tatsui did not leave his missionary zeal behind in London when he returned to Japan the following year; he soon became involved in the "Movement for the People's Freedom and Rights," which eventually led to his arrest and a six-month stay in a detention center.[14] Following his release, he fled to the United States, where he published articles exposing the conditions in the Japanese penal system and expressed his doubts as to whether the Japanese government would ever convince any "civilized nation" that it had undertaken any fundamental penal reform.[15]

What makes Japanese treaty revision noteworthy in a comparative perspective is the fact that the discussion on treaty revision was not only a policy concern in government circles and other elite contexts; it penetrated almost every level of the political debate, attaining a powerful momentum of its own. The "Movement for the People's Freedom and Rights" was not limited to advocates from the former samurai class; the movement also included many rural activists. For instance, in 1881, a "Learning and Debating Society" in Itsukaichi, west of Tokyo, drew up and discussed different drafts for the new Japanese constitution. In their deliberations, extraterritoriality and the government's power to conclude and revise treaties figured prominently; this group believed that only the Japanese people should have the right to conclude treaties through their elected representatives.[16]

Even though Japan did not yet have a representative form of government, many ambitious politicians would soon learn that the area of treaty revision could make or break their careers and sometimes even their physical well-being. On 14 May 1878, the leading Meiji statesman Ōkubo Toshimichi was slain in Kioichō ward on his way to the imperial palace. The assassins of this last surviving member of the "three heroes of the Meiji restoration" were a group of discontented lower samurai (*ashigaru*) who hailed from the former Kaga domain. Their immediate motive for killing Ōkubo was to avenge the death of Saigō Takamori, who had died in the abortive Satsuma Rebellion one year earlier, but among the grievances listed in their apologia (*zankanjō*) was also the failure of the Meiji oligarchs to revise the unequal treaties. Judging by their letter, they were not particularly concerned with the urgency of legal reform but saw the failure of the government to revise the treaties as a reflection of the government's unwillingness to increase military spending.[17]

Attempts at Reform

From the Meiji oligarchs' perspective, the first step to achieve treaty revision was to acquire legal expertise from abroad, and in the 1870s a number of government agencies employed foreign legal experts: the ministries of foreign affairs and justice took on Henry Willard Denison and Gustave Émile Boissonade, respectively, and the Ministry of Technology and Industry hired the Briton John Richard Davidson as their advisor. The relationship between these agencies and their handsomely remunerated advisors was not always cooperative, and sometimes they competed openly, contributing to the volatile political climate of the early Meiji era.[18]

Armed with their knowledge of international law, Japanese policy-makers set out to draw limits on the extension of extraterritoriality. As early as 1873, the Foreign Ministry argued that although foreigners were under the jurisdiction of their own consuls, they were still obliged to follow municipal laws and regulations, and the Japanese government reserved the right to inflict administrative punishments on foreigners.[19] According to a later formulation of this doctrine, Japan had only granted "consular jurisdiction" (*ryōji saibanken*) to foreign residents in Japan but not "extraterritoriality" (*chigai hōken*); only accredited diplomats enjoyed extraterritoriality, here understood as complete immunity from local laws and jurisdiction.[20] While foreigners may have given their extraterritorial privileges a wider interpretation in China, this was a result of how the treaties were implemented rather than the actual contents of the treaties. Indeed, the Meiji and Qing governments had much in common regarding the fundamental attitude toward extraterritoriality, and in the circular from the Zongli yamen of 1878, Qing authorities made it explicit that they never agreed to give foreigners complete immunity from Chinese laws and jurisdiction. Many foreigners agreed with the Japanese position.[21] As early as in 1861, Captain F. Howard Vyse, the acting British consul to Kanagawa, took his compatriots to task for thinking that they enjoyed complete immunity from the laws of Japan.

> To carry out this argument to its legitimate conclusion it would follow, that the government of Japan, has made a Treaty, by which Foreigners are privileged to come within their territory and outrage or trample under foot all laws and customs of the country, which may not happen to be in accordance with those of another race or nation; and to do so wholly regardless of the obvious inconvenience and danger to society, by an immunity which not only would expose the laws of the State to continual infraction but must unavoidably expose its government to degradation in the eyes of their own subjects to the subversion of all order.[22]

An integral part of the efforts to abolish extraterritoriality was to study how the practice operated outside East Asia, and the mixed courts in Egypt attracted most of the attention of Japanese policy-makers. These mixed courts, which ruled in civil and commercial suits, had been created by the Egyptian statesman Nūbār

Pasha in order to reclaim powers that had been lost to the numerous consular courts that were in operation in Egypt in the 1870s.²³ The Japanese Foreign Ministry sent one of the members of the Iwakura mission, the junior diplomat Fukuchi Gen'ichirō, to Egypt in order to investigate the mixed courts. On his return to Japan in 1873, he filed a report to the Japanese government in which he recommended that the Japanese follow the Egyptian example.²⁴ Four years later, the Japanese government sent Davidson to make another on-the-spot investigation. In his report, Davidson urged the Japanese government not to emulate the Egyptian mixed courts. He argued that such a move would perpetuate extraterritoriality rather than undermining it, since the foreign judges in the mixed courts were only accountable to their respective governments. He suggested that if the Japanese government were to appoint foreign judges to mixed courts in order to reassure the treaty powers, the judges should be accountable to the Japanese government only.²⁵ The recommendations made by Hasegawa Takashi, who made another trip to Egypt in 1885–86, were largely in line with Davidson's.²⁶

It is noteworthy that the Japanese did not show any interest in the Qing legal system or in the operation of the Mixed Court in Shanghai, although they were certainly aware of their existence. They also chose to ignore the experiences of the Sino-Japanese mixed tribunals in Japan, which Qing diplomats insisted were the only legal way of trying mixed cases under the Sino-Japanese Treaty of Tianjin. Japanese statesmen clearly aimed to distance themselves from their neighbor in the West, and they even created two new Sino-Japanese compounds for mixed courts, first *tachiai saibansho* and then *kongō saibansho*. The latter compound is clearly a translation loan from the European and Arabic words for "mixed court," and this term is now the accepted generic term for "mixed courts" in both Chinese and Japanese.²⁷

In the 1880s, treaty revision developed into an extremely delicate foreign policy issue and claimed a number of political casualties. The foreign minister Terajima Munenori tried to negotiate treaty revision by focusing on recovering tariff autonomy from the treaty powers, but he was forced to resign in 1879 because of his failure to address the question of extraterritoriality. His successor, Inoue Kaoru, carried out extensive preparations and consultations with the Western powers for the partial recovery of Japanese jurisdiction over foreigners between 1882 and 1887. His proposal suggested opening the entire country to foreigners (*naichi zakkyo*) as a quid pro quo for the abolition of extraterritoriality; the promulgation of new national legal codes, which the treaty powers would be encouraged to comment on; and the appointment of foreign judges to Japanese mixed courts, which would rule in cases involving foreigners. The negotiations were mostly held in secret, but when the public found out the contents of the proposal, Inoue was seen as a sellout and was opposed from almost every part of society.²⁸

The press mounted a massive campaign against Inoue's plan for treaty revision, and the conservative minister for agriculture and commerce, Tani Kanjō, added further pressure to the campaign by tendering his resignation from the cabinet. Tani had just returned from a research trip to Europe, and following his resignation he published a memorial in which he castigated both Inoue and the "Movement for the People's Freedom and Rights" for being overly indulgent to Western demands for legal reform. Although Tani did not oppose an overhaul of the Japanese legal system, he felt that Inoue's reforms represented an unnecessary westernization of the national polity and that it would damage Japan's prestige to carry out reforms in order to please foreign powers. Instead, he suggested that the Japanese government renounce the treaties unilaterally and strengthen armaments, in case the treaty powers threatened to take military action in response to such a move. Tani suspected that any such threat would likely be a bluff, and in any case, he was confident that Japan could avert an invasion by playing the European treaty powers against each other. He had found the European countries increasingly divided during his trip, and he suggested that the Japanese government appeal to European public opinion in order to signal the determination of the Japanese people.[29] While liberal reformers saw treaty revision as an opportunity to argue in favor of legal reform and representative government, conservatives like Tani regarded it as a way to rally the people against excessive westernization.[30] Inoue was eventually forced to resign from his post as foreign minister in September 1887.[31]

Political satirists took aim at the persistent efforts of the Japanese government to revise the treaties. Georges Bigot portrayed treaty revision in *Tôbaé* in a variety of ways. In one cartoon of 1887, treaty revision was represented as an orchestra, with Foreign Minister Inoue acting as the conductor and the Western consuls playing different instruments, trying to keep in unison.[32] In another series of cartoons that year, treaty revision was depicted as an acrobatic stunt: Inoue, followed by the German minister in a grotesque Prussian hussar outfit, is standing on a wall inviting the foreign ministers to jump through a paper screen called "good sense justice." On the other side of the wall—called "treaty revision"—the greedy diplomats are able to avail themselves of different kinds of material rewards in return for their agreements to revise the treaties.[33]

Manufacturing Incidents and Obtaining Treaty Revision

Even though legal reform was widely conceived as a necessary precondition for treaty revision, the Japanese authorities were able to wrest a number of concessions from the treaty powers in regard to the limits of extraterritoriality. This was

Treaty revision as an acrobatic stunt. The German minister to Japan—portrayed in a Prussian hussar outfit—is helping the Japanese foreign minister, Inoue Kaoru, to kick foreign diplomats through a screen named "good sense justice," over the symbolic wall of "treaty revision." On the other side of the wall, the foreign dignitaries are helping themselves to their ample rewards, such as new concessions, geishas, decorations, and industrial contracts. Cartoon by Georges Bigot, *Tôbaé*, 15 March 1887. http://dewey.sfc.keio.ac.jp/tobae/tobae/1035. accessed 17 January 2004.

true even while the Chinese-style *Shinritsu kōryō* and its supplements were still in force, preliminary criminal codes that were hardly satisfactory in the eyes of the treaty powers. At the same time that the Japanese government was doing its utmost to achieve early treaty revision, a string of extraterritorial incidents gave the government several opportunities to challenge the treaty powers and push its own interpretation of the limits of foreign privilege. In contrast to their Qing counterparts, who tended to see extraterritoriality as an administrative problem, Japanese politicians regarded extraterritoriality as a serious political problem, and they made every effort to politicize extraterritorial cases involving Westerners. On the other hand, extraterritorial incidents were a risky game to play, since they tended to increase the pressure on the Japanese government to take a hardline stance toward the treaty powers.

On 5 June 1872, inclement weather forced the Peruvian steamer *María Luz* to land in Yokohama harbor with the permission of the Japanese government. The night after the ship had landed, a Chinese passenger left the ship and boarded a British gunboat anchored nearby. He told the British crew that the Peruvian ship was carrying a load of more than two hundred Chinese "coolie" laborers who were being mistreated and abused by the Peruvian crew. When the British chargé d'affaires learned of the event, he contacted the Japanese government, urging it to take action for humanitarian reasons. Japan and Peru had not concluded any commercial treaty, so any legal action against the Peruvian crew had to be taken by the Japanese authorities in consultation with the consular body, according to the Yokohama land regulations—just as the Sino-Japanese forgery case had been handled two years earlier.[34]

There were still no appropriate Japanese laws in place that could be invoked to rule in a matter of this magnitude to the complete satisfaction of the treaty powers. However, after some hesitation, the Japanese government resolved to take legal action and instructed the local court in Yokohama to adjudicate the case without consulting the foreign consuls. The court dismissed any criminal charges against the crew but declared that the employment contract signed by the Chinese laborers in Macau was null and void and released the laborers. With the exception of the British chargé d'affaires, the consular body protested the unilateral action of the Japanese government. The Peruvian government sued for damages through its specially appointed representatives. In order to resolve the diplomatic deadlock, the case was referred for arbitration to the Russian czar, Alexander II, for arbitration, who eventually ruled completely in favor of the Japanese government in 1875.[35]

The management of the "*María Luz* Incident" created a certain degree of good will toward Japan in official Chinese circles, and when the Japanese minister plenipotentiary Soejima Taneomi left for Tianjin in 1873 to exchange ratifications of the Sino-Japanese Treaty of Tianjin and discuss the Ryukyu incident, he could use the case as an example of Japanese evenhandedness.[36] In the meantime, the ever-present Mixed Court magistrate Chen Fuxun was given temporary diplomatic status as Qing consul (*lishiguan*) and was sent to Yokohama to repatriate the Chinese laborers, which earned him the praise of his superiors.[37]

One consequence of the incident was that Japan and Peru concluded a commercial treaty in 1873, according to which Peruvian citizens gained extraterritorial privileges under the most-favored-nation clause in the treaty. However, these provisions were not put into effect, since Peru was in no hurry to send consuls. The treaty also stipulated that once Japan had negotiated treaty revisions with the other treaty powers, Japan and Peru should agree on a new treaty.[38] The most lasting legacy of the event was that the Japanese authorities had set a precedent that it could claim sole jurisdiction over unrepresented foreigners, thus undermining the consultative prerogatives of the consular body, laid down in the Yokohama land regulations of 1867.[39] Whereas a similar agreement on the jurisdiction over unrepresented foreigners had been one of the legal foundations for the Mixed Court rules in Shanghai in 1869, the budding Meiji régime used the

María Luz incident to forestall any further consolidation of mixed jurisdiction in Japan.

As the legal experts of the Russian czar were examining the *María Luz* incident in Saint Petersburg, another extraterritorial case was in the making in Yokohama whose ultimate resolution would further destabilize foreign jurisdiction in Japan. Foreign-language newspapers had long been an integral part of life in the Japanese treaty ports, just as in China. However, beginning in 1872, the Scottish journalist John Reddie Black launched a series of mostly unsuccessful Japanese-language newspapers. As the "Movement for People's Freedom and Rights" advocates were agitating for an elected legislature and attacking the Meiji oligarchs for their failure to revise the unequal treaties, the Japanese government soon realized that a foreign-run Japanese-language press could pose a serious threat to the prestige of the government. When the industrious Scotsman launched the *Bankoku shimbun* in January 1876, the Japanese government decided to take action and asked the British consular authorities to suppress the paper. The government also threatened to file criminal charges against any Japanese who had dealings with the newspaper.[40]

Foreign Minister Terajima Munenori managed to persuade the British minister, Harry Parkes, that it was not in anybody's interest to allow British subjects to challenge the Japanese government in the Japanese language, using extraterritoriality as a protective shield. Consequently, Parkes issued a consular regulation, which the Foreign Office eventually sanctioned, forbidding Britons from publishing Japanese-language newspapers. As far as the Japanese authorities were concerned, the British minister's action was an important affirmation of the fact that Japanese laws were binding on foreigners, something the Japanese had tried to implement with relation to opium importation with a much smaller degree of success. Western diplomats demurred at this interpretation, arguing that Japanese laws were only binding on foreigners to the extent that they were given explicit sanction by their respective governments, but another momentous precedent had been set, further undermining extraterritorial jurisdiction in Japan.[41]

The Japanese government continued to pursue treaty revision single-mindedly, but in 1886 Inoue's efforts to revise the treaties were distracted by yet another extraterritorial incident. On 24 October 1886, the British freight steamer *Normanton,* bound for Kobe, sank outside the coast of Wakayama prefecture. The whole foreign crew was saved, with the exception of one member, but none of the twenty-five Japanese passengers survived. A naval court of inquiry that was held in the British consulate in Kobe, found that the officers and the crew "did all in their power to save the lives of the passengers." Although the naval court had no criminal jurisdiction, the Japanese public quite understandably interpreted the court's findings as a whitewash. The Japanese government decided to pursue criminal charges against the British captain, John William Drake, in the British consular court in Kobe.⁴²

By the time the trial was set to begin, the atmosphere was so emotionally charged that the hearings were moved from Kobe to the British consular court in Yokohama. Drake's legal counsel tried to blame the victims for their failure to save themselves. According to Drake, the Japanese passengers had not understood English and had not followed his instructions. However, as more witnesses were heard, his guilt became increasingly obvious, and he was sentenced to three months' imprisonment for manslaughter. Although the sentence was appropriate according to contemporary English law, the Japanese public suspected that the sentence would have been harsher had the victims been European. The ruling provoked outrage in Japanese mass media, and it even inspired a popular song that warned that Inoue's proposal to allow foreigners to reside in the Japanese interior would lead to Japan being flooded with foreigners.⁴³ The aftermath of the "*Normanton* incident" made it difficult to make any concessions to the treaty powers, and the incident largely contributed to Inoue's failure to implement his plan of treaty revision and his subsequent resignation from the cabinet.⁴⁴ Today, the *Normanton* incident is a classic example of how consular jurisdiction allowed foreigners to get away with murder which no textbook on the subject fails to mention.⁴⁵

The next foreign minister, Ōkuma Shigenobu also tried his luck on treaty revision, suggesting proposals that were strikingly similar to those of his predecessor. However, he was attacked by a bomb shortly after taking office. While it did not kill him, he lost his leg, and he resigned from the cabinet after having served less than a year.⁴⁶ Aoki Shūzō, who had negotiated the settlement of the Nagasaki Incident in his capacity as an undersecretary, was promoted to succeed Ōkuma.⁴⁷ He proved marginally more successful in winning over public opinion, but in 1890 the newly convened National Diet signaled its opposition to excessive Westernization by rejecting the new civil code, which was designed to pave the way for treaty revision. On 11 May 1891, the Russian crown prince narrowly survived an attempt on his life in Ōtsu, which eventually forced Aoki to resign from his post. However, during the assailant's trial, the Japanese judiciary impressed the treaty powers by asserting its independence from the Japanese government. The "Ōtsu incident" is often described as a turning point in the campaign for treaty revision.⁴⁸

Treaty revision was eventually realized under the stewardship of Mutsu Munemitsu, who had made the journey from rebel to statesman twice in his political career. Mutsu managed to devise a proposal for treaty revision that was not seen as demeaning of Japanese sovereignty but still satisfied the treaty powers, many of which feared that Japan would withdraw from the treaties unilaterally.⁴⁹ Shortly after Mutsu received word that Britain had accepted his plan to abolish extraterritoriality within five years, hostilities between Japan and the Qing Empire commenced. Japan's subsequent victory immortalized Mutsu as the hero of both the Sino-Japanese war and treaty revision. When extraterritoriality was finally abolished in 1899, two years after Mutsu's death, none of the anticipated traumas were realized, and harassment of foreigners was no more common than before.[50]

Japan's successful revision of the unequal treaties and the conclusion of the Treaty of Shimonoseki are usually regarded as the beginning of Japan's status as an imperialist treaty power in East Asia. Many scholars have regarded that treaty as the beginning of Japanese extraterritorial rights in China,[51] and timelines of the "treaty port system" in East Asia usually exclude the preceding Sino-Japanese Treaty of Tianjin,[52] which had governed Sino-Japanese relations for almost a quarter of a century. Yet the Chinese and Japanese had been involved in complex extraterritorial disputes for more than three decades prior to the new treaty. Far from being the introduction of Japanese extraterritoriality into China, the Treaty of Shimonoseki marked the shift from a bilateral to a unilateral extraterritorial régime, which made it possible for Japan to join the ranks of the Western treaty powers. Now the Japanese were not only able to share all the privileges the other treaty powers had gained through most-favored-nation arrangements; they also gave the treaty port system a further impetus by opening new treaty ports and expanding the scope of foreign privilege.[53]

From the point of view of legal history, 1895 was an important watershed not only because of the abolition of Chinese extraterritoriality in Japan. It also represents another turning point: Japan's acquisition of its first overseas colony, Taiwan. During the previous treaty régime with China, the Japanese had not shown any serious interest in Chinese jurisprudence. However, as the Japanese government now ruled over a territory with a Chinese population, the Japanese colonial authorities started to chart and codify Chinese laws and customs as they understood they were applied in Taiwan.[54] This quest for knowledge and power resulted in a large body of scholarship that is of tremendous value for historians today.[55] Having abolished legal pluralism internally, the Japanese government now created a legally pluralistic régime under colonial conditions. A new chapter in Sino-Japanese relations was about to be written.

The Elephant in the Room

Compared to the Japanese calls for treaty revision, Chinese arguments against extraterritoriality look more tentative, and rather than calling for the immediate abolition of the practice as such, Chinese policy-makers usually directed their criticism against unjust outcomes and specific abuses of consular jurisdiction.[56] Lin Zexu's famous letter to Queen Victoria, in which he argued that English should be subject to the same laws as Chinese, is often quoted as an example of official Chinese opposition to personal jurisdiction.⁵⁷ However, Lin did not use the Chinese word for "jurisdiction" (*guanxia*) but the more normative word *fadu*, whose meaning is closer to "legal order" or "law and order." The wording in this letter was very similar to that of Ying Baoshi's general injunction to Japanese sojourners in Shanghai in the 1860s, instructing them to follow Chinese laws and customs in the absence of duly appointed Japanese consular authorities.⁵⁸ This statement in no way prevented Ying from taking part in drafting a commercial treaty that contained provisions for extraterritorial jurisdiction for both Chinese and Japanese; nor did it prevent him from cooperating in setting up the Mixed Court in Shanghai.

When Qing officials voiced objections to extraterritoriality while the treaties were in operation, they often centered on the impracticality of allowing unlimited extraterritorial privileges, such as granting extraterritorial privileges to foreigners alongside the right to take up residence in the interior of the country. For instance, a document the Zongli yamen sent to a number of prominent officials in 1867 regarding upcoming revision of a number of treaties stated that the only way foreigners could be allowed to trade in the interior of China was if they submitted to local Chinese jurisdiction (*gui difangguan guanxia*).⁵⁹ This position is consistent with that taken by Wenxiang when he argued with Alcock over the limits of extraterritoriality in 1868.⁶⁰

Most objections to extraterritoriality in the mid-nineteenth century did not come from official circles in the capital but from the private writings of Han Chinese officials and other literati. Perhaps the earliest objection to the legal privileges granted to the British came from the official Liu Yunke, who pointed out in a memoir on the war that it might be difficult to quell public outrage if British criminals were allowed to get away with murder as in the infamous Lin Weixi case in 1839,⁶¹ yet he did not make any overall argument about the necessity of asserting jurisdiction over foreigners. The dissident journalist Wang Tao, who had lived in Scotland for a number of years, is also credited with being one of the first to call for the abolition of consular jurisdiction as early as 1870–71, in a letter to Ding Richang.⁶² However, a close reading of his letter reveals that Wang actually proposed to put foreigners in the interior under the jurisdiction of Chinese officials, who would punish Westerners according to Western law and in so doing deprive them of their argument for consular jurisdiction.⁶³ Thus, Wang Tao was experimenting with ideas of allowing two parallel bodies of law to operate in the Qing Empire, albeit administered by Chinese officials. He would later realize the impracticality of these suggestions and argue for the complete abolition of extraterritoriality.⁶⁴

Singapore-born Wu Tingfang had the honor to be the first Chinese called to the bar in London, which coincidentally happened just as the lay jurist Baba Tatsui was publishing his famous tracts against extraterritoriality. Unlike his combative Japanese contemporary, Wu did not use his legal expertise to make a cogent argument to the British public for abolishing consular jurisdiction. In one instance, he asked the British government to reconsider the legalization of opium under the new tariff regulations without engaging in broader legal issues.[65] When Wu returned to China in 1877, officials from Li Hongzhang's group of "foreign affairs" (*yangwu*) officials wooed the Cantonese barrister to take up a minor position in Li's camp, but many more senior officials were suspicious of, or outright hostile, toward foreign-born and foreign-educated people like Wu, and Wu's supporters never managed to raise enough money to pay him the salary he felt his qualifications merited. Instead, he took a job in the service of the colonial government in Hong Kong, where he waged a low-key struggle to improve the position of the Chinese community.[66]

Like other countries grappling with Western imperialism, Chinese who made "bureaucratic pilgrimages" to the imperial metropoles would eventually form a more profound understanding of international relations in a Western context.[67] Following the dispatch of Qing diplomats abroad in late 1870s, there was a noticeable shift in attitudes toward extraterritoriality and representations of the practice. Most of the arguments against extraterritoriality emerged from the ranks of the "foreign affairs" officials in the camp of Li Hongzhang, the same group of people who had tried to enlist the talents of Wu Tingfang.

In 1877, the Qing minister to Britain, Guo Songtao, submitted a memorial in which he suggested solutions to the legal conundrums besetting the treaty ports that had been opened between 1842 and 1876. As he saw it, one reason why it was difficult to reach consensus between foreign consuls and magistrates in mixed suits was the absence of a common legal standard. In contrast to Western countries, which regarded commercial and international law as important parts of any legal system, the Qing Empire had not engaged in these questions seriously but had improvised solutions and ceded more power to the consuls than was necessary even under the treaties. To remedy this increasingly vexing situation, he argued in favor of drafting a commercial code in order to create common ground and regain some lost rights.[68]

Guo's careful argument undoubtedly suggested the need for sweeping legal reforms, but he also framed them within the existing legal order. For instance, the strong emphasis on corporal punishments in the Qing Code had long been a source of contention in the Shanghai Mixed Court, and the foreign assessors had been able to introduce monetary punishments with some degree of success.[69] With this in mind, Guo pointed out that the Court of Colonial Affairs (*Lifanyuan*) allowed the commutation of exile with imprisonment and caning to fines in relation to Mongol banners, and he suggested that this could be used as a precedent for introducing a system of punishments more closely aligned with Western models.[70] But even this cautious approval of Western institutions was too radical for some elements of Qing officialdom, and when his admiration for things

Western became widely known in official circles, he and his proposal became the target of attack.[71]

Another example of this new approach was He Ruzhang, who witnessed Japanese treaty revision firsthand during his tenure as a minister from the Qing Empire in Tokyo. He identified tariff autonomy and abolition of extraterritoriality as two priorities, the former being of far greater importance.[72] He was arguably the first Chinese to use the Sino-Japanese term *zhiwai faquan* for extraterritoriality instead of *bugui guanxia*, which implies that he was moving to an understanding of the practice within an international context. He realized that the way extraterritoriality was practiced in China had very little foundation in the treaties, received little support in international law, and infringed on the sovereignty of the Qing Empire as it was understood by contemporary standards of international law.[73] On the other hand, he never used these observations to argue for fundamental institutional changes in China,[74] and he does not seem to have reflected on the fact that part of his own job was to ensure that the Chinese communities enjoyed full extraterritorial privileges under the Sino-Japanese Treaty of Tianjin.

Many individuals who traveled to territories controlled by the treaty powers in Southeast Asia made observations similar to those of He Ruzhang. One of them was the scholar Li Pingshu, who visited the British Crown Colony of Singapore in 1887. In his travelogue he pointed out that foreign consuls in the colonies did not exercise jurisdiction over their nationals and that mixed courts were not commonly practiced in the West.[75] Notwithstanding all these important contributions to an emerging critique of extraterritoriality, it is noteworthy that the discussion remained separate from day-to-day policy-making and was seldom part of public debate, even in the treaty ports.

When Qing officials discussed treaty revision and legal reform, there was an elephant in the room: Manchu privilege. It was one thing to reflect on the inequities of extraterritoriality after a trip abroad or to suggest some changes for a gradual reform of the legal system in order to prepare for treaty revision. However, revising the treaties was not only a question of convincing the treaty powers that China's legal system was "up to the mark"; it also involved undertaking far-reaching institutional reforms, which were bound to affect the relationships between ruler and subject, and between Manchus and Chinese. Despite the fact that the Qing court had introduced some halfhearted reforms of Manchu privilege, the problem would simply not disappear by itself, and no one was yet prepared to challenge the banner system head-on. So long as this systemic tension in the Qing legal order went unaddressed, no constituency for treaty revision emerged in China as in Meiji Japan. Whenever an extraterritorial incident occurred, Qing officials usually shied away from mobilizing public opinion, and instead they did their utmost to secure the best possible outcome within the confines of the existing legal order.

Extraterritoriality at Sea

Despite the rich literature on treaty revision and extraterritorial incidents in Japan, extraterritorial incidents in China were often more severe and involved more people than Japanese incidents. Consider, for instance, an event in 1863 related by the Harvard geologist Raphael Pumpelly after a trip outside Shanghai on the steamer *Surprise*:

> As we were steaming full speed, we saw some distance ahead of us a large scow loaded so heavily with bricks as to be almost unmanageable by the oars of four Chinamen who were propelling it. They saw the steamer coming, and knowing well how narrow was the channel, worked with all their force to get out of it and let the boat pass. As we all stood watching the slow motion of the scow which we were rapidly approaching, I listened every instant for the order to stop the engine. The unwieldy craft still occupied half the channel, the coolies straining every muscle to increase her slow motion, and uttering cries which evidently begged for a few instants' grace. There was yet time to avoid collision, when the pilot called out, "Shall I stop her, sir?" "No," cried the captain, "go ahead." There was no help for it. Horrified at hearing this cold-blooded order, I waited breathlessly for the crash, which soon came.[76]

Pumpelly then proceeded to describe the way the four Chinese were killed and the indifference of the crew, who seemed to be more concerned about possible damage to their ship than the fate of the victims. The incident gave rise to a strident debate in the pages of the *Nation* between Pumpelly and one of the owners of the *Surprise*, who indignantly dismissed Pumpelly's charges that the foreign community in Shanghai was infested with racial prejudice toward the Chinese and frequently abused their privileges with impunity.[77] The Qing authorities were deeply concerned by incidents such as this, and in 1867 Zeng Guofan approached the foreign consular body in Shanghai with a request to prohibit British ships from navigating in certain dangerous waters outside Shanghai.[78] The British consul responded that the consular body did not have the authority to issue any such proclamation,[79] but following consultations within the diplomatic body, Alcock issued a proclamation the following year to the effect that the British ships were no longer allowed to navigate a stretch of the Yangtze River known as the "Straw Shoe Channel" (*Caoxiexia*).[80]

The new regulations were not able to forestall even more lethal incidents in the waters surrounding the treaty port. On the morning of 4 April 1875, the British steamer *Ocean* collided with the Chinese-owned passenger ship *Fusing* (*Fuxing*) 120 miles north of Shaweishan island (Sheshandao) outside Shanghai.[81] The net tonnage of the *Ocean* was almost twice that of the *Fusing*, which suffered extensive damage and sank in just a few minutes.⁸² The *Fusing* carried 125 passengers; all European passengers but one were saved, while an estimated sixty-three Chinese passengers died, either by drowning or being crushed by the bow of the *Ocean*. The *North-China Herald* blamed the failure of Robert Morton Andrews, the captain of the *Fusing*, to save more Chinese passengers on how crowded the ship was at the time.⁸³ The fledgling Chinese-language newspaper *Shenbao*, however, gave the impression that European passengers had been anything but helpful in rescuing the Chinese passengers.⁸⁴ The *Ocean* was also severely damaged and barely made the journey back to Shanghai with the surviving passengers and crew, after which the facts of the case became known.⁸⁵

Not only the large number of casualties ensured that the accident would attract the media's attention; in addition, many of the victims were prominent Qing officials, and their obituaries produced even more publicity.⁸⁶ Furthermore, the wrecked steamships belonged to competing firms, Jardine & Matheson and the China Merchants' Steam Navigation Company (CMSNC; *Zhongguo lunchuan zhaoshangju*), an officially sponsored enterprise with close ties to the Qing government. As was customary at the time,⁸⁷ foreign commanders and officers staffed both ships, but while the crew of the *Ocean* was mixed, the crew of the *Fusing* consisted of Chinese only.⁸⁸

At the request of Captain Brown of the *Ocean*, a naval court of inquiry was held on the premises of the British Supreme Court, presided over by Captain A. Buller of H.M.S. *Modeste* in the presence of the British consul W. H. Medhurst. The circuit intendant sent the Shanghai district magistrate, the Mixed Court magistrate Chen Fuxun, and an interpreter to attend the hearings, and representatives from the CMSNC were also present at the inquest. The prominent British barrister William Venn Drummond appeared on the behalf of the CMSNC, and Robert Earnest Wainewright represented Brown.⁸⁹ Despite the strong Chinese presence in the courtroom, only Europeans were heard as witnesses, and *Shenbao* noted with disappointment that the naval court was "not a mixed court" (*fei huishen*) and that the Qing officials were "only allowed to observe the proceedings" (*jin ling zai pang ting an*).⁹⁰ The hearings went on for two days before the naval court concluded that the accident could be equally blamed on both parties and further commended the crew of the *Ocean* for its efforts to save the crew of the *Fusing*, concluding that "all that could possibly be done for the survivors had been accomplished."⁹¹

Quite understandably, this outcome did not please the victims' families or the owners of the CMSNC, who filed a series of lawsuits to redress their grievances. One of the managers of the CMSNC, the famous comprador Tang Jingxing (Tong King-sing), sued the *Ocean* for 200,000 taels in damages in the British Supreme Court, still presided over by its first incumbent judge, Edmund Hornby. Drummond and I. B. Eames represented the plaintiffs, whereas Wainewright pleaded the case of the defendants together with Hannen, who had defended

Robert Willis George in the capital case six years earlier. Despite this impressive lineup of legal counsel for the plaintiffs, the Supreme Court supported the findings of the naval court, and Tang Jingxing's request for compensation was denied; instead costs related to the accident were to be divided between the two parties.[92]

The failure of Tang's civil suit led to a second attempt. This time, the circuit intendant Feng Jun'guang represented the families of the victims and sued Captain Brown, asking for 1,000 taels per victim, totaling 63,000 taels. Medhurst presided over the court in the presence of the circuit intendant, the vice-consul Arthur Davenport, and the Mixed Court magistrate Chen Fuxun. The same lawyers represented Jardine in this suit; Drummond was hired by the circuit intendant to plead the case of the victims, and he produced a letter of instruction from the Shanghai district magistrate to that effect. The first line of defense in consular courts cases was usually to dispute the jurisdiction of the court, and Wainewright and Hannen moved that the court suspend its hearings due to its lack of competence to rule in the matter. In response to these claims, Drummond declared that in pursuance of article 17 in the Sino-British Treaty of Tianjin, the court was a "mixed court," which had full jurisdiction in the case. Realizing that Drummond's shrewd maneuver might set a precedent, Medhurst prevaricated:

> We are here by virtue of the Article in the Treaty. I do not say it is a Mixed court, like that in the Maloo [i.e. Nanking Road]; it is a Consular Court, but I rule that subject to the correction of my superiors. It is practically a Court to go into claims against a British subject, and I sit as Consul. Not being able of myself [sic] to settle the matter satisfactorily, I have called in the assistance of the Chinese authority.[93]

As the district magistrate's instructions made clear, it was the circuit intendant who had summoned Medhurst to hear the case, not the other way around, but the consul refused to deliberate in the matter. This somewhat inconclusive exchange of views speaks volumes about how a court could constitute itself as a Chinese mixed court or a consular court, depending on expediency.[94] Notwithstanding his refusal to deliberate on the nature of the court, Medhurst allowed the proceedings to continue, and almost all the previous witnesses were heard once more to establish the liability of the *Ocean*.[95] Despite the many indications that the crew had been negligent in its rescue of the passengers, no one seemed to consider the role of Captain Andrews, who had survived the loss of the *Fusing* while sixty-three of his Chinese passengers had drowned. Andrews did not seem to reflect on his own role or responsibility for the outcome of the accident to any considerable extent. This was typical: "I cannot say how many passengers and others were lost. It is the compradore's business to know that; he was drowned, and all books and accounts were lost with the ship."[96]

These callous remarks did not stir up any emotions, but when the *Shenbao* attributed the large number of casualties to the supposedly incompetent Chinese sailors of the *Fusing*, the CMSNC considered filing libel charges against the popular newspaper.[97] The consul was impressed by the evidence and ruled in favor of the CMSNC but decreased the amount of compensation to 11,000 taels.[98] Facing financial ruin, Captain Brown quickly left Shanghai without making any payment to the victims. In the end, the British government reportedly disbursed the full amount of the compensation through Drummond but did not allow media to publish this.[99]

The steamboat incident of 1875 was but one among many accidents that beset the busy waters around Shanghai in the late nineteenth century. At 6 o'clock in the morning of 20 January 1887, the British-owned steamship *Nepaul* collided with the Chinese man-of-war *Wan Nien Ching* (*Wannian qing*), which was anchored on an island in the mouth of the Yangtze River waiting for the fog to clear.[100] The *Wan Nien Ching* carried almost three hundred Chinese passengers who were on their way to celebrate Spring Festival, and between eighty and one hundred lives were lost in the crash.[101] The Chinese ship was owned by none other than the industrious governor of Taiwan, Liu Mingchuan. When he learned about the disaster, he promptly hired Drummond, who had just returned from Shanghai after defending the riotous sailors in Nagasaki.

In the naval court, the Swedish commander of the *Wan Nien Ching*, Captain Damström, displayed a typical lack of interest in his Chinese passengers, and one of his English subordinates openly admitted that he had "made no effort to get out our boats, because I saw it was completely useless as they were completely crowded with Chinese."[102] No one seemed to react to these admissions of negligence. The case instead focused on the reckless operation of the *Nepaul*, which had traveled at high speed despite the thick fog. Drummond made a convincing case that the captain of the *Nepaul* had violated existing regulations and that the *Wan Nien Ching* could not be held liable for supposedly violating some minor points of naval law, since the ship was only bound by Chinese laws. The counsel for the defendant vehemently disagreed with Drummond but refused to elaborate on what laws the *Wan Nien Ching* was subject to. After Drummond dealt this devastating blow, the British Supreme Court in Admiralty declared the *Nepaul* entirely at fault,[103] which meant that the owner of the *Wan Nien Ching* could sue for compensation. Judging by the press reaction, the victory in the case came as a surprise to the Chinese community,[104] and the *Dianshizhai Pictorial* greeted this as a great victory for the Chinese in the International Settlement.[105]

The Shanghai public learns about the settlement of the *Wan Nien Ching* case. *Dianshizhai huabao*, 107:82 (1887). Reprinted in *Dianshizhai huabao* (Guangzhou: Guangdong renmin chubanshe, 1983).

報論之詳且書無
候償
聲言懇試思所以能勝
之者未嘗亟故也從前中國積
弱久
歐西人滔以謀我故難間
兩人
自強之機日起而有功而
近則
以爭利故各國猜忌不
似從
前之見好事異而勢殊
故得
所藉手以告成功者
實在
十年之前然以未失
如此
之大公無我也
然而
英已加人一
等矣

萬年青勝

去臘二十六日,我萬年青船為你包而公司撞沉,勢不得不入訟之兩,竟得直滬上諸日

Events That Never Became "Incidents"

The *Fusing* and the *Wan Nien Ching* cases had all the ingredients of explosive extraterritorial incidents, and the indifference of Western crews toward the lives of Chinese passengers was often touched on in the Chinese-language press. For instance, following a steamboat accident in 1885, the *Dianshizhai Pictorial* complained about foreign callousness and racial prejudice, quoting the classic paragraph in the *Zuo Commentary* to *the Spring and Autumn Annals:* "If he be not our kin, he is sure to have a different mind."[106] The contrast with the contemporaneous "*Normanton* incident" is instructive. Both Chinese and Japanese authorities appealed to the consular authorities for redress, but they approached the matter in different ways. When the Japanese government was not satisfied with the findings of the naval court in Kobe, it produced criminal charges against Captain Drake for manslaughter; at the same time, both the government and public opinion used the incident to put pressure on the treaty powers to revise the unequal treaties. In China, the concerned parties employed the best lawyers they could find to secure an acceptable outcome in the courts, but they stopped short of filing criminal charges, even though there were ample indications of negligence in the rescuing operations. No one took the opportunity to use these incidents to challenge extraterritoriality or to campaign for treaty revision. The Chinese steamship incidents remained local events, and there is no evidence that they impacted policy-making circles or any national audience to any greater extent. When Li Hongzhang submitted a palace memorial on the *Fusing* case that was published in the *Shenbao* before the emperor had even responded to it, he did not reflect any opposition to the way the matter was settled as such.[107]

The role of the Shanghai bar is also intriguing. If Qing officialdom was hostile to foreign educated Chinese like Wu Tingfang, Shanghai was a city where foreign legal counsel could develop and prosper. To be sure, the fact that people like Drummond could practice law at all was due to their extraterritorial status, since Chinese law banned "litigation tricksters," effectively preventing an indigenous legal profession from developing. On the other hand, it was the circuit intendant of Shanghai, supported by the Zongli Yamen, who had finally legalized the appearance of lawyers in the Mixed Court over the objections of the consular body, which had wanted the lawyers to stay in the consular courts and had not wanted the Chinese community to have the benefits of Western legal counsel.[108] Drummond was handsomely remunerated for his services to the Chinese community, and the Qing court even awarded him with honorary ranks in the Qing civil service.[109] But just like the Qing statesmen, who mainly used international law to solve discrete problems, Drummond played a role in the hybrid legal order of the treaty ports that was more that of a troubleshooter than reformer. Whereas his French contemporary Boissonade was deeply involved in reshaping the Japanese legal system, Drummond never played such a role in China. After the treaty port archipelago was submerged by the rising Chinese nation-state in the twentieth century, Drummond left no durable legacy, and he and his clients were forgotten. In Japan a number of monuments have been named after Boissonade, but no law school in China is adorned with a bust of Drummond. Incidentally, this well-connected barrister paid a steep price for providing legal counsel to the Chinese community. When leading members of the British community in Shanghai learned that he had been nominated for a prominent post in the British consular service in China in 1894, they called a meeting urging the Foreign Office to reconsider its nomination, and one participant castigated Drummond as a "notoriously philo-Chinese lawyer."[110]

In retrospect, the Japanese reaction to the "*Normanton* incident" may seem "hyperemotional," and it might very well have been the case that most Japanese commentators had a crude understanding of the English legal system as it was manifested in the consular and naval courts.[111] However, the Japanese response sent a strong political signal to Britain and other foreign powers that Japanese lives could not be squandered with impunity under the protective shield of extraterritoriality. In Japan, the *Normanton* incident is still discussed in school textbooks and popular historical works; the *Fusing* and the *Wan Nien Ching* cases have not been accorded the same iconic status as extraterritorial incidents in the Chinese literature of the treaty ports.[112]

The fact that these steamboat incidents did not penetrate the emerging national consciousness of late Qing China cannot be attributed to the supposed lack of a public debate in the late nineteenth century. The Shanghai press was circulated widely in the empire and reached a large readership. At the same time that the *Fusing* case was being tried in the courts of Shanghai, the reading public of China was engrossed in stories about the "Yang Naiwu case," a case of miscarriage of justice that inspired officials from all over the country to submit memorials to the throne and journalists to write editorials in the *Shenbao*.[113]

Further illustrating how the extraterritorial régimes in Shanghai seemed to operate by default is the fact that the Qing government failed to restrict the operation of extraterritoriality when the Japanese government managed to persuade the British minister to prohibit the publication of Japanese-language newspapers, a precedent the Qing government was well aware of.[114] The British-owned Chinese-language daily *Shenbao* was a nuisance to many groups in Shanghai, both foreign and native. Local officials and guilds were often offended by reports in the newspapers, and foreigners, for their part, often charged that the newspaper was a mouthpiece of Chinese xenophobia operating under the shield of extraterritoriality. The consuls were content with the existence of a foreign-language press and were not likely to defend the *Shenbao* at this point in time. However, despite lobbying from local officials in Shanghai, the central government did not seize the opportunity to shut down the newspaper by using the precedent set in

Japan. The reason was not just that the Qing court reluctantly accepted extraterritoriality but also that it regarded the *Shenbao* as a relatively innocuous and useful source of information. Even the Empress Dowager herself reportedly read the newspaper on a regular basis. The *Shenbao* would survive a number of crises and foreign consuls' and local officials' attempts to shut it down.[115]

In order to operate, the consular and mixed courts in the treaty ports depended not only on coercion but also on collaboration. Hornby, who had once faced an irate crowd in connection with a consular court case, remarked in his memoirs: "Of course, I never tried another British subject accused of killing a Chinaman at an outlying port, unless there was a gun-boat near at hand."[116] On the other hand, the resources of the imperial powers were limited, and the foreign consuls made it clear to their constituencies that they could not expect gunboats to come to their rescue every time they ran into trouble with the Chinese authorities.[117] When Wainewright summed up his unsuccessful defense for the *Nepaul* in 1887, he touched a nerve when he said that he "had a horrible misgiving that the case was going to be turned into another Nagasaki affair, but happily that had been averted," provoking laughter in the courtroom.[118]

The Struggle over the Mixed Court

The fragile consensus over extraterritoriality and the treaty ports would be shaken to its foundations by the emergence of a new treaty power: Japan. The defeat of the Qing Empire in the Sino-Japanese War initiated a scramble for rights and concessions, giving the treaty port system "a new lease of life."[119] Many of the people who had smarted under the incursions of the foreign powers came out in the open, agitating against the unequal treaties and the Manchu Qing government, which signed yet another humiliating treaty after the Boxer débâcle in 1900.

One of the most significant foreign violations of Qing sovereignty over its own subjects was the effort to expand the scope of extraterritoriality and the jurisdiction of the Mixed Court. Extraterritoriality had originally been justified as protecting foreigners from Chinese punishments and practices; now it was being used to extend foreign jurisdiction to the Chinese residents of Shanghai. A major point of contention between Qing and foreign authorities in the Mixed Court was whether a foreign assessor should be allowed to observe the proceedings in purely "Chinese cases" in order to defend the interests of the foreign community, and there were constant and mainly unsuccessful efforts from the Shanghai Municipal Council to renegotiate the agreement to that effect. Another source of conflict was the foreign assessors' assertion that Chinese suspects could be extradited to Qing authorities only if the Mixed Court had established the case against the suspects. For most of the nineteenth century, Qing authorities were able to resist these foreign incursions, and in so doing they were on solid ground from the point of view of the Qing legal system, which recognized the personality principle but not the nebulous concept of "foreign interests." However, in the wake of the setbacks around the turn of century, the balance tipped decisively in favor of the foreign assessors. The famous *Subao* case was indicative of how much power the assessors of the Mixed Court had been able to claw back from the Qing side.

In 1903, two Chinese nationalists, Zhang Binglin and Zou Rong, published a number of articles in the journal *Subao* in which they reviled the Guangxu emperor and called for the overthrow of the Manchus. According to the treaties, their case was subject to Qing jurisdiction, and under the current criminal code the two could be tried for lèse-majesté, a crime punishable by death. However, the two activists were in the custody of the foreign-controlled police force of the International Settlement, and they were able to use the publicity of the case in order to avoid extradition. The case had important diplomatic repercussions and was even debated in the House of Commons. In the end it became politically impossible for the authorities in the International Settlement to extradite Zhang and Zou to a certain death, and the Mixed Court sentenced them to light prison sentences and expulsion from the International Settlement. Zhang and Zou's successful use of "court shopping" had important implications for the operation

Scene from the Shanghai Mixed Court around the turn of the century. The Mixed Court magistrate is seated in the center, surrounded by *yamen* runners, spectators, and foreign police officers, including a Sikh police constable on the right. Courtesy of Shanghai Muncipal Archives.

of the Mixed Court, as it established foreign jurisdiction in political cases that had little or nothing to do with the interests of the foreign community.[120]

When full-scale war broke out between Russia and Japan in early 1904, the weakness of the Qing government was further exposed during the many confrontations between the two powers that took place on Chinese territory. Tensions soon spilled over in Shanghai; two drunken Russian sailors' killing of a Chinese bystander in a scuffle with a rickshaw driver led to riots in December and prompted the powerful Ningbo guild to demand justice for the victim.[121] The following year, a coalition of native place associations stepped up their campaign against imperialism by leading a boycott against the United States to protest its Chinese exclusion acts.[122]

Against this backdrop of increased antiforeign feeling, it was only a matter of time before the Mixed Court became the target of nationalist agitation. For a long time it had been accepted practice for male prisoners to be sent to the Municipal Jail in Shanghai, and the consular body had long requested that the same be done for female prisoners. Thus in December 1905, when the Mixed Court charged a woman from Guangdong with kidnapping, the assessor demanded that she be sent to the Municipal Jail. The Mixed Court magistrate refused to comply, and a violent fight broke out between the municipal police and Chinese detectives. The behavior of the circuit intendant and his subordinates may have been erratic or inconsistent, as some foreigners claimed, but the position of the Municipal Council and the consular body had little or no support in the treaties. When the foreign community represented their case to the ministers in Beijing, the Municipal Council in Shanghai was ordered to return to the 1869 Mixed Court rules in the absence of any alternatives that the Qing authorities could accept.[123] As a direct response to the events in 1904–5, the U.S. government finally established a Supreme Court in China in order to enhance the image of the United States in China by tightening the administration of consular jurisdiction.[124] The most lasting outcome of these turbulent years was not a weakening of the consular courts but a strengthening. Neither were the consular courts the prime target of nationalist propaganda, which centered on the Mixed Court, an institution that could still be seen as a Chinese institution, however marred by foreign influence. In other words, extraterritoriality was only opposed to the extent that it directly affected Chinese communities, and a full-scale attack on the practice in all its expressions had yet to emerge.

Legal Reform

The same events that led to repeated riots in Shanghai and increased anti-Manchu propaganda across the country also prompted the Qing court to take action. Already in 1898, the Confucian visionary and reformer Kang Youwei had tried to assist the Guangxu emperor in reforming the Qing polity in the "hundred days of reform," which were partly inspired by Japan's success in treaty revision.[125] However, the Empress Dowager, Cixi, halted the reforms and ousted Kang Youwei's group from the Qing court, and other more moderate officials were soon recruited to take over the reform projects, many of them without any experience in policymaking. The Boxer débâcle added new urgency to institutional reform, and the moderate nationalist Wu Tingfang, who had finally found a position in the Qing foreign service, was enlisted to negotiate new treaties in 1902.[126] One of the resulting treaties, the Sino-British "Mackay treaty," was the first treaty China concluded with a foreign power that directly addressed Chinese concerns about extraterritoriality.[127] Article 12 of the new treaty read:

> China having expressed a strong desire to reform her judicial system and to bring it into accord with that of Western nations, Great Britain agrees to give every assistance to such reform, and she will also be prepared to relinquish her extra-territorial rights when she is satisfied that the state of the Chinese laws, the arrangement for her administration, and other considerations warrant her in so doing.[128]

Concurrent with these efforts, the prominent legal scholar Shen Jiaben and Wu Tingfang were put in charge of legal reform, and in 1904 Shen was made the head of the newly established "Bureau for the Compilation of Law" (*Falü bianzuanguan*). For the first time, the Qing court agreed that sweeping reforms were necessary for treaty revision, and in a steady stream of ambitious memorials, Shen and his subordinates addressed not only questions such as penal reform, criminal procedure, the revision of the mixed court regulations, and constitutional reform but also the sensitive question of Manchu privilege, which was the subject of a large part of their reform proposals. However, the suggested reforms proved too ambitious for many senior officials, who blocked the initiative, and Wu Tingfang resigned from his position in disgust.[129]

The first wave of institutional reform was followed by a second, and this time Shen Jiaben set out to realize the more pragmatic goal of revising the existing Qing Code instead of replacing it with an entirely new code, and he managed to enlist the support of more senior statesmen.[130] In the summer of 1907, the Manchu bannerman and governor-general of Liangjiang, Duanfang, memorialized the throne urging the abolishment of the judicial subprefect and the integration of all Manchus into the same jurisdiction as Han Chinese.[131] In response to this and other calls for reform, the Empress Dowager issued two decrees in the fall of 1907 that disbanded the banner garrisons and abolished all differences between Manchus and Han, without, however, explicitly mentioning the judicial subprefect.[132]

On 10 January 1908, the indefatigable Shen Jiaben responded to a request from the Empress Dowager to give more detailed suggestions for abolition of

Manchu privilege. In the memorial, he gave a long list of all the statutes and substatutes that needed to be revised in order to abolish all remaining Manchu privileges, with the notable exception of the prerogatives of the imperial nobility. In the beginning of the memorial, he justified his proposals in the following way:

> Now that communications between China and the outside world (have been established) and laws and thoughts are progressing in new directions, if we still adhere to the old laws which mark of the spheres of Manchus and Chinese, such will not only arouse an attitude of contempt on the part of the foreigners, but also greatly impede the future of the establishment of a constitution.[133]

What Shen spelled out here was not only the fact that treaty revision was dependent on the approval of foreigners but also that maintaining the legal distinction between Manchus and Han would make it impossible to constitute a modern nation—a necessary precondition for treaty revision and the abolition of extraterritoriality. The centrality of Manchu-Han relations for the success of constitutional reform is further illustrated by the fact that Shen suggested that the Mongol Code (*Menggu lüli*) be retained for the time being, pending further legal reforms.

Both Duanfang's and Shen Jianben's suggestions were accepted by the throne, but the new policies backfired at the local level, and the government eventually failed to disband the banner garrisons.[134] Most of the reforms were never implemented, and as some extant local archives indicate, the judicial subprefect was retained right until the end of the dynasty in some prefectures. From the records, it appears that apart from his judicial duties, he also served as a kind of welfare worker and was in charge of supervising banner schools.[135]

After Cixi's death in November 1908, Zaifeng, who acted as prince regent in the infant Xuantong emperor's stead, inherited the responsibility for constitutional reforms. Although he did not reverse the reforms entirely, his regency would be known for the extensive promotion of Manchu interest within the Qing government, which contributed to the fall of the dynasty in 1911. Thus, even though Manchus and Han were nominally equal at the end of the Qing dynasty, the bannermen remained an "occupational caste" or a separate ethnic group until the end.

Dénouement

The Republican revolution in 1911–12 unleashed a wave of anti-Manchu violence, which attained genocidal dimensions in some parts of the country, such as Xi'an, Nanjing, and Taiyuan, where Manchu men, women, and children were systematically targeted for killings.[136] Duanfang, who died trying to reassure a vengeful crowd that his ancestors were originally of Han Chinese origin, was one of the first casualties of the revolution.[137] As order was restored in the country, Wu Tingfang took part in negotiating a historic compromise on the behalf of the new Republican government, allowing the banner garrisons to continue to exist and the infant emperor and his retinue to stay the Forbidden City, which they did until 1924.[138] The new government also promulgated a new draft constitution, which heralded a new era in Chinese constitutional thought. Although all previous Qing draft constitutions had emphasized the personal sovereignty of the emperor and the continuity of the imperial house, they had never specified the territorial extents of the empire. The new Republican draft constitution, on the other hand, emphasized the territorial extent of the Chinese republic and the popular sovereignty of the Chinese people, a pattern that would prevail in all constitutions throughout the republic.[139]

Although the new government vowed to abolish extraterritoriality and renegotiate all of the unequal treaties, the most immediate consequence of the Republican revolution in Shanghai was yet another setback for Chinese jurisdiction. Following the collapse of the local Qing authorities in Shanghai, the Municipal Council of the International Settlement and the French Concession stepped into the power vacuum and appointed the Chinese magistrates to their Mixed Courts, putting the Chinese residents in Shanghai under de facto foreign jurisdiction. China's new régime was not able to reclaim the jurisdiction of the Qing government, and Shanghai became a safe haven for criminals, who continued to use extraterritoriality as a protective shield. The following three decades would be the classical gangster age of Shanghai.

Instead of the "barbarity" of traditional Chinese practices, it was now the weakness of the central government that served as justification of extraterritoriality. Undeterred by these setbacks, the Republican governments, which followed one other in swift succession, continued to work on legal reform, and a number of international conferences on extraterritoriality and foreign privileges in China were convened in the decades to come. However, these reforms were not what weakened the system; the first serious blow to extraterritoriality was dealt by World War I, which removed German and Austro-Hungarian subjects from consular jurisdiction as China joined the Allies in the hope of sharing the spoils of war. As many contemporaries noted, the main consequence of this change of legal régime was not that this group of foreigners became easy prey for arbitrary Chinese government practices but that they were able to forge closer relationships with Chinese authorities and businesses, giving them a certain competitive edge over other Western actors.[140] The second major blow to consular jurisdiction was the Russian revolutions of 1917, which removed Russia from consular jurisdiction and led to an influx of Russian émigrés into Shanghai.

However, the surviving treaty powers still protected the extraterritorial privileges of their citizens jealously, and the Chinese delegation left the peace conference in Versailles bitterly disappointed, thoroughly discrediting the warlord-dominated Beijing government and paving the way for China's two competing revolutionary nationalist parties: the Guomindang and the Communist Party. The Nationalist groundswell that laid the ground for Chiang Kai-shek's Northern Expedition in 1925–27 claimed a number of victories for Chinese national sovereignty. The British government realized the futility of defending all treaty ports and simply gave up a number of concessions without a fight.[141] However, the treaty powers were not prepared to give up Shanghai, the heart of the treaty port order, and a violent confrontation between the Shanghai police force and Nationalist demonstrators outside the Mixed Court claimed a number of casualties in 1925. This spelled the end of the Mixed Court. From then on, local Chinese authorities simply refused to enforce the verdicts of the Mixed Court outside the International Settlement. This rendered the thoroughly discredited institution largely ineffective, and a Chinese-run local court finally replaced it in 1927.[142] For a moment it looked as if Chiang Kai-shek's Nationalists would be able to roll back the entire treaty port system, but in the early 1930s the Nanjing government was challenged by Japan, which postponed further efforts to revise the treaties. China would have to wait another decade to abolish extraterritoriality.

Conclusion

The circumstances surrounding the eventual abolition of extraterritoriality in China are full of ironies. The Japanese, who had given the treaty port system a "new lease of life" in the wake of the First Sino-Japanese War, would render the practice inoperative in large parts of the country following their full-scale invasion of China in 1937. Later, as the Japanese government and the Allies were clamoring to win the support of the Chinese, extraterritoriality was officially abolished in both the Nationalist and Japanese-occupied areas with great fanfare in early 1943. In the British Embassy in Chongqing, the temporary capital of Nationalist China, representatives from the British and Chinese governments signed a new Sino-British treaty on 11 January 1943, and Wang Jingwei's pro-Japanese régime soon followed suit with a similar agreement with the Japanese government.[1] However, it was not the Nationalists who would enjoy the fruits of this foreign policy victory, as they would be expelled to the island of Taiwan six years later. Instead, the People's Republic of China would claim the credit for unifying China under one government exercising full jurisdiction over all its inhabitants. On the other shore of the East China Sea, the same legal system and constitution that had been deemed sufficient for the abolition of extraterritoriality sixty years earlier were now condemned as products of Japan's "failed modernity." A new constitution was drafted under the supervision of General Douglas MacArthur, and the U.S. forces stationed in Japan were removed from local jurisdiction under Status of Forces Agreements. Thus the appraisals of what constituted an internationally acceptable legal system had shifted in the past hundred years, and legal reform cannot fully account for the vicissitudes of extraterritoriality in East Asia. War, revolution, and Great Power politics usually shaped the framework of a given legal régime, but the extent to which a controversial practice such as extraterritoriality managed to take root in China and Japan depended on the degree to which it did—or did not—resonate with the indigenous legal order, and on how that legal order changed over time.

By examining extraterritoriality in East Asia in general and China in particular, this book has offered a number of opportunities to reconsider questions of law, Sino-Japanese relations, and the East Asian encounter with colonialism. Extraterritoriality was not implanted into East Asia as a ready-made product but developed in a dialogue with local precedents, local understandings of power, and local institutions, which are best understood within the complex triangular relationship between China, Japan, and the West. This insight does not mitigate the reality of Western imperialism in East Asia, but it displaces the privileged position of European imperial centers over the "peripheries" in the history of East Asian state-building. Manchu-Chinese relations were of great significance when the Qing Empire accommodated foreign demands for consular jurisdiction and opened diplomatic relations with Japan. The Manchu military conquest elite enjoyed extensive legal privileges that placed them outside the criminal jurisdiction of local Chinese administration. A close reading of treaty texts and other relevant documents suggested that a Qing institution for the adjudication for Manchu-Chinese disputes served as the model for both the International Mixed Court in Shanghai and the extraterritorial arrangements in the Sino-Japanese Treaty of Tianjin in 1871. Thus the adaptability of Qing legal procedure provided for a relatively seamless transition into the treaty port era, which would have momentous consequences for China's national sovereignty in the twentieth century. Instead of setting clear limits for foreign jurisdiction, Qing officials became increasingly entangled in different extraterritorial arrangements, not least through their willingness to participate in mixed courts in China and to establish mixed courts in Japan.

There was no parallel to this development in the Japanese case. Instead, Japanese authorities chose *not* to integrate consular courts and mixed courts into the indigenous legal order, and the fact that the Bakufu collapsed within fifteen years after the conclusion of the first commercial treaty meant that Bakufu laws and institutions never asserted any discernable influence over the way extraterritoriality evolved in Japan, which could have formed a counterpart to the evolution of hybrid Sino-foreign institutions in China. The Bakufu did tolerate the practice of extraterritoriality, and there is little evidence of any principled resistance to foreign jurisdiction during the first fifteen years of the treaty port order. However, the Bakufu insisted that extraterritoriality and consular jurisdiction did not imply that foreigners enjoyed complete immunity from municipal laws, and it managed to persuade the foreign consular body to adopt its approach to a certain extent. The early Meiji state continued where the Bakufu had left off and drew clear limits beyond which it did not wish foreign privilege to extend itself. In contrast to Qing China, where officials evinced a certain degree of tolerance toward foreigners resolving conflicts among themselves, the ever-expanding Japanese state became increasingly reluctant to cede jurisdiction in any area. By the time the Qing Empire and Meiji Japan entered into treaty relations in 1871, Japanese statesmen were preoccupied with reforming the legal system and centralizing the government, and they were not likely to look to Japan's past to find models to accommodate—or resist—demands for extraterritorial privileges. Thus, in contrast to China, consular jurisdiction remained an alien body in the Tokugawa state and its early Meiji counterpart, and Japanese policy-makers were determined to keep it that way.

In analyzing the conclusion of the Sino-Japanese Treaty of Tianjin as well as the implementation of extraterritorial jurisdiction under the treaty, this book has narrated a relatively unknown chapter in Sino-Japanese relations. As the two countries followed very different trajectories during the last decades of the nineteenth century, their policies on extraterritorial jurisdiction clashed in a number of arenas. The Japanese government never accepted the Sino-Japanese Treaty of Tianjin in 1871 as a permanent basis of intercourse with the Qing Empire, and it clearly did its utmost to push for interpretation in its favor and to exclude what was regarded as undue Chinese interference in Japan's internal affairs. The problems were compounded by the fact that the very content of Japanese consular jurisdiction was a moving target, as the Japanese legal system underwent a whole cycle of reform in the 1870s and 1880s. The Qing government, on the other hand, was quite satisfied with the Treaty of Tianjin and had little or no understanding of the type of legal reforms the Japanese government was carrying out. Indeed, the Treaty of Tianjin constituted a dangerous stumbling block for Japanese efforts in treaty revision in relation to the Western powers, since it was by no means certain that Japanese legal reforms would persuade the Qing Empire to abolish the extraterritorial privileges of the Chinese communities in Japan.

The implementation of the treaty also had very different consequences for the two countries. The Japanese community in the Chinese treaty ports remained relatively small prior to 1895, and the Qing government was much more concerned with preventing conflicts between Western and Chinese residents in the treaty ports, as well as trying to restrain missionary activities in the Chinese interior. Still, the treaty sheds much new light on how flexible Qing statesmen were in dealing with questions of consular jurisdiction and provides an important corrective to a historical narrative on the treaty port era in which China is usually portrayed as a rather passive and reactive power. The Qing Empire was an absolutely central concern to Japanese statesmen, and the Treaty of Tianjin regulated Japan's relations with its numerically largest foreign community. The Chinese communities in the treaty ports played a crucial role in Japan's foreign trade, both on their own and as compradors for Western merchants, and the Treaty of Tianjin effectively shielded this economically important group from Japanese jurisdiction.

The importance of the Sino-Japanese Treaty of Tianjin has been underestimated, because the histories of the treaty ports in China and Japan have usually been written within the framework of national histories, which are largely focused on the encounter with the West. The scholarship on extraterritoriality has also stressed the impact of the West rather than the triangular relationship between China, Japan, and the West, because this scholarship has rested predominantly on Western-language primary sources. This has produced a skewed narrative that attributes too much importance to the agency of foreign actors in the treaty ports and has failed to see that consular jurisdiction rested not only on the presence of Western gunboats but also on the active participation and cooperation of Qing authorities.

Having provided a springboard for foreign domination, extraterritoriality has left many policy-makers in mainland China with a legacy of deeply felt suspicions toward international law, international organizations, and more recently human rights. The Communist Party of China decided that its legitimacy as the ruling political party on the Chinese mainland ultimately rested on its ability to ward off real and perceived threats to China's national sovereignty and territorial integrity. China's "hundred years of humiliation" forms an integral part of the prevailing nationalist narrative, and the struggle against the semicolonial status of China under the "unequal treaties" has been enshrined in every constitution since 1954. Furthermore, article 32 of the current constitution explicitly states that "while on Chinese territory foreigners must abide by the law of the People's Republic of China"—which is a rather curious affirmation of China's territorial sovereignty, given the fact that current international practices are very restrictive toward extraterritorial legal immunities. The idea that foreigners seemed to be able to commit grave crimes with impunity on Chinese soil has provided subsequent Chinese governments with powerful arguments against "foreign interference" in China's internal affairs. In contemporary political discourse in China, extraterritoriality and its colonial legacy have been invoked in a number of ways in order to delegitimize foreign criticism of China's human rights record.[2] Indeed, few countries emphasize the importance of national sovereignty more aggressively than China does today. Yet against the backdrop of an increasingly globalized world, where many problems can only be resolved on an international level, Chinese claims sometimes stand out as rather odd. The ideal type of the Westphalian nation-state—if it ever existed—increasingly looks like an interlude in state formation that reached its zenith during the second half of the twentieth century. Today, the extraterritorial application of laws and jurisdiction are not primarily associated with immunity from local jurisdiction, but more with different countries claiming jurisdiction over their own nationals when they have committed crimes abroad—some countries even reserving the right to prosecute foreign "unlawful combatants." The People's Republic of China is not an exception from this trend. Under article 10 in the nation's Criminal Code, the

Chinese authorities may prosecute Chinese citizens for crimes against the Criminal Code that are committed abroad, even if they have already been punished for the crime, and China's assertion of this right has led to widely publicized cases in New Zealand and Norway.[3]

Japan, on the other hand, no longer challenges the international world order but is an active participant in international institutions and organs. The relatively short duration of the treaties as well as Japan's own history of territorial and colonial expansion in China and Korea have largely overshadowed the legacy of the unequal treaties, and extraterritoriality has not left an imprint in Japan comparable to that of the continent. Still, radical critics of the postwar alliance with the United States have often used the "unequal treaties" as a trope to criticize the Mutual Security Assistance Pact,[4] and its successor the Treaty of Mutual Cooperation and Security, two controversial treaties that put Japan under the defense umbrella of the United States' armed forces. The continued presence of U.S. armed forces in Japan makes the question of extraterritoriality persistently newsworthy, since military personnel enjoy limited immunity from Japanese jurisdiction under a "Status of Forces Agreement" included in article 6 of the treaty.[5] Critics have charged that such agreements provide U.S. military personnel with a legal comfort zone in which they can commit crimes with impunity.

This book has suggested that there is a conceptual link between the way the Chinese state has treated foreigners and ethnic "minorities," a link that is still relevant. Seen from the vantage point of new Qing history, the establishment of the People's Republic of China can be understood as the reconstruction of Han Chinese identity and the establishment of Han Chinese rule over the entire territory of China proper, as well as over peripheral regions that have usually been subject to different forms of indirect rule. When the Communist Party seized power in 1949, it professed to be an internationalist and multiethnic party that sought to build brotherly relations with the rest of world and safeguard the rights of ethnic minorities through an elaborate system of regional and ethnic autonomy. Even though the Party claimed to be the legitimate successor to the polyethnic Qing Empire, it produced very few non-Han statesmen of a stature comparable to Mujangga, Qiying, or Wenxiang. Instead, Han Chinese officials and cadres came to dominate the party, government, and military in all key sectors and in all regions of the People's Republic, even in regions where Han Chinese had not been in a majority historically.[6]

Following the strengthening of Han Chinese rule over the territories of the former Qing dynasty, the new government also undertook to expel all foreigners from China, a step going far beyond what was necessary to rid China of foreign imperialism. The new régime repatriated not only representatives of foreign imperialism but also missionaries, teachers, academics, and even some people who were sympathetic to the Communist cause. The only exception was a tiny group of tightly monitored foreign friends and experts who lived relatively privileged lives segregated from the majority population. These arrangements, which look rather similar to the shielded existence of foreigners during the treaty port era, are an innovation that also took inspiration from the Eastern Bloc.[7] As a result, both the relative and absolute number of foreigners in China are still significantly smaller than they were in 1919.[8]

The post-1949 development was not a foregone conclusion or an inevitable consequence of China's recent and distant history. There were resources both in China's past and in Marxist doctrine to conceive different ways of interacting with foreigners and ethnic minorities. Marxism is an ideology with cosmopolitan ambitions, and the rights of ethnic minorities were very much part and parcel of the Leninist legacy, which the Communist Party inherited after taking power. It is tempting to see the People's Republic's emphasis on centralist government as a mere continuation of the Qing state, which did not allow the articulation of any sectional interests in the body politic, but as this book has shown, the Qing state was never a unitary nation-state that enacted one kind of political and legal order throughout its territory.

Deng Xiaoping's policy of economic reform and opening to the world after 1979 changed many of the parameters of the old system to manage foreigners. Today, China is more open than it has ever been since 1949, and foreigners can travel without restriction to most parts of the People's Republic. Many of the hallmarks of the old order—separate residential areas for foreigners, the notorious dual currency system, and a separate pricing system for foreigners—have been dismantled, and in many cities, many foreigners reside and work side by side with Chinese. The Chinese legal order has gone through what looks like an almost complete transformation, and Chinese are increasingly prone to use the court system to resolve disputes. Having been occluded by the binaries of the Cold War for a quarter of a century, the relationship between China and the rest of the world is once again framed as a legal encounter, where the health of the overall relationship is judged in terms of intellectual property rights, treaty obligations, human rights, and consumer protection.

Chinese law is also surrounded by a number of uncertainties that challenge the legitimacy of the entire system. The legal rights of China's own citizens are often violated by the government, and dramatic policy reversals wreak havoc on agreements that have been entered into in good faith. The strong Chinese state seems to have resolved the status of foreigners in China once and for all, yet foreigners are still surrounded both by restrictions on their activities and special treatments, which create a powerful logic of segregation from Chinese society at large. For instance, foreigners are largely excluded from direct involvement in many areas such as media and law,[9] in which foreigners such the British journalist

Ernest Major and the French lawyer Jean Escarra made pioneering contributions during the Qing and Republican eras.[10] The Chinese government can no longer maintain the old system of nurturing a carefully monitored group of "foreign friends" in closed settings,[11] but neither the government nor the diplomatic corps in China have been able to imagine a new system.

No one wishes the return of the old treaty port system to China and East Asia, but it is not clear how long extraterritoriality will leave a stigmatizing legacy on the presence of foreigners in China. Globalization does not only mean that China will have a greater role in the world, it also means that "the world"—in all its different incarnations—will assert itself in China. It is no longer possible to assume that a foreigner on the streets of Beijing or Shanghai is a wealthy businessman or a privileged expert from a Western country; today foreigners are active in a broad range of sectors and come from a large number of different countries.[12] Many foreigners have lived in China for decades, marry local people, and have children with mixed ancestry,[13] which poses some fundamental questions of what it means to be Chinese abroad or foreign in China. Yet, save for the tentative introduction of a "green card" system, the assumption is still that foreigners should eventually return to where they came from, and current parameters of Chinese public opinion give very little room for the articulation of foreign voices. However, many of the restrictions surrounding foreigners in China are no longer tenable, and in the long term, it is not realistic to expect that foreigners will reconcile themselves to the severe restrictions on free speech, political rights, and freedom of movement that still persist in China. Nor is it realistic to expect that the majority of Chinese would accept any accommodation to foreign sensibilities that would entail special rights or privileges that would be out of reach for most Chinese. Perhaps the answer to these questions is that foreigners should defend their own rights in China, not as colonial sojourners or privileged foreign experts but as legitimate and equal residents of China, just as Nils Möller claimed to do in the late nineteenth century.

GLOSSARY OF CHINESE AND JAPANESE TERMS

Abe Masahiro 阿部正弘

Ajia-fū no besshu naru kokusaihō 亞細亞風ノ別種ナル国際法

anchasi 按察司

Andō Shōeki 安藤昌益

Ansei 安政

Aoki Shūzō 青木周藏

Ao yi 澳夷

aqimu boke 阿奇木伯克

ashigaru 足輕

Ashikaga Yoshimitsu 足利義満

Baba Tatsui 馬場辰猪

Bamin dongshi 八閩董事

Bamin huisuo zongli 八閩會所總理

Bamin huisuo 八閩會所

bang 幫

bankoku kokuhō 萬國公法

banshi dachen 辦事大臣

bayi 八議

biekai shengmian 別開生面

Bogui 柏貴

boke 伯克

bu zhi fadu, bu zhi liyi 不知法度,不知禮義

bugui guanxia 不歸管轄

Buke shohatto 武家諸法度

buneng anjing shoufa 不能安靜守法

Cai Xuan 蔡軒

Caoxiexia 草鞋峽

Celeng 策楞

Changshan 長善

Chao Tingzuo 晁廷佐

Chen Dezhui 陳德錐

Chen Fuxun 陳福勳

Chen Qin 陳欽

Chenglin 成林

chigai hōken 治外法權

chihōkan 地方官

Glossary of Chinese and Japanese Terms

Chinsai Nippō 鎮西日報

chitsuroku shobun 秩禄處分

chuanxi xueshu 傳習學術

Chūgokujin 中國人

Chūka kaigisho 中華會議所

Chūka kaikan 中華會館

Cixi 慈禧

Da Qingguo lishifu 大清國理事府

Da Qing lichao Shilu 大清歷朝實錄

daimyō 大名

daishin 大審

daotai 道臺

Daqing huidian shili 大清會典事例

dashen 大審

Date Munenari 伊達宗城

Deng Wei 鄧偉

Dian'an 滇案

Difangguan 地方官

Ding Richang 丁日昌

Ding Ruchang 丁汝昌

Dingyuan 定遠

Duanfang 端方

duijindian 兌金店

Duli cunyi 讀例存疑

duliang tongzhi 督糧同知

Du Yuesheng 杜月笙

ekken 越權

fadu 法度

Falü bianzuanguan 法律編纂館

Fan Ximing 范錫明

fanzui mian faqian 犯罪免發譴

Feng Jun'guang 馮焌光

fu 府

fudai daimyō 譜代大名

fudutong 副都統

Fukuchi Gen'ichirō 福地源一郎

Fukumoto Makoto 福本誠

Fukuwara Hanjūrō 福原伴十郎

Furukawa Yoshimasa 古川吉正

fūsetsugaki 風説書

Fuxing 福星

fuyi tongzhi 撫夷同知

fuyi 賦役

gai gui gai sheng guanxia 改歸該省管轄

gaitu guiliu 改土歸流

gangkou 港口

ganjie 甘結

geguo lingshiguan wuyong ganyu 各國領事官勿庸干預

ginmi 吟味

Gong Mujiu 宮慕九

Gongbuju 工部局

gongci 供詞

gongsuo 公所

gongtong chaming qi shi 公同查明其事

gongxie 公廨

Guangfu temple 廣福寺

Guangzhou Tiaoyue 廣州條約

guanshen 觀審

guanshu 管束

guanxia 管轄

Guiliang 桂良

gui difangguan guanxia 歸地方官管轄

Guo Songtao 郭嵩燾

Guo Wanjun 郭萬俊

haifang fenfu 海防分府

haifang tongzhi 海防同知

haihan chiken 廢藩置縣

haitōrei 廢刀令

Hanabusa Yoshimoto 花房義質

hanseki hōkan 版籍奉還

Hasegawa Takashi 長谷川喬

hatamoto 旗本

Hatoyama Kazuo 鳩山和夫

He Ruzhang 何如璋

heding 核定

heimin 平民

hei-nō bunri 兵農分離

hikiaimono 引合物

Honda Toshiaki 本多利明

huabang sishi 華幫司事

Huang Chengyi 黃承乙

Huang Juezi 黃爵滋

Huang Zonghan 黃宗漢

Huangpu tiaoyue 黃埔條約

Huaren 華人

Huashana 花沙納

Huawairen 化外人

huayang lishi tongzhi 華洋理事同知

Huayang tongzhi 華洋同知

huayi jiaoshe shijian 華夷交涉事件

Hubu 戶部

huiguan 會館

Huijiang zeli 回疆則例

huishen fenfu 會審分府

Huishen gongxie 會審公廨

huishen tongzhi 會審同知

huishen weiyuanhui 會審委員會

huishen 會審

huitong banli 會同辦理

huitong shenli 會同審理

huixunju 會訊局

Humen Tiaoyue 虎門條約

ichiryō ikkachū 一領一家中

Ii Naosuke 井伊直弼

Ikokusen uchiharai rei 異國船打拂令

Inoue Kaoru 井上馨

Inoue Kiyonao 井上清直

Inoue Masashi 井上政

Ishin no san ketsu 維新の三傑

Iwakura Tomomi 岩倉具視

Iwase Tadanari 岩瀬忠震

jiangji 匠籍

Jiangning tiaoyue 江寧條約

jianmin 賤民

jiaoshe anjian 交涉案件

jiaoshi 教士

jibun shioki 自分仕置

jin ling zai pang ting an 僅令在旁聽案

Jingbao 京報

jinshi 進士

jipai 籍牌

jishu 自首

Jiyū minken undō 自由民權運動

Jiyuan 濟遠

jōkamachi 城下町

jōyaku kaisei 條約改正

jōyaku misai no gaikokujin 條約未濟ノ外國人

junliu tuzui yishang 軍流徒罪以上

junmin yuehui cisong 軍民約會詞訟

kaishin iinkai 會審委員會

Kanagawa bugyō 神奈川奉行

kanbun 漢文

Kang Youwei 康有為

kanshin 觀審

kari jōyaku 假條約

Kawaji Toshiaki 川路聖謨

Kawakami Kin'ichi 河上謹一

Kawano Michitomo 河野通倫

Kawazu Sukekuni 河津祐邦

kazoku 華族

ken 縣

kenji 檢事

Kido Takayoshi 木戶孝允

Kinjū narabini kuge shohatto 禁中並公家諸法度

kinsatsu 金札

kirisute gomen 切捨御免

Koga Tōan 古賀侗庵

Komine Suzu 小嶺鈴

kongō saibansho 混合裁判所

Konshuru saidanjo コンシユル裁斷所

Kōtaiji 晧臺寺

Kujikata osadamegaki 公事方御定書

kunten 訓點

Kurokawa Koshirō 黑川小四郎

Kusaka Yoshio 日下義雄

kyōshu 梟首

Li Hongzhang 李鴻章

Li Pingshu 李平書

Li Shuchang 黎庶昌

Glossary of Chinese and Japanese Terms

liangguo jiaoshe shijian bici jun xu huitong gongping shenduan yi zhao yundang 兩國交涉事件彼此均須會同公平審斷以昭允當

liangmin 良民

Lianrui 廉瑞

Libu 吏部

lifan tongzhi 理番同知

Lifanyuan 理藩院

li Miao tongzhi 理苗同知

Lin Weixi 林維喜

Lin Zexu 林則徐

Lin'gui 麟桂

Lingnan huisuo 嶺南會所

lingshi gongtang 領事公堂

lingshi yamen 領事衙門

lingshi 領事

lishi fenfu 理事分府

lishi fu 理事府

lishi ting 理事廳

lishi tongpan 理事通判

lishi tongzhi 理事同知

lishi yamen 理事衙門

lishi 理事

lishiguan 理事官

Liu Mingchuan 劉銘傳

Liu Yunke 劉韻珂

li Yao tongzhi 理猺同知

lüli 律例

Mancheng 滿城

Manque 滿缺

Menggu lüli 蒙古律例

mianzhi shou bi jifeng 免致受彼譏諷

Miaoli 苗例

Mine Susumu 峯進

Minren 民人

Mo Xiangzhi 莫祥芝

Mori Arinori 森有禮

Moriyama Takichirō 森山多吉郎

Muzhang'a 穆彰阿

Mutsu Munemitsu 陸奧宗光

Nagasaki bugyō 長崎奉行

naichi zakkyo 内地雜居

Nedachi Sukeshichirō 根立助七郎

niban 擬辦

niesi 臬司

Nihon yakusho e toritatsu beshi 日本役所へ取立へし

ninen mo naku 二念無く

Niu Chunbin 紐春彬

Numa Heirokurō 沼間平六郎

Ōkubo Tadahiro 大久保忠恕

Ōkubo Toshimichi 大久保利通

Ōkuma Shigenobu 大隈重信

Omoto Jūtarō 尾本壽太郎

pai yangguan huishen 派洋官會審

pangzuo guanshen 旁坐觀審

Prince Gong 恭親王

qi niu xun niu 騎牛尋牛

qiejie 切結

qie 妾

qiji 旗籍

qimin fenzhi 旗民分治

qimin jiaoshe anjian 旗民交涉案件

qimin lishi tongzhi 旗民理事同知

Qing Shilu 清實錄

Qingguo jimin 清國籍民

Qingguoren 清國人

Qingshang 清商

qiren 旗人

Qishan 琦善

Qiying 耆英

rijikan 理事官

rōjū 老中

ru anzhong bing bu qianshe yangren zhe, bude ganyu 如案中並不牽涉洋人者不得干預

ryōji saibanken 領事裁判權

ryōji 領事

saibankan 裁判官

Saidan wa sōhō ni oite hempa nakaru beshi 裁斷は雙方に於て偏頗なかるへし

Saigō Takamori 西鄉隆盛

Saikai Shimbun 西海新聞

Saitō Chikudō 齋藤竹堂

Sakoku 鎖國

Sanfan zhi luan 三藩之亂

Sanjiang 三江會所

Sanjō Sanetomi 三條實美

sankin kōtai 參勤交代

Sei-i tai shōgun 征夷大將軍

Seitaisho 政體書

seitō bōgyo 正當防禦

seitō no bōei 正當ノ防衛

sekihai 籍牌

semu ren 色目人

Senzaimaru 千歲丸

Shanghai Yangjingbang sheguan huishen zhangcheng 上海洋涇浜設官會審章程

Shanghai zudi zhangcheng 上海租地章程

Sheshandao 佘山島

Shen Bingyuan 沈炳垣

Shen Guanfu 沈關福

Shen Guifen 沈桂芬

Shen Jiaben 沈家本

shi shu wuli, qingmie zhi zhi 寔屬無禮, 輕蔑之至

shihai chigae kakaru deiri 支配違え懸る出入

shihai 支配

shimatsusho 始末書

Shimazu Hisamitsu 島津久光

Shinajin 支那人

Glossary of Chinese and Japanese Terms

Shinkoku sekimin 清國籍民

Shinkokujin 清國人

shi-nō-kō-shō 士農工商

Shinritsu kōryō 新律綱領

Shinshō 清商

shizoku 士族

shūkō jōki 修好條規

shunmin 順民

sizi chujing 私自出境

Soejima Taneomi 副島種臣

Songbu 送部

Songyun 松筠

Subao 蘇報

sui Yao tongzhi 綏猺同知

Susongtai dao 蘇松太道

tachiai saibansho 立会裁判所

tai laoye 太老爺

Taixi 泰西

Takasugi Shinsaku 高杉晋作

Tang Jingxing 唐景星

Tangren 唐人

Tani Kanjō 谷干城

taryō tashihai no mono 他領他支配の者

Tei Einei 鄭永寧

Tenryō 天領

Terajima Munenori 寺島宗則

Tōjin yashiki 唐人屋敷

Tokugawa Ieyoshi 德川家慶

Tokugawa Nariaki 德川齊昭

Tokugawa Yoshinobu 德川慶喜

tongli 通例

Tongshang dachen 通商大臣

Tōtsūji 唐通事

toumu 頭目

tozama daimyō 外様大名

Tsimshatsui 尖沙嘴

Tsuda Mamichi 津田真道

Tsuruhara Sadayoshi 鶴原定吉

Tsutsui Masanori 筒井政憲

Tu Zongying 涂宗瀛

tuliu yishang 徒流以上

tusi 土司

waga Kōkoku no chijoku 我カ皇国ノ恥辱

Waiguo shiwu xingming fu da toumu tai laoye 外國事務刑名府大頭目太老爺

Wang Aran 王阿然

Wang Fa 王發

Wang Tao 王韜

wanguo gongfa 萬國公法

Wangxia tiaoyue 望廈條約

wannian heyue 萬年和約

Wannian qing 萬年青

Watanabe Kazan 渡邊崋山

Wei Pengcheng 魏鵬程

Wei Xiangshu 魏象樞

Wei Yi'ao 魏亦鰲

weiyuan 委員

Weiyuan 威遠

Wenxiang 文祥

woguo conglai wu ci zhengti 我國從來無此政體

Wu A'er 吳阿二

Wu Jianzhang 吳健章

Wu Tingfang 伍廷芳

Wu Xu 吳煦

wugu qianlian ren 無辜牽連人

wuxing zhi zhigu 無形之桎梏

xi en shi ji ge guo 新恩施及各國

xian 縣

xiangyue huitong shenli 相約會同審理

Xiaodaohui 小刀會

xiuhao tiaogui 修好條規

Xu Chengzu 徐承祖

Xu Chunfu 許春甫

Xue Huan 薛煥

Xue Yunsheng 薛允生

Yafu 亞福

yakunin 役人

Yamada Akiyoshi 山田顕義

Yamaguchi Shakujirō 山口錫次郎

Yanagihara Sakimitsu 柳原前光

Yang Shu 楊樞

Yangjingbang lishi gongxie 洋涇浜理事公廨

yangwu 洋務

Yantai tiaoyue 煙台條約

Yantai 煙台

Ye Mingchen 葉名琛

yi fu gong fa 以符公法

yi jia liang ji 一家兩籍

yi qi ya min 倚旗壓民

yi qiji wei hushenfu 以旗籍為護身符

Yilibu 伊里布

Ying Baoshi 應寶時

Ying niesi yamen 英臬司衙門

Yinghan 英翰

Yinghe 英和

yiti junzhan 一體均霑

yiti yuewen 一體約問

yoshin 豫審

you ming wu shi 有名無實

youmin mei jie rujiao wei hufu 莠民每借入教為護符

Yu Qiong 余璚

yu zu wo xingjiao wu yi 與阻我行教無異

yu 諭

Yuan dianzhang 元典章

Yuan Shuxun 袁樹勛

yuehui 約會

Glossary of Chinese and Japanese Terms

yueshu 約束

Zaifeng 載灃

Zankanjō 斬奸状

Zeng Guofan 曾國藩

Zhang Binglin 章炳麟

Zhang Jixin 張集馨

Zhang Sigui 張斯桂

zhangcheng 章程

zhangjing 章京

Zheng Renrui 鄭仁瑞

Zheng Xiaoxu 鄭孝胥

Zhenyuan 鎮遠

zhifu 知府

Zhifu 芝罘

zhongchen 忠臣

Zhongguo fadu 中國法度

Zhongguo lunchuan zhaoshangju 中國輪船招商局

Zhongguo 中國

Zhonghua huiguan 中華會館

Zhongtu 中土

zhou 州

Zhu Xi 竹溪

zhuangtun 莊屯

zhuanzhu 專主

zishou 自首

Zongli Yamen 總理衙門

Zongrenfu 宗人府

Zou Rong 鄒容

zuihuiguo daiyu 最惠國待遇

zuihuiguo tiaokuan 最惠國條款

NOTES

Introduction

1. NCH, 1 November 1877, 405.
2. NCH, 10 July 1891, 51.
3. NCH, 10 July 1891, 51.
4. For a study of Sino-Korean relations during late Qing, when Qing subjects enjoyed extraterritorial privileges in Korea, see Larsen, *Tradition, Treaties and Trade*.
5. The classic narrative of the "treaty system" can be found in Fairbank, "Creation of the Treaty System," 213–63.
6. Fishel, *End of Extraterritoriality*, 4–7.
7. Hoare, *Japan's Treaty Ports*.
8. Feuerwerker, "Foreign Presence in China," 129.
9. This aspect of foreign privilege has been called "the Midas touch" of extraterritoriality by Eileen Scully in *Bargaining with the State*, 5.
10. Lee, "Law and Local Autonomy," 113.
11. Scully, *Bargaining with the State*, 97; Wakeman, *Policing Shanghai*.
12. Soulié de Morant, *Exterritorialité*, 33–46; see also Willoughby, *Foreign Rights*, 44–45, 568 (n. 25).
13. Willoughby, *Foreign Rights*, 2–8; Wang, *China's Unequal Treaties*, 2.
14. Lethbridge, *All about Shanghai*, 55. Today this street is known as "Yan'an East Road" (Yan'an Donglu).
15. As to the question whether the presence of force invalidates an international agreement, Immanuel Hsü has made the following comment: "'Under duress' in international law applies to a threat to the life of the delegate, and not to the state. Kuei-liang and the emperor were not threatened by Elgin insofar as their personal lives were concerned; the state was threatened." Hsü, *China's Entrance*, 231 n. 98. See also Wang, *China's Unequal Treaties*.
16. Hevia, *English Lessons*, 60.
17. Liu, *Clash of Empires*, 112–13.
18. Sebes and Pereira, *Jesuits and the Sino-Russian Treaty*.
19. Lewis, *Frontier Contact*.
20. Sahlins, *Boundaries*, 6–7, 28–29, 54–59; Herman, *Amid the Clouds and Mist*, 11, 16; Strauss, *Law, Resistance, and the State*; Thongchai, *Siam Mapped*.
21. In continental Western Europe, legal pluralism is known as *Rechtspluralismus* (German), *rechtspluralisme* (Dutch), *pluralisme légal* (French), and *rättspluralism* (Swedish). For a classic treatment of legal pluralism in English, see Hooker, *Legal Pluralism*.
22. Of course, the word *adat* is derived from the Arabic word *'ādāt* which means "customs." Griffiths, "Recent Anthropology of Law"; Merry, "Law and Colonialism," 897–906.
23. "Any human society, I postulate, does not possess a single consistent legal system, but as many such systems as there are functioning subgroups." Pospíšil, *Anthropology of Law*, 98.

24. Merry, "Legal Pluralism," 881.
25. To my knowledge, the first scholar to apply the concept of legal pluralism to Qing China is Dorothea Heuschert, who used it in relation to Qing policy toward Mongolia. See Heuschert's seminal article, "Legal Pluralism" and *Die Gesetzgebung der Qing*. I am indebted to Mark C. Elliott for introducing me to Heuschert's important work on legal pluralism.
26. Hu, *Common Descent Group*; Cohen, "Writs of Passage."
27. Griffiths, "What Is Legal Pluralism?"
28. Merry, "Law and Colonialism," 871.
29. Peter Sahlins preferred to use the term "jurisdictional sovereignty."
30. For a recent contribution to this debate, which makes use of the concept of legal pluralism, see Shah, *Legal Pluralism in Conflict*.
31. Fairbank, "Creation of the Treaty System," 244.
32. Hsü, *China's Entrance*, 139.
33. Wagner, "*Shenbao* in Crisis."
34. For a survey of some of these objections, see Wang, *China's Unequal Treaties*, 25–27.
35. Guo, *Zhuanzhe*, 488.
36. "Until 1902 no honest attempt had been made by China to nullify in any way the limitation imposed upon her territorial jurisdiction." Mah, "Foreign Jurisdiction in China," 677.
37. Cohen, *Between Tradition and Modernity*, 231–32.
38. Guo, *Zhuanzhe*; Wang, *China's Unequal Treaties*.
39. Callery, *Correspondance diplomatique*, 64, 66.
40. This point is also made in Elman, *On Their Own Terms*, xxii–xxiii, 392–93.
41. These themes are developed in further length in Fogel, *Teleology of the Modern Nation-State*.
42. Bergère, *Shanghai*; Coates, *China Consuls*.
43. Malmsten, *Sjöfolk och fartyg från Nordvästskåne*, 3:136–59.
44. For a historical map of both existing and no longer existing historical buildings in Shanghai, see Kinouchi, *Shanhai rekishi gaidomappu*.
45. Ottosson, "Möller och hans sagoslott." The villa is now known as "Heng Shan Moller Villa Hotel" and is located at 30 Shaanxi South Road in Shanghai.

Chapter 1

1. Sayre, "Passing of Extraterritoriality."
2. Deuchler, *Confucian Gentlemen*.
3. Ch'ü, *Local Government*, 193; Wong, *China Transformed*, 193, 201.
4. China proper is here defined as the eighteen provinces that the Qing dynasty conquered from the Ming.
5. Ch'ü, *Local Government*, 1–13.
6. Confucius, *Analects*, 13:18 (p. 121).
7. Bodde and Morris, *Law in Imperial China*, 39–43.
8. Tao, "Traditional Chinese Social Ethics"; Jansen, *China in the Tokugawa World*, 68.
9. Bodde and Morris, *Law in Imperial China*, 34–35.
10. The functions of these different legal entities have been the subject of a number of seminal works in English, even though scholars have generally not expressed themselves in terms of legal pluralism. Two of the first scholars to treat this topic at any length were Hu Hsien-chin and Sybille van der Sprenkel, who delved deeply into the role of common descent groups and the interplay between informal and formal legal institutions. See Hu, *Common Descent Group*; van der Sprenkel, *Legal Institutions*, 80–96. Conflicts between the Qing government and local society in Southeast China have been covered extensively by Melissa Macauley, who has drawn on the works of legal anthropologists such as Leopold Pospíšil and Clifford Geertz. Macauley, *Social Power and Legal Culture*, 325–42. In their works, Bryna Goodman and Linda Cooke Johnston have uncovered the tremendous importance of guilds in the

treaty port of Shanghai. See Goodman, *Native Place*; Johnson, *Shanghai*. A group of historians centered on Philip C. Huang and Kathryn Bernhardt have also done groundbreaking work in analyzing the relationship between local custom and civil law the Qing legal order. See Bernhardt and Huang, *Civil Law*; for a critique of this school, see Bourgon, "Uncivil Dialogue."

11. Perhaps the strongest statement regarding the Qing state as a "unitary state" is given in R. Bin Wong's seminal work on Chinese state-building, *China Transformed*.
12. Ye and Esherick, *Chinese Archives*, 5. One of the major exceptions to this is the archives of the Huizhou merchants. Wilkinson, *Chinese History*, 955–64.
13. Wittfogel and Fêng, *History of Chinese Society*, 465–67.
14. Took, *Native Chieftaincy*; Giersch, *Asian Borderlands*; Herman, *Amid the Clouds*.
15. Ch'en, *Chinese Legal Tradition*, 80–88; Huang, *Yuandai falü*, 150–51, 272, 275.
16. Qiu, *Yuanshi cidian*, 637.
17. As far as I know there are no precedents for calling this kind of institution *yuehui* in Chinese prior to the Yuan dynasty. On the language of the Mongol Code, see Ch'en, *Chinese Legal Tradition*, 32.
18. *Da Yuan dianzhang*, 53:21a–24b.
19. Escarra, *La Chine et le droit international*, 5–6. Many of Escarra's arguments most likely derive from Paul Ratchnevsky's groundbreaking work on Mongol law. See for instance Ratchnevsky, *Un code des Yuan*, 1:lxxviii, 55, 200. For one objection to Escarra's claims, see Irie, *Chūgoku ni okeru gaikokujin no chii*, 453. I am indebted to Kishimoto Mio for directing my attention to Irie's work.
20. Farmer, *Zhu Yuanzhang*, 81–83; for a divergent view of the Ming legal project, see Bourgon, "De quelques tendances."
21. Jiang, *Great Ming Code*, 88.
22. Took, *Native Chieftaincy*; Herman, *Amid the Clouds and Mist*.
23. Ho, "Significance of the Ch'ing."
24. Roth [Li], "Manchu-Chinese Relationship."
25. Kuhn, *Soulstealers*, 34–36; see also Kuhn, "Chinese Views."
26. Farmer, *Zhu Yuanzhang*, 33, 72.
27. Kuhn, *Soulstealers*, 34–36; see also Sommer, *Sex, Law and Society*, 260–72.
28. See for instance, Giersch, *Asian Borderlands*. I am indebted to James Lee for directing my attention to this work.
29. Heuschert, "Legal Pluralism."
30. Shimada, *Shinchō Mōko rei*, 90, 148–49, 482; Heuschert, "Legal Pluralism," 318–19.
31. Heuschert, "Legal Pluralism," 317.
32. Newby, "Begs of Xinjiang"; Newby, *Empire*, 18, 146.
33. The precise nature of these local judges and Islamic law in China are still understudied topics. A. R. Dicks, "New Lamps for Old"; Lipman, *Familiar Strangers;* and Lipman, "Fierce and Brutal People."
34. For a reprint of the Mongol Code and the regulations for the Moslem regions, see Zhongguo bianjiang shidi yanjiu zhongxin, *Menggu lüli, Huijiang zeli*.
35. French, *Golden Yoke*.
36. One such case dates from 1728, when two Tibetan clergymen were slow-sliced for treason. See Petech, *China and Tibet*, 134. See also Brook et al., *Death by a Thousand Cuts*, 36.
37. Ho, "Men Who Would Not Be Amban"; Millward, *Eurasian Crossroads*.
38. Zheng, "Pursuing Perfection."
39. DQHS, 739:1a–6b.
40. Hua, "Qing wangchao."
41. A search of Academia Sinica's database, Scripta Sinica, for the *Qing shilu* yields a wealth of entries for either of these terms, but not the two terms used together. For more information of this database, see hanchi.ihp.sinica.edu.tw.proxy.lib.umich.edu/ihp/hanji.htm.

42. Roth, *Manchu-Chinese Relationship*, 2–38.
43. Rhoads, *Manchus and Han*, 37; Stapleton, *Civilizing Chengdu*, 28–31.
44. Rhoads, *Manchus and Han*, 42.
45. It is also important to keep in mind that most Manchus were subject to mainly unwritten Manchu clan laws. For more on the Manchu clan organization, see Shirokogoroff, *Social Organization of the Manchus*.
46. Elliott, *Manchu Way*, 39–88.
47. Jones, *Great Qing Code*, 42. In referring to the Qing Code, I will use Jones's translation unless otherwise noted.
48. Lin, "Qingdai qimin falü," 41.
49. This has been observed by both Jean Escarra and Paul Ratchnevsky. See Escarra, *La Chine*, 5, and Ratchnevsky, *Un code des Yuan*, 1:lxxviii, 55, 200.
50. Jiang, *Great Ming Code*, 201; *Da Minglü zhijie suozai Minglü*, 585–86.
51. Philastre, *Le code annamite*, 2:452.
52. Elliott, *Manchu Way*, 254–55.
53. Rhoads, *Manchus and Han*, 36–37; Im, *Qingchao baqi*, 119.
54. Baller, *Sacred Edict*, 143–46.
55. Zhou and Gu, *Shengyu guangxun*, 128.
56. Elliott, *Manchu Way*, 339.
57. DQLS, Yongzheng, 48:1a–b (27 September 1726); also quoted in Lin, "Qingdai qimin falü," 43.
58. Rhoads, *Manchus and Han*, 290. To what extent Manchu bannermen are an ethnic group is open to debate. For alternative views see Elliott, *Manchu Way*, 1–35, and Crossley, "Thinking about Ethnicity."
59. Elliott, *Manchu Way*, 333–42; Rhoads, *Manchus and Han*, 292.
60. Zhongguo diyi lishi dang'anguan, *Kangxi qiju zhu*, 1:544; see also Lin, "Qingdai qimin falü," 42, 50.
61. Ding, "Qingdai lishi tongzhi," 264. I am indebted to Mark C. Elliott for introducing me to Ding Yizhuang's work. I have chosen to translate *lishi tongzhi* as "judicial subprefect" in order to demonstrate the institutional continuity. Elliott prefers to translate it as "civil commissioner"; see Elliott, *Manchu Way*, 226. Elliott's translation has a long history and can be traced back to Giles, *Chinese-English Dictionary*, 865.
62. Ding, "Qingdai lishi tongzhi," 264–65.
63. DQLS, Kangxi, 104:20b–21a (6 October 1682); see also Ding, "Qingdai lishi tongzhi," 264.
64. DQLS, Kangxi, 125:4b–5a (28 March 1686); see also Ding, "Qingdai lishi tongzhi," 264.
65. Changshan, *Zhu Yue baqi zhi*, 17:6a–6b.
66. Jones, *Qing Code*, 326; Ding, "Qingdai lishi tongzhi," 265–66.
67. Xinzhu, *Fuzhou zhufang zhi*, 6:15b–16a.
68. DQHS, 25–27.
69. Zheng, "Yongzheng, Qianlong shiqi," 647–48; Isett, *State, Peasant, and Merchant*, 61.
70. DQHS, 819:18b–23b.
71. Xue, *Duli cunyi dianzhu*, 705–706.
72. DQHS, 819:18b–23b; see also Elliott, *Manchu Way*, 199.
73. Li, "Ming-Qing de falü zhidu," 248–50.
74. See, for instance, *Huijiang zeli*, 6:18 in Zhongguo bianjiang shidi yanjiu zhongxin, *Menggu lüli, Huijiang zeli*.
75. Alabaster, *Notes and Commentaries*, 11.
76. Ch'ü, *Local Government*, 125.
77. Geertz, *Local Knowledge*, 195.
78. For more on how the "checks and balances" in the Qing legal order worked in theory and practice, see Alford, "Of Arsenic and Old Laws."
79. Elliott, *Manchu Way*, 226.

80. Ding, "Qingdai lishi tongzhi," 264.
81. Hucker, *Dictionary*, 553–54.
82. Hucker, "Governmental Organization," 45, 58–59.
83. Mayers, *Chinese Government*, 38; Zhang, *Qingdai fazhi yanjiu*, 1:170–71; for a survey of how the subprefect worked in the treaty port of Hankou, see Rowe, *Hankow*, 31–35.
84. Brunnert and Hagelström, *Political Organization*, 460; Lee, *Manchurian Frontier*, 73.
85. DQHS, 1:337b.
86. DQLS, Qianlong, 204:18a–b, translated in Fu, *Documentary Chronicle*, 176; see also Edwards, "Ch'ing Legal Jurisdiction," 227.
87. Changshan, *Zhu Yue baqi zhi*, 1:7b–7a.
88. See sections "Rehe lishi tongzhi" and "Bagou lishi tongzhi," in *Zhili Rehe tongzhi fuyi quanshu*.
89. Xinzhu, *Fuzhou zhufang zhi*, 6:15b–16a.
90. As Lin Qian has pointed out, this important point has eluded Zheng Qin. Lin, "Qingdai qimin falü," 50 n. 45; Zheng, *Qingdai falü zhidu yanjiu*, 304.
91. On the importance of "clarity of language" under the Qing, see Metzger, *Internal Organization*, 105.
92. Fortunately for the historian, the occurrences of words and their contexts can now be tested empirically by searching databases. A search of the Scripta Sinica database for the Xianfeng (1851–61), Tongzhi (1862–74), and Guangxu (1875–1908) reigns shows that *lishi* was almost always prefixed to *tongzhi* or *tongpan* and related compounds. From the beginning of the Guangxu period, *lishi* starts to be used for consuls in compounds such as *lishi shu*, *fu lishi* and *lishiguan*. Note that *lishiguan* could refer both to a judge in the imperial clan court and to Qing consuls in Japan (*lishi fu*). Out of twenty-nine hits for *lishi* in the Xianfeng period, nineteen referred to *lishi tongzhi, lishi tongpan, lishiguan,* or *lishi siyuan*. The same figures for the Tongzhi period are thirty-seven hits out of forty-four and for the Guangxu period 107 hits out of 115. (Search of *Qing Shilu* in Scripta Sinica for the Xianfeng, Tongzhi, and Guangxu periods; hanchi.ihp.sinica.edu.tw.proxy.lib.umich.edu/ihp/hanji.htm, 24 September 2010.) As with many other Qing titles and names, it is also useful to compare the term with its Manchu counterpart. (See Nie, "Man'guan hanshi," 6; Chen, *Manchu Archival Materials*, 5.) In this case, the nature of the office becomes somewhat clearer when one examines the Manchu name: *weile beidere tungjy* or *weile beidere uhei saraci*, the meaning of which roughly corresponds to "crime-punishing subprefect." (Elliott, *Manchu Way*, 461 n. 82; Hu, *Xin Manhan dacidian*, 810.)
93. Mayers, *Chinese Government*, 38.
94. Ding, "Qingdai lishi tongzhi," 266.
95. Ibid.
96. See maps of Qingzhou garrison and Fuzhou garrison. Elliott, *Manchu Way*, 113; Im, *Qingchao baqi*, 215.
97. Deposition from Chao Tingzuo, Shuntian fu, 28-4-201-005.
98. Communication from district magistrate Wang to judicial subprefect, 5 August 1803, Shuntian fu, 28-4-201-020.
99. Shuntian fu, 28-4-2-1-061.
100. See for instance Yinghe's memorial to the throne in 1825, quoted in He, *Huangchao jingshi wenbian*, 35:11b–14a.
101. Lin, "Qingdai qimin falü," 47.
102. Zhang, *Daoxian huanhai jianwen*, 36–8; quoted in Ding, "Qingdai lishi tongzhi," 267, and Elliott, *Manchu Way*, 227.
103. Fairbank, "Synarchy under the Treaties," 204–31.
104. DQLS, Tongzhi, 144:26a–27a (23 July 1865); the edict is translated in Kingsmill, "Retrospect of Events," 139–40.
105. Lin, "Qingdai qimin falü," 47; DQLS, Tongzhi, 181 (4 September 1866).

106. *Dianshizhai huabao*, 235:54 (1890). In order to correctly date issues in this important journal, I have used the table in Mohr, *Die moderne chinesische Tagespresse*, 2:161–62.
107. See regulations from Zongli yamen on missionary activities, 24 March 1896, reprinted in Chen, *Qingdai dongbei*, 285–86.
108. Isett, *State, Peasant and Merchant*, 111–15.
109. China Maritime Customs, *Decennial Reports*, 21.
110. Plaint filed by Deng Wei, 23 October 1882, Lishi fumin fu, 2.31.
111. Bond (*ganjie*), 31 October 1882, Lishi fumin fu, 2.31.
112. Im, *Qingchao baqi*, 123–125, 182 n. 166. I have been unable to track down the source Im relied on for her account of this event, but the incident was deemed important enough to be included in the Qing *Veritable Records*; DQLS, Guangxu, 436:19b–20a (8 February 1899).
113. Zhou and Gu, *Shengyu guangxun jijie*, 424.
114. The Tokugawa social order has alternatively been described as a centralized form of feudalism or as a federal system of government. This is not the place to take a stand in that discussion, except to say that unlike feudal kingdoms in Europe, where kings did not always have an unrestricted right to interfere with the privileges of the aristocracy, the shogun did have the power to dismiss and remove territorial lords who did not please him. "Centralized feudalism" is first used by George Bailey Sansom, in *Japan: A Short Cultural*, 444–458. The term "federalism" comes from Berry, *Hideyoshi*, 147–67. See also Ishii, *Nihonjin*, 233–36.
115. As Howell has demonstrated, Japan did not have any clearly delimited territorial boundaries prior to the Meiji restoration. Howell, *Geographies of Identity*.
116. For more on the *kokudaka* system, see Howell, *Geographies of Identity*, 22–24.
117. Botsman, *Punishment and Power*, 59–61.
118. Haley, *Authority without Power*, 46.
119. "The status system was therefore decidedly not a caste system in which birth permanently determined one's station in life, nor was status the Tokugawa era's functional equivalent of race." Howell, *Geographies of Identity*, 21. For a different view on the concept of race during the Tokugawa period, see Ooms, *Tokugawa Village Practice*, 302.
120. As David L. Howell has pointed out, this "mobility was not constrained by an ideology of essential identity such as race or caste." Howell, *Geographies of Identity*, 21, 25.
121. Henderson, *Conciliation and Japanese Law*, 1:15–17.
122. Henderson, "Chinese Legal Studies."
123. Kobayakawa, *Kinsei minji soshō*, 700; Howell, *Geographies of Identity*, 20–44.
124. Kobayakawa, *Kinsei minji soshō*, 703.
125. Botsman, *Punishment and Power*, 79–84.
126. Hiramatsu, *Kinsei keiji soshō*, 20–21. I am indebted to Dani Botsman for directing my attention to this important work on Tokugawa law.
127. Katō, "Governing Edo," 47; see also the Japanese version of the same article, "Edo no shihai to sono tokushitsu."
128. Botsman, *Punishment and Power*, 80–82.
129. Henderson, *Conciliation and Japanese Law*, 1:92–97; Whereas Henderson prefers to call this category of cases "diversity cases," I have chosen to call them "mixed cases" in consonance with my general argument.
130. Kobayakawa, *Kinsei minji soshō*, 700.
131. Kobayakawa, *Kinsei minji soshō*, 767.
132. For a brief list of possible combinations, see Henderson, *Conciliation and Japanese Law*, 1:94; for a more exhaustive treatment, see Kobayakawa, *Kinsei minji soshō*, 697–768, and Hiramatsu, *Kinsei keiji soshō*, 65–88.
133. Kobayakawa, *Kinsei minji soshō*, 156–60.
134. Kobayakawa, *Kinsei minji soshō*, 77, 703; the perhaps most accessible treatment of mixed jurisdiction is Kikuyama, "Meiji shonen," 169–214.

135. Kobayakawa, *Kinsei minji soshō*, 723.
136. Henderson, *Conciliation and Japanese Law*, 1:77, 92, 95.
137. "It never occurred to shogunal policy makers that Japan could be a multiethnic empire in which non-Japanese (that is, uncivilized) peoples would be subject to sovereignty of the Japanese state in the same manner as the core population." Howell, *Geographies of Indentity*, 198.
138. Lehmann, "Léon Roches."
139. Entry for 28 July 1871, in Kido, *Diary of Kido Takayoshi*, 48.
140. Ravina, *Last Samurai*, 168–72; for a more exhaustive treatment, see Kikuyama, *Meiji kokka no keisei*. On a journey to France, a Japanese passenger informed the Qing official Zhang Deyi about the reforms, which Zhang interpreted as a shift from a "feudal" (*fengjian*) to a "prefectural" (*junxian*) form of government. See entry for 16 November 1870, in Zhang Deyi, *Suishi Faguo ji*, 61.
141. Ravina, *Last Samurai*, 166–72.
142. Howell, *Geographies of Identity*, 67–69.
143. This process forms an interesting counterpart to the state-building projects in sixteenth-century Germany, where Roman law was used as a vehicle to assert the territorial sovereignty (*Landeshoheit*) of German states such as Saxony. See Strauss, *Law, Resistance, and the State*.
144. Ch'en, *Formation*, 3–30.
145. Tsunoda, *Sources of Japanese Tradition*, 704; see also Ravina, *Last Samurai*, 2–3.
146. Henderson, *Conciliatioon and Japanese Law*, 1:87.
147. Fukuzawa Yukichi's mention of *kirisute gomen* actually antedates this edict by a year; see *Gakumon no susume* (1871), in Fukuzawa, *Fukuzawa Yukichi chosakushū*, 3:20.
148. Bix, *Hirohito*, 27, 30, 693.
149. For an instructive discussion on modern citizenship and different concepts of citizenship, see Caldwell, "Citizen and the Republic."
150. Ch'en, *Formation*, 73; for more on Boissonade and his influence on Japanese law, see Antonetti et al., *Boissonade*; Ikeda, "French Legal Advisor."
151. One attempt is Chiba, *Legal Pluralism*; see also Haley, *Spirit of Japanese Law*.
152. Haley, *Authority without Power*, 69.
153. On the limits of using German models as an explanation for institutional change in Japan, see Mehl, "Meiji shigaku."
154. Although I agree with the main thrust of Mark Ravina's argument about the character of the Meiji restoration, I disagree with some of the parallels between Japan, Italy, and Germany that he draws in Ravina, *Land and Lordship*, 200–201. Whereas the duke of Parma and grand duke of Tuscany were deposed during the Risorgimento in 1859–60, the king of Württemberg and the two grand dukes of the Mecklenburg states retained power in Bismarcks's imperial German state, and they were not deposed until 1918, in the wake of the German revolution.
155. Incidentally, his archives are today one of our major sources of knowledge about the local Qing legal order.
156. This plural legal order has left behind a rich repository of local archives, such as village and temple records, that have given material to a rich literature on the relationship between different legal entities and the state. See, for instance, Henderson, *Village "Contracts."*
157. Hooker, *Legal Pluralism*, 158–81. Hooker is however careful to point out that the Chinese "customary law," which was enforced in the British colonies, was "wholly the invention of the colonial courts." For more on colonial courts and the invention of tradition, see Bourgon, "Le droit coutumier."
158. Even after the establishment of the People's Republic of China in 1949, the Chinese criminal code has retained a lot of terminology that dated from the imperial era. See Finkelstein, "Language of Communist China's Criminal Law," 190; for a contrasting view, see van der Valk, "Previous Chinese Legal Language."
159. This point has been eloquently made by Edward Farmer as regards early Ming legislation. See Farmer, *Zhu Yuanzhang* 103–4.

Chapter 2

1. Wakeman, *Policing Shanghai*, 289.
2. Alcock, "China and Its Foreign Relations."
3. Rutherford Alcock to Lord Stanley, 24 December 1868, in Foreign Office of Great Britain, *Correspondence*, 271.
4. Jiang, *Ming Code*, 43.
5. Johnson, *T'ang Code*, 1:252. See also Kuwabara, "On P'u Shou-kêng," 46.
6. Jiang, *Ming Code*, 43.
7. Jiang, *Ming Code*, lxii.
8. Jones, *Qing Code*, 67–68; Xue Yunsheng, *Duli cunyi*, 89–91.
9. Edwards, "Ch'ing Legal Jurisdiction," 225.
10. Alabaster, "Notes on Chinese Law," 94. Indeed, the section on "peoples outside of civilization" in the *Supplement to the Collected Statutes of the Great Qing Dynasty* only deals with Mongols, Miao, and Moslems. DQHS, 739:1a–6b.
11. Edwards, "Ch'ing Legal Jurisdiction," 225.
12. Edwards, "Ch'ing Legal Jurisdiction," 226.
13. Ljungstedt, *Historical Sketch*, 75–76.
14. Edwards, "Ch'ing Legal Jurisdiction," 226–27.
15. Ljungstedt, *Historical Sketch*, 110–11.
16. Edwards, "Ch'ing Legal Jurisdiction," 226–28.
17. Dzereng's memorial, 27 December 1743, DQLS, Qianlong, 204:18a–b; English translation in Fu, *Documentary Chronicle*, 1:176.
18. Edwards, "Ch'ing Legal Jurisdiction," 227–32; the decree is also quoted in Ljungstedt, *Historical Sketch*, 81.
19. Fu, *Documentary Chronicle*, 1:193–94; also quoted in Edwards, "Ch'ing Legal Jurisdiction," 252–55. The Qianlong emperor's pragmatic approach stands in contrast to Lin Zexu, who quoted the aforementioned Franco-British case as a precedent when he argued that the British suspected murderer of Lin Weixi should be surrendered in 1839. See the English translation of Lin's proclamation, 2 August 1839, in "Proclamation of the High Imperial Commissioner, concerning the murder of Lin Weihe," *Chinese Repository* 8, no. 4 (August 1839), 213–15.
20. Edwards, "Ch'ing Legal Jurisdiction," 259.
21. Koo, *Status of Aliens*, 47.
22. Sousa, *Capitulatory Régime*, 84–86. The term "dragoman" derives from the Arabic word *turjumān*, meaning "translator" or "interpreter."
23. For an interesting treatment of the question of collective responsibility, see Chen, "Law, Empire and Historiography."
24. "After the Lady Hughes case in 1784, the English resolved never again to submit to Chinese criminal jurisdiction." Edwards, "Ch'ing Legal Jurisdiction," 260.
25. Chen, "Law, Empire and Historiography."
26. An exhaustive study of Qing border policies, covering all jurisdictions that were contiguous to the vast Manchu Empire, is yet to be written.
27. Perdue, *China Marches West*, 161–73.
28. Mancall, *Russia and China*, 157, 282–83. For the Manchu version of article 6, see SDRK, 9.
29. In the second edict to King George III in September 1793, the Qianlong emperor did indeed draw a parallel between the Portuguese settlement in Macau and the Russian trading station in Kiahkta. Cheng and Lestz, *Search for Modern China*, 107.
30. Harrison, *Man Awakened from Dreams*, 22. For an intriguing account of the trade at Kiakhta in the mid-eighteenth century, see Liljevalch, *Chinas handel*, 301–7.
31. Mancall, *Russia and China*, 253.
32. The Manchu version of the article can be found in SDRK, 61–62; for an English translation from the Chinese version, see Mancall, *Russia and China*, 302.

33. SDRK, 65–66; Mancall, *Russia and China,* 304–5.
34. SDRK, 71–72; Mancall, *Russia and China,* 309. See also Hsü, *China's Entrance,* 139.
35. Since there is no single English term that would do full justice to the office known in Manchu as *Tulergi golo dasara jurgan* and in Chinese as *Lifanyuan,* I have chosen to use the well-established term "Court of Colonial Affairs" for reasons of simplicity. If we are conformable using "Grand Council" as the English name for the *Junjichu* (Manchu: *Coohai nashūn i ba*), which literally translates as "Council for Military Secrets," I see little reason why we should invent a new term for the *Lifanyuan.*

    The question to what extent the Qing Empire should be termed a "colonial empire" is a separate issue, which is subject to an interesting discussion in Perdue, "Comparing Empires," and in Hostetler, *Qing Colonial Enterprise.*
36. DQLS, Qianlong, 202:32a–32b; for an English translation, see Fu, *Documentary Chronicle,* 1:176.
37. The Manchu text of the article can be found in SDRK, 88–89; for a French translation, see Hertslet, *Treaties between Great Britain and China,* 1:302–3. Wellington Koo's insistence that the Chinese translation of the treaty is the most valid (*Status of Aliens,* 52 n. 1) is somewhat misplaced, given the fact that there was no official Chinese text of the treaty at the time of its conclusion. The only major discrepancy between Hertslet's French translation and the Manchu version of the article deals with the manner of reporting executions, which should read in English: "If they be people from the Central Kingdom (*Dulimbai gurun*), they should be beheaded after the matter has been reported to the Court of Colonial Affairs; if they are Russians, they should be beheaded after the matter has been reported to the Russian senate." The translation from Manchu is my own.
38. Mancall, *Russia and China,* 269.
39. Fletcher, "Heyday of the Ch'ing Order," 377–79.
40. Pan, *Zhongya Haohanguo,* 22.
41. In her recent work on Qing relations with Khoqand, Laura J. Newby basically concurs with Pan Zhiping's assertion that the Khoqandi settlement had little to do with extraterritoriality. See Newby, *Empire,* 184–99. However, it is noteworthy that elsewhere in her book, she actually refers to a legal suit between a Kashgari and a Khoqandi merchant, which was resolved with the *hakim beg*—the local Muslim official—acting "in conjunction with the akhunds and the Khoqandi aqsaqal." This actually provides strong evidence to the effect that Qing authorities were indeed inclined to devolve jurisdiction in Inner Asia. See Newby, *Empire,* 218 n. 31. I am indebted to Scott Levi for directing my attention to this important work.
42. Communication from Changling, 13 April 1832, LFZZ 3-161-7701-45.
43. Memorial from Songyun, 3 March *1831,* LFZZ, 3-161-7701-34 and memorial from Songyun, 1 October *1831,* LFZZ 3-161-7701-36. On the costs of maintaining Qing rule in Xinjiang, see for instance Fletcher, "Sino-Russian Relations," 60–61.
44. Some Qing officials evidently felt that the emperor had gone too far in granting these concessions. Polachek, *Inner Opium War,* 349 n. 26.
45. Interview with Khoqandi envoy, 13 April 1832, LFZZ, 3-161-7701-44. The English translation is excerpted from Newby, *Empire,* 189–90 (Chinese terms in brackets are inserted by me).
46. In a seminal article on Inner Asian diplomacy, Pan Zhiping and Jiang Lili have made systematic comparisons between some Chinese and Turkic archival material, where they show how Qing officials softened the tone in Khoqandi communications without changing the contents when they reported them to the throne. See Pan and Jiang, "1832 nian Qing yu Haohan"; for a similar conclusion, see Millward, *Eurasian Crossroads.*
47. Stephens, *Order and Discipline,* 61.
48. Petition from Khoqandi beg, 13 April *1832,* LFZZ, 3-161-7701-43.
49. Transcript of *note verbal* from Qing envoys He Ruzhang and Zhang Sigui to Japanese foreign minister Terajima Nunenori, 14 January 1878, GKS 4.1.1.14.

50. This forms an interesting parallel to Philip Huang's observation that the Qing code was not just employed a set of carefully drafted criminal laws but also could be used as a normative guide on how to resolve private disputes in a noncriminal way. See Philip C. Huang, *Civil Justice in China*, 8. For more on how the Confucian family system informed penal law, see Jiang, *Ming Code*, lxxii–lxxiii.
51. Guo, *Zhuanzhe*, 481.
52. "The change in legal theory in the West is an important factor in explaining British behavior in China in the nineteenth century in contrast to Russian behavior in the seventeenth and eighteenth." Mancall, *Russia and China*, 271.
53. Frederic Wakeman, Jr., "Canton Trade," 175–78.
54. Chang, *Commissioner Lin*, 186.
55. For a list of important imperial edicts against opium, see Chang, *Commissioner Lin*, 219–21.
56. For an interesting interpretation of Qing policy-making at the eve of the Opium War, see Polachek, *Inner Opium War*, 89–102.
57. See Chang, *Commissioner Lin*, 85–111, and Polachek, *Inner Opium War*, 101–35, for exhaustive treatments of the debate. For a more recent account, see Mao Haijian, *Tianchao de bengkui*, 89–102.
58. Wakeman, "Opium Trade," 181.
59. Chang, *Commissioner Lin*, 92.
60. The full text of the regulations can be found in YPZZ, 1:557–81, and in Liang, *Yue haiguan*, 19:10–59. For an extended discussion of the rules, see Bello, *Opium and the Limits of Empire*, 114–76.
61. Chang, *Commissioner Lin*, 97–98.
62. Lin's memorial to the throne, 18 May 1839, YPZZ, 2:149.
63. Têng and Fairbank, *China's Response to the West*, 26–27; for an alternative translation, see Liu, *Clash of Empires*, 229–241.
64. YPZZ, 2:171, 2:243.
65. Luo, *Hanyu dacidian*, 5:1041. The term can alternatively be translated as "legal standards"; see Brook et al., *Death by a Thousand Cuts*, 77.
66. YPZZ, 4:18–21.
67. The term *guanxia* was one of the most usual terms to describe "jurisdiction" in Qing dynasty administrative Chinese. For instance, the term occurs no fewer than 2,368 times in the *Veritable Records of the Qing Dynasty* (search on Scripta Sinica, 8 May 2009). Deborah Cao is thus mistaken in considering *guanxia* one of the terms that W. A. P. Martin coined in his famous translation of the *Law of Nations*; see Cao, *Chinese Law*, 163.
68. Sir R. Alcock to Lord Stanley, Peking, 23 December 1868, in Foreign Office of Great Britain, *Correspondence*, 261–68. Many of Li Zexu's most precise statements against "extraterritoriality" that Chang Hsin-pao quotes are actually taken from the English translations that were published in the *Chinese Repository*. See for instance Chang, *Commissioner Lin*, 182.
69. See for instance, the Grand Council's comments on the demands on treaty revision from the four great treaty powers in 1858, in DCYPZZ, 3:351–52.
70. This point is made convincingly in Mao, *Tianchao de bengkui*.
71. For instance, when Sir Rutherford Alcock responded to Zeng Jize's impassioned appeal to the English public to redress the inequities of the commercial treaties, he interpreted Zeng's statement as an attack on extraterritoriality and felt compelled to justify a practice that he actually had deep reservations about, despite the fact that Zeng did not mention law or extraterritoriality in the original statement. Zeng Jize, "China," and Alcock, "China and Its Foreign Relations."
72. Guo, *Zhuanzhe*, 490.
73. Chang, *Commissioner Lin*, 179–88.
74. Chang, *Commissioner Lin*, 195–202; Waley, *Opium War*, 61–64.
75. Lord Palmerston to Sir Henry Pottinger, 21 May 1841, in Morse, *International Relations*, 1:655–59.

76. Historian Guo Weidong has recovered the Chinese text of the draft regulations on extraterritoriality. See Guo, *Zhuanzhe*, 475–86.
77. Guo suggests that the Chinese rejected British demands for participation in mixed trials. However, the sources Guo quotes do not bear out this claim; the only thing we can say with certainty is that the question was shelved for the time being. Guo, *Zhuanzhe*, 482.
78. See for instance, the note from Qiying, Ilibu, and Niu Jian to Sir Henry Pottinger, 1 September 1842, in Sasaki, *Ahen sensō*, 218.
79. Tsiang, "Extension of Equal Commercial Privileges"; for a recent treatment of most-favored-nations status, see Guo, *Zhuanzhe*, 560–88.
80. Thus Lydia Liu, who seems to be unaware of T. F. Tsiang's seminal article on the topic, is mistaken in claiming that Fairbank was engaging in "speculation" on the origins of most-favored-nation treatment. Liu, *Clash of Empires*, 5.
81. Wang, *China's Unequal Treaties*, 4.
82. "XIII.—Disputes between British subjects and Chinese. Whenever a British subject has to complain of a Chinese he must first proceed to the Consulate and state his grievance. The Consul will thereupon enquire into the merits of the case and do his utmost to arrange it amicably. In like manner, if a Chinese have reason to complain of a British subject, he shall no less listen to his complaint, and endeavour to settle it in a friendly manner. If unfortunately, any disputes take place of such a nature that the Consul cannot arrange them amicably, then he shall request the assistance of a Chinese Officer that they may together examine into the merits of the case, and decide it equitably. Regarding the punishment of English criminals, the English Government will enact the laws necessary to attain that end, and the Consul will be empowered to put them into force; and regarding the punishment of Chinese criminals, these will be tried and punished by their own laws, in the way provided for by correspondence which took place at Nanking, after the concluding of the peace." TCCF, 1:388.
83. This was also the case, as we will see in chapter 4, in the Japanese treaties, as was eloquently argued by Sheppard in *Extra-territoriality in Japan*.
84. For an interesting case study on this issue, see Wagner, "*Shenbao* in Crisis."
85. Guo, *Zhuanzhe*, 483–84.
86. Fairbank, *Trade and Diplomacy*, 1:119–27.
87. Hietala, *Manifest Design*, 59–60.
88. Pinkney, *Decisive Years in France*, 128; Maybon and Fredet, *Histoire*, 4.
89. What is believed to be the table where the treaty as signed can still be admired in the Kun Iam temple today. For a picture, see Shipp, *Macau, China*, 69.
90. TCCF, 1:690.
91. Caleb Cushing to Calhoun, 29 April 1844, in ADPP1, 8:20.
92. "Article XXXIII.—Citizens of the United States who shall attempt to trade clandestinely with such of the ports of China as are not open to Foreign commerce, or who shall trade in opium or any other contraband articles of merchandise, shall be subject to be dealt with by the Chinese Government, without being entitled to any countenance or protection from that of the United States; and the United States will take measures to prevent their flag from being abused by the subjects of other nations as a cover for the violation of the laws of the empire." TCCF, 1:689.
93. "Article XXV.—All questions in regard to rights, whether of property or person, arising between citizens of the United States in China, shall be subject to the jurisdiction of, and regulated by the authorities of their own Government; and all controversies occurring in China between citizens of the United States and subjects of any other Government shall be regulated by the treaties existing between the United States and such Governments, respectively, without interference on the part of China." TCCF, 1:687.
94. Keeton, *Development of Extraterritoriality*, 1:285.
95. "Article XXVII.—Si malheureusement, il s'élevait quelque rixe ou quelque querelle entre des Français et des Chinois, comme aussi dans le cas où, durant le cours d'une semblable

querelle, ou un plusieurs individus seraient tués ou blessés. Soit par des coups de feu soit autrement, les Chinois seront arrêtés pat l'Autorité Chinoise, qui se chargera de les faire examiner et punir, s'il y a lieu, conformément aux lois du pays. Quant aux Français, ils seront arrêtés à la diligence du Consul, et celui-ci prendra toutes les mesures nécessaires pour que les prévenus soient livrés à l'action régulière des lois françaises dans la forme et suivant les dispositions qui seront ultérieurement déterminées par le Gouvernement Français.

"Il en sera de même en toute circonstance analogue et non prévue dans la présent Convention, le principe étant que, pour la répression des crimes et délits commis par eux en Chine, les Français seront constamment régis par les lois Françaises." TCCF, 1:785.

96. Grosse-Aschhoff, *Negotiations*, 64.
97. Qiying's memorial, 28 July 1844, YWSM, Daoguang, 72:18b; for an English translation, see Swisher, *China's Management*, 164. Callery, *Correspondance diplomatique*.
98. Qiying to Lagrené, 16 and 21 October 1844; Lagrené to Qiying, 22 October 1844, in Callery, *Correspondance diplomatique*, 51–74.
99. Guo, *Zhuanzhe*, 470–511.
100. Grosse-Aschhoff, *Negotiations*, 79; Morse, *International Relations*, 1:331–32.
101. Lagrené to Qiying, 25 December 1844, Callery, *Correspondance diplomatique*, 108–9; Morse, *International Relations*, 1:332.
102. Qiying's memorial to the throne, rescripted 27 April 1847. YPZZDASL, 7:785–86.
103. Mende, "Norges økonomiske interesser," 3.
104. NCDN, 31 October 1877.
105. This ambiguity would not be resolved until Sweden and China concluded a new treaty in 1908, which was duly ratified by both parties the following year. Cassel, "Traktaten som aldrig var."
106. Joseph Fletcher, "Sino-Russian Relations," 330–32. The treaty was concluded in a Russian and Manchu version; no official Chinese version exists. For the official texts of the treaty, see SDRK, 69–109; a Chinese translation is reprinted in Wang, *Zhongwai jiu yuezhang*, 1:78–80.
107. Hsü, *China's Entrance*, 142.
108. Mujangga's memorial, 15 August 1844, translated in Swisher, *China's Management*, 168.
109. For a summary of the most important incidents, see Morse, *International Relations*, 1:366–99.
110. Liljevalch, *Chinas handel*, 172; the translation from the Swedish original text is my own.
111. Fairbank, *Trade and Diplomacy*, 1:201–2; Wong, *Deadly Dreams*, 115.
112. Fairbank, "Creation of the Treaty System," 244–46.
113. Harry Parkes's manipulation of the "Arrow incident" has been carefully analyzed by John Y. Wong in his magisterial work *Deadly Dreams*, 43–66.
114. Morse, *International Relations*, 1:414–15.
115. For a summary of the case, see Morse, *International Relations*, 1:479–82.
116. Cohen, "Christian Missions," 550.
117. Wei, *La politique missionnaire*, 488–91.
118. For an entertaining account of the vicissitudes of Huc's missionary ventures in China, see Leys, *Burning Forest*, 47–94.
119. Memorial by the governor-general of Sichuan, Baoxing, to the throne, 14 July 1846, YPZZDASL, 7:675–77.
120. This policy would in due course lead to the loss of central control over capital punishment. For more on this, see Zheng, *Qingdai falü zhidu yanjiu*, 13.
121. Cooke, *China and Lower Bengal*, 430–31; for Chaloner Alabaster's notes on Ye's comments, see Wong, *Deadly Dreams*, 267 n. 37.
122. For a sympathetic portrait of this intriguing figure, see Wong, *Yeh Ming-ch'en*.
123. Morse, *International Relations*, 1:483–485.
124. Morse, *International Relations*, 1:504–5. In this work, Bogui is called "Pikwei."
125. Report from Huang Zonghan on conditions in Guangzhou under the British occupation, 8 June 1858, DCYPZZ, 3:378.

126. "With only five thousand troops and two Chinese interpreters, the Allies had to have the cooperation of the existing authorities if they hoped to rule a hostile and turbulent population of one million." Wakeman, *Strangers at the Gate*, 161.
127. "Article XVI.—Chinese subjects who may be guilty of any criminal act towards British subjects shall be arrested and punished by the Chinese authorities according to the Laws of China. British subjects who may commit any crime in China shall be tried and punished by the Consul or other Public Functionary authorized thereto according to the Laws of Great Britain. Justice shall be equitably and impartially administered on both sides." TCCF, 1:409.
128. Swisher, *China's Management*, 505; see also Spence, *To Change China*, 102.
129. Sir Thomas Wade's report to the earl of Denby, 14 July 1877, in Foreign Office of Great Britain, *Further Correspondence*, 143.
130. Chiang, *China's Destiny*, 55–56; Guo, *Zhuanzhe*, 481–82.
131. The French sinologist and diplomat Georges Soulié de Morant blamed the deficiencies of this article on Chinese influence: "Nous trouvons, dès le début, d'assez grandes divergences; et nous constatons, là comme dans les autres parties des traités, un grand manque de clarté dans les idées et une absence regrettable des termes précis de la phraséologie juridique européenne: l'influence chinoise a imposé ses expressions nébuleuses et vagues." *Droits conventionnels*, 76.
132. "Article XVII.—A British subject having reason to complain of a Chinese must proceed to the Consulate and state his grievance. The Consul will inquire into the merits of the case, and do his utmost to arrange it amicably. In like manner, if a Chinese have a reason to complain of a British subject, the Consul shall no less listen to his complaint, and endeavour to settle it in a friendly manner. If disputes take place, then he shall request the assistance of the Chinese authorities, that they may together examine into the merits of the case and decide it equitably." TCCF, 1:409.
133. Memorial from Guiliang, Huashana, and Qiying to the throne, 9 June 1858, DCYPZZ, 3:389. For a classic account of the negotiations, see Hsü, *China's Entrance*, 46–70.
134. For more on this point, see Liu, *Clash of Empires*, 112; see also Wong, *Anglo-Chinese Relations*, 7–8.
135. Cohen, "Christian Missions," 552–53.
136. "Article XI.—All citizens of the United States of America in China peaceably attending to their affairs, being placed on a common footing of amity and goodwill with subjects of China, shall receive and enjoy, for themselves and everything appertaining to them, the protection of the local authorities of Government, who shall defend them from all insult or injury of any sort. If their dwellings or property be threatened or attacked by mobs, incendiaries, or other violent or lawless persons, the local officers, on requisition of the Consul, shall immediately despatch a military force to disperse the rioters, apprehend the guilty individuals, and punish them with the utmost rigour of the law. Subjects of China shall be punished by the Chinese authorities according to the laws of China; and citizens of the United States who may insult, trouble or wound the persons or injure the property of Chinese, or commit any other act in China shall be punished only by the Consul or other public functionary thereto authorized according to the laws of the United States. Arrests in order to trial may be made by either the Chinese or the United States authorities." TCCF, 1:717–8. The Sino-American Treaty of Tianjin was concluded on 18 June 1858.
137. The Sino-Russian Treaty of Tianjin was concluded on 13 June 1858. For the original Manchu, Chinese, Russian, and French versions of the treaties with Russia, see SDRK, 122–58.
138. Hao and Wang, "Changing Chinese Views," 194.
139. Rutherford Alcock to Lord Stanley, 24 December 1868, in Foreign Office of Great Britain, *Correspondence*, 271.
140. The convention was concluded in 1869 as a supplement to the Treaty of Tianjin but never ratified, due to merchant opposition to the stationing of Qing consuls in Hong Kong.
141. Cohen, "Christian Missions," 552. The Sino-French convention of Beijing was concluded on 18 October 1860.

142. When the Qianlong emperor opposed banning Islam in 1782, he took a similar rhetorical stance, arguing that Moslems were no different from Daoists, Buddhists, or lamas. Lipman, "Fierce and Brutal People," 102. For the original edict, see DQLS, Qianlong, 1159:10b–12b.
143. YWSM, Tongzhi, 82:13a–14a.
144. Cohen, *China and Christianity*, 257.

Chapter 3

1. Wright and Cartwright, *Twentieth Century Impressions*, 401.
2. Memorial from Mujangga to the throne, 12 May 1843, YPZZDASL, 7:134–35.
3. Fairbank, *Trade and Diplomacy*, 1:210–12.
4. In the Shanghai dialect, *Yangjingbang* often means "broken English" or "broken Shangainese." See Min, *Wu fangyan*, 224. Yangjingbang was filled in 1914–15 and became Edward VII Avenue, today's Yan'an East Road.
5. The English version of the Land Regulations can be found in Xu and Qiu, *Shanghai gonggong zujie zhidu*, 200–208; for a Chinese translation, see Wang, *Zhongwai jiu yuezhang*, 1:65–70.
6. Leung, *Shanghai Taotai*, 46–49.
7. Keeton, *Development of Extraterritoriality*, 1:345; Kotenev, *Shanghai*, 4–6.
8. Kotenev, *Shanghai*, 55–56.
9. "Description of Shánghái," *Chinese Repository* 16, no. 11 (1847), 545. The curious accents are found in the original.
10. Maybon and Fredet, *Histoire*, 35–39; Bergère, *Shanghai*, 12–14.
11. Kotenev, *Shanghai*, 7–8.
12. Kotenev, *Shanghai*, 46–47.
13. Kotenev, *Shanghai*, 69.
14. "A concession comprises land, the whole of which has been leased to the foreign government, at a ground rent, the land then being sub-let to the foreign residents." Keeton, *Development of Extraterritoriality*, 321 n. 1.
15. Soulié de Morant, *Exterritorialité*, 173–74.
16. For a brief case study based on documents from the British foreign office archives, see Hammond, "Shanghai Mixed Court."
17. Kotenev, *Shanghai*, 11–13.
18. Lane-Poole, *Harry Parkes*, 1:482.
19. Keeton, *Development of Extraterritoriality*, 348.
20. Lane-Poole, *Harry Parkes*, 1:483.
21. Kotenev, *Shanghai*, 56.
22. Keeton, *Development of Extraterritoriality*, 1:348; Yao and Wu, *Shanghai xian xuzhi*, 2:4b.
23. The description of the assessors as "enthusiasts" comes from Barton, "Shanghai Mixed Court," 40.
24. Alabaster and Alabaster, *Notes and Commentaries*.
25. For a list of the first subprefects, see Ying and Yu, *Shanghai xianzhi*, 12:24b–25b; see also Leung, *Shanghai Taotai*, 58–59, 149.
26. Kotenev, *Shanghai*, 53.
27. Kotenev, *Shanghai*, 55–56.
28. Zou, *Zhapu beizhi*, 5:3b.
29. Keeton, *Development of Extraterritoriality*, 1:243.
30. *Times* (London), 13 July 1863, quoted in Keeton, *Development of Extraterritoriality*, 1:240–41.
31. For the rules regulating the court, see "Order in Council for the Better Government of Her Majesty's Subjects in the Dominions of the Emperor of China and the Tycoon of Japan. Windsor, 9th March 1865," in Hertslet, *Treaties*, 2:424–61.
32. Hornby, *Autobiography*, 191; Kayaoğlu, *Legal Imperialism*, 124–26.

33. Tahirih Lee claims that "Chinese authorities never approved this court as consistent with Treaty provisions," and quotes Kotenev as support for this. Lee, "Law and Local Autonomy," 112 n. 93. However, there is no basis for such a claim in Kotenev, *Shanghai,* 80, 85.
34. Edwards, "Ch'ing Legal Jurisdiction," 250.
35. Yao and Wu, *Shanghai xian xuzhi,* 14:9a–9b.
36. Motono, "Sino-British Conflict," 138.
37. Kotenev, *Shanghai,* 75; Kinouchi, *Shanhai rekishi,* 123. Kinouchi gives 1869 as the date of the move. The premises of the first Mixed Court were torn down long ago, and the location now houses Shanghai No 1 Food Store.
38. R. J. Forrest's second memorandum to Consul Charles A. Winchester (November 1868), in Foreign Office of Great Britain, *Correspondence,* 169.
39. Soulié de Morant, *Droits conventionnels,* 90–92; Kotenev, *Shanghai,* 60–68.
40. Kotenev, *Shanghai,* 69–70; Keeton, *Development of Extraterritoriality,* 400. *Tidjaret* derives from the Arabic word *tijāra,* meaning "commerce."
41. The French Mixed Court in Shanghai is an interesting topic that deserves more attention by scholars. For a brief introduction to the operation of the French Mixed Court, see Soulié de Morant, *Exterritorialité,* 146–68.
42. Chinese note from Sir Rutherford Alcock to Prince Gong, 14 December 1866 (Tongzhi 5.11.8), FO 230/80.
43. Chinese note from Prince Gong to Alcock, 22 December 1866 (Tongzhi 5.11.16), FO 230/81. It is not clear from the sources whether the Qing counterpart in these discussions was Li Hongzhang or Zeng Guofan, both of whom held the position of superintendent of trade and governor-general of Liangjiang in 1866. See Qian, *Qingdai zhiguan,* 2:1478.
44. Chinese note from Prince Gong to sir Rutherford Alcock, 3 May 1867 (Tongzhi 6.3.29), FO 230/81; an English translation of this document can be found in FO233/96.
45. R. J. Forrest's memorandum to Winchester (November 1868), in Foreign Office of Great Britain, *Correspondence,* 168.
46. Letter from Alcock to Hornby, 21 March 1868, FO 656/10. For more on Hornby's appraisal of the Ottoman legal system, see Kayaoğlu, *Legal Imperialism,* 124–26.
47. Letter from Alcock to Hornby, 21 March 1868, FO 656/10.
48. Wright, *Chinese Conservatism,* 21–42.
49. Prince Gong to Alcock, 20 October 1868, FO 230/81. An English translation can be found in ADPP2, 18:190–97. My Chinese quotes have been taken from the articles in the approved Chinese version of the Mixed Court rules that remained unchanged. See Kotenev, *Shanghai,* 70–71. For the Chinese text of the "Provisional Rules for the Mixed Court," see Yao and Wu, *Shanghai xian xuzhi,* 2:4b–6b, and Wang, *Zhongwai jiu yuezhang,* 269–70.
50. Ross Browne to Prince Gong, 17 November 1868, in ADPP2, 18:185–86.
51. E. Perkins [?], Bureau of Claims, commenting on the rules, 17 February 1869, in ADPP2, 18:202, 204.
52. NCDN, 20 April 1869.
53. Kotenev, *Shanghai,* 72.
54. Jean Escarra was the first scholar to point out that the Yuan court system could be seen as a precursor to the Mixed Courts in China; see Escarra, *Chine,* 5–6. Indeed, many of Escarra's arguments most likely derive from Paul Ratchnevsky's groundbreaking work on Mongol law, which was published later in the 1930s. See for instance, Ratchnevsky, *Code,* 1:lxxviii, 55, 200.
55. For more on the mixed courts in Egypt, see for instance Nathan J. Brown, "Mixed Courts of Egypt."
56. Wang, *Zhongwai jiu yuezhang,* 1:269.
57. Mark Elvin regarded these limitations on the powers of the Mixed Court subprefect as "anomalous from a Chinese point of view," but in the light of the highly specialized nature of the subprefects, this appears perfectly normal. Elvin, "Mixed Court," 149.

58. Court summons and arrest warrants of the International Mixed Court are reproduced in Lee, "Law and Local Autonomy," 390 and 392, respectively. For different appellations of the subprefect, see Mayers, *Chinese Government*, 38.
59. Yao, *Huayang susong*, 1:560.
60. Yao and Wu, *Shanghai xian xuzhi*, 14:9a. Wang, *Shanghai zujie*, 3:3a.
61. British vice-consul Arthur Davenport, quoted in Seward, "Memorandum on the Mixed Court at Shanghai" (14 October 1879), reprinted in ADPP2, 18:236.
62. Report by circuit intendant Yuan Shuxun, 1905, in Yao, *Huayang susong*, 2:566–67.
63. See for instance, Zeng Guofan's memorial, received 9 March 1871, YWSM, Tongzhi, 80:9b–13b. See also the set of rules for the handing of criminal cases in Japan, issued in February 1881. Xu, *Tongshang yuezhang*, 4:12–14.
64. NCDN, 25, 26, 28, 29 June and 6 July 1869. Xu, *Tonghang yuezhang*, 26:23–25.
65. NCH, 26 June 1869. *NCDN*, 25 June 1869.
66. NCDN, 25, 26, 28, 29 June and 6 July 1869.
67. NCH, 31 July and 7 August 1869; see also Hornby, *Autobiography*, 281–82. For more on "judicial rituals" in colonial courts, see Katz, *Divine Justice*, 118–32.
68. On Hornby's anguish over handing out capital sentences, see Hornby, *Autobiography*, 255–56.
69. NCDN, 1 September 1869.
70. Scully, *Bargaining with the State*, 68–9.
71. Xu, *Tongshang yuezhang*, 26:23–25. The case is also related in Yao, *Huayang susong*, 99–102, and Yao et al., *Minguo Shanghai xianzhi*, 14:27a.
72. The republican jurist Yao Zhihe commented on the naïveté of such an understanding of the most-favored-nation principle. Yao, *Huayang susong*, 1:98–99.
73. Keeton, *Development of Extraterritoriality*, 1:359.
74. Report of Sir Thomas Wade to the Earl of Denby, 14 July 1877, in Foreign Office of Great Britain, *Further Correspondence*, 143; also quoted in Kotenev, *Shanghai*, 81.
75. Hornby to the Earl of Clarendon, 27 July 1869, FO 228/484.
76. Seward, "Memorandum on the Mixed Court at Shanghai," in ADPP2, 18:236. One twentieth-century Chinese account contends that it was due to the lack of English-speaking staff that the Qing authorities let the issue of Chinese assessors slip. Chao, "Opinion of Chao Shih-en," 3. See also Lee, "Law and Local Autonomy," 60 and n. 62.
77. "Lun Yingguan huishen shi," *Shenbao*, 19 October 1872 (Tongzhi 11.9.18), 1.
78. Arthur Davenport, "Memorandum by Mr. Davenport on the Mixed Court at Shanghae," in Parliament of Great Britain and Foreign Office of Great Britain, *Commercial Reports*, 59; see also Kotenev, *Shanghai*, 84.
79. Ye Xiaoqing, "Shanghai before Nationalism," 46; Lee, "Law and Local Autonomy," 14.
80. Ying and Yu, *Shanghai xian zhi*, 12:24b–25b; Yao and Wu, *Shanghai xian xuzhi*, 8b–11b.
81. For an intriguing treatment of the colonial discourse on cruel Chinese punishments both before and during in the treaty port era, see Brook et al., *Death by a Thousand Cuts*, 169–202.
82. See the reports that U.S. consul Matthew Tyson Yates, Austro-Hungarian consul Joseph Haas, and the British consul Chaloner Alabaster submitted to the Municipal Council in 1875, reprinted in NCH, 12 June 1875, 582–84.
83. Kotenev, *Shanghai*, 87; on appellate system, see Edwards, "Ch'ing Legal Jurisdiction," 229
84. Kotenev, *Shanghai*, 72–79.
85. Hsü, "Late Ch'ing Foreign Relations," 83.
86. Prince Gong's memorial to the throne, 26 April 1875, LFZZ, 3-156-7612-2.
87. Wang, *Margary Affair*, 72–75.
88. Chefoo is an English rendering of the island of Zhifu, which is situated outside the city of Yantai and had come to stand for the whole city itself.
89. Section 2(2), TCCF, 1:494.
90. "Huishen guan'an lun," *Shenbao*, 19 October 1872, 1.

Notes to Pages 79–87

91. Section 2(2), TCCF, 495.
92. Ibid.
93. See for instance Hevia, *English Lessons*, 60.
94. For a similar observation, Liu, *Clash of Empires*, 112.
95. For more on the tension between British merchants and the Foreign Service, see Pelcovits, *Old China Hands*.
96. Morse, *International Relations*, 2:303–6.
97. Kotenev, *Shanghai*, 79–82.
98. Hinckley, *American Consular Jurisdiction*, 159.
99. The original Chinese text and an official English translation are reprinted in a circular called "The Tsung-Li Yamên to the Chinese Ministers Abroad" (March 1878), reprinted in ADPP2, 3:400–413.
100. Koo, *Status of Aliens*, 212–28.
101. As Rune Svarverud has pointed out, W. A. P. Martin elected to use the expression *bugui difang guanxia* to translate "extraterritoriality" when he rendered Henry Wheaton's *Elements of International Law* into Chinese (Svarverud, *International Law*, 108). Yet the construction *gui . . . guanxia* has a solid foundation in Qing administrative language. For instance, when the Governor of Guizhou, Zhao Tingchen, memorialized the Board of Revenue in 1659, he stated "all places that originally belonged to Guangxi province should be changed back to the jurisdiction [*gai gui gai sheng guanxia*] of the said province"; DQLS, Shunzhi, 130:3b–4a.
102. George F. Seward, "Memorandum, October 4, 1879," in ADPP2, 18:224.
103. George F. Seward, "Memorandum on the Mixed Court at Shanghai, October 14, 1879," in ADPP2, 18:240.
104. Keeton, *Development of Extraterritoriality*, 1:341–43. Hinckley, *American Consular Jurisdiction*, 159–61.
105. Kotenev, *Shanghai*, 88.
106. Kotenev, *Shanghai*, 14–16.
107. Kotenev, *Shanghai*, 84–93.
108. Motono, "Sino-British Conflict," 142.
109. Motono, "Sino-British Conflict,"152.
110. Scully, *Bargaining with the State*, 21–48.

Chapter 4

1. Toby, *State and Diplomacy*, 11–22.
2. Wakabayashi, *Anti-foreignism*, 58–68.
3. Toby, *State and Diplomacy*, 13–14.
4. Wakabayashi, *Anti-foreignism*, 62–63. The original Japanese text of the "expulsion edict" can be found in Takayanagi and Ishii, *Ofuregaki Tenpō Shūsei*, 2:858–59.
5. Morse, *International Relations*.
6. Massarella, *World Elsewhere*, 115–16; see also Auslin, *Negotiating with Imperialism*, 26.
7. The clinic itself has been torn down, but the site today houses a Siebold Museum.
8. Siebold's life and the "Siebold incident" has been the subject of many works and monographs over the years. This narrative is based on Kouwenhoven and Forrer, *Siebold and Japan*.
9. Wakabayashi, *Anti-foreignism*, 162.
10. Quoted in Jansen, *China in the Tokugawa World*, 23.
11. Jansen, *China in the Tokugawa World*, 71. For more on the Tokugawa trade with China, see Ōba, *Tōsen Mochiwatarisho*, and Ōba, *Chūgoku bunka juyō*.
12. Bastid-Bruguière, "Currents of Social Change," 582–89; Kamachi, *Reform in China*, 188.
13. Kamachi, "Nagasaki kakyō," 2–3.
14. Nakamura, "Tōtsūji ni tsuite"; see also Kamachi, "Nagasaki kakyō," 2.

15. Shionoya Tōin made this point in his political tract *Kakkaron,* which was published in 1859. Part of the text and annotated translation have been published by van Gulik in "Kakkaron."
16. Abiko, "Persecuted Patriot"; Cassel, "Koga Tōan."
17. Katō, *Kurofune,* 278–79; Keene, *Japanese Discovery of Europe,* 46.
18. Kouwenhoven and Forrer, *Siebold and Japan,* 61–62; the original sources as well as English translations can be found in Greene, "Correspondence." The Japanese texts are also available in Hayashi and Yanai, *Tsūkō ichiran zokushū,* 2:505–6, 527–28.
19. Hayashi and Yanai, *Tsūkō ichiran zokushū,* 5:24–25.
20. For a discussion on Japanese sources on the opium war, see Katō, *Kurofune,* 261–84; see Wakabayashi, "From Peril to Profit."
21. For more on this intriguing question, see Masuda, *Japan and China.*
22. Saitō, "Ahen Shimatsu" (1843), in Sumida, *Nihon kaibō shiryō,* 3:203–10.
23. A standard narrative of this crisis can be found in Beasley, *Select Documents*; see also Mitani, *Meiji Ishin.*
24. This is my translation of a passage from the Russian text of article 8, which reads as follows: "Как Русский в Японии, так и Японец в России всегда свободны и не подвергаются никаким стеснениям. Учинивший преступление может быть арестован, но судится не иначе, как по законам своей страны." TCEJ, 570. The Japanese and Dutch texts follow the Russian closely. I am indebted to Martin Feldmann and Whit Gray for double-checking my Russian translation.
25. Article 9 of the Treaty of Shimoda, 1855. It is not entirely clear to what extent the most-favored-nation arrangement in the Treaty of Shimoda actually did cover extraterritorial rights. See also Hoare, *Japan's Treaty Ports,* 55.
26. Wakabayashi, *Anti-foreignism,* 62.
27. Wong, *Deadly Dreams.*
28. Beasley, *Select Documents,* 43.
29. TCEJ, 734–35. The rest of the article concerned itself with the adjudication of commercial disputes and read as follows: "The Consular Courts shall be open to Japanese creditors, to enable them to recover their just claims against American citizens, and the Japanese Courts shall in like manner be open to American citizens for the recovery of their just claims against Japanese.

    "All claims for forfeitures or penalties for violations of this treaty, or of the articles regulating trade, which are appended hereunto, shall be sued for in the consular courts, and all recoveries shall be delivered to the Japanese authorities.

    "Neither the American or Japanese governments are to be held responsible for the payment of any debts, contacted by their respective citizens or subjects."
30. Caleb Cushing to Calhoun, 29 April 1844, in ADPP1, 8:20.
31. "Memorandum by Mr. Davenport on the Mixed Court at Shanghae," Parliament of Great Britain and Foreign Office of Great Britain, *Commercial Reports,* 59.
32. TCEJ, 422.
33. Morita, "'Fubyōdō' jōyaku to ryōji saibanken," 59–62.
34. Beasley, *Select Documents,* 162.
35. Satow, *Diplomat in Japan,* 275. A similar point is made in Hishida, *International Status of Japan as a Great Power,* 133. I am grateful to Douglas Howland for this reference.
36. Morita, "Bakuhan kankei ni miru saibanken," 58–81; Morita, *Kaikoku to chigai hōken,* 18–54.
37. Lane-Poole and Dickins, *Harry Parkes,* 2:314.
38. Morita, "'Fubyōdō' jōyaku to ryōji saibanken," 59–62; "Tsung-Li Yamên to the Chinese Ministers Abroad" (March 1878), reprinted in ADPP2, 3:400–413.
39. Botsman, *Punishment and Power,* 133–34. For Alcock's own account of the incident and his role in it, see Alcock, *Capital of the Tycoon,* 2:15–25.
40. The rules are quoted in full in Paske-Smith, *Western Barbarians,* 250–51.

41. According to the American geologist Raphael Pumpelly, an outspoken critic of consular jurisdiction, Richardson was known for his arrogant behavior toward locals. He was once prosecuted by a British consular court for his brutal treatment of one his Chinese servants. Richardson was sentenced to pay a fine of mere 5 dollars, but the British minister was reportedly so outraged by the inadequate punishment that he reversed the verdict and imposed a more fitting punishment. Pumpelly did not, however, tell us what that punishment was supposed to be. See Pumpelly's letter to the editor, *Nation,* 17 March 1870, 173.
42. Morita, "'Fubyōdō' jōyaku to ryōji saibanken," 72–73.
43. Botsman, *Punishment and Power,* 138. A reproduction of the original imperial letter can be seen in Meiji jingū, *Meiji ishin,* 53.
44. Auslin, *Negotiating with Imperialism,* 154–156; Ottosson, "Svensk frihandelsimperialism."
45. Auslin, *Negotiating with Imperialism,* 157.
46. Letter to Sanjō Sanetomi, 9 April 1869, in Tada, *Iwakura-kō jikki,* 2:699; Auslin, *Negotiating with Imperialism,* 156–57.
47. Masuda, *Japan and China,* 2–3.
48. Auslin, *Negotiating with Imperialism,* 180; Marlene J. Mayo, "Rationality in the Restoration."
49. Paske-Smith, *Western Barbarians,* 249.
50. Fujimura, "Jōyaku reikōron."
51. Zhu, "Shanhai kyoryū Nihonjin shakai," 402–3.
52. Hishitani, *Nagasaki gaikokujin kyoryūchi,* 275–312 and 778–805; figures for 1864 and 1870: 736.
53. Zhu, "Shanhai kyoryū Nihonjin shakai," 402–3.
54. Kamachi, "Chinese in Meiji Japan," 59.
55. F. G. Myburgh to Rutherford Alcock, 12 December 1861, quoted in Paske-Smith, *Western Barbarians,* 247–48. See also Hishitani, *Nagasaki gaikokujin kyoryūchi,* 727–34 and 739.
56. Hayashi et al., *Hōki bunrui taizen,* 25:343.
57. Kotenev, *Shanghai,* 61–62.
58. Hayashi et al., *Hōki bunrui taizen,* 25:84; see also Usui, "Yokohama kyoryūchi," 3b:861, and Tabohashi, "Nisshin shin kankei," 165.
59. Proclamation from local Japanese authorities in Kanagawa prefecture, 16 December 1870, "Jōyaku misaikoku oyobi Shinkokujin torishimekata sankōsho," GKS, 3.9.4.4.
60. See for instance, Hooker, *Law and the Chinese.*
61. Undated petition from Guangdong association, Nagasaki Kenritsu Nagasaki Toshokan, "Shinajin ōfuku," NKS 14-170-4; see also Kamachi, "Nagasaki kakyō," 6, and Kamachi, "Chinese in Meiji Japan," 61–62.
62. Petition from the Fujian Guild, February-March 1869, "Shinajin ōfuku," NKS 14-170-4.
63. Usui, "Yokohama kyoryūchi," 863.
64. Instructions from foreign affairs bureau (*Gaimukyoku*) to Fujian and Guangdong guilds, 9 February 1871, "Shinkokujin ōfuku, Meiji 3 nen," NKS 14-249-2.
65. Instruction from foreign affairs bureau, September 1870, "Shinkokujin ōfuku, Meiji 3 nen," NKS 14–249–2.
66. Fogel, *Cultural Dimension,* 83.
67. Takasugi Shinsaku, "Yūshin goroku," in Takasugi, *Takasugi Shinsaku zenshū,* 2:141–16.
68. Wang, *Li Hongzhang,* 6–7; Chow, *China and Japan,* 23–30.
69. Wang, *Li Hongzhang,* 7–8, and Chow, *China and Japan,* 27; Fogel, *Articulating the Sinosphere,* 70. The regulation Ying consulted is in all likelihood the regulation that can be found in the *Hubu zeli,* 54:1. Blurring the distinction between domestic and foreign trade, this directive also regulates trade with ships coming from Shandong, Fujian-Guangdong, and Vietnam.
70. Wang, *Li Hongzhang,* 8–10; Chow, *China and Japan,* 28.
71. Ying Baoshi's response to Kawazu, March 1868, GKS 3.9.4.4.
72. Wang, *Li Hongzhang,* 9–10.

73. Anatol Kotenev, the main authority on the Mixed Court in Shanghai, is silent on the role of Japanese in the 1860s. See Kotenev, *Shanghai*.
74. See entry on Tei Einei in *Nihon jinmei daijiten, Gendai*, 4:330.
75. Chow, *China and Japan*, 32–36; Tsiang, "Sino-Japanese," 4–6.
76. Cohen, *China and Christianity*, 229–33.
77. Hsü, "Late Ch'ing Foreign Relations," 77; Wright, *Chinese Conservatism*, 286–95.
78. Fujimura, "Meiji shonen," 10–13; Wang, *Li Hongzhang*, 57.
79. Memorial from Yinghan, received 18 December 1870, YWSM, Tongzhi, 79:7b–8a. The translation from the Chinese is my own; see also Chow, *China and Japan*, 37.
80. Chow, *China and Japan*, 36–37.
81. Deuchler, *Confucian Gentlemen*, 14–15.
82. Memorial from Li Hongzhang, received 22 January 1871, YWSM, Tongzhi 79:46b–48b; see also Chow, *China and Japan*, 37–38.
83. Memorial from Zeng Guofan, received 9 March 1871, YWSM, Tongzhi, 80:9b–13b; see also Chow *China and Japan*, 39.
84. Tsiang, "Sino-Japanese," 7.
85. Memorial from Zeng Guofan, received 9 March 1871, YWSM, Tongzhi, 80:9b–13b.
86. Ibid.
87. As I pointed out in the first chapter, jurists have not been unanimous on the question as to whether most-favored-nation arrangements applied to extraterritoriality. For the Japanese case, Murase, "Most-Favored-Nation Treatment."
88. Tsiang T'ing-fu has argued that Qing officials only realized that treaty port extraterritoriality was a unilateral privilege in 1873. See Tsiang, "Sino-Japanese," 15.
89. Tsiang, "Sino-Japanese," 7.
90. Fairbank, *Trade and Diplomacy*, 128–29.
91. Tsiang, "Sino-Japanese," 8–9.
92. Fujimura, "Meiji shonen," 13; see also Kim, *Last Phase*, 136–53.
93. Wang, *Li Hongzhang*, 59–60.
94. See, for instance, the note from Qing consul Ruan Zutang to Oki Morikata, governor of Kanagawa, 15 November 1887, GKS 7.1.8.6, vol. 1.
95. For a more exhaustive discussion on the significance of equivalence, which differs in some respects from my own, see Liu, "Legislating the Universal," 152–53.
96. Wheaton, *Wan'guo Gongfa*, preface, 1b.
97. Wang, *Li Hongzhang*, 87–88.
98. Tabohashi, "Nisshin shin kankei," 170.
99. Kim, *Last Phase* 147; Fujimura, "Meiji shonen," 16–21.
100. Ying Baoshi and Chen Qin to Yanagihara Sakimitsu, 7 August 1871, in Li, *Li Wenzhong, Zougao* (Memorials), 18:46a–46b; translation from Kim, "Last Phase," 148.
101. Fujimura, "Meiji shonen."
102. Murase, "Most-Favored-Nation Treatment," 284–86.
103. Fujimura, "Meiji shonen," 22.
104. Wakabayashi, "From Peril to Profit," 68–69.
105. For the official Chinese and Japanese texts of the treaty, see TCEJ, 77–86. For an unofficial translation of the treaty, see TCCF, 2:507–14.
106. For more on the role of language in the Chinese character sphere, see Dudden, "Japan's Engagement."
107. "At the ports appointed in the territory of either government, it will be competent for the other to station Consuls for the control of its own merchant community. All suits in which they [the Consul's nationals] are the only parties, the matter in dispute being money or property, it will fall to the Consul to adjudicate according to the law of his own state. In mixed suits, the plaint having been laid before the Consul, he will endeavour, in the first instance, to prevent litigation by friendly counsel. If this be not possible, he will write officially to the local authority, and in concert with him will fairly try the case and decide it.

Where acts of theft or robbery are committed, and where debtors abscond, the local authorities can do no more than make search for and apprehend the guilty parties. They shall not be held liable to make compensation." This unauthorized translation is taken from TCCF, 2:510; the original Chinese and Japanese texts of the article are found in TCEJ, 80. The Chinese and Japanese terms inserted in the text here are taken from the original Chinese and Japanese texts, respectively.
108. "At any of the ports appointed, at which no Consul shall have been stationed, the control and care of the traders reporting thither shall devolve on the local authorities. In the case of the commission of the any act of crime, the guilty party shall be apprehended, and the particulars of his offence communicated to the Consul at the nearest port, by whom he shall be tried and punished according to law." Unauthorized translation from TCCF, 2:510; for the original text of article 9, see TCEJ, 81.
109. Communication to Rutherford Alcock, 1 September 1871, YWSM, Tongzhi, 82:13a–14a.
110. Notification by Sir Rutherford Alcock, 6 October 1868, in Hertslet, *Treaties*, 2:558. The notification was based on section 85 in the "Order in Council for the Better Government of Her Majesty's Subjects in the Dominions of the Emperor of China and the Tycoon of Japan. Windsor, 9th March 1865," but this section was removed in 1881. Hertslet, *Treaties*, 2:444.
111. The unofficial English translation of the full article reads: "If any subject of either power connect himself at any of the open ports with lawless offenders for purposes of robbery or other wrongdoing, or if any work his way into the interior and commit acts of incendiarism, murder, or robbery, active measures for his apprehension shall be taken by the proper authority, and notice shall at the same time be given without delay to the Consul of the offender's nationality. Any offender who shall venture with weapons of a murderous nature to resist capture may be slain in the act without farther consequences; but the circumstances which have led to his life being thus taken shall be investigated at an inquest which will be held by the Consul and local authority together. In the event of the occurrence taking place in the interior, so far from the port that that the Consul cannot not arrive in time for the inquest, the local authority shall communicate a report of the facts of the case to the Consul.

"When arrested and brought up for trial, the offender, if at a port shall be tried by the local authority and the Consul together. In the interior he shall be tried and dealt with by the local authority, who will official communicate the facts of the case to the Consul.

"If subjects of either power shall assemble to the number of ten or more to foment disorder and commit excesses in the dominions of the other, or shall induce subjects of the other therein to conspire with them fore the doing of injury to the other power, the authorities of the latter shall be free at once to arrest them, If at a port, their Consul shall be informed, in order that he may take part in their trial. If in the interior, the local authority shall duly try them, and shall officially communicate particulars to the Consul. In either case capital punishment shall be inflicted at the scene of the offence." Unauthorized translation of article 8, TCCF, 2:512; for the original text, see TCEJ, 82–84.
112. Xu, *Tongshang yuezhang*, 4:12a–14b.
113. TCEJ, 83.
114. This was the official British position, which was most eloquently articulated by Sir Thomas Wade when the Chefoo Convention negotiated. See Morse, *International Relations*, 2:303–6. As we saw in the case of the Mixed Court in Shanghai, Wade's position was not respected, and foreign assessors often acted as cojudges in practice.
115. Photograph of Date Munenari and the delegation to China, September 1871, NKS, 18-115.
116. Hyōdō, *Date Munenari kō*, 313; Fujimura, "Meiji shoki," 24.
117. See for instance, Nakayama, *Shinbun shūsei*, 2:90.
118. English note to Li Hongzhang from Soejima and Terajima, January-February 1872, DNGB, 4:265.

119. See, for instance, "Yi zhu Riben gekou lishiguan lixing shiyi qi tiao," an anonymous and undated policy document on the Sino-Japanese Treaty of Tianjin preserved in the National Library of China, Beijing (no. 51026). It describes the Japanese legal reforms as a threat to the preservation of order in the Chinese community in Japan.
120. Memorandum from Inoue Kaoru to Shioda Saburō, Japanese minister to Beijing, 18 April 1887, DNGB, 20:133–38.
121. Chow, *China and Japan*, 42; see also DNGB, 5:239–303.
122. For instance, in 1929 Wu Songgao claimed that there was no treaty basis for giving foreign assessors the privilege of *huishen*, ignoring the fact that the Sino-Japanese Treaty of Tianjin had extensive stipulations on mixed jurisdiction in mixed suits. Wu, *Zhiwai faquan*, 266.
123. Kang and Pan, *Jindai wairen*, 118.
124. George F. Seward, "Memorandum, October 4, 1879," in ADPP2, 18:230.
125. Tending to regard Japan's subsequent success in revising the unequal treaties as a foregone conclusion, historians have usually focused on the aspects in early Meiji foreign policy that foreshadowed Japanese penetration of China at the expense of other perspectives. Wayne C. McWilliams's otherwise exhaustive article on the Soejima mission is a prime example of this. McWilliams, "East Meets East."
126. Not even when McWilliams relates a discussion on extraterritoriality between Soejima and Li Hongzhang does he make clear that the Sino-Japanese Treaty of Tianjin provided for mutual extraterritorial privileges. McWilliams, "East Meets East," 249. For a transcript of Soejima's discussions with Li, see DNGB, 4:262–66.
127. *Hōki bunrui taizen*, 24:352–54; Gaimushō Gaikō Shiryōkan, *Nihon gaikōshi jiten*, 75, 1014. For a full list of Chinese and Japanese envoys and consuls, see Gugong bowuyuan, *Qingji Zhongwai shiling*, 67.
128. *Hōki bunrui taizen*, 24:404–25; Gugong bowuyuan, ed. *Qingji Zhongwai shiling*, 195–205.
129. Howland, *Borders of Chinese Civilization*, 41.
130. McWilliams, "East Meets East," 246.
131. Chow, *China and Japan*, 45–48. See also "Lun qian guan zhu Riben," 24 September 1875, in Li, *Li Wenzhong*, Yishu han'gao (Papers from the Zongli Yamen), 4:24a–25b; the appeal is also mentioned in Xu, *Tongshang yuezhang*, 4:46b.
132. Hsü, *China's Entrance*, 176–79.
133. Chow, *China and Japan*, 48–51.
134. Hsü, *China's Entrance*, 186; Wheaton, *Wan'guo Gongfa*.
135. He Ruzhang and Zhang Sigui to Terajima Nunenori, 14 January 1878, GKS 4.1.1.14.
136. RSNE, 1 December 1877, 2. I am indebted to Lane R. Earns for this reference.
137. RSNE, 18 September 1878, 2.
138. Two examples can be seen in Fukken kaikan (Fuijian Huiguan) and Kōfukuji, which functioned as community centers for the Fujian association and Sanjiang association, respectively. Personal visits, July 2005. See also Chen Donghua (Chin Tōka), "Nagasaki kyoryūchi no Chūgokujin shakai," in Nagasaki kenritsu Nagasaki toshokan, *Nagasaki kyoryūchi gaikokujin meibo*, 495.
139. Machida, *Meiji no kangakushatachi*, 62–82.
140. Note from Yu Qiong to Nagasaki prefect, 18 March 1879, NKS 14–435–3; see also Kamachi, "Nagasaki kakyō," 9, and Kamachi, "Chinese," 67.
141. This is the case for archival material in both Tokyo and Nagasaki.
142. Petition from Fujian merchants and Fujian association, 12 June 1875, "Shinkokujin shonegai," NKS 14-382-2.
143. My distinction between "membership" and "citizenship" has drawn on Brubaker, *Citizenship and Nationhood*, 21–34; for a different treatment of the topic of citizenship, see Caldwell, "Citizen and the Republic."
144. Ch'en, *Formation*, 57.
145. Letter from Masaki Shōnosuke to minister of justice Yamada Akiyoshi, 1 April 1885, GKS, 4.1.1.14.
146. Mayo, "Rationality in the Restoration," 355–56.

147. Circular from Foreign Ministry, 1 October 1878, Daijōkan furei benran, National Archives of Japan, 2A.033.09. The Japanese meaning of the word ("commissioner, manager") has now replaced the old meaning in the Chinese language, and the word is now listed as a Sino-Japanese word. See entry for *lishiguan* in Liu, *Hanyu wailaici*.
148. See entries in *Chinsai Nippō*, 26 October 1883, and *Shenbao*, 25 August 1886, respectively.
149. A prime example of this policy is the "Nagasaki Affair" of September 1883, which will be analyzed in chapter 5.
150. Hu, *Common Descent Group*.
151. Chen, "Tei Kōshō," 24.
152. Johnson, *Shanghai*, 202–6.
153. For a similar observation on the "judicial continuum" of the Qing legal order, see Katz, *Divine Justice*.
154. Memorial from Qing legation, 2 February 1888, LFZZ, 3-164-7744-69.
155. Zheng Xiaoxu (1860–1938) is more known today for his collaboration with the Japanese in "Manchukuo" than for his career as Qing consul in Japan. For his role in establishing the Chinese association in Kobe, see Chen, "Tei Kōshō." For a more extensive treatment of the first decades of his life, see Xu, *Zheng Xiaoxu*.
156. The figures for Shanghai and Yokohama are taken from Zhu, *Shanhai kyoryū Nihonjin shakai*, 402; the figures for Nagasaki are based on numbers found in Hishitani, *Nagasaki gaikokujin kyoryūchi*, 736, and Nagasaki kenritsu Nagasaki toshokan, *Nagasaki kyoryūchi gaikokujin meibo*, 3:357.
157. Peattie, "Japanese Treaty Port Settlements," 168.
158. Wray, *Mitsubishi and the N.Y.K.* I am indebted to Anne Reinhardt at Williams College for directing me to this source. On the Japanese entry into the shipping industry in the 1880s, see Fogel, *Articulating the Sinosphere*, 83–84.
159. The Sino-Japanese Treaty of Tianjin has been the subject of a number of monographs over the years. Evidently occasioned by the publication of the YWSM, Tabohashi Kiyoshi (February-March 1933) and Tsiang T'ing-fu (April 1933) published the two first full-length articles on the treaty. Fujimura ("Meiji shonen ni okeru Ajiya seisaku no shūsei to Chūgoku") and Wang (*Li Hongzhang yu Zhong-Ri dingyue*) have written the best monographs on the drafting of the treaties, drawing on newly available archival material. Chow (*China and Japan*) and Kim (*Last Phase*) have also written seminal works that touch on the treaties. Yet both Chinese and Japanese standard works are curiously silent on the 1871–96 period in Sino-Japanese relations in general and the actual application of the treaty in particular. See for instance Inō, *Higashi Ajia*. Some works even give the impression that consular jurisdiction only became a factor in Sino-Japanese relations after 1895, while others only devote passing mention to the fact that an important group of overseas Chinese enjoyed extraterritorial privileges. (See, for instance, Kang and Pan, *Jindai wairen*, Brooks, *Japan's Imperial Diplomacy*, and Guo, *Zhuanzhe*.) The only group of scholars that has produced works of any length on the topic are Japanese local historians and scholars studying the overseas Chinese. (Usui, "Yokohama kyoryūchi"; Chen, "Tei Kōshō"; Hishitani, *Nagasaki gaikokujin kyoryūchi*; Kamachi, "Chinese in Meiji Japan.") For one attempt to discuss the Sino-Japanese Treaty of Tianjin within the framework of the "tributary system," see Hamashita, "Tribute Trade System."

Chapter 5

1. Wu A'er's deposition to Consul Yu Qiong, 4 November 1881, GKS 4.2.5.135.
2. Note from Yu to Kawano, 7 December 1881, GKS 4.2.5.135.
3. Due to the fact that foreigners were subject to a number of different jurisdictions in the treaty port era, it is impossible to obtain exact statistics for foreign crime in the Japanese treaty ports. To my knowledge, Richard T. Chang is the only person who has tried to undertake such a task. Chang, *Justice of the Western Consular Courts*.

4. Hishitani, *Nagasaki gaikokujin kyoryūchi*, 285.
5. GKS 7.1.8.4, 5 vols.
6. Johnson, *Shanghai*, 123–54; Goodman, *Native Place*, 84–118; Ronquillo, "Administration of Law."
7. Undated petition from Cantonese community, NKS 14-170-4; see Kamachi, "Chinese in Meiji Japan," 62.
8. Ibid.
9. Petition from Fukienese community, February-March 1869, NKS 14-170-4; see Kamachi, "Chinese in Meiji Japan," 62.
10. Note from Zongli *yamen* to Tei Einei, 26 November 1875, in DNGB, 9:449–51; "Lun qian guan zhu Riben," 24 September 1875, in Li, *Li Wenzhong*, Yishu han'gao (Papers from the Zongli Yamen), 4:24a–25b.
11. Petition from Wei Shouli, 29 July 1870, NKS 14-289.
12. Petition from Zheng Renrui and Niu Chunbin, 27 August 1869, NKS 14-170-4.
13. Usui, "Yokohama kyoryūchi," 861; Tanaka, "Shinkokujin Chōkai-ra nisesatsu jiken."
14. Hayashi et al., *Hōki bunrui taizen*, 25:84.
15. For more on this punishment and its relation to forgery, see Ch'en, *Formation*, 33–34, 84, and 160.
16. English note from Geisenheimer to the governor of Kanagawa prefecture, 14 August 1870, GKS, 4.1.4.3–1, vol. 1; see also Usui, "Yokohama kyoryūchi," 873.
17. Usui, "Yokohama kyoryūchi," 474–77; Ying's letter, dated 22 December 1868, is reprinted in DNGB, 2.1:262.
18. Usui, "Yokohama kyoryūchi," 41–47.
19. List of Chinese convicted by Tokyo district court, "Honpō ni Shinkoku ryōjikan setchi ni tsuki kakkō zairyū dōkokujin hanzai sono hoka toriatsukai kankei zakken," GKS, 4.1.1.14; Usui, "Yokohama kyoryūchi," 877.
20. Ch'en, *Formation*, 166 n. 160.
21. Note from Zongli *yamen* to Tei Einei, 26 November 1875, DNGB, 9:449–51.
22. Note from Tei Einei, 28 November 1875, DNGB, 9:451–53.
23. Note from Zongli *yamen* to Tei Einei, 12 February 1876, DNGB, 9:458–59.
24. Wakabayashi, "From Peril to Profit," 55–75.
25. Hayashi et al., *Hōki bunrui taizen*, 22:165. Consequently, Richard T. Chang is wrong when he states that the Dutch treaty was "the first treaty embodying a prohibition" on the importation of opium. Chang, *Justice of the Western Consular Courts*, 45.
26. Hayashi et al., *Hōki bunrui taizen*, 22:98, 102.
27. Chang, *Justice of the Western Consular Courts*, 39–79.
28. Joint petition from Cantonese and Fukienese associations, dated March 1875, NKS, 14–382–2. Kamachi, "Nagasaki kakyō," 6–7, and Kamachi, "Chinese in Meiji Japan," 62.
29. Letter to the editor, *Yokohama mainichi shimbun*, 25 June 1875; see also Usui, "Yokohama kyoryūchi," 866.
30. Letters to the editor, *Yokohama mainichi shimbun*, 2, 3, and 13 July 1875.
31. Letter to the editor, *Yokohama mainichi shimbun*, 2 July 1875.
32. The extent to which Chinese availed themselves of the Japanese press is a question that needs to be investigated further. For more on the role of the treaty port press in the creation of a Chinese "public sphere," see Vittinghoff, "Readers, Publishers and Officials."
33. Proclamation from He Ruzhang and Zhang Sigui, 14 January 1878, GKS, 4.1.1.14.
34. "Yi zhu Riben gekou lishiguan lixing shiyi qi tiao." An undated draft of the regulations with a commentary is preserved in the National Library of China, Beijing. The regulations are dated February 1881 and are published in Xu, *Tongshang leizuan yuezhang*, 4:12–14.
35. Kamachi, "Chinese in Meiji Japan," 63–67.
36. See, for instance, memorial from Zhou Zupei et al., 11 June 1858, in YWSM, Xianfeng, 26:13a–15b; the memorial is also quoted in Banno, *China and the West*, 26–27.
37. Brooks, *Japan's Imperial Diplomacy*, 85–86.

38. Note from Yang Shu to Kusaka Yoshio, 15 January 1889, GKS 7.1.8.4, vol. 4.
39. Usui, "Yokohama kyoryūchi," 867; note from Japanese consul general in Shanghai to foreign minister, 22 August 1883, DNGB, 16:278.
40. A similar point is made in Buoye, *Manslaughter, Markets, and Moral Economy*, 7.
41. For instance, in 1871, Shanghai and Nagasaki were connected by telegraph. Yang, *Technology of Empire*, 21.
42. Wu's deposition, 4 November 1881, GKS 4.25.135.
43. Kawano to Yu, November 1881, GKS 4.25.135.
44. Ricket, "Voluntary Surrender and Confession"; see "Offenders Surrendering Voluntarily" in the *Shinritsu kōryō*, translated in Ch'en, *Formation*, 95.
45. Legal brief by Yu, 19 September 1882, GKS 4.2.5.135.
46. Telegram from foreign minister Inoue Kaoru to consul Kawakami Kin'ichi, 2 May 1887, DNGB, 20:468.
47. *Saikai shimbun*, 9 November 1881.
48. DNGB, 9:439–60; see Kamachi, "Chinese in Meiji Japan," 68.
49. Note from Terajima Munenori to He Ruzhang, 29 January 1878, DNGB, 11:248–250.
50. Note from He Ruzhang and Zhang Sigui to Terajima Munenori, 7 February 1878, DNGB, 11:252; see Kamachi, "Chinese in Meiji Japan," 68 n. 40.
51. Terajima to He, February 1878, DNGB, 11:258–261.
52. Opinion from Denison, 8 October 1883, GKS 4.2.5.83, vol 1.
53. RSNE, 30 June 1883, 2.
54. Ibid.
55. Ibid. See also *Japan Mail*, quoted in RSNE, 21 July 1883, 2.
56. "Late Affair in Nagasaki," JWM, 29 September 1883, 528–29.
57. Deposition by Wei Pengcheng, September 1883, GKS 4.2.5.83.
58. Deposition by Chen Dezhui, September 1883, GKS 4.2.5.83.
59. Mine Susumu's letter of explanation (*shimatsusho*), 16 September 1883, GKS 4.2.5.83; see also "Late Affair in Nagasaki," JWM, 29 September 1883, 528–29.
60. Medical report by W. Renwick, 4 October 1883, GKS 4.2.5.83.
61. An English translation of such a search warrant is reproduced in RSNE, 27 October 1883.
62. Petition from Fujian Association to Guo Wanjun, 16 September 1883, GKS 4.2.5.83.
63. Note from Guo to Nagasaki public prosecutor, with attachment, 20 September 1883, GKS 4.2.5.83.
64. Note from Li Shuchang to Foreign Ministry, 27 September 1883, GKS 4.2.5.83.
65. Sasama, *Zusetsu Edo machibugyōsho jiten*, 132–43. I am indebted to Dani Botsman for this reference.
66. On the relative autonomy of status groups in relation to the state, see Howell, *Geographies of Identity*, 42–44.
67. Pou Lin Sing, "Nagasaki Affair," JWM, 27 October 1883, 625.
68. Opinion from Boissonade, 4 October 1883, GKS 4.2.5.83, vol. 1. The translation from French is my own.
69. Opinion from Denison, 8 October 1883, GKS 4.2.5.83, vol. 1.
70. Opinion from Denison, 15 November 1883, GKS 4.2.5.83, vol. 1.
71. Opinion from Denison, 15 November 1883, GKS 4.2.5.83, vol. 1.
72. "Tsung-Li Yamên to the Chinese Ministers Abroad" (March 1878), reprinted in ADPP2, 3:406–7.
73. See, for instance, Zeng Guofan's memorial to the throne, received 9 March 1871, YWSM, Tongzhi, 80:9b–13b; see also the original Chinese text of "Tsung-Li Yamên to the Chinese Ministers Abroad" (March 1878), in ADPP2, 3:409.
74. For more on the "territorial dimensions" of extraterritoriality, see Scully, "Historical Wrongs and Human Rights."
75. "Tsung-Li Yamên to the Chinese Ministers Abroad" (March 1878), in ADPP2, 3:408–9.
76. Editorial (*shasetsu*), *Chinsai nippō*, 21 October 1883.

77. Editorial, *Chinsai nippō*, 24, 25, 26, 27, 28, 30 ... October 1883.
78. RSNE, 17 November 1883, 2.
79. "Late Affair at Nagasaki," JWM, 29 September 1883, 528–29.
80. "Status of Chinese in Japan," JWM, 27 October 1883, 623–24.
81. As Natascha Vittinghoff has shown, the English-language press in the treaty ports had a wide Chinese readership, and vice versa. As the examples in this chapter indicate, there is little reason to assume that Japan was any different in this respect. Vittinghoff, "Readers, Publishers and Officials."
82. Pou Lin Sing, letter to the editor, JWM, 27 October 1883, 625. Emphasis in original.
83. For more on treaty port customary practices, see Cassel, "Traktaten som aldrig var och fördraget som nästan inte blev."
84. Morita, "'Fubyōdō' jōyaku to ryōji saibanken," 71; Alcock, *Capital of the Tycoon*, 2:391.
85. Chen, "On Analogy in Ch'ing Law."
86. Note from Li Shuchang to Inoue Kaoru, 23 October 1883, GKS 4.2.5.83.
87. Copy of note from Inoue Kaoru to Li Shuchang, 29 October 1883, GKS 4.2.5.83.
88. Note from Li Shuchang to Inoue Kaoru, 26 October 1883, GKS 4.2.5.83.
89. "Murder in Shanghai," JWM, 1 August 1891; for more on criminal procedure in Meiji Japan, see Quigley, *Japanese Government and Politics*, 283–84.
90. For more on criminal procedure in Edo, see Botsman, *Punishment and Power*, 33–38.
91. Ch'en, *Formation*, 78–79.
92. Johnson, *Instance of Treason*, 186.
93. Ch'ü, *Local Government in China*, 124–29.
94. Mittler, *Newspaper for China*, 220–21.
95. For more on this, see Kuhn, *Soulstealers*, 187–222.
96. Macauley, *Social Power and Legal Culture*.
97. Note from Li Shuchang to Inoue Kaoru, 10 November 1883, GKS 4.2.5.83.
98. RSNE, 20 February 1886, 2.
99. Communication from public prosecutor Okamoto to foreign minister Inoue Kaoru, 28 January 1884, GKS 4.2.5.83.
100. Communication from public prosecutor Okamoto to foreign minister Inoue Kaoru, 28 January 1884, GKS 4.2.5.83.
101. RSNE, 2 February 1884, 2.
102. Kamachi, "Chinese in Meiji Japan," 69.
103. Note from foreign minister Inoue Kaoru to Qing minister Xu Chengzu, 3 March 1886, GKS 4.2.5.83.
104. Xu to Inoue, 1 March 1886, GKS 4.2.5.83.
105. Inoue to Xu, 3 March 1886, GKS 4.2.5.83.
106. DNGB, 22:649–65; Kamachi, "Chinese in Meiji Japan," 72 (n. 50).
107. Lee, *New History of Korea*, 276–78. For more on Sino-Japanese rivalries in Korea, see Larsen, *Tradition, Treaties, and Trade*.
108. RSNE, 6 March 1886, 2.
109. For more information on these ships, see Gardiner et al., *Conway's All the World's Fighting Ships*, 395–401. I am indebted to Prof. Y. W. Ma for this reference.
110. JWM, 21 August 1886, 180.
111. RSNE, 21 August 1886; JWM, 11 September 1886; *Hōchi Shimbun* quoted in JWM, 21 August 1886. See also Nakamura, *Kusaka Yoshio den*, 140–157.
112. These figures come from Yasuoka, "Meiji 19 nen," 50–51. See also JWM, 21 August 1886. Kamachi, "Chinese in Meiji Japan," 69–71.
113. Xu Chengzu to Foreign Ministry, 18 August 1886, DNGB, 20:534.
114. Xu Chengzu to Foreign Ministry, 24 August 1886. DNGB, 20:534.
115. Yasuoka, "Meiji 19 nen," 61–63.
116. Notes of conversation between Aoki and Qing minister, 1 September 1886, DNGB, 20:535.

117. Fukuzawa Yukichi, "Datsuaron," *Jiji shimpō*, 16 March 1885; reprinted in Fukuzawa, *Fukuzawa Yukichi zenshū*, 10:238–40.
118. RSNE, 29 September 1886. This claim probably came from the Japanese press as it occurs in Nakayama, *Shinbun shūsei*, 6:343; also quoted in Yasuoka, "Meiji 19-nen," 63, 90 (n. 35).
119. Japanese transcript of conversation between Xu and Inoue, 26 September 1886. DNGB, 20:537–38.
120. *Tōkyō nichinichi shimbun*, 18 August 1883, reprinted in Nakayama, *Shinbun Shūsei*, 6:318–19.
121. *Shenbao*, 25 August 1886. It is true that *Shenbao* and *Dianshizhai Pictorial* were run by a British businessman, Ernest Major, but all available evidence indicates that the newspaper took a "Chinese point of view" when reporting on foreign affairs. Ye, *Dianshizhai Pictorial*, 6–8.
122. *Hōchi Shimbun* quoted in JWM, 21 August 1886.
123. Yasuoka, "Meiji 19-nen," 58–59.
124. Cartoon published in *Tôbaé*, no. 2, 1 March 1887. See also Shimizu, *Zoku Bigō sobyōshū*, 126–27.
125. See for instance JWM, 21 August 1886, 178.
126. Ibid.
127. Summary of conversation, 12 October 1886, DNGB, 20:539–41.
128. DQLS, Guangxu, 234:156a (29 November 1886).
129. Yasuoka, "Meiji 19-nen," 70.
130. Yasuoka, "Meiji 19-nen," 76.
131. Chow, *China and Japan*, 170; see also DQLS, Guangxu, 259:477b (13 October 1888).
132. Telegram from Inoue Kaoru to Kusaka Yoshio, 22 November 1886, GKS 4.2.5.103, vol. 4.
133. Wakabayashi, *Anti-foreignism*, 140.
134. Yasuoka, "Meiji 19-nen," 45.
135. *Hōchi Shimbun* quoted in JWM, 21 August 1886.
136. Yoshino, *Nikka kokkō ron*, 4–5.
137. For one example of how the Nagasaki incident is interpreted against the background of subsequent Japanese aggression in China, see Pomerantz-Zhang, *Wu Tingfang*, 77–80. Throughout her narrative of Sino-Japanese relations in this otherwise thoroughly researched book, Pomerantz-Zhang seems to be totally unaware of the fact that Chinese enjoyed extraterritorial privileges in Japan before 1895.
138. Yasuoka, "Meiji 19-nen," 82–83.
139. Murata, *Kōbe kaikō sanjūnenshi*, 2:435–36.
140. RSNE, 17 August 1892, 2. I am indebted to Lane R. Earns for this reference.
141. Inoue's deposition, 18 April 1887, DNGB, 20:464–65. See also Kawakami's report to foreign minister Inoue Kaoru, 21 April 1887, DNGB, 20:458–60.
142. Fukumoto's deposition, 19 April 1887, DNGB, 20:465–66.
143. Mo to Kawakami, 11 April 1887, DNGB, 20:460.
144. Kawakami to Mo, 12 April 1887, DNGB, 20:460–61.
145. Mo to Kawakami, 12 April 1887, DNGB, 20:461.
146. Mo to Kawakami, 15 April 1887, DNGB, 20:462–63.
147. Inoue to Kawakami, 2 May 1887, DNGB, 20:467–68.
148. Lee "Law and Local Autonomy," 118.
149. Bodde and Morris, *Law in Imperial China*, 113–22.
150. When the same problem was broached in a consular courts case in 1875, British consul Charles A. Sinclair declared: "No act of domestic legalization can overrule a clause in a Treaty, which is an act between nations." NCH, 11 February 1875, 129; see also "Alleged Murder by Japanese," NCH, 17 July 1891, 73.
151. Sentence by Nagasaki Court (*Nagasaki jūzai saibansho*), 30 June 1887, GKS 4.2.5.110.
152. The foregoing narrative is based on "A Chinaman Killed by Japanese" and "Murder in the City," NCH, 10 July 1891, 55–56. The Guangfu Temple was located near the intersection of Fangbin Middle Road and Laonan South Road; it has been torn down. Kinouchi, *Shanhai rekishi gaidomappu*, 6.

153. NCH, 10 July 1891.
154. GKS 4.2.5.135.
155. A communication from Yuan to Tsuruhara was published in *Shenbao*, 1 September 1891. An abridged translation of the statement was published in NCH, 4 September 1891, 316.
156. "Alleged Murder by Japanese," NCDN, 13 July 1891.
157. Verdict from Nagasaki Court, 18 December 1891, GKS 4.2.5.135.
158. "Murder in the City," NCH, 27 November 1891, 731–32. This article was reprinted in extenso in RSNE, 2 December 1891, 2–3.
159. "Murder of a Chinese by Japanese," NCH, 4 September 1891, 316.
160. Kim, *Last Phase*, 150.
161. None of the cases analyzed in this chapter has any prominent place in the literature on Japanese treaty revision, if mentioned at all. A prime example this is Inoue Kiyoshi's classic work *Jōyaku Kaisei*.
162. Memorandum in English from Inoue to Shioda, 18 April 1887, DNGB, 20:133.

Chapter 6

1. For a fascinating inside account of these two events, see Mutsu, *Kenkenroku*, 68–76.
2. The *Dingyuan* and *Weiyuan* were sunk by the Japanese in the battle of Weihaiwei in February 1895, whereas the *Zhenyuan* and *Jiyuan* were captured and renamed the *Chin'en* and *Sai'en*, respectively. Gardiner et al., *Conway's All the World's Fighting Ships*, 395–401; Guo, *Jindai Zhongguo shishi rizhi*, 2:901–6.
3. The famous Japanese author Miyake Setsurei devoted a whole chapter to Ding Ruchang in his book on great men and women. Miyake, *Ijin no ato*, 6–23.
4. Soulié de Morant, *Exterritorialité*, 146–47; Padoux, review of Liu Shih-shun, *Extraterritoriality*.
5. Auslin, *Negotiating with Imperialism*, 24–29.
6. Lane-Poole, *Harry Parkes*, 2:313.
7. Chang, *Justice of the Western Consular Courts*.
8. Iriye, "Japan's Drive to Great-Power Status," 737.
9. Tsuda, "Gōmon ron no ichi" (17 May 1874), reprinted in Yamahiro and Nakano, *Meiroku zasshi*, 259–62. The translation is taken from Braisted et al., *Meiroku zasshi*, 96. See also Botsman, *Punishment and Power*, 167–68.
10. Baba, Tatui [Baba Tatsui], *Treaty between Japan and England* (London: Trübner, 1876), reprinted in Baba, *Baba Tatsui zenshū*, 1:133–64 (English part). A facsimile is also reprinted in Inō, *Jōyaku kaiseiron*, 1:1–28.
11. For more information on how these acts influenced one of Baba's Chinese contemporaries, see Luk, "Hong Kong Barrister," 342.
12. Baba, *Baba Tatsui zenshū*, 1:142 (English part).
13. As Richard Chang has noted, Baba's pamphlet has had an enormous impact on the historiography of extraterritoriality. Chang, *Justice of the Western Consular Courts*, xi. For one example, see Inoue, *Jōyaku kaisei*.
14. Mitchell, *Janus-Faced Justice*, 23.
15. Baba, "In a Japanese Cage: The Horrors of Life in a Prison in Tokio," *Evening Star* (Washington, DC), 25 June 1887, reprinted in Baba, *Baba Tatsui zenshū*, 3:5–13; see also Botsman, *Punishment and Power*, 190.
16. For more on this society and the "Itsukaichi constitution," see Irokawa, *Culture of the Meiji Period*, 99–108.
17. Apologia signed by Shimada Ichirō et al., 14 May 1878, in Ishikawa kenritsu rekishi hakubutsukan, *Kioichō jiken*, 92–95.
18. Ikeda, "French Legal Advisor in Meiji Japan," 217.
19. Chang, *Justice of the Western Consular Courts*, 48, 158 n. 22.

20. Mutsu, *Kenkenroku*, 113–16; for the original Japanese text, see Mutsu, *Shintei Kenkenroku*, 183–87. This contention that the Japanese government had only granted "consular jurisdiction" to foreigners has influenced contemporary scholarship on extraterritoriality, and some historians have also taken a further step arguing that whereas consular jurisdiction operated in Japan, foreigners in China enjoyed complete extraterritoriality, ignoring the fact that the Chinese and Japanese extraterritorial régimes partially overlapped in the period between 1871 and 1895. Morita, "'Fubyōdō' jōyaku to ryōji saibanken."
21. Eli T. Sheppard, who was consulting for the Japanese government, put forward one of the most coherent articulations of the official Japanese position. Sheppard, *Extra-territoriality in Japan*.
22. Letter from F. Howard Vyse to British residents of Yokohama, 13 December 1860, reprinted in NCH, 19 January 1861.
23. Brown, "Precarious Life and Slow Death of the Mixed Courts."
24. Nakaoka, "Japanese Research on the Mixed Courts." I am indebted to Cemil Aydin for providing me with this reference.
25. Davidson, *Second Report by John R. Davidson*.
26. Nakaoka, *Hasegawa Takashi no Ejiputo kongō saibanjo chōsa*. I am indebted to Cemil Aydin for providing me with this reference.
27. The Japanese diplomat Nishida Kōichi once pointed out that unlike *huishen yamen*, the English "mixed court" and Japanese *kongō saibansho* both derive from words meaning "mixed" and "court," respectively. See Nishida's report in Chinese translation in Yao, *Huayang susong*, 2:753. To this observation, we can add that the same is true for the French word *cour mixte* and the Arabic counterpart *mahkama mukhtalita*, which were used for the Egyptian mixed courts.
28. Inoue, *Jōyaku kaisei*, 79–95. For an official Japanese account of Japan's way to treaty revision, see Gaimushō Ajiakyoku, *Ryōji saibanken teppai mondai*, 331–99.
29. Tani Kanjō's memorial is quoted in Itagaki, *Jiyūtō shi*, 3:219–25.
30. Kenneth B. Pyle, "Meiji Conservatism," 688–96.
31. Inoue, *Jōyaku kaisei*, 79–128; Ikeda, "French Legal Advisor in Meiji Japan," 187–218.
32. *Tôbaé*, 15 September 1887, reprinted with comments in Shimizu, *Zoku Bigō sobyōshū*, 122–25.
33. *Tôbaé*, 15 March 1887; see Shimizu, *Zoku Bigō sobyōshū*, 138–39.
34. Tanaka, "Maria Rusu-gō jiken."
35. Ibid. For one example of a coolie contract, see Stewart, *Chinese Bondage in Peru*, 42–44.
36. McWilliams, "East Meets East," 247.
37. Memorial from Liu Kunyi, 15 October 1880, reprinted in Liu, *Liu Kunyi yiji*, 2:573–74.
38. Gardiner, *Japanese and Peru*, 16.
39. Tanaka, "Maria Rusu-gō jiken," 287–89.
40. Hoare, "'Bankoku Shimbun' Affair."
41. Ibid.
42. Chang, *Justice of the Western Consular Courts*, 81–98; Tanaka, "Norumanton-gō jiken."
43. Shimizu, *Zoku Bigō sobyōshū*, 132. The song, "Norumanton-gō no uta," can be found in collections of popular Meiji songs on the Internet.
44. Chang, *Justice of the Western Consular Courts*, 81.
45. For two examples, see Inoue, *Jōyaku kaisei*, 38–41, and Ide, *Meiji minshūshi*, 151–68.
46. Inoue, *Jōyaku kaisei*, 139–48.
47. Inoue, *Jōyaku kaisei*, 171–84.
48. Osadake, *Ōtsu Jiken*.
49. Auslin, *Negotiating with Imperialism*, 194–200.
50. Hoare, *Japan's Treaty Ports*, 168–69.
51. Brooks, *Japan's Imperial Diplomacy*, 80.
52. See for instance, the history book that a commission of Japanese, Chinese, and Korean historians has produced: Nitchūkan sangoku kyōtsū rekishi kyōzai iinkai, *Mirai o hiraku rekishi*.

53. Hoare, *Japan's Treaty Ports*, 172–75.
54. For more on legal reform in Taiwan under Japanese rule, see Wang, *Legal Reform in Taiwan*.
55. For one example, see Oda and Yamane, *Shinkoku gyōseihō*.
56. Hao and Wang, "Changing Chinese Views of Western Relations," 194; Cohen, *Between Tradition and Modernity*, 231–32.
57. Chang, *Commissioner Lin*, 136.
58. See Ying's letter, 22 December 1868, reprinted in DNGB, 2.1:262.
59. Letter from Zongli *yamen* (17 September 1867), YWSM, Tongzhi, 50:34a. See also Reinhardt, "Navigating Imperialism in China," 73–75; Knight Biggerstaff, "Secret Correspondence of 1867–1868."
60. Hao and Wang, "Changing Chinese Views of Western Relations, 1840–95," 194.
61. Guo, *Zhuanzhe*, 479–80.
62. Cohen, *Between Tradition and Modernity*, 231–32.
63. Letter to Ding Richang, n.d., in Wang, *Taoyuan chidu*, 338.
64. Wang, *Taoyuan wenlu waibian*, 73–74.
65. "What the Chinese Think about Opium," *Friend of China*, October 1875, 192–201; see also Pomerantz-Zhang, *Wu Tingfang*, 34.
66. Pomerantz-Zhang, *Wu Tingfang*, 38–40.
67. For more on these "bureaucratic pilgrimages," see Anderson, *Imagined Communities*, 114.
68. Guo Songtao's memorial (3 October 1877), in Wang and Wang, *Qingji waijiao shiliao*, 11:10–13; also quoted in Pomerantz-Zhang, *Wu Tingfang*, 39.
69. For more on this episode, see Kotenev, *Shanghai*, 61.
70. Wang and Wang, *Qingji waijiao shiliao*, 11:11b.
71. Pomerantz-Zhang, *Wu Tingfang*, 40.
72. Dai Dongyang, "Riben xiugai tiaoyue jiaoshe."
73. Letter to Liu Xianzhuang, n.d., in Wen, *Chayang sanjia wenchao*, 3:9.
74. Chow, *China and Japan*, 69.
75. Li et al., *Li Pingshu qishi zixu, Ouchu wushi zishu, Wang Xiaolai shulu*, 24; also quoted in Ye Xiaoqing, "Shanghai before Nationalism," 47.
76. Pumpelly, *Across America and Asia*, 205.
77. Edward Cunningham, "Mr. Pumpelly and the Foreigners in China," *Nation*, 3 March 1870, 139.
78. "Taotai to Consul," 30 June 1867, FO 228–433.
79. "Consul to Taotai," 6 July 1867, FO 228–433.
80. Printed notification from Rutherford Alcock, 4 June 1868, FO 228–433. For the identification of place names, see Inspectorate General of Customs, *Names of Places on the China Coast*. Today, the Straw Shoe Channel is more known for being one of the sites where the Nanjing Massacre took place in December 1937.
81. "Fatal Collision at Sea between the 'Ocean' and the 'Fusing,'" NCH, 8 April 1875, 340–41.
82. NCH, 29 May 1875, 524.
83. NCH, 8 April 1875, 340.
84. *Shenbao*, 9 April 1875, 2.
85. NCH, 8 April 1875, 341.
86. *Shenbao*, 12 April 1875, 3.
87. During the nineteenth century, practically all skilled positions on both Chinese and foreign steamships were reserved to foreigners, a practice that endured several decades into the twentieth century. For more on the hiring practices on nineteenth-century steamship companies, see Anne Reinhardt, "Navigating Imperialism in China," 179–233.
88. NCH, 29 May 1875, 535.
89. "Naval Court of Enquiry," NCH, 15 April 1875, 363.
90. *Shenbao*, 14 April 1875, 2.
91. NCH, 15 April 1875, 367.
92. "H.B.M.'s Supreme Court," NCH, 29 May 1875, 524–36.

93. NCH, 19 June 1875, 615.
94. For another example of the malleable nature of courts in the treaty ports, see the report on a mixed case that was tried in Fuzhou the same year. NCH, 11 February 1875, 129–31.
95. For a short sketch of the *Fusing* case, see Chen Tong, "Shehui bianqian zhong de Shanghai lüshi," 56–59.
96. NCH, 19 June 1875, 616.
97. NCH, 24 July 1875, 83; for an English translation of the *Shenbao* editorial, see ibid., 95; for the Chinese original of the text, *Shenbao,* 11 May 1875.
98. NCH, 17 July 1875.
99. Chen, "Shehui bianqian zhong de Shanghai lüshi," 58–59.
100. For more information on this ship, see Gardiner et al., *Conway's All the World's Fighting Ships*, 398.
101. NCH, 26 January 1887, 94; NCH, 23 February 1887, 207–21.
102. NCH, 23 February 1887, 208, 210.
103. NCH, 2 March 1887.
104. *Shenbao,* 26 February 1887.
105. *Dianshizhai huabao,* 107:82 (1887); see also Ye, *Dianshizhai Pictorial,* 150.
106. *Dianshizhai huabao,* 37:6 (1885); see also Ye, *Dianshizhai Pictorial,* 8. The translation from the *Zuo Commentary* comes from Legge, *Chinese Classics,* 5.1:355. For more on this important passage, see Dikötter, *Discourse of Race,* 3, and Liu, *Clash of Empires,* 72–73.
107. Palace memorial from Li Hongzhang, 16 May 1875, in *Shenbao,* 3 June 1875; see also DQLS, Guangxu, 7:11a–12a.
108. This was established in the "Swatow Opium Guild Case" in September 1879. See Kotenev, *Shanghai,* 201–5.
109. For a photograph of Drummond and a short biography of this "leading resident of Shanghai," see Wright and Cartwright, *Twentieth Century Impressions,* 516. Two of his honorary ranks are recorded in DQLS, Guangxu, 274:1a (25 September 1889), and DQLS, Guangxu, 577:4a (9 September 1907).
110. "Mr. Drummond's Appointment," NCH, 26 January 1894; see also Chen, "Shehui bianqian zhong de Shanghai lüshi," 59–60.
111. Chang, *Justice of the Western Consular Courts,* 82.
112. The Fusing incident has been almost completely forgotten, whereas the sinking of the *Wan Nien Ching* has mainly been studied by specialists in Chinese maritime history and is not widely known outside of the field. For instance, only one paragraph is devoted to the *Fusing* case in Xue Liyong's *Jiu Shanghai zujie shihua,* 53. One relatively exhaustive treatment of the *Wan Nien Ching* case can be found in Chen Yue, "Heng kong chu shi." I am indebted to Prof. Y. W. Mah for this reference. One incident that has attracted some attention is the "Kowshing Incident," which took place at the early stages of the First Sino-Japanese War. See Howland, "Sinking of the S.S. Kowshing."
113. Alford, "Of Arsenic and Old Laws"; Dong, "Communities and Communication."
114. Another case of an extraterritorial régime operating by default is the Swedish-Norwegian treaty with the Qing Empire from 1847, which the Qing government respected in practice, despite the fact that the Qing never formally ratified the treaty. See Cassel, "Traktaten som aldrig var och fördraget som nästan inte blev."
115. Wagner, "Shenbao in Crisis," *Late Imperial China* 20, no. 1 (1999): 107–43.
116. Hornby, *Sir Edmund Hornby,* 245.
117. Pelcovits, *Old China Hands and the Foreign Office,* 30.
118. NCH, 23 February 1887, 220.
119. This description comes from Hoare, *Japan's Treaty Ports,* 172.
120. For an outline of the *Subao* case, see Lust, "'Su-Pao' Case," and Rankin, *Early Chinese Revolutionaries,* 88–95. See also Kotenev, *Shanghai,* 109–13 and 239, and Keeton, *Development of Extraterritoriality,* 1:365–66.
121. Wang, *In Search of Justice,* 79–80.

122. For more on the role of the guilds, or the native place organizations, see Goodman, "Locality as Microcosm of the Nation?"
123. Kotenev, *Shanghai*, 126–32; see also Goodman, *Native Place*.
124. Scully, *Bargaining with the State from Afar*, 97–98.
125. For more on the Japanese connection, see Reynolds, *China, 1898–1912*.
126. Pomerantz-Zhang, *Wu Tingfang*, 141–48.
127. Chen, "'Zhong-Ying xuyi tongshang xingchuan tiaoyue.'"
128. TCCF, 1:557.
129. For the most complete account of Shen Jiaben's efforts to abolish the separate status of Manchus, see Rhoads, *Manchus and Han*, 70–120; for an account of Wu Tingfang's contributions to legal reform, see Pomerantz-Zhang, *Wu Tingfang*, 172–79, and Luk, "Hong Kong Barrister."
130. Most of these memorials can be found in Gugong bowuyuan, *Qingmo choubei lixian dang'an shiliao*.
131. Duanfang's memorial, 31 July 1907, in Gugong bowuyuan, *Qingmo choubei lixian dang'an shiliao*, 2:915–18; also quoted in Rhoads, *Manchus and Han*, 110–12.
132. Rhoads, *Manchus and Han*, 117–18.
133. Shen Jiaben's memorial to the throne, 10 January 1908, as translated in Meijer, *Introduction of Modern Criminal Law in China*, 186; the original can be found in Shen, and Yu, *Zunyi Man-Han tongxing xinglü*.
134. Rhoads, *Manchus and Han*, 121–25.
135. Shuntian fu (Archives of Shuntian Prefecture), Zhongguo diyi lishi dang'anguan (First Historical Archives of China), 28.1.12.018; see also Zheng, *Qingdai falü zhidu yanjiu*, 305.
136. The characterization of some aspects of the 1911 revolution as genocidal comes from Rhoads, *Manchus and Han*, 204.
137. Rhoads, *Manchus and Han*, 202–3.
138. Rhoads, *Manchus and Han*, 252–70.
139. For English translations of Chinese draft constitutions from 1908 through 1943, see Pan, *Chinese Constitution*.
140. Kirby, *Germany and Republican China*, 17, 24, 226; Scully, *Bargaining with the State*, 82–83.
141. Bickers, *Britain in China*, 139–43.
142. Stephens, *Order and Discipline in China*, 62.

Conclusion

1. Chan, "Abrogation of British Extraterritoriality in China 1942–43"; Ma, "Invisible War between the United States and Japan over China."
2. Angle and Svensson, *Chinese Human Rights Reader*, 359; Kang and Pan, *Jindai wairen zai-Hua zhiwai faquan yanjiu*, 3; For a stimulating treatment on the relationship between extraterritoriality and the human rights debate, see Scully, "Historical Wrongs and Human Rights."
3. Edward Gay, "China Murder Trial 'Insult to NZ Jurisdiction,'" nzherald.co.nz, www.nzherald.co.nz/nz/news/article.cfm?c_id=1&;objectid=10699328, 13 January 2011, accessed 8 March 2011; Arild M. Jonassen, "Kina har løslatt Zhao Fei," *Aftenposten*, www.aftenposten.no/nyheter/uriks/article3857418.ece, 14 October 2010, accessed 18 March 2011.
4. Inoue, *Jōyaku kaisei*, i–v; see also Johnson, "Three Rapes."
5. Cochran and Chiu, *U.S. Status of Force Agreements with Asian Countries*.
6. William C. Kirby, "When Did China Become China: Thoughts on the Twentieth Century," in Fogel, *Teleology of the Modern Nation-State*, 108.
7. Brady, *Making the Foreign Serve China*.
8. Dikötter, *Age of Openness: China before Mao*, 39–40.

9. According to current Chinese legislation, foreign lawyers are not permitted to engage in any legal advice concerning Chinese law. See "China May Crack Down on Foreign Law Firms," China Daily.com.cn, 16 May 2006.
10. Wagner, "Role of the Foreign Community in the Chinese Public Sphere."
11. The most exhaustive treatment of this neglected topic can be found in Brady, *Making the Foreign Serve China*.
12. Tania Branigan, "Africans Protest in China after Nigerian Dies in Immigration Raid," guardian.co.uk, 16 July 2006.
13. Simon Elegant and Chengcheng Jiang, "Can a Mixed-Race Contestant Become a Chinese Idol?" Time.com, 23 September 2009.

BIBLIOGRAPHY

Abiko, Bonnie. "Persecuted Patriot: Watanabe Kazan and the Tokugawa Bakufu." *Monumenta Nipponica* 44, no. 2 (1989): 199–219.
ADPP1. Davids, Jules, ed. *American Diplomatic and Public Papers, the United States and China.* Series 1. *The Treaty System and the Taiping Rebellion, 1842–1860*. 21 vols. Wilmington, Del.: Scholarly Resources, 1973.
ADPP2. Davids, Jules, ed. *American Diplomatic and Public Papers, the United States and Chin.* Series 2. *The United States, China, and Imperial Rivalries, 1861–1893*. 18 vols. Wilmington, Del.: Scholarly Resources, 1979.
Alabaster, Ernest. "Notes on Chinese Law and Practice Preceding Revision." *Journal of the North China Branch of the Royal Asiatic Society* 38 (1906): 83–100.
Alabaster, Ernest, and Chaloner Alabaster. *Notes and Commentaries on Chinese Criminal Law, and Cognate Topics*. London: Luzac & Co., 1899. Reprint, Taipei: Ch'eng-Wen, 1968.
Alcock, Rutherford. *The Capital of the Tycoon: A Narrative of a Three Years' Residence in Japan*. 2 vols. London: Longman, Green, Longman, Roberts, & Green, 1863. Reprint, St. Clair Shores, Mich.: Scholarly Press, 1969.
Alcock, Rutherford. "China and Its Foreign Relations." *Asiatic Quarterly Review* 3 (1887): 443–66.
Alford, William P. "Of Arsenic and Old Laws: Looking Anew at Criminal Justice in Late Imperial China." *California Law Review* 72, no. 6 (1984): 1180–1256.
Anderson, Benedict R. *Imagined Communities: Reflections on the Origin and Spread of Nationalism*. Rev. and extended ed. London: Verso, 1991.
Angle, Stephen, and Marina Svensson, eds. *The Chinese Human Rights Reader: Documents and Commentary, 1900–2000*. Armonk, N.Y.: M. E. Sharpe, 2001.
Antonetti, Guy, ed. *Boissonade et la réception du droit français au Japon: Colloque*. Paris: Société de législation comparée, 1991.
Askew, Joseph Benjamin. "Re-visiting New Territory: The Terranova Incident Re-examined." *Asian Studies Review* 28, no. 4 (2004): 351–71.
Auslin, Michael R. *Negotiating with Imperialism: The Unequal Treaties and the Culture of Japanese Diplomacy*. Cambridge, Mass.: Harvard University Press, 2004.
Baba Tatsui. *Baba Tatsui zenshū*. Edited by Nishida Taketoshi. 4 vols. Tokyo: Iwanami shoten, 1987.
Baller, F. W., ed. *The Sacred Edict*. Shanghai: American Presbyterian Mission Press, 1892.
Banno, Masataka. *China and the West, 1858–1861: The Origins of the Tsungli Yamen*. Cambridge, Mass.: Harvard University Press, 1964.
Barton, Sydney. "The Shanghai Mixed Court." *Chinese Social and Political Science Review* 5, no. 1 (1919): 31–41.
Bastid-Bruguière, Marianne. "Currents of Social Change." In *Cambridge History of China: Late Ch'ing, 1800–1911*, pt. 1, vol. 11, edited by Denis C. Twitchett and John K. Fairbank, 536–602. Cambridge: Cambridge University Press, 1978.

Beasley, W. G., ed. *Select Documents on Japanese Foreign Policy, 1853–1868*. London: Oxford University Press, 1955.
Bello, David Anthony. *Opium and the Limits of Empire: Drug Prohibition in the Chinese Interior, 1729–1850*. Cambridge, Mass.: Harvard University Asia Center, distributed by Harvard University Press, 2005.
Benton, Lauren A. *Law and Colonial Cultures: Legal Regimes in World History, 1400–1900*. Cambridge: Cambridge University Press, 2002.
Bergère, Marie-Claire. *Shanghai: China's Gateway to Modernity*. Translated by Janet Lloyd. Stanford, Calif.: Stanford University Press, 2009.
Bernhardt, Kathryn, and Philip C. Huang, eds. *Civil Law in Qing and Republican China*. Stanford, Calif.: Stanford University Press, 1994.
Berry, Mary Elizabeth. *Hideyoshi*. Cambridge, Mass.: Harvard University Press, 1982.
Bickers, Robert A. *Britain in China: Community, Culture and Colonialism, 1900–1949*. Manchester, UK: St. Martin's Press, 1999.
Biggerstaff, Knight. "The Secret Correspondence of 1867–1868: Views of Leading Chinese Statesmen Regarding the Further Opening of China to Western Influence." *Journal of Modern History* 22, no. 2 (1950): 122–36.
Bix, Herbert P. *Hirohito and the Making of Modern Japan*. New York: HarperCollins, 2000.
Bodde, Derk, and Clarence Morris. *Law in Imperial China: Exemplified by 190 Ch'ing Dynasty Cases*. Cambridge, Mass.: Harvard University Press, 1967.
Boorman, Howard L., Richard C. Howard, and Joseph K. H. Cheng, eds. *Biographical Dictionary of Republican China*. 5 vols. New York: Columbia University Press, 1967.
Botsman, Daniel V. *Punishment and Power in the Making of Modern Japan*. Princeton, N.J.: Princeton University Press, 2005.
Bourgon, Jérôme. "De quelques tendances récentes de la sinologie juridique américaine." *T'oung Pao* 84, no. 4–5 (1998): 380–414.
Bourgon, Jérôme. "Le droit coutumier comme phénomène d'acculturation bureaucratique au Japon et en Chine." *Extrême-Orient, Extrême-Occident* 23 (2001): 125–43.
Bourgon, Jérôme."Uncivil Dialogue: Law and Custom Did Not Merge into Civil Law under the Qing." *Late Imperial China* 23, no. 1 (2002): 50–90.
Brady, Anne-Marie. *Making the Foreign Serve China: Managing Foreigners in the People's Republic*. Lanham, Md.: Rowman & Littlefield, 2003.
Braisted, William Reynolds, Yasushi Adachi, and Yuji Kikuchi, eds. *Meiroku zasshi: Journal of the Japanese Enlightenment*. Cambridge, Mass.: Harvard University Press, 1976.
Brook, Timothy, and Bob Tadashi Wakabayashi, eds. *Opium Regimes: China, Britain, and Japan, 1839–1952*. Berkeley: University of California Press, 2000.
Brook, Timothy, Bourgon Jérôme, and Gregory Blue. *Death by a Thousand Cuts*. Cambridge, Mass.: Harvard University Press, 2008.
Brooks, Barbara J. *Japan's Imperial Diplomacy: Consuls, Treaty Ports, and War in China, 1895–1938*. Honolulu: University of Hawai'i Press, 2000.
Brown, Nathan J. "The Precarious Life and Slow Death of the Mixed Courts of Egypt." *International Journal of Middle East Studies* 25, no. 1 (1993): 33–52.
Brubaker, Rogers. *Citizenship and Nationhood in France and Germany*. Cambridge, Mass.: Harvard University Press, 1992.
Brunnert, S., V. V. Hagelström, and N. F. Kolesov. *Present Day Political Organization of China*. Translated by A. Biel'chenko and E. E. Moran. Shanghai: Kelly and Walsh, 1912. Reprint, Oxford: Routledge, 2007.
Buoye, Thomas M. *Manslaughter, Markets, and Moral Economy: Violent Disputes over Property Rights in Eighteenth Century China*. Cambridge: Cambridge University Press, 2000.
Caldwell, Peter C. "The Citizen and the Republic in Germany, 1918–1935." In *Citizenship and National Identity in Twentieth-Century Germany*, edited by Geoff Eley and Jan Palmowski, 40–56. Stanford, Calif.: Stanford University Press, 2008.
Callery, Joseph-Marie, ed. *Correspondance diplomatique Chinoise relative aux négotiations du traité de Whampoa conclu entre la France et la Chine le 24 octobre 1844*. Paris: Seringe Frères, 1879.

Cao, Deborah. *Chinese Law: A Language Perspective = Shuo Fa*. Aldershot, England: Ashgate, 2004.
Cassel, Pär. "Excavating Extraterritoriality: The 'Judicial Sub-prefect' as a Prototype for the Mixed Court in Shanghai." *Late Imperial China* 24, no. 2 (2003): 156–82.
Cassel, Pär. "Koga Tōan, *Suppositions on Naval Defense* and the Opium War Debate." Paper presented at the Harvard Graduate Student Conference for Japanese Studies, Cambridge, Massachusetts, 16 March 2002.
Cassel, Pär. "Traktaten som aldrig var och fördraget som nästan inte blev: De svensk-norsk-kinesiska förbindelserna, 1847–1909" [The Treaty that never was and the Treaty that almost never became: Swedish-Norwegian-Chinese relations, 1847–1909]. *Historisk tidskrift* 130, no. 3 (2010): 437–66.
Chan, K. C. "The Abrogation of British Extraterritoriality in China 1942–43: A Study of Anglo-American-Chinese Relations." *Modern Asian Studies* 11, no. 2 (1977): 257–91.
Chang Hsin-pao. *Commissioner Lin and the Opium War*. Cambridge, Mass.: Harvard University Press, 1964.
Chang, Richard T. *The Justice of the Western Consular Courts in Nineteenth-Century Japan*. Westport, Conn.: Greenwood Press, 1984.
Changshan. *Zhu Yue baqi zhi*. 1879 ed. Reprinted in *Xuxiu Siku quanshu*, vols. 859–60. Shanghai: Shanghai guji chubanshe, 1995.
Chao Shih-en (Zhao Shi'en). "The Opinion of Chao Shih-En, Delegate of the Shanghai General Chamber of Commerce." *Falü pinglun* [Law Weekly Review], 22 June 1924, 2–3.
Chen Chieh-hsien (Chen Jiexian). *Manchu Archival Materials*. Taipei: Linking, 1988.
Chen Donglin, ed. *Qingdai Dongbei Acheng Hanwen dang'an xuanbian*. Beijing: Zhonghua shuju, 1994.
Chen, Fu-mei Chang. "On Analogy in Ch'ing Law." *Harvard Journal of Asiatic Studies* 30 (1970): 212–24.
Chen Laixing. "Tei Kōsho nikki ni miru Chūka kaikan sōkenki no Kōbe kakkyō shakai." *Jinbun ronshū* 32, no. 2 (1996): 1–25.
Chen Li. "Law, Empire, and Historiography of Modern Sino-Western Relations: A Case Study of the *Lady Hughes* Controversy in 1784." *Law and History Review* 27, no. 1 (2009): 1–53.
Ch'en, Paul Heng-Chao. *Chinese Legal Tradition under the Mongols: The Code of 1291 as Reconstructed*. Princeton, N.J.: Princeton University Press, 1979.
Ch'en, Paul Heng-Chao. *The Formation of the Early Meiji Legal Order: The Japanese Code of 1871 and Its Chinese Foundation*. London Oriental Series, vol. 35. Oxford: Oxford University Press, 1981.
Chen Tong. "Shehui bianqianzhong de Shanghai lüshi." Ph.D. diss., Chinese University of Hong Kong, 2004.
Chen Yaping. "'Zhong-Ying xuyi tongshang xingchuan tiaoyue' yu Qingmo xiulü bianxi." *Qingshi yanjiu* 1 (2004): 58–65.
Chen Yue. "Heng kong chu shi: Fujian chuanzheng 'Wannian Qing' paojian." *Xiandai jianchuan* 313 (2007): 47–55.
Cheng, Pei-kai, Michael Elliot Lestz, and Jonathan D. Spence, eds. *The Search for Modern China: A Documentary Collection*. New York: Norton, 1999.
Chia Ning. "The Li-Fan Yuan in the Early Ch'ing Dynasty." Ph.D. diss., Johns Hopkins University, 1992.
Chiang Kai-shek. *China's Destiny and Chinese Economic Theory*. Translated by Philip J. Jaffe. New York: Roy, 1947.
Chiba Masaji. *Legal Pluralism: Toward a General Theory through Japanese Legal Culture*. Tokyo: Tokai University Press, 1989.
China Maritime Customs. *Decennial Reports on the Trade, Industries, etc. of the Ports Open to Foreign Commerce, and on Conditions and Development of the Treaty Port Provinces 1902–11, Third Issue*. Vol. 1. *Northern and Yangzte Ports*. Shanghai: Statistical Dept. of the Inspectorate General of Customs, 1913.
The Chinese Repository. Guangzhou (Canton), 1832–51.
Chinsai Nippō. Nagasaki.

Chow Jen Hwa. *China and Japan: The History of Chinese Diplomatic Missions in Japan, 1877–1911.* Singapore: Chopmen Enterprises, 1975.

Ch'ü T'ung-tsu (Qu Tongzu). *Law and Society in Traditional China.* Paris: Mouton, 1965.

Ch'ü T'ung-tsu (Qu Tongzu). *Local Government in China under the Ch'ing.* Cambridge, Mass.: Harvard University Press, 1962.

Coates, P. D. *The China Consuls: British Consular Officers, 1843–1943.* New York: Oxford University Press, 1988.

Cochran, Charles L., and Hungdah Chiu, eds. *U.S. Status of Force Agreements with Asian Countries: Selected Studies.* Occasional Papers/Reprints Series in Contemporary Asian Studies, no. 7 (28). Baltimore: University of Maryland School of Law, 1979.

Cohen, Jerome Alan, ed. *China's Practice of International Law: Some Case Studies.* Cambridge, Mass.: Harvard University Press, 1972.

Cohen, Myron L. "Writs of Passage in Late Imperial China: The Documentation of Practical Understandings in Minong, Taiwan." In *Contract and Property in Early Modern China*, edited by Madeleine Zelin, Jonathan K. Ocko, and Robert Gardella, 37–93. Stanford, Calif.: Stanford University Press, 2004.

Cohen, Paul A. *Between Tradition and Modernity: Wang T'ao and Reform in Late Ch'ing China.* Harvard East Asian Monographs 133. Cambridge, Mass.: Council on East Asian Studies, 1987.

Cohen, Paul A. *China and Christianity: The Missionary Movement and the Growth of Chinese Antiforeignism, 1860–1870.* Cambridge, Mass.: Harvard University Press, 1963.

Cohen, Paul A. "Christian Missions and Their Impact to 1900." In *Cambridge History of China: Late Ch'ing, 1800–1911*, pt. 1, vol. 10, edited by Denis C. Twitchett and John K. Fairbank, 543–90. Cambridge: Cambridge University Press, 1978.

Confucius. *The Analects.* Translated by D. C. Lau. Harmondsworth, England: Penguin Books, 1979.

Cooke, George Wingrove. *China and Lower Bengal: Being "the Times" Special Correspondence from China in the Years 1857–58.* 5th ed. London: G. Routledge, 1861. Reprint, Wilmington, Del.: Scholarly Resources, 1972.

Crossley, Pamela Kyle. "Thinking About Ethnicity in Early Modern China." *Late Imperial China* 11, no. 1 (1990): 1–35.

Dai Dongyang. "Riben xiugai tiaoyue jiaoshe yu He Ruzhang de tiaoyue renshi." *Jindaishi yanjiu*, no. 6 (2004): 161–97.

Daijōkan furei benran (Compendium of Proclamations from the Council of State), Kokuritsu kōbunshokan (National Archives of Japan), Tokyo.

Da Minglü zhijie suozai Minglü. In *Zhongguo zhenxi falü dianji jicheng*, edited by Liu Hainian and Yang Yifan, 2.1:397–632. Beijing: Kexue chubanshe, 1994.

Davidson, John Richard. *Second Report by John R. Davidson Being an Examination of the Question of Japanese Judicial Reform and Codification Viewed in the Light of His Report on the Egyptian System of Mixed Courts Dated June 1877.* N.p., 1877.

Da Yuan Shengzheng Guochao Dianzhang. 1303 ed. Reprint, 3 vols., Taipei: Guoli gugong bowuyuan, 1976.

DCYPZZ. Qi Sihe, ed. *Di'er ci Yapian zhanzheng.* 6 vols. Shanghai: Shanghai renmin chubanshe, 1978–79.

Denby, Charles. "Extraterritoriality in China." *American Journal of International Law* 18, no. 4 (1924): 667–75.

Deuchler, Martina. *Confucian Gentlemen and Barbarian Envoys: The Opening of Korea, 1875–1885.* Seattle: University of Washington Press, 1977.

Dianshizhai huabao. Shanghai. 528 issues in 44 vols. Reprint, Guangzhou: Guangdong renmin chubanshe, 1983.

Dicks, A. R. "New Lamps for Old: The Evolving Legal Position of Islam in China, with Special Reference to Family Law." In *Islamic Family Law*, edited by Chibli Mallat and Jane Frances Connors, 347–87. London: Graham & Trotman, 1990.

Dikötter, Frank. *The Age of Openness: China before Mao*. Berkeley: University of California Press, 2008.
Dikötter, Frank. *The Discourse of Race in Modern China*. Stanford, Calif.: Stanford University Press, 1992.
Ding, Yizhuang. *Qingdai baqi zhufang yanjiu*. Shenyang: Liaoning minzu chubanshe, 2003.
Ding, Yizhuang. "Qingdai lishi tongzhi kaolüe." In *Qingzhu Wang Zhonghan xiansheng bashi shouchen xueshu lunwenji*, edited by Chang Jiang, 263–74. Shenyang: Liaoning daxue chubanshe, 1993.
DNGB. Gaimushō chōsabu, ed. *Dai Nihon gaikō bunsho*. 73 vols. Tokyo: Nihon Kokusai Kyōkai, 1936–63.
Dong, Madeleine Yue. "Communitities and Communication: A Study of the Case of Yang Naiwu (1873–77)." *Late Imperial China* 16, no. 1 (1994).
DQHS. Kun'gang and Liu Qiduan, eds. *Qinding Da Qing huidian shili*. 1899 ed. 1220 vols. (*juan*). Reprinted in *Xuxiu Siku quanshu*, vols. 798–814. Shanghai: Shanghai guji chubanshe, 1995–98.
DQLS. *Da Qing lichao shilu*. Arranged according to imperial reign. Tokyo, 1937. Reprint, Taipei: Huawen shuju, 1964.
Dudden, Alexis. *Japan's Colonization of Korea: Discourse and Power*. Honolulu: University of Hawai'i Press, 2005.
Dudden, Alexis. "Japan's Engagement with International Terms." In *Tokens of Exchange: The Problem of Translation in Global Circulations*, edited by Lydia He Liu, 165–91. Durham, N.C.: Duke University Press, 1999.
Edwards, R. Randle. "Ch'ing Legal Jurisdiction over Foreigners." In *Essays on China's Legal Tradition*, edited by Jerome Alan Cohen, R. Randle Edwards, and Fu-mei Chang Chen, 222–69. Princeton, N.J.: Princeton University Press, 1980.
Elliott, Mark C. *The Manchu Way: The Eight Banners and Ethnic Identity in Late Imperial China*. Stanford, Calif.: Stanford University Press, 2001.
Elman, Benjamin A. *On Their Own Terms: Science in China, 1550–1900*. Cambridge, Mass.: Harvard University Press, 2005.
Elvin, Mark. "The Mixed Court of the International Settlement at Shanghai (until 1911)." *Papers on China* 17 (1963): 131–59.
Escarra, Jean. *La Chine et le droit international*. Paris: A. Pedone, 1931.
Fairbank, John King. "The Creation of the Treaty System." In *Cambridge History of China: Late Ch'ing, 1800–1911*, pt. 1, edited by John K. Fairbank, 213–63. Cambridge: Cambridge University Press, 1978.
Fairbank, John King. "Synarchy under the Treaties." In *Chinese Thought and Institutions*, edited by John K. Fairbank, 204–31. Chicago: University of Chicago Press, 1957.
Fairbank, John King. *Trade and Diplomacy on the China Coast: The Opening of the Treaty Ports, 1842–1854*. 2 vols. Cambridge, Mass.: Harvard University Press, 1953.
Falü pinglun [Law weekly review]. Beijing.
Farmer, Edward L. *Zhu Yuanzhang and Early Ming Legislation: The Reordering of Chinese Society Following the Era of Mongol Rule*. New York: Brill, 1995.
Feuerwerker, Albert. "The Foreign Presence in China." In *The Cambridge History of China: Republican China, 1912–1949*, pt. 1, edited by John King Fairbank and Albert Feuerwerker, 128–207. Cambridge: Cambridge University Press, 1986.
Finkelstein, David. "The Language of Communist China's Criminal Law." In *Contemporary Chinese Law: Research Problems and Perspectives*, edited by Jerome Alan Cohen, 188–209. Cambridge, Mass.: Harvard University Press, 1970.
Fishel, Wesley R. *The End of Extraterritoriality in China*. Berkeley: University of California Press, 1952.
Fletcher, Joseph. "The Heyday of the Ch'ing Order in Mongolia, Sinkiang and Tibet." In *Cambridge History of China: Late Ch'ing, 1800–1911*, pt. 1, vol. 10, edited by Denis C. Twitchett and John K. Fairbank, 351–408. Cambridge: Cambridge University Press, 1978.
Fletcher, Joseph. "Sino-Russian Relations, 1800–62." In *Cambridge History of China: Late Ch'ing, 1800–1911*, pt. 1, edited by Denis C. Twitchett and John K. Fairbank, 318–50. Cambridge: Cambridge University Press, 1978.

FO. Foreign Office, National Archives, Kew, England.
Fogel, Joshua A. *Articulating the Sinosphere: Sino-Japanese Relations in Space and Time.* Cambridge, Mass.: Harvard University Press, 2009.
Fogel, Joshua A. *The Cultural Dimension of Sino-Japanese Relations: Essays on the Nineteenth and Twentieth Centuries.* Armonk, N.Y.: M. E. Sharpe, 1995.
Fogel, Joshua A., ed. *The Teleology of the Modern Nation-State: Japan and China, Encounters with Asia.* Philadelphia: University of Pennsylvania Press, 2005.
Foreign Office of Great Britain, ed. *Correspondence Respecting the Revision of the Treaty of Tien-tsin. China: A Collection of Correspondence and Papers Relating to Chinese Affairs, 1871–75.* No. 5. London: Printed by Harrison and Sons, 1871.
Foreign Office of Great Britain, ed. *Further Correspondence Respecting the Attack on the Indian Expedition to Western China and the Murder of Mr. Margary.* London: Harrison, 1877.
French, Rebecca Redwood. *The Golden Yoke: The Legal Cosmology of Buddhist Tibet.* Ithaca, N.Y.: Cornell University Press, 1995.
Fu, Lo-shu, ed. *A Documentary Chronicle of Sino-Western Relations, 1644–1820.* 2 vols. Tucson: University of Arizona Press, 1966.
Fujimura Michio. "Jōyaku reikōron no zentei: Jōyaku kaiseishi no kenkyū (1)." *Nagoya daigaku bungakubu kenkyū ronshū* 29 (1963): 1–20.
Fujimura Michio. "Meiji shonen ni okeru Ajiya seisaku no shūsei to Chūgoku: Nisshin shūkō jōki sōan no kentō." *Nagoya daigaku bungakubu kenkyū ronshū 44: Shigaku* 15 (1967): 3–26.
Fukuzawa Yukichi. *Fukuzawa Yukichi chosakushū.* 12 vols. Tokyo: Keiō Gijuku Daigaku shuppankai, 2002.
Fukuzawa Yukichi. *Fukuzawa Yukichi zenshū.* 2nd ed. 22 vols. Tokyo: Iwanami Shoten, 1958.
Gaimushō Ajiakyoku, ed. *Ryōji saibanken teppai mondai.* Tokyo: Gaimushō Ajiakyoku, n.d.
Gaimushō Gaikō Shiryōkan, ed. *Gaikō shiryōkan shozō Gaimushō kiroku sōmokuroku, senzenki.* 3 vols. Tokyo: Hara shobō, 1992.
Gaimushō Gaikō Shiryōkan, ed. *Nihon gaikōshi jiten.* New ed. Tokyo: Yamakawa shuppansha, 1992.
Gardiner, C. Harvey. *The Japanese and Peru, 1873–1973.* 1st ed. Albuquerque: University of New Mexico Press, 1975.
Gardiner, Robert, Roger Chesneau, and Eugene M. Kolesnik, eds. *Conway's All the World's Fighting Ships, 1860–1905.* London: Conway Maritime Press, 1979.
Geertz, Clifford. *Local Knowledge: Further Essays in Interpretive Anthropology.* New York: Basic Books, 1983.
Giersch, Charles Patterson, Jr. *Asian Borderlands: The Transformation of Qing China's Yunnan Frontier.* Cambridge, Mass.: Harvard University Press, 2006.
Giles, Herbert A. *A Chinese-English Dictionary.* London: B. Quaritch, Kelly & Walsh, Limited, 1892.
GKS. Gaimushō kiroku, Senzenki. (Diplomatic Records. Pre-war Period.) Gaimu honshō gaikō shiryōkan (Diplomatic Records' Office of the Ministry of Foreign Affairs of Japan), Tokyo.
Goodman, Bryna. "The Locality as Microcosm of the Nation? Native Place Networks and Early Urban Nationalism in China." *Modern China* 21, no. 4 (1995): 387–419.
Goodman, Bryna. *Native Place, City, and Nation: Regional Networks and Identities in Shanghai, 1853–1937.* Berkeley: University of California Press, 1995.
Greene, D. C. "Correspondence between William II of Holland and the Shōgun of Japan A.D. 1844." *Transactions of the Asiatic Society of Japan,* first series, 34, no. 4 (1907): 99–132.
Griffiths, John. "Recent Anthropology of Law in the Netherlands and Its Historical Background." In *Anthropology of Law in the Netherlands: Essays on Legal Pluralism,* edited by Keebet von Benda-Beckmann and A. K. J. M. Strijbosch, 11–66. Dordrecht: Foris, 1986.
Griffiths, John. "What Is Legal Pluralism?" *Journal of Legal Pluralism and Unofficial Law* 24 (1986): 1–50.
Grosse-Aschhoff, Angelus Francis J. *The Negotiations between Ch'i-Ying and Lagrené, 1844–1846.* St. Bonaventure, N.Y.: Franciscan Institute, 1950.

Gugong bowuyuan, ed. *Qingmo choubei lixian dang'an shiliao*. 2 vols. Beijing: Zhonghua shuju, 1979.
Gugong bowuyuan, ed. *Qingji Zhongwai shiling nianbiao*. Beijing: Zhonghua shuju, 1985.
Gulik, Robert Hans van. "Kakkaron: A Japanese Echo of the Opium War." *Monumenta Serica* 4 (1939): 478–545.
Guo Tingyi, ed. *Jindai Zhongguo shishi rizhi: Qingji*. 2 vols. Taipei: Zhengzhong shuju, 1963.
Guo Weidong. "'Jiangnan shanhou zhangcheng' ji xiangguan wenti." *Lishi yanjiu* 1 (1995).
Guo Weidong. "Jindai Zhongguo liquan sangshi de ling yizhong yinyou: Lingshi caipanquan zai-Hua queli guocheng yanjiu." *Jindaishi Yanjiu* 2 (1997): 216–36.
Guo Weidong. "Lun lingshi caipanquan zai jindai Zhongguo de queli." *Beida shixue* 3 (1995): 200–213.
Guo Weidong. "Yapian zhanzheng qianhou waiguo funü jinru Zhongguo tongshang kou'an wenti." *Jindaishi yanjiu* 1 (1999): 242–67.
Guo Weidong. "'Zhaohui' yu Zhongguo waijiao wenshu jindai fanshi de chugou." *Lishi Yanjiu* 3 (2000): 92–102.
Guo Weidong. *Zhuanzhe: Yi zaoqi Zhong-Ying guanxi he "Nanjing tiaoyue" wei kaocha zhongxin*. Shijiazhuang: Hebei renmin chubanshe, 2003.
Haley, John Owen. *Authority without Power: Law and the Japanese Paradox*. New York: Oxford University Press, 1991.
Haley, John Owen. *The Spirit of Japanese Law*. Athens: University of Georgia Press, 1998.
Hamashita, Takeshi. "The Tribute Trade System and Modern Asia." *Memoirs of the Research Department of the Toyo Bunko* 46 (1988): 7–25.
Hammond, Kelly. "The Shanghai Mixed Court 1863–1880: Colonial Institution Building and the Creation of Legal Knowledge as a Process of Interaction and Mediation between the Chinese and the British." Master's thesis, Simon Fraser University, 2007.
Harrison, Henrietta. *The Man Awakened from Dreams: One Man's Life in a North China Village, 1857–1942*. Stanford, Calif. Stanford University Press, 2005.
Hao Yen-p'ing and Wang Erh-min. "Changing Chinese Views of Western Relations, 1840–95." In *The Cambridge History of China: Late Ch'ing, 1800–1911*, pt. 2, vol. 11, edited by John King Fairbank and Kwang-Ching Liu, 142–201. Cambridge: Cambridge University Press, 1980.
Harootunian, Harry D. *Toward Restoration: The Growth of Political Consciousness in Tokugawa Japan*. Berkeley: University of California Press, 1970.
Hayashi Fukusai and Yanai Kenji, eds. *Tsūkō ichiran zokushū*. 5 vols. Osaka: Seibundō, 1968–73.
Hayashi Shōzō, Ishii Ryōsuke, and Naikaku kirokukyoku, eds. *Hōki bunrui taizen*. 88 vols. Tokyo: Naikaku kirokukyoku, 1891–94. Reprint, Tokyo: Hara Shobō, 1977.
He Changling, ed. *Huangchao jingshi wenbian*. Reprint, Taipei: Shijie shuju, 1964.
Henderson, Dan Fenno. "Chinese Legal Studies in Early 18th Century Japan: Scholars and Sources." *Journal of Asian Studies* 30, no. 1 (1970): 21–56.
Henderson, Dan Fenno. *Conciliation and Japanese Law, Tokugawa and Modern*. 2 vols. Seattle: Published for the Association for Asian Studies by University of Washington Press, 1965.
Henderson, Dan Fenno. *Village "Contracts" In Tokugawa Japan : Fifty Specimens with English Translations and Comments*. Seattle: University of Washington Press, 1975.
Herman, John E. *Amid the Clouds and Mist: China's Colonization of Guizhou, 1200–1700*. Cambridge, Mass.: Harvard University Asia Center: Distributed by Harvard University Press, 2007.
Hertslet, Edward, ed. *Treaties, &C., between Great Britain and China; and between China and Foreign Powers; Orders in Council, Rules, Regulations, Acts of Parliament, Decrees, and Notifications Affecting British Interests in China, in Force on the 1st January, 1896*. 2 vols. London: Homson, 1896.
Heuschert, Dorothea. *Die Gesetzgebung der Qing für die Mongolen Im 17. Jahrhundert: Anhand des Mongolischen Gesetzbuches aus der Kangxi-Zeit (1662–1722)*. Wiesbaden: Harrassowitz Verlag, 1998.
Heuschert, Dorothea. "Legal Pluralism in the Qing Empire: Manchu Legislation for the Mongols." *International History Review* 20, no. 2 (1998): 310–24.

Hevia, James Louis. *English Lessons: The Pedagogy of Imperialism in Nineteenth-Century China.* Durham, N.C.: Duke University Press, 2003.

Hietala, Thomas R. *Manifest Design: Anxious Aggrandizement in Late Jacksonian America.* Ithaca, N.Y.: Cornell University Press, 1985.

Hinckley, Frank Erastus. *American Consular Jurisdiction in the Orient.* Washington, D.C.: W. H. Loudermilk, 1906.

Hiramatsu Yoshirō. *Kinsei keiji soshō hō no kenkyū.* Tokyo: Sōbunsha, 1960.

Hishida, Seiji George. *The International Position of Japan as a Great Power.* New York: Columbia University Press, 1905.

Hishitani Takehira. *Nagasaki Gaikokujin kyoryūchi no kenkyū.* Fukuoka: Kyūshū Daigaku Shuppankai, 1988.

Ho, Dahpon David. "The Men Who Would Not Be Amban and the One Who Would: Four Frontline Officials and Qing Tibet Policy, 1905–1911." *Modern China* 34, no. 2 (2008): 210–46.

Hoare, James E. "The 'Bankoku Shimbun' Affair: Foreigners, the Japanese Press and Extraterritoriality in Early Meiji Japan." *Modern Asian Studies* 9, no. 3 (1975): 289–302.

Hoare, James E. *Japan's Treaty Ports and Foreign Settlements: The Uninvited Guests, 1858–1899.* Folkestone, Kent, England: Japan Library, 1994.

Hooker, M. Barry, ed. *Law and the Chinese in Southeast Asia.* Singapore: Institute of Southeast Asian Studies, 2002.

Hooker, M. Barry, ed. *Legal Pluralism: An Introduction to Colonial and Neo-colonial Laws.* Oxford: Clarendon Press, 1975.

Ho Ping-ti (He Bingdi). "The Significance of the Ch'ing Period in Chinese History." *Journal of Asian Studies* 26, no. 2 (1967): 189–95.

Hornby, Edmund Grimani. *Sir Edmund Hornby: An Autobiography.* Boston: Houghton Mifflin, 1928.

Hostetler, Laura. *Qing Colonial Enterprise: Ethnography and Cartography in Early Modern China.* Chicago: University of Chicago Press, 2001.

Hourani, Albert Habib. *A History of the Arab Peoples.* Cambridge, Mass.: Harvard University Press, 1991.

Howell, David L. *Geographies of Identity in Nineteenth-Century Japan.* Berkeley: University of California Press, 2005.

Howell, David L. "Territoriality and Collective Identity in Tokugawa Japan." *Daedalus* 127, no. 3 (1998): 105–32.

Howland, Douglas R. *Borders of Chinese Civilization: Geography and History at Empire's End, Asia-Pacific.* Durham, N.C.: Duke University Press, 1996.

Howland, Douglas R. "Japan's Civilized War: International Law as Diplomacy in the Sino-Japanese War (1894–1895)." *Journal of the History of International Law* 9, no. 2 (2007): 179–201.

Howland, Douglas R. "Samurai Status, Class, and Bureaucracy: A Historiographical Essay." *Journal of Asian Studies* 60, no. 2 (2001): 353–80.

Howland, Douglas R. "The Sinking of the S.S. *Kowshing*: International Law, Diplomacy, and the Sino-Japanese War." *Modern Asian Studies* 42, no. 4 (2008): 673–703.

Howland, Douglas, and Luise White, eds. *The State of Sovereignty: Territories, Laws, Populations.* Bloomington: Indiana University Press, 2009.

Hsia Ching-lin. *The Status of Shanghai: A Historical Review of the International Settlement: Its Future Development and Possibilities through Sino-Foreign Co-operation.* Shanghai: Kelly and Walsh, 1929.

Hsü, Immanuel Chung-yüeh. *China's Entrance into the Family of Nations: The Diplomatic Phase, 1858–1880.* Cambridge, Mass.: Harvard University Press, 1960.

Hsü, Immanuel Chung-yüeh. "Late Ch'ing Foreign Relations, 1866–1905." In *The Cambridge History of China: Late Ch'ing, 1800–1911,* pt. 2, vol. 10, edited by John King Fairbank and Kwang-Ching Liu, 70–141. Cambridge: Cambridge University Press, 1980.

Hsü, Immanuel Chung-yüeh. *The Rise of Modern China.* 3rd ed. New York: Oxford University Press, 1983.

Hua Li. "Cong qiren biancha baojia kan Qing wangchao 'qi-min fenzhi' zhengce de bianhua." *Minzu yanjiu* 5 (1988): 97–106.
Huang, Philip C. *Civil Justice in China: Representation and Practice in the Qing*. Stanford, Calif. Stanford University Press, 1996.
Huang Shijian, ed. *Yuandai falü ziliao jicun*. Hangzhou: Zhejiang guji chubanshe, 1988.
Hubu zeli. N.p., 1851–61.
Hucker, Charles O. *A Dictionary of Official Titles in Imperial China*. Stanford: Stanford University Press, 1985.
Hucker, Charles O. "Governmental Organization of the Ming Dynasty." *Harvard Journal of Asiatic Studies* 21 (1958): 1–66.
Hu Hsien-chin. *The Common Descent Group in China and Its Functions*. New York: Johnson Reprint, 1964.
Hummel, Arthur William, ed. *Eminent Chinese of the Ch'ing Period (1644–1912)*. 2 vols. Washington, D.C.: United States Government Printing Office, 1943.
Hu Zengyi, ed. *Xin Man-Han dacidian*. Ürümqi: Xinjiang renmin chubanshe, 1994.
Hyōdō Ken'ichi. *Date Munenari kō den*. Tokyo: Sōsendō shuppan, 2004.
Ide Magoroku. *Meiji minshūshi*. Tokyo: Tokuma shoten, 1988.
Ikeda, Masako Kobayashi. "French Legal Advisor in Meiji Japan (1873–1895): Gustave Emile Boissonade de Fontarabie." Ph.D. diss., University of Hawai'i, 1986.
Im Kaye Soon (Ren Guichun). *Qingchao Baqi Zhufang Xingshuai Shi*. 1st ed. Beijing: Sanlian shudian, 1993.
Im Kaye Soon (Ren Guichun). "The Rise and Decline of the Eight Banner Garrisons in the Ch'ing Period (1644–1911): A Study of the Kuang-chou, Hang-chou, and Ching-chou Garrisons." Ph.D. diss., University of Illinois at Urbana-Champaign, 1981.
Inō Tentarō, ed. *Higashi Ajia ni okeru fubyōdō jōyaku taisei to kindai Nihon*. Tokyo: Iwata Shoin, 1995.
Inō Tentarō, ed. *Jōyaku kaisei naichi zakkyo kankei bunken mokuroku*. Tokyo: Ōshima shoten, 1958.
Inō Tentarō, ed. *Jōyaku kaiseiron shiryō shūsei*. 6 vols. Tokyo: Hara shobō, 1994.
Inoue Kiyoshi. *Jōyaku kaisei: Meiji no minzoku mondai*. Iwanami Shinsho. Tokyo: Iwanami Shoten, 1955.
Inspectorate General of Customs, ed. *Names of Places on the China Coast and the Yangtze River First Issue*. Shanghai, 1882.
Irie Keishirō. *Chūgoku ni okeru gaikokujin no chii*. Tokyo: Nikka kankei hōritsu jimusho: Hatsubaijo Tōkyō, 1937.
Iriye, Akira. "Japan's Drive to Great-Power Status." In *The Cambridge History of Japan: The Nineteenth Century*, edited by Marius B. Jansen, 5:721–782. Cambridge: Cambridge University Press, 1989.
Irokawa, Daikichi. *The Culture of the Meiji Period*. Translated by Stephen Vlastos Noboru Hiraga, Futani Eiji, and Carol Gluck. Edited by Marius B. Jansen. Princeton, N.J.: Princeton University Press, 1985.
Isett, Christopher Mills. *State, Peasant, and Merchant in Qing Manchuria, 1644–1862*. Stanford, Calif.: Stanford University Press, 2006.
Ishii Shirō. *Nihonjin no kokka seikatsu*. Tokyo: Tōkyō daigaku shuppankai, 1986.
Ishikawa kenritsu rekishi hakubutsukan, ed. *Kioichō jiken: Bushi no kindai to chiiki shakai*. Kanazawa: Ishikawa kenritsu rekishi hakubutsukan, 1999.
Itagaki, Taisuke. *Jiyūtō shi*. Edited by Tōyama Shigeki and Satō Shigerō. 3 vols. *Iwanami Bunko*. Tokyo: Iwanami shoten, 1997.
Jansen, Marius B. *China in the Tokugawa World*. Cambridge, Mass.: Harvard University Press, 1992.
Johnson, Chalmers A. *An Instance of Treason: Ozaki Hotsumi and the Sorge Spy Ring*. Expanded ed. Stanford, Calif.: Stanford University Press, 1990.
Johnson, Chalmers A. "Three Rapes: The Status of Forces Agreement and Okinawa." *Japan Focus*, 7 December 2003.

Johnson, Linda Cooke. *Shanghai: From Market Town to Treaty Port, 1074–1858*. Stanford, Calif.: Stanford University Press, 1995.
Johnson, Wallace Stephen, ed. *The T'ang Code*. 2 vols. Princeton, N.J.: Princeton University Press, 1979.
Jones, William C. *The Great Qing Code*. New York: Oxford University Press, 1994.
JWM. *Japan Weekly Mail*. Tokyo.
Kamachi, Noriko. "The Chinese in Meiji Japan: Their Interactions with the Japanese before the Sino-Japanese War." In *The Chinese and the Japanese: Essays in Political and Cultural Interactions*, edited by Akira Iriye, 58–73. Princeton, N.J.: Princeton University Press, 1980.
Kamachi, Noriko. "Meiji shoki no Nagasaki kakyō." *Ochanomizu shigaku* 20 (1976): 1–19.
Kamachi, Noriko. *Reform in China: Huang Tsun-hsien and the Japanese Model*. Cambridge, Mass.: Council on East Asian Studies, 1981.
Kang Dashou and Pan Jiade. *Jindai wairen zai-Hua zhiwai faquan yanjiu*. Chengdu: Sichuan renmin chubanshe, 2002.
Katō Takashi. "Edo no shihai to sono tokushitsu." In *Edo to Pari*, edited by Kaoru Ugawa, James L. McClain, and John M. Merriman, 63–83. Tokyo: Iwata Shoin, 1995.
Katō Takashi. "Governing Edo." In *Edo and Paris: Urban Life and the State in the Early Modern Era*, edited by James L. McClain, John M. Merriman, and Kaoru Ugawa, 41–67. Ithaca, N.Y.: Cornell University Press, 1994.
Katō Yūzō. *Kurofune zengo no sekai*. Tokyo: Iwanami Shoten, 1985.
Katz, Paul R. *Divine Justice: Religion and the Development of Chinese Legal Culture*. London: Routledge, 2009.
Kayaoğlu, Turan. *Legal Imperialism: Sovereignty and Extraterritoriality in Japan, the Ottoman Empire, and China*. New York: Cambridge University Press, 2010.
Keene, Donald. *The Japanese Discovery of Europe, 1720–1830*. Rev. ed. Stanford, Calif.: Stanford University Press, 1969.
Keeton, George Williams. *The Development of Extraterritoriality in China*. 2 vols. London: Longmans, Green, 1928. Reprint, New York: Howard Fertig, 1969.
Kido, Takayoshi. *The Diary of Kido Takayoshi*. Translated by Sidney Devere Brown and Akiko Hirota. 3 vols. Tokyo: University of Tokyo Press, 1983–86.
Kikuyama Masaaki. *Meiji kokka no keisei to shihō seido*. Tokyo: Ochanomizu shobō, 1993.
Kikuyama Masaaki. "Meiji shonen no shihō kaikaku." *Waseda hōgaku* 62, no. 2 (1986): 169–214.
Kim, Key-hiuk. *The Last Phase of the East Asian World Order: Korea, Japan, and the Chinese Empire, 1860–1882*. Berkeley: University of California Press, 1980.
Kingsmill, Thomas W. "Retrospect of Events in China and Japan during the Year 1865." *Journal of the North China Branch of the Royal Asiatic Society*, new series, no. 2 (1865): 135–70.
Kinouchi Makoto, ed. *Shanhai rekishi gaidomappu*. Tokyo: Taishūkan, 1999.
Kirby, William C. *Germany and Republican China*. Stanford: Stanford University Press, 1984.
Kobayakawa Kingo. *Kinsei minji soshō seido no kenkyū*. Enl. and rev. ed. Tokyo: Meicho fukyūkai, 1988.
Koo, V. K. Wellington (Gu Weijun). *The Status of Aliens in China*. Studies in History, Economics and Public Law, no. 126. New York: Columbia University, 1912.
Kotenev, Anatol M. *Shanghai: Its Mixed Court and Council*. Shanghai: North-China Daily News & Herald, 1925. Reprint, Buffalo, N.Y.: Wm. S. Hein, 1987.
Kouwenhoven, Arlette, and Matthi Forrer. *Siebold and Japan: His Life and Work*. Translated by Mark Poysden. Leiden: Hotei, 2000.
Kuhn, Philip A. "Chinese Views on Social Classification." In *Class and Social Stratification in Post-revolution China*, edited by James L. Watson, 16–28. Cambridge: Cambridge University Press, 1984.
Kuhn, Philip A. *Soulstealers: The Chinese Sorcery Scare of 1768*. Cambridge, Mass.: Harvard University Press, 1990.

Kuwabara, Jitsuzō. "On P'u Shou-kêng." *Memoirs of the Research Department of the Toyo Bunko*, 2, 7 (1928, 1935): 1–79, 1–104.
Lane-Poole, Stanley, and F. Victor Dickins. *The Life of Sir Harry Parkes: K.C.B., G.C.M.G., Sometime Her Majesty's Minister to China and Japan*. 2 vols. London: Macmillan, 1894.
Larsen, Kirk W. *Tradition, Treaties, and Trade: Qing Imperialism and Chosŏn Korea, 1850–1910*. Cambridge, Mass.: Harvard University Asia Center, distributed by Harvard University Press, 2008.
Lee Ki-baik. *A New History of Korea*. Translated by Edward W. Wagner and Edward J. Schultz. Cambridge, Mass.: published for the Harvard-Yenching Institute by Harvard University Press, 1984.
Lee, Robert H. G. *The Manchurian Frontier in Ch'ing History*. Cambridge, Mass.: Harvard University Press, 1970.
Lee, Tahirih Victoria. "Law and Local Autonomy at the International Mixed Court of Shanghai." Ph.D. diss., Yale University, 1990.
Legge, James. *The Chinese Classics: With a Translation, Critical and Exegetical Notes, Prolegomena and Copious Indexes*. 2nd rev. ed. 7 vols. Oxford: Clarendon Press, 1893–95.
Lehmann, Jean-Pierre. "Léon Roches—Diplomat Extraordinary in the Bakumatsu Era: An Assessment of His Personality and Policy." *Modern Asian Studies* 14, no. 2 (1980): 273–307.
Lethbridge, Henry J., ed. *All About Shanghai: A Standard Guidebook*. N.p., 1934. Reprint, New York: Oxford University Press, 1986.
Leung Yuen-sang. *The Shanghai Taotai: Linkage Man in a Changing Society, 1843–90*. Honolulu: University of Hawai'i Press, 1990.
Lewis, James B. *Frontier Contact between Chosŏn Korea and Tokugawa Japan*. London: Routledge-Curzon, 2000.
Leys, Simon. *The Burning Forest: Essays on Chinese Culture and Politics*. 1st American ed. New York: Holt, 1986.
LFZZ. Lufu zouzhe (Copies of memorials to the Grand Council Archives). Zhongguo diyi lishi dang'anguan (First Historical Archives of China), Beijing.
Liang Tingnan, ed. *Yue haiguan zhi*. 1874. Reprint, Taipei: Chengwen chubanshe, 1968.
Li Hongzhang. *Li Wenzhong Gong quanji*. 165 vols., divided into six categories. Edited by Wu Rulun. 1905. Reprint, Taipei: Wenhai chubanshe, 1962.
Liljevalch, Carl Fredrik. *Chinas handel industri och statsförfattning jemte underrättelser om chinesernes folkbilding, seder och bruk samt notiser om Japan, Siam m. fl.* Stockholm: J. Beckman, 1848.
Lin Qian. "Qingdai qimin falü guanxi de tiaozheng—Yi 'fanzui mian faqian' lü wei hexin." *Qingshi yanjiu* (2004): 39–50.
Li Pingshu, Mu Xiangyue, and Wang Xiaolai. *Li Pingshu qishi zixu, Ouchu wushi zishu, Wang Xiaolai shulu*. Edited by Fang Ertong and Chen Zhengshu. Shanghai: Shanghai guji chubanshe, 1989.
Lipman, Jonathan N. *Familiar Strangers: A History of Muslims in Northwest China*. Studies on Ethnic Groups in China. Seattle: University of Washington Press, 1997.
Lipman, Jonathan N. "A Fierce and Brutal People: On Islam and Muslims in Qing Law." In *Empire at the Margins: Culture, Ethnicity, and Frontier in Early Modern China*, edited by Pamela Kyle Crossley, Helen F. Siu, and Donald S. Sutton, 83–110. Berkeley: University of California Press, 2006.
Li Shengyu. "Ming-Qing de falü zhidu." In *Zhongguo fazhi shi*, edited by Zeng Daiwei and Luo Hongying, 192–252. Beijing: Falü chubanshe, 2001.
Lishi fumin fu (Archives of the Subprefect's Yamen). Shuangcheng shi dang'anju (Shuangcheng City Archives), Shuangcheng.
Liu Kunyi. *Liu Kunyi Yiji*. 6 vols. Zhongguo Jindaishi Ziliao Congshu. Beijing: Zhonghua shu ju, 1959.
Liu, Lydia He. *The Clash of Empires: The Invention of China in Modern World Making*. Cambridge, Mass.: Harvard University Press, 2004.

Liu, Lydia He. "Legislating the Universal: The Circulation of International Law in the Nineteenth Century." In *Tokens of Exchange: The Problem of Translation in Global Circulations*, edited by Lydia He Liu, 127–64. Durham, N.C.: Duke University Press, 1999.

Liu Shih-shun. *Extraterritoriality: Its Rise and Its Decline*. Studies in History, Economics and Public Law. New York: Columbia University, 1925.

Liu Zhengtan, Gao Mingkai, Mai Yongqian, and Shi Youwei, eds. *Hanyu wailaici cidian*. Shanghai: Shanghai cishu chubanshe, 1984.

Li Yi. "The Bureau That Invites Merchants: An Examination of the Bureaucratic Characteristics of the China Merchants' Steam Navigation Company, 1864–1883." Ph.D. diss., University of Washington, 1993.

Ljungstedt, Anders. *Contribution to an Historical Sketch of the Roman Catholic Church at Macao; and the Domestic and Foreign Relations of Macao*. Boston: J. Munroe & Co., 1836. Reprint, Adamant Media, 2004.

Luk, Bernard Hung-kay (Lu Hongji). "A Hong Kong Barrister in Late-Ch'ing Law Reform." *Hong Kong Law Journal* 11, no. 3 (1981): 339–55.

Luo Zhufeng et al., eds. *Hanyu dacidian*. 12 vols. Shanghai: Hanyu daician chubanshe, 1990–93.

Lust, J. "The 'Su-Pao' Case: An Episode in the Early Chinese Nationalist Movement." *Bulletin of the School of Oriental and African Studies, University of London,* 27, no. 2 (1964): 408–29.

Ma, Xiaohua. "The Invisible War between the United States and Japan over China: A Study of the Abolition of Extraterritoriality in 1943." *Journal of American and Canadian Studies*, no. 15 (1997): 93–111.

Macauley, Melissa Ann. *Social Power and Legal Culture: Litigation Masters in Late Imperial China*. Stanford, Calif.: Stanford University Press, 1998.

Machida, Saburō. *Meiji no kangakushatachi*. Tokyo: Kenbun shuppan, 1998.

Mah, N. Wing. "Foreign Jurisdiction in China." *American Journal of International Law* 18, no. 4 (1924): 676–95.

Malmsten, Bror B. *Sjöfolk och fartyg från Nordvästskåne: Tidsperioden 1836—1960*. Vol. 3. Viken, Sweden: n.p., 1989.

Mancall, Mark. *Russia and China: Their Diplomatic Relations to 1728*. Cambridge, Mass.: Harvard University Press, 1971.

Mao Haijian. *Tianchao de bengkui: Yapian zhanzheng zaiyanjiu*. Beijing: Sanlian shudian, 1995.

Maruyama, Masao. *Studies in the Intellectual History of Tokugawa Japan*. Translated by Mikiso Hane. Princeton, N.J.: Princeton University Press, 1989.

Massarella, Derek. *A World Elsewhere: Europe's Encounter with Japan in the Sixteenth and Seventeenth Centuries*. New Haven, Conn.: Yale University Press, 1990.

Masuda, Wataru. *Japan and China: Mutual Representations in the Modern Era*. Translated by Joshua A. Fogel. New York: St. Martin's Press, 2000.

Maybon, Charles B., and Jean Fredet. *Histoire de la concession française de Changhai*. Paris: Plon, 1929.

Mayers, William Frederick. *The Chinese Government: A Manual of Chinese Titles, Categorically Arranged and Explained, with an Appendix*. 3rd ed. rev. by G. M. H. Playfair. Shanghai: Kelly & Walsh, 1897. Reprint, Taipei: Ch'eng-Wen, 1966.

Mayo, Marlene J. "Rationality in the Restoration: The Iwakura Embassy." In *Modern Japanese Leadership: Transition and Change*, edited by Bernard S. Silberman and Harry D. Harootunian. Tucson: University of Arizona Press, 1966.

McWilliams, Wayne C. "East Meets East. The Soejima Mission to China, 1873." *Monumenta Nipponica* 30, no. 3 (1975): 237–75.

Mehl, Margaret. "Meiji shigaku ni okeru Doitsu no eikyō: Dore hodo igi aru eikyō datta no ka." In *Rekishigaku to shiryō kenkyū*, edited by Tōkyō Daigaku shiryō hensanjo, 182–201. Tokyo: Yamakawa Shuppansha, 2003.

Meijer, Marinus Johan. *The Introduction of Modern Criminal Law in China*. Batavia (Jakarta), Indonesia: De Unie, 1950. Reprint, Arlington, Va.: University Publications of America, 1976.

Meiji jingū, ed. *Meiji ishin hyakusanjū-nen kinen: Meiji ishin ten, kindai Nihon no dansei*. Tokyo: Meiji jingū, 1998.

Mende, Erling von. "Norges økonomiske interesser i Kina i det 19. århundre og unionsregjeringens holdning til disse." In *Norge-Kina: Kompendium fra seminar våren og høsten 1972*, 1–29. Oslo: Østasiatisk institutt, Universitetet i Oslo, n.d.
Merry, Sally Engle. "Law and Colonialism." *Law and Society Review* 25, no. 4 (1991): 889–922.
Merry, Sally Engle. "Legal Pluralism." *Law and Society Review* 22, no. 5 (1988): 869–96.
Metzger, Thomas A. *The Internal Organization of Ch'ing Bureaucracy: Legal, Normative, and Communication Aspects*. Cambridge, Mass.: Harvard University Press, 1973.
Min Jiaqi, ed. *Jianming Wu fangyan cidian*. Shanghai: Shanghai cishu chubanshe, 1986.
Mitani Hiroshi. *Meiji ishin to nashonarizumu: Bakumatsu no gaikō to seiji hendō*. Tokyo: Yamakawa shuppansha, 1997.
Mitchell, Richard H. *Janus-Faced Justice: Political Criminals in Imperial Japan*. Honolulu: University of Hawai'i Press, 1992.
Mittler, Barbara. *A Newspaper for China? Power, Identity, and Change in Shanghai's News Media, 1872–1912*. Cambridge, Mass.: Harvard University Asia Center, distributed by Harvard University Press, 2004.
Miyake, Setsurei. *Ijin no ato*. Tokyo: Heigo shuppansha, 1910.
Mohr, Wolfgang. *Die moderne chinesische Tagespresse: ihre Entwicklung in Tafeln und Dokumenten*. 3 vols, Münchener Ostasiatische Studien: Sonderreihe; Bd. 2. Wiesbaden: Steiner, 1976.
Morita Tomoko. "Bakuhan kankei ni miru saibanken—Nagasaki Eikan suifu satsugai jiken o chūshin ni." In *Bakumatsu ishinki no chian to jōhō*. Tokyo: Taiga Shobō, 2003.
Morita Tomoko. "'Fubyōdō' jōyaku to ryōji saibanken—Kaikō chokugo no Nichi-Ei kōshō o chūshin toshite." *Shigaku Zasshi* 105, no. 4 (1996): 59–81.
Morita Tomoko. *Kaikoku to chigai hōken: Ryōji saiban seido no un'yō to Maria Rusu-gō jiken*. Tokyo: Yoshikawa kōbunkan, 2005.
Morse, Hosea Ballou. *The International Relations of the Chinese Empire*. 3 vols. London: Longmans, Green, 1910–18.
Motono, Eiichi. "H. A. Giles versus Huang Chengyi: Sino-British Conflict over the Mixed Court, 1884–85." *East Asian History* 12 (1996): 135–57.
Murase, Shin'ya. "The Most-Favored-Nation Treatment in Japan's Treaty Practice during the Period 1854–1905." *American Journal of International Law* 70, no. 2 (1976): 273–97.
Murata Seiji, ed. *Kōbe kaikō sanjūnenshi*. 2 vols. Kōbe: Kaikō sanjūnen kinenkai, 1898.
Mutsu Munemitsu. *Kenkenroku: A Diplomatic Record of the Sino-Japanese War, 1894–95*. Translated by Gordon Mark Berger. Princeton, N.J.: Princeton University Press, 1982.
Mutsu Munemitsu. *Shintei Kenkenroku: Nisshin sensō gaikō hiroku*. Edited by Nakatsuka Akira. Iwanami Bunko. Tokyo: Iwanami shoten, 1999.
Nagasaki kenritsu Nagasaki toshokan, ed. *Bakumatsu Meiji ni okeru Nagasaki kyoryūchi gaikokujin meibo*. Kyōdo Shiryō Sōsho. Nagasaki: Nagasaki kenritsu Nagasaki toshokan, 2004.
Nakamura Tadashi. "Sakoku jidai no zai-Nichi kakyō: Tōtsūji ni tsuite." *Shigaku kenkyū* 77–79 (1960): 493–505.
Nakaoka San'eki. *Hasegawa Takashi no Ejiputo kongō saibanjo chōsa*. Nishi to Higashi to: Maejima Shinji sensei tsuitō ronbunshū. Tokyo: Kyūko Shoin, 1985.
Nakaoka San'eki. "Japanese Research on the Mixed Courts of Egypt in the Earlier Part of the Meiji Period in Connection with the Revision of the 1858 Treaties." *Journal of Sophia Asian Studies* 6 (1988): 11–47.
Nakayama Yasumasa, ed. *Shinbun shūsei meiji hennen shi*. 15 vols. Tokyo: Zaisei Keizai Gakkai, 1941.
NCDN. *North China Daily News*. Shanghai.
NCH. *North-China Herald and Supreme Court & Consular Gazette*. Shanghai.
Newby, Laura J. "The Begs of Xinjiang: Between Two Worlds." *Bulletin of the School of Oriental and African Studies, University of London* 61, no. 2 (1998): 278–97.
Newby, Laura J. *The Empire and the Khanate: A Political History of Qing Relations with Khoqand c. 1760–1860*. Brill's Inner Asian Library 16. Leiden: Brill, 2005.
Nie Chongqi. "Man'guan Hanshi." *Yenching Journal of Chinese Studies* 32 (1947): 97–116.
Nihon jinmei daijiten, Gendai. Tokyo: Heibonsha, 1979.

Niida Noboru. *Chūgoku hōsei shi kenkyū*. Tokyo: Tōkyō daigaku shuppankai, 1959.
Nitchūkan sangoku kyōtsū rekishi kyōzai iinkai, ed. *Mirai o hiraku rekishi: Higashi Ajia sangoku no kin-gendaishi*. Tokyo: Kōbunken, 2005.
NKS. Nagasaki kyōdo shiryō (Nagasaki local history archives). Nagasaki kenritsu Nagasaki toshokan (Nagasaki Prefectural Nagasaki Library).
Norman, E. Herbert. *Andō Shōeki and the Anatomy of Japanese Feudalism*. Washington, D.C.: University Publications of America, 1979.
Ōba, Osamu. *Edo jidai ni okeru Chūgoku bunka juyō no kenkyū*. Kyoto: Dōhōsha, 1984.'
Ōba, Osamu. *Edo jidai ni okeru Tōsen Mochiwatarisho no kenkyū*. Suita: Kansai Daigaku shuppanbu, 1967.
Oda Yorozu and Yamane Yukio, eds. *Shinkoku gyōseihō: Rinji Taiwan kyūkan chōsakai dai 1-bu hokoku*. 6 vols. N.p.: Rinji Taiwan kyūkan chōsakai, 1905–15. Reprint, Tokyo: Taian, 1965.
Ooms, Herman. *Tokugawa Village Practice: Class, Status, Power, Law*. Berkeley: University of California Press, 1996.
Osadake Takeshi. *Ōtsu jiken: Roshia kōtaishi Ōtsu sōnan*. Edited by Mitani Taiichiro. *Iwanami Bunko*. Tokyo: Iwanami shoten, 1991.
Ottosson, Ingemar. "Möller och hans sagoslott—ett blad ur Shanghais förflutna." *Kinarapport* 4 (2009): 12–17.
Ottosson, Ingemar. "Svensk frihandelsimperialism: Det ojämlika fördraget med Japan 1868–1896." *Historisk Tidskrift* 2 (1997): 199–223.
Ōyama Azusa and Inō Tentarō, eds. *Jōyaku kaisei chōsho shūsei*. 2 vols. Tokyo: Hara shobō, 1991.
Padoux, Georges. Review of Liu Shih-shun, *Extraterritoriality, Its Rise and Decline*, New York, Columbia University, 1925. *Chinese Social and Political Science Review* 10, no. 3 (1926): 755–63.
Pan Wei-tung. *The Chinese Constitution: A Study of Forty Years of Constitution-Making in China*. Washington, D.C.: Catholic University of America Press, 1945.
Pan Zhiping. *Zhongya Haohanguo yu Qingdai Xinjiang*. Beijing: Zhongguo shehui kexue chubanshe Xinhua shudian jingxiao, 1991.
Pan Zhiping and Jiang Lili. "1832 nian Qing yu Haohan yihe kao." *Xibei shidi* 1 (1989): 100–109.
Parliament of Great Britain and Foreign Office of Great Britain. *Commercial Reports from Her Majesty's Consuls in China, 1870*. London: Printed by Harrison and Sons, 1872.
Paske-Smith, Montague. *Western Barbarians in Japan and Formosa in Tokugawa Days, 1603–1868*. Kobe: J. L. Thompson, 1930.
Peattie, Mark R. "Japanese Treaty Port Settlements in China, 1895–1937." In *The Japanese Informal Empire in China, 1895–1937*, edited by Peter Duus, Ramon Hawley Myers, and Mark R. Peattie, 166–209. Princeton, N.J.: Princeton University Press, 1989.
Pelcovits, Nathan Albert. *Old China Hands and the Foreign Office*. New York: pub. under the auspices of American Institute of Pacific Relations by the King's Crown Press, 1948.
Perdue, Peter C. *China Marches West: The Qing Conquest of Central Eurasia*. Cambridge, Mass: Belknap Press of Harvard University Press, 2005.
Perdue, Peter C. "Comparing Empires: Manchu Colonialism." *International History Review* 20, no. 2 (1998): 255–62.
Petech, Luciano. *China and Tibet in the Early 18th Century: History of the Establishment of Chinese Protectorate in Tibet*. 2nd ed. Leiden: Brill, 1972.
Philastre, Paul Louis Félix, ed. *Le Code Annamite: Nouvelle traduction complète*. 2 vols. Paris: E. Leroux, 1909. Reprint, Taipei: Ch'eng-Wen, 1967.
Pinkney, David H. *Decisive Years in France, 1840–1847*. Princeton, N.J.: Princeton University Press, 1986.
Polachek, James M. *The Inner Opium War*. Cambridge, Mass.: Harvard University Press, 1992.
Pomerantz-Zhang, Linda. *Wu Tingfang (1842–1922): Reform and Modernization in Modern Chinese History*. Hong Kong: Hong Kong University Press, 1992.
Pospíšil, Leopold J. *Anthropology of Law: A Comparative Theory*. New York: Harper & Row, 1971.
Pumpelly, Raphael. *Across America and Asia: Notes of a Five Years' Journey around the World, and of Residence in Arizona, Japan, and China*. New York: Leypoldt & Holt, 1870.

Pyle, Kenneth B. "Meiji Conservatism." In *The Cambridge History of Japan: The Nineteenth Century*, edited by Marius B. Jansen, 674–720. Cambridge: Cambridge University Press, 1989.
Qian Shifu. *Qingdai zhiguan nianbiao*. 4 vols. Beijing: Zhonghua shuju, 1980. Reprint, 2005.
Qian Tai. *Zhongguo bupingdeng tiaoyue zhi yuanqi ji qi feichu zhi jingguo*. Yangmingshan: Guofang yanjiuyuan, 1961.
Qiu Shusen, ed. *Yuanshi cidian*. Jinan: Shandong jiaoyu chubanshe, 2002.
Quigley, Harold Scott. *Japanese Government and Politics*. New York: Century, 1932.
Rankin, Mary Backus. *Early Chinese Revolutionaries: Radical Intellectuals in Shanghai and Chekiang, 1902–1911*. Cambridge, Mass.: Harvard University Press, 1971.
Ratchnevsky, Paul. *Un code des Yuan*. 4 vols. Paris: E. Leroux, 1937–85.
Ravina, Mark. *Land and Lordship in Early Modern Japan*. Stanford, Calif.: Stanford University Press, 1999.
Ravina, Mark. *The Last Samurai: The Life and Battles of Saigō Takamori*. Hoboken, N.J.: Wiley, 2003.
Reinhardt, Anne. "Navigating Imperialism in China: Steamship, Semicolony, and Nation, 1860–1937." Ph.D. diss., Princeton University, 2002.
Reynolds, Douglas Robertson. *China, 1898–1912: The Xinzheng Revolution and Japan*. Cambridge, Mass.: Council on East Asian Studies, distributed by Harvard University Press, 1993.
Rhoads, Edward J. M. *Manchus and Han: Ethnic Relations and Political Power in Late Qing and Early Republican China, 1861–1928*. Seattle: University of Washington Press, 2000.
Ricket, W. Allyn. "Voluntary Surrender and Confession in Traditional Chinese Law: The Problem of Continuity." *Journal of Asian Studies* 30, no. 4 (1971): 797–814.
Ronquillo, Remigio B. "The Administration of Law among the Chinese in Chicago." *Journal of Criminal Law and Criminology* (1931–1951) 25, no. 2 (1934): 205–24.
Roth [Li], Gertraude. "The Manchu-Chinese Relationship, 1618–1636." In *From Ming to Ch'ing: Conquest, Region, and Continuity in Seventeenth-Century China*, edited by Jonathan D. Spence and John E. Wills, 3–37. New Haven, Conn.: Yale University Press, 1979.
Rowe, William T. *Hankow: Commerce and Society in a Chinese City, 1796–1889*. Stanford, Calif.: Stanford University Press, 1984.
RSNE. *Rising Sun & Nagasaki Express*. Nagasaki.
Ruskola, Teemu. "Colonialism without Colonies: On the Extraterritorial Jurisprudence of the U.S. Court for China." Emory Public Law Research Paper no. 09-67 (2008).
Sahlins, Peter. *Boundaries: The Making of France and Spain in the Pyrenees*. Berkeley: University of California Press, 1989.
Saikai shimbun. Nagasaki.
Sansom, George Bailey. *Japan: A Short Cultural History*. Rev. ed. London: Barrie and Jenkins, 1976.
Sasaki Masaya, ed. *Ahen sensō no kenkyū: Shiryō hen*. Tokyo: Kindai Chūgoku kenkyū iinkai, 1964.
Sasama Yoshihiko. *Zusetsu Edo machibugyōsho jiten*. Tokyo: Kashiwa Shobō, 1991.
Satow, Ernest Mason. *Diplomat in Japan: The Inner History of the Critical Years in the Evolution of Japan When the Ports Were Opened and the Monarchy Restored*. Philadelphia: Lippincott, 1921.
Sayre, Francis Bowes. "The Passing of Extraterritoriality in Siam." *American Journal of International Law* 22, no. 1 (1928): 70–88.
Scully, Eileen P. *Bargaining with the State from Afar: American Citizenship in Treaty Port China, 1844–1942*. New York: Columbia University Press, 2000.
Scully, Eileen P. "Historical Wrongs and Human Rights in Sino-Foreign Relations: The Legacy of Extraterritoriality." *Journal of American-East Asian Relations* 9, nos. 1–2 (2000): 129–46.
SDRK. Ministerstvo inostrannykh del, ed. *Sbornik dogovorov Rossii s Kitaem, 1689–1881 Gg*. Saint Petersburg: Tipografia imperatorskoi akademii nauk, 1889. Reprinted as Michael Weiers, ed., *Die Verträge zwischen Russland und China, 1689–1881*. Bonn:Wehling, 1979.
Sebes, Joseph, and Thomas Pereira. *The Jesuits and the Sino-Russian Treaty of Nerchinsk (1689): The Diary of Thomas Pereira*. Bibliotheca Instituti Historici S.I., vol. 18. Rome: Institutum Historicum S.I., 1962.
Shah, Prakash. *Legal Pluralism in Conflict: Coping with Cultural Diversity in Law*. Portland, Ore.: Glass House Press, 2005.

Shenbao. Shanghai.
Shen Jiaben, and Yu Liansan. *Zunyi Man-Han tongxing xinglü.* Beijing: Xiuding falüguan, 1908.
Sheppard, Eli T. *Extra-territoriality in Japan, an Inquiry with Particular Reference to the Immunity of Foreigners in Japan from the Municipal Laws of the Territory, by Virtue of Existing Treaty Stipulations.* Tokyo: n.p., 1879.
Shimada Masao. *Shinchō Mōko rei no kenkyū.* Tokyo: Sōbunsha, 1982.
Shimizu Isao, ed. *Bigō sobyōshū, Iwanami Bunko.* Tokyo: Iwanami shoten, 2003.
Shimizu Isao, ed. *Wāguman Nihon sobyōshū.* Tokyo: Iwanami Shoten, 2003.
Shimizu Isao, ed. *Zoku Bigō sobyōshū, Iwanami Bunko.* Tokyo: Iwanami shoten, 2001.
Shipp, Steve. *Macau, China: A Political History of the Portuguese Colony's Transition to Chinese Rule.* Jefferson, N.C.: McFarland, 1997.
Shirokogoroff, S. M. (Shirokogorov, Sergeï Mikhaïlovich). *Social Organization of the Manchus: A Study of the Manchu Clan Organization.* Shanghai: Royal Asiatic Society, North China Branch, 1924.
Shuntian fu (Archives of Shuntian Prefecture). Zhongguo diyi lishi dang'anguan (First Historical Archives of China), Beijing.
Sommer, Matthew H. *Sex, Law, and Society in Late Imperial China.* Stanford, Calif.: Stanford University Press, 2000.
Soulié de Morant, Georges. *Exterritorialité et intérêts étrangers en Chine.* Paris: Paul Geuthner, 1925.
Soulié de Morant, Georges. *Les droits conventionnels des étrangers en Chine.* Paris: Léon Tenin, 1916.
Sousa, Nasim (Nasīm Susa). *The Capitulatory Régime of Turkey, Its History, Origin, and Nature.* Baltimore: Johns Hopkins Press, 1933.
Spence, Jonathan D. *To Change China: Western Advisers in China, 1620–1960.* Harmondsworth, England: Penguin Books, 1980.
Sprenkel, Sybille van der. *Legal Institutions in Manchu China: A Sociological Analysis.* Monographs on Social Anthropology no. 24. London: Athlone Press, 1966.
Stapleton, Kristin Eileen. *Civilizing Chengdu: Chinese Urban Reform, 1895–1937.* Cambridge, Mass.: Harvard University Press, 2000.
Stephens, Thomas B. *Order and Discipline in China: The Shanghai Mixed Court, 1911–27.* Seattle: University of Washington Press, 1992.
Stewart, Watt. *Chinese Bondage in Peru: A History of the Chinese Coolie in Peru, 1849–1874.* Westport, Conn.: Greenwood Press, 1970.
Strauss, Gerald. *Law, Resistance, and the State: The Opposition to Roman Law in Reformation Germany.* Princeton, N.J.: Princeton University Press, 1986.
Sumida Shōichi, ed. *Nihon kaibō shiryō sōsho.* 10 vols. Tokyo: Kaibō shiryō kankōkai, 1932–33.
Svarverud, Rune. *International Law as World Order in Late Imperial China: Translation, Reception and Discourse, 1847–1911.* Leiden: Brill, 2007.
Swisher, Earl, ed. *China's Management of the American Barbarians; A Study of Sino-American Relations, 1841–1861, with Documents.* New Haven, Conn.: Published for the Far Eastern Association by Far Eastern Publications, Yale University, 1953.
Tabohashi Kiyoshi. "Nisshin shin kankei no seiritsu." *Shigaku zasshi* 44, nos. 2–3 (1933): 163–99, 314–38.
Tada Kōmon, ed. *Iwakura-kō jikki.* 3 vols. Tokyo: Iwakura-kō kyūseki hozonkai, 1927.
Takasugi Shinsaku. *Takasugi shinsaku zenshū.* Edited by Hori Tetsusaburō. 2 vols. Tokyo: Shin Jinbutsu raisha, 1974.
Takayanagi Shinzō and Ishii Ryōsuke, eds. *Ofuregaki Tenpō Shūsei.* 2 vols. Tokyo: Iwanami Shoten, 1937.
Tanaka, Tokihiko. "Maria Rusu-gō jiken: Miteiyaku kokujin ni tai-suru hōken dokuritsu no ichi katei." In *Nihon Seiji Saiban Shiroku,* edited by Sakae Wagatsuma, 1:273–298. Tokyo: Daiichi Hōki Shuppan, 1968.
Tanaka, Tokihiko. "Norumanton-gō jiken: Kakka sōyō no ryōji saiban." In *Nihon Seiji Saiban Shiroku,* edited by Sakae Wagatsuma, 2:125–142. Tokyo: Daiichi Hôki Shuppan, 1968.
Tanaka, Tokihiko. "Shinkokujin Chōkai-ra nisesatsu jiken: Miteiyakukokujin saiban to shihōken no yōgo." In *Nihon Seiji Saiban Shiroku,* edited by Sakae Wagatsuma, 1:134–153. Tokyo: Daiichi Hôki Shuppan, 1968.

Tan Poh-Ling, ed. *Asian Legal Systems: Law, Society, and Pluralism in East Asia*. Sydney: Butterworths, 1997.
Tao De-min. "Traditional Chinese Social Ethics in Japan, 1721–43." *Gest Library Journal* 4, no. 2 (1991): 68–84.
TCCF. Inspectorate General of Customs, ed. *Treaties, Conventions, etc., between China and Foreign States*. 2nd ed. 2 vols. Shanghai: Statistical Department of the Inspectorate General of Customs, 1917.
TCEJ. Kaijō Gijutsu Anzenkyoku, ed. *Treaties and Conventions between the Empire of Japan and Other Powers: Together with Universal Conventions, Regulations and Communications since March, 1854*. Rev. ed. Tokyo: Printed at the "Kokubunsha" Printing Office by order of the Foreign Office, 1884.
Têng, Ssu-yü, and John King Fairbank. *China's Response to the West: A Documentary Survey, 1839–1923*. Cambridge, Mass.: Harvard University Press, 1979.
Thongchai, Winichakul. *Siam Mapped: A History of the Geo-Body of a Nation*. Honolulu: University of Hawai'i Press, 1994.
Toby, Ronald P. *State and Diplomacy in Early Modern Japan: Asia in the Development of the Tokugawa Bakufu*. Princeton, N.J.: Princeton University Press, 1984.
Took, Jennifer. *A Native Chieftaincy in Southwest China: Franchising a Tai Chieftaincy under the Tusi System of Late Imperial China*. Sinica Leidensia, Leiden: Brill, 2005.
Tsiang T'ing-fu (Jiang Tingfu). "Sino-Japanese Diplomatic Relations, 1870–94." *Chinese Social and Political Science Review* 17, no. 1 (1933): 1–106.
Tsunoda Ryūsaku, William Theodore De Bary, and Donald Keene, eds. *Sources of Japanese Tradition*. New York: Columbia University Press, 1958.
Usui Katsumi. "Yokohama kyoryūchi no Chūgokujin." In *Yokohama-Shi Shi*, 3b:860–913. Yokohama: Yokohama-shi, 1963.
Valk, Marc H. van der. "Previous Chinese Legal Language and Communist Chinese Legal Language." *Monumenta Serica* 29 (1970–71): 589–630.
Vittinghoff, Natascha. "Readers, Publishers and Officials in Contest for a Public Sphere and the Shanghai Newspaper Market in Late Qing China (1860–1880)." *T'oung Pao* 4–5 (2001): 393–455.
Wagner, Rudolf G. "The Role of the Foreign Community in the Chinese Public Sphere." *China Quarterly* 142 (1995): 423–43.
Wagner, Rudolf G. "The *Shenbao* in Crisis: The International Environment and the Conflict between Guo Songtao and the *Shenbao*." *Late Imperial China* 20, no. 1 (1999): 107–43.
Wakabayashi, Bob Tadashi. *Anti-foreignism and Western Learning in Early-Modern Japan: The New Theses of 1825*. Cambridge, Mass.: Council on East Asian Studies, 1986.
Wakabayashi, Bob Tadashi. "From Peril to Profit: Opium in Late-Edo to Meiji Eyes." In *Opium Regimes: China, Britain, and Japan, 1839–1952*, edited by Timothy Brook and Bob Tadashi Wakabayashi, 55–75. Berkeley: University of California Press, 2000.
Wakeman, Frederic E. "The Canton Trade and the Opium War." In *Cambridge History of China: Late Ch'ing, 1800–1911*, pt. 1, vol. 10, edited by Denis C. Twitchett and John K. Fairbank, 163–212. Cambridge: Cambridge University Press, 1978.
Wakeman, Frederic E. *Policing Shanghai, 1927–1937*. Berkeley: University of California Press, 1995.
Wakeman, Frederic E. *Strangers at the Gate: Social Disorder in South China, 1839–1861*. Berkeley: University of California Press, 1966.
Waley, Arthur. *The Opium War through Chinese Eyes*. Stanford, Calif.: Stanford University Press, 1968.
Wang Dong. *China's Unequal Treaties: Narrating National History*. Lanham, Md.: Lexington Books, 2005.
Wang Guanhua. *In Search of Justice: The 1905–1906 Chinese Anti-American Boycott*. Cambridge, Mass.: Harvard University Asia Center, distributed by Harvard University Press, 2001.
Wang Jiajian. *Zhongguo jindai haijun shilun ji*. Taipei: Wenshizhe chubanshe, 1984.
Wang, Shên-tsu. *The Margary Affair and the Chefoo Agreement*. New York: Oxford University Press, 1940.

Wang Tao. *Taoyuan chidu*. 1876. Reprint, Taipei: Wenhai chubanshe, 1983.
Wang Tao. *Taoyuan wenlu waibian*. Shanghai, 1897. Reprint, Shanghai: Shanghai shudian chubanshe, 2002.
Wang Tay-sheng. *Legal Reform in Taiwan under Japanese Colonial Rule, 1895–1945: The Reception of Western Law*. Seattle: University of Washington Press, 2000.
Wang Tieya, ed. *Zhongwai jiu yuezhang huibian*. 3 vols. Beijing: Sanlian chubanshe, 1982.
Wang Xi. *Li Hongzhang yu Zhong-Ri dingyue, 1871*. Taibei shi Nan'gang: Zhongyang yanjiuyuan jindaishi yanjiusuo, 1981.
Wang Yanwei and Wang Liang, eds. *Qingji waijiao shiliao*. Beiping: Waijiao shiliao bianzuanchu, 1932. Reprint, Taipei: Wenhai chubanshe, 1964.
Wang Yitang. *Shanghai Zujie Wenti*. 3 vols. Shanghai: s.n., 1919.
Wei, Tsing-sing Louis. *La politique missionnaire de la France en Chine, 1842–1856*. Paris: Nouvelles Éditions latines, 1961.
Wen, Tingjing, ed. *Chayang sanjia wenchao: He Ruzhang, Lin Daquan, Qiu Jinxin*. N.p., 1910–11. Reprint, Taipei: Wenhai chubanshe, 1966.
Wheaton, Henry. *Wan'guo gongfa*. Translated by William Alexander Parsons Martin (Ding Weiliang). Beijing: Chongshiguan, 1864. Reprinted in *Xuxiu Siku quanshu*, vol. 1299. Shanghai: Shanghai guji chubanshe, 1995.
Wilkinson, Endymion Porter. *Chinese History: A Manual*. Rev. and enl. ed. Cambridge, Mass.: Harvard University Press, 2000.
Willoughby, Westel Woodbury. *Foreign Rights and Interests in China*. Rev. and enl. ed. 2 vols. Baltimore: The Johns Hopkins Press, 1927.
Wirgman, Charles. *The Japan Punch*. Reprint, Tokyo: Yūshōdō shoten, 1975.
Wittfogel, Karl August, and Chia-shêng Fêng. *History of Chinese Society: Liao, 907–1125*. Philadelphia: American Philosophical Society, distributed by the Macmillan Co., 1949.
Wong, J. Y. (Huang Yuhe), ed. *Anglo-Chinese Relations, 1839–1860: A Calendar of Chinese Documents in the British Foreign Office Records*. Oxford: Published for the British Academy by Oxford University Press, 1983.
Wong, J. Y. (Huang Yuhe), ed. *Deadly Dreams: Opium, Imperialism, and the Arrow War (1856–1860) in China*. Cambridge Studies in Chinese History, Literature, and Institutions. Cambridge: Cambridge University Press, 1998.
Wong, J. Y. (Huang Yuhe), ed. *Yeh Ming-Ch'en: Viceroy of Liang Kuang 1852–8*. Cambridge: Cambridge University Press, 1976.
Wong, Roy Bin. *China Transformed: Historical Change and the Limits of European Experience*. Ithaca, N.Y.: Cornell University Press, 1997.
Wray, William D. *Mitsubishi and the N.Y.K., 1870–1914: Business Strategy in the Japanese Shipping Industry*. Cambridge, Mass.: Harvard University Press, 1984.
Wright, Arnold, and H. A. Cartwright. *Twentieth Century Impressions of Hongkong, Shanghai, and Other Treaty Ports of China: Their History, People, Commerce, Industries, and Resources*. London: Lloyds Greater Britain, 1908.
Wright, Mary Clabaugh. *The Last Stand of Chinese Conservatism: The T'ung-chih Restoration, 1862–1874*. Stanford, Calif.: Stanford University Press, 1957.
Wu Songgao. *Zhiwai faquan*. Shanghai: Shangwu yinshuguan, 1929.
Xinzhu (Sinju), ed. *Fuzhou Zhufang Zhi*. 1745 ed. Reprinted in *Jinwu shili: Fuzhou zhufangzhi*. Haikou: Hainan chubanshe, 2000.
Xue Liyong. *Jiu Shanghai zujie shihua*. Shanghai: Shanghai shehui kexueyuan chubanshe, 2002.
Xue Yunsheng. *Duli cunyi dianzhu*. Edited by Hu Xingjiao, Deng Youtian, and Wang Qingxi. Beijing: Zhongguo renmin Gong'an daxue chubanshe, 1994.
Xu Gongsu, and Qiu Jinzhang. *Shanghai Gonggong zujie zhidu/Shanghai International Settlement*. Nanjing: Guoli zhongyang yanjiuhui kexue yanjiusuo, 1933.
Xu Linjiang. *Zheng Xiaoxu qianbansheng pingzhuan*. Shanghai: Xueling chubanshe, 2003.
Xu Xiaoqun. *Trial of Modernity: Judicial Reform in Early Twentieth Century China, 1901–1937*. Stanford, Calif.: Stanford University Press, 2008.

Xu Zongliang, ed. *Tongshang yuezhang leizuan*. 10 vols. *Jindai Zhongguo shiliao congkan xubian*. N.p.: Beiyang shiyin guanshuju, 1898. Reprint, Taipei: Wenhai chubanshe, 1977.
Yamahiro Shinichi and Metooru Nakano, eds. *Meiroku zasshi*. 2 vols. *Iwanami Bunko*. Tokyo: Iwanami shoten, 1999.
Yang Daqing. *Technology of Empire: Telecommunications and Japanese Expansion in Asia, 1883–1945*. Cambridge, Mass.: Harvard University Asia Center, distributed by Harvard University Press, 2010.
Yao Wennan and Wu Xin, eds. *Shanghai xian xuzhi*. Shanghai: n.p., 1918. Reprint, Taipei: Chengwen chubanshe, 1970.
Yao Wennan, Wu Xin, and Jiang Jiamei, eds. *Minguo Shanghai xianzhi*. Shanghai: Shanghai xian zhengfu, 1936. Reprinted in *Zhongguo difangzhi jicheng: Shanghai fu xian zhi ji 4*. Shanghai: Shanghai shudian, 1991.
Yao Zhihe, ed. *Huayang susong li'an huibian*. 2 vols. Shanghai: Shangwu yinshuguan, 1915.
Yasuoka Akio. "Meiji 19 nen Nagasaki Shinkoku suihei sōtō jiken." *Hōsei Daigaku bungakubu kiyō* 36 (1988): 41–94.
Ye Wa and Joseph Esherick. *Chinese Archives: An Introductory Guide*. Berkeley: Institute of East Asian Studies, University of California Center for Chinese Studies, 1996.
Ye Xiaoqing. "Shanghai before Nationalism." *East Asian History* 3 (1992): 33–52.
Ye Xiaoqing. *The Dianshizhai Pictorial: Shanghai Urban Life, 1884–1898*. Ann Arbor: Center for Chinese Studies, University of Michigan, 2003.
Ying Baoshi and Yu Yue, eds. *Shanghai xian zhi*. Shanghai: Wumen xianshu, 1871. Reprint, Taipei: Chengwen chubanshe, 1975.
Yi zhu Riben gekou lishiguan lixing shiyi qi tiao. Undated manuscript. National Library of China (Zhongguo guojia tushuguan).
Yokohama mainichi shimbun. Yokohama.
Yoshino Sakuzō. *Nikka kokkō ron*. Tokyo: Shin Kigensha, 1948.
YPZZ. Qi Sihe, Lin Shuhui, and Shou Jiyu, eds. *Yapian zhanzheng*. 6 vols. Shanghai: Shenzhou guoguang she, 1954.
YPZZDASL. Zhongguo diyi lishi dang'anguan, ed. *Yapian zhanzheng dang'an shiliao*. 7 vols. Shanghai: Shanghai renmin chubanshe, 1987.
Yu Yue, ed. *Chongxiu Shanghai xianzhi*. Shanghai: Wumen xianshu, 1871.
YWSM. Wenqing, Jia Zhen, and Baoyun, eds. *Chouban yiwu shimo*. Arranged according to imperial reign. Beiping: Beiping bowuyuan, 1923. Reprint, Taipei: Wenhai chubanshe, 1970–71.
Zeng Jize (Marquis Tseng). "China: The Sleep and the Awakening," *Asiatic Quarterly Review* 3 (1887): 1–10.
Zhang Deyi. *Suishi Faguo ji: San shu qi*. Edited by Zuo Buqing and Zhong Shuhe. Changsha: Hunan renmin chubanshe, 1982.
Zhang Jinfan, ed. *Qingchao fazhi shi*. Beijing: Zhonghua shuju Xinhua shudian jingxiao, 1998.
Zhang Jixin. *Daoxian huanhai jianwen*. Edited by Du Chunhe and Zhang Xiuqing. Beijing: Zhonghua shuju, 1981.
Zhang Weiren (Wejen Chang), ed. *Qingdai fazhi yanjiu: Zhongyang yanjiuyuan lishi yuyan yanjiusuo xiancun Qing neige daku yuancang Qingdai fazhi dang'an xuanji fuzhu ji xiangguan zhi lunshu*. 3 vols. Taipei: Taiwan shangwu yinshuguan, 1983.
Zheng Qin. "Pursuing Perfection: Formation of the Qing Code." *Modern China* 21, no. 3 (1995): 310–44.
Zheng Qin. *Qingdai falü zhidu yanjiu*. Beijing: Zhongguo zhengfa daxue chubanshe, 2000.
Zheng Qin. "Yongzheng, Qianlong shiqi de sifa zhidu." In *Zhongguo fazhi tongshi*, vol. 8, edited by Zhang Jinfan, 637–84. Beijing: Falü chubanshe, 1999.
Zhili Rehe tongzhi fuyi quanshu. N.p., n.d. [Late Qianlong period]. Copy in Zhongguo guojia tushuguan (National Library of China), Beijing.
Zhongguo bianjiang shidi yanjiu zhongxin, ed. *Menggu lüli, Huijiang zeli*. Zhongguo bianjiang shidi ziliao congkan. Zonghe juan. Beijing: Quanguo tushuguan wenxian suowei fuzhi zhongxin, 1988.

Zhongguo diyi lishi dang'anguan, ed. *Kangxi qiju zhu*. 3 vols. Beijing: Zhonghua shuju, 1984.
Zhou Zhenhe and Gu Meihua, eds. *Shengxun guangxun jijie yu yanjiu*. Shanghai: Shanghai shudian chubanshe, 2006.
Zhu Rong. "Shanhai kyoryū Nihonjin shakai to Yokohama kakyō shakai no hikaku kenkyū." In *Yokohama to Shanhai: Kindai toshi keiseishi hikaku kenkyū*, edited by Yokohama kaikō shiryōkan. Yokohama: Yokohama kaikō shiryō fukyû Kyōkai Yokohama Kaikō Shiryōkan, 1995.
Zou Jing, ed. *Zhapu Beizhi*. Zhapu: n.p., 1843. Reprinted in *Zhongguo difangzhi jicheng: Xiangzhen* 20. Shanghai: Shanghai shudian, 1992.

INDEX

Abe Masahiro, 89
Alabaster, Chaloner, 67, 71
Alcock, Rutherford, 10, 39, 61, 70–71, 206n71
 dress code and, 105
 Japan and, 92–93, 132
Alcock Convention, 61, 99
Alexander II, 157
alien registration, 96
Andrews, Robert Morton, 165–66
Ansei Treaties, 88–94
Aoki Shūzō, 137, 159
Arrow War, 57–58, 90
article 12, of Mackay Treaty, 175
article 13, in Treaty of the Bogue, 52
articles, in Sino-British Treaty of Tianjin
 article 16, 59, 75, 78–79
 article 17, 166
 article 50, 79
articles, in Sino-Japanese Treaty of Tianjin
 article 8, 105
 article 11, 105
 article 13, 105, 124, 131, 142–44
Ashikaga Yoshimitsu, 86–87

Baba Tatsui, 151–52, 161
Bakufu, 30–32, 85–94, 180
Balfour, George, 64
Bankoku shimbun, 158
bannermen, 20–29, 176
Belgium, 55, 118
Bigot, Georges Ferdinand, 138, *139*, 155
Black, John Reddie, 158
Boissonade, Gustave Émile, 129, 153, 170
Brandt, Max von, 140
Brazil, 8

Britain. *See also* Sino-British Treaty of Tianjin
 China and, 47–53, 56–60
 commercial treaties with, 4, 7
 EIC of, 42–43, 47
 Japan and, 90–93
 treaty revision and, 159–60
British Supreme Court
 in Hong Kong, 68
 Ocean incident and, 165
 in Shanghai, 63–84, 105–6, 142, 165–66
Brown, Captain, 165–67
Browne, Ross, 61, 71
Bruce, Frederick, 66
bureaucratic pilgrimages, 162
Bureau for the Compilation of Law (*Falü bianzuanguan*), 174

Cai Xuan, 137
Cantonese association, 116
capital punishment, 124, 126, 143
 George and, 73–77, 106, 142, 166
 Zhu Xi and, 118–19
Capitulations, 12
Changshan, 28
Chao Tingzuo, 26–27
Chapdelaine, Auguste, 56–58
Chefoo Convention, 12
 conclusion of, 108
 Li Hongzhang and, 78
 name of, 212n88
 reform and, 77–80
 repercussions, 80–84
Chen Dezhui, 128
Chen Fuxun
 of Mixed Court, 68, 83, 98, 109, 157, 165–66
 Ocean incident and, 165–66

Chenglin, 99, 118–19
Chen Qin, 101–4
Chiang Kai-shek, 178
China. *See also* Han Chinese; Qing Empire; Sino-Japanese cases; Treaties of Tianjin
  Belgium and, 55
  Britain and, 47–53, 56–60
  Communist Party of, 178, 182–84
  consular jurisdiction in, 3–4, 13, 61, 81, 100–105, 143–44, 180
  draft constitutions of, 177
  extraterritoriality in, 5–6, 10–11, 13, 39–84, 141–48, 160–81, 185, 225n20
  in First Sino-Japanese War, 149, 172, 179
  foreigners in, 40–43, 46–58, 83, 184–85
  France and, 54, 56–57, 99
  imperial nobility, prerogatives of, 176
  Japanese relations with, 11, 84, 86–88, 94–148
  Korea and, 135
  legal tradition of, 7, 16, 203n157
  linguistic hegemony of, 7, 110
  María Luz incident and, 156–58
  missionaries in, 56–57, 62, 105, 150
  modern, 182–85
  Nagasaki and, 85, 95–97, 110, 113, 115–17, 125–41
  Nationalists in, 178
  opium and, 48, 53–54, 120–22
  People's Republic of, 179, 182–83, 203n158
  personal jurisdiction in, 12
  Republican revolution in, 176–78
  Russia and, 43–45, 60, 204n29
  Treaty of Shimonoseki and, 13, 114, 149, 160
  treaty revisions by, 160–78
  U.S. and, 53–54, 56, 65, 71–72, 174
China Merchants' Steam Navigation Company (CMSNC; *Zhongguo lunchuan zhaoshangju*), 165–67
Chinese associations, 113, 116, 120–22
Chinese exclusion acts, 174
Chongqing, 179
Christianity
  ban on, 54
  George's trial and, 74
  missionaries, 56–57, 62, 105, 150
Cixi (empress dowager), 175
CMSNC. *See* China Merchants' Steam Navigation Company
colonies
  forms of law in, 6–7

  Japanese, 160
  in Southeast Asia, 163
commercial treaties, 4–7, 47, 84, 161. *See also* specific treaties
Communist Party, 178, 182–84
concessions, 55
Confucius, 16, 47
consular courts, 6, 100, 131, 172, 174
consular jurisdiction
  in China, 3–4, 13, 61, 81, 100–105, 143–44, 180
  extraterritoriality compared to, 153
  over homicide, 125–26
  in Japan, 13, 100–108, 113–14, 125, 130–31, 225n20
  Normanton incident and, 159
  strengthening of, 174
  Wang Tao against, 161
consuls, 91, 102, 105–6, 109–14
Cooke, George Wingrove, 57
"Coordinating Litigation Involving Military Personnel and Civilians," 21
corporal punishment, 162
counterfeit money, 117–19
Court of Colonial Affairs (*Lifanyuan*), 45, 162, 205n35
Court of Joint Trials, 72
Criminal Code, 34
criminal jurisdiction, 105–6, 219n3
Cushing, Caleb, 53, 90

Damström, Captain, 167
Daoguang reign, 27
Date Munenari, 104, *106*, 106–7
Davenport, Arthur, 166
Davidson, John Richard, 153
death sentences, 105–6
Deng Wei, 29
Deng Xiaoping, 184
Denison, Henry Willard, 129–30, 153
dialect-group organizations (*bang*), 113, 116, 120
Ding Ruchang
  in First Sino-Japanese War, 149
  in Nagasaki Incident, 135, 138, 141
Drake, John William, 159, 170
dress code, 105
Drummond, William Venn, 137, 165–67, 170–71
Duanfang, 175, 177
Du Yuesheng, 39
Dzereng, 25, 41

Eames, I. B., 165
East Asia, diplomatic order of, 4
East India Company (EIC), 42–43, 47
Egyptian mixed courts, 153–54
EIC. *See* East India Company
Eight Banners, 20–24
1895, turning point of, 160
Elements of International Law (Wheaton), 93–94, 103, 109
Elliot, Charles, 50
emigration, 87
English-language press, in treaty ports, 132, 222n81
envoys, Sino-Japanese cases and, 122–27, *123*
equal treaties, 60, 108
Escarra, Jean, 211n54
exclusion acts, Chinese, 174
exclusionary edicts, 85
expulsion edict (*Ikokusen uchiharai rei*), 85–86
"extend benefits equally" (*yiti junzhan*), 51
extraterritoriality. *See also* treaty revision
    Baba Tatsui attacking, 151–52, 161
    in China, 5–6, 10–11, 13, 39–84, 141–48, 160–81, 185, 225n20
    codified, 39–62
    colonial forms of law and, 6–7
    consular jurisdiction compared to, 153
    Guangzhou and, 42–43
    impracticality of, 161
    indeterminacy of, 4
    inequality of, 5
    Inoue Kaoru and, 133–35, 137–40, 143, 154–55, *156*, 158
    in Japan, 5, 7, 11–13, 63–84, 89–148, 180–81, 225n20
    justification of, 177
    in Korea, 5
    legal pluralism and, 12
    limited extension of, 153
    in Macau, 41–42
    most-favored-nation treatment and, 61, 101–4, 157, 216n87
    native legal order and, 6–8
    objections to, 160–62
    Peru and, 156–57
    as practice, 6
    public debate over, 150–52
    in Siam, 5
    in Sino-Japanese Treaty of Tianjin, 97–114, 131–32, 144–45, 180

terminology, 163
Wu Tingfang against, 161–62

Fairbank, John King, 10, 207n80
Fan Ximing, 110
feudalism, 202n114
First Opium War, 48–51
First Sino-Japanese War, 149, 172, 179
Forbes, Frank B., 3
foreign affairs officials, 162
forgery, 117–19
Forrest, R. J., 68, 70
France
    China and, 54, 56–58, 99
    commercial treaties with, 4
    Japan and, 90–91
French Concession, 65
Fukuchi Gen'ichirō, 154
Fukumoto Makoto, 141–42
Fukuwara Hanjūrō, 144–45
Fukuzawa Yukichi, 137
Furukawa Yoshimasa, 115, 125–26, 143
Fusing (*Fuxing*) incident, 164–66, 170–71, 227n112

Gabet, Joseph, 57
Geisenheimer, F., 118
General Regulations of Trade, 51–52
genocide, 176–77
George, Robert Willis, 73–77, 106, 142, 166
Giles, Herbert A., 83
globalization, 182, 185
Gong (prince), 70–71, 211n49
Gong Mujiu, 64
Guangxi province, 57
Guangzhou
    banner garrison, 23, 25
    extraterritoriality and, 42–43
    foreigners in, 55–58
    Kearny in, 51
    Treaty of, 55
guanxia terminology, 206n67
gunboat diplomacy, 84
Guomindang party, 178
Guo Songtao, 162–63
Guo Wanjun, 129, 133–34
Guo Weidong, 10, 207n76

Haley, John, 35
Hanabusa Yoshimoto, 98

Han Chinese
  Manchus and, 20–23, 176
  Mongols and, 19
  rule of, 183
Hannen, Nicholas John, 74, 165–66
Harris, Townsend, 89–91, 120
Harris Treaty, 90–91
Hatoyama Kazuo, 137
He Ruzhang, 109, 122, *123*, 127, 163
Heuschert, Dorothea, 198n25
hiring practices, on steamships, 226n87
homicide, consular jurisdiction over, 125–26
Hong Kong
  jurisdiction in, 101
  Supreme Court, 68
  Wu Tingfang in, 162
Hornby, Edmund, 68, 70, 74, 76, 165, 172
Hsü, Immanuel, 197n15
Huang Chengyi, 83
Huang Juezi, 48
Huang Zonghan, 58
Huc, Évariste, 56–57

Ii Naosuke, 91
Imperial Clan Court, 21
imperial nobility, prerogatives of, 176
Inner Asian frontier, foreign jurisdiction on, 43–45
inner lords, 30
Inoue Kaoru
  extraterritoriality and, 133–35, 137–40, 143, 154–55, *156*, 158
  treaty revision and, 154–55, *156*, 158
Inoue Kiyonao, 90
Inoue Masashi, 141–42
International Settlement, 65–66
Iwakura Tomomi, 93–94
Iwase Tadanari, 90

Japan. *See also* Meiji Japan; Sino-Japanese cases; Sino-Japanese Treaty of Tianjin; Tokugawa Japan
  Alcock and, 92–93, 132
  Ansei Treaties of, 88–94
  Bakufu in, 30–32, 85–94, 180
  Belgium and, 118
  Britain and, 90–93
  Chinese relations with, 11, 84, 86–88, 94–148
  colonies of, 160
  consular jurisdiction in, 13, 100–108, 113–14, 125, 130–31, 225n20
  Dutch dealings with, 85–87
  emigration and, 87
  English-language press in, 132
  extraterritoriality in, 5, 7, 11–13, 63–84, 89–148, 180–81, 225n20
  in First Sino-Japanese War, 149, 172, 179
  foreigners residing in, 150
  France and, 90–91
  jurisdiction in, 12, 31, 115–22, 130, 143–44, 219n3
  Korea and, 135
  legal pluralism in, 15, 29–38, 149–50, 160
  María Luz incident and, 156–58
  Mixed Court and, 98, 100, 142–43, 149, 154
  modern, 183
  movement limited in, 150
  opium and, 120–22, 126–27
  personal jurisdiction in, 12, 130
  Rules and Regulations for the Peace, Order, and Good Government of British Subjects within the Dominions of the Tycoon of Japan and, 92–93
  Russia and, 174
  Shanghai and, 113–14
  Sino-British Treaty of Tianjin and, 90
  state-building in, 29–38
  Treaty of Shimonoseki and, 13, 114, 149, 160
  treaty port system and, 85, 123–24, 160, 179
  U.S. and, 88–90, 183
Jardine & Matheson, 165–66
joint conferences, 17
joint trials, 24–25, 72, 120, 142
Judicature Acts, 151
judicial subprefect (*lishi tongzhi*)
  Chen Fuxun, 68, 83, 98, 109, 157, 165–66
  established, 22–27
  Mixed Court, 72–73, 77
  power of, 211n57
  translation of, 200n61, 201n92
jurisdiction. *See also* consular jurisdiction
  criminal, 105–6, 219n3
  in Hong Kong, 101
  in Japan, 12, 31, 115–22, 130, 143–44, 219n3
  in Nagasaki, 91–92
  Opium War and, 48–51
  personal, 9, 12, 130
  in Shanghai, 3–4
  terminology, 160–61, 206n67

Kang Youwei, 174–75
Kawakami Kin'ichi, 142
Kawazu Sukekuni, 97–98
Kearny, Lawrence, 51
Khoqand settlement, 45–46, 205n41
Kido Takayoshi, 33–34
Kirkwood, Montague, 137
Kobe, *Normanton* incident at, 159, 170
Komine Suzu, 125
Korea. *See also* First Sino-Japanese War
    commercial treaties with, 4, 84
    extraterritoriality in, 5
    legal order in, 8
    Sino-Japanese rivalry over, 135
Kotenev, Anatol, 72, 216n73
Kuhn, Philip A., 18
Kurokawa Koshirō, 135
Kusaka Yoshio, 135, 137

Lady Hughes case, 43
Lagrené, Théodore de, 53–54, 62
Land Regulations, 64
Lang, William, 138
lawyers, legality of, 170, 229n9
legal order
    in Korea, 8
    of Ming dynasty, 17–19, 21, 40
    native, 6–8
    of Qing Empire, 15–20, 36–39, 47, 59–60
    terminology, 161
    of Tokugawa Japan, 7–8, 30–31, 37
legal pluralism
    classical, 9
    Daoguang reign and, 27
    development of, 8–9
    extraterritoriality and, 12
    in Japan, 15, 29–38, 149–50, 160
    in Qing Empire, 15–20, 38–39, 149–50, 198n25
    terminology, 197n21, 198n10
legal reform, 174–76
legal sovereignty, 9
Lianrui, 29
Liao dynasty, 17
Li Hongzhang, 139, 170
    bureaucratic network of, 109, 162
    Chefoo Convention and, 78
    Sino-Japanese Treaty of Tianjin and, 97, 99–100, 104, 107–8
Liljevalch, Carl Fredrik, 55–56

Lin'gui, 65
Lin Weixi, 50, 74, 87, 161
Lin Zexu, 10, 48–50, 160, 204n19, 206n68
Li Pingshu, 163
Li Shuchang, 129, 133
literary examinations, 105
Liu Mingchuan, 167
Liu Yunke, 161
loyalty, to the emperor, 16

MacArthur, Douglas, 179
Macau
    extraterritoriality in, 41–42
    labor agreements signed in, 157
    Portuguese settlement at, 41–42, 204n29
Mackay Treaty, 175
Manchus. *See also* Qing Empire
    cities of, 28
    clan laws of, 200n45
    genocide of, 176–77
    Han Chinese and, 20–23, 176
    privilege of, 25–29, 163, 176, 180, 200n45
    in Qing dynasty, 20–22, 24–29
Margary, Augustus Raymond, 78, 109
María Luz incident, 156–58
Martin, W. A. P., 93–94, 103, 213n101
Mayers, William Frederick, 97
Medhurst, W. H., 165–66
Meiji Japan
    alien registration in, 96
    constitution of, 36
    Criminal Code of, 34
    legal pluralism in, 29–38
    María Luz incident and, 156–58
    Meiji restoration and, 5, 7, 13, 32, 203n154
    modern society of, 35–36
    secretive criminal procedure of, 133
    treaty revision in, 93–94, 149–78
Meiji restoration, 5, 7, 13, 32, 203n154
Merry, Sally, 9
Mine Susumu, 128–29, 134–35
Ming dynasty, legal order of, 17–19, 21, 40
missionaries, 56–57, 62, 105, 150
mixed cases, 23, 31–32, 62, 72
    with Chinese associations, 120
    obligation to carry out, 142
Mixed Court, 4, 14, 105–6
    of Appeal, 67
    Chen Fuxun of, 68, 83, 98, 109, 157, 165–66
    corporal punishment and, 162

Mixed Court (*continued*)
   end of, 178
   importance of, 82
   Japanese and, 98, 100, 142–43, 149, 154
   lawyers legalized at, 170
   location, 69
   model for, 180
   Parkes and, 56–59, 66–67, 96
   precursor to, 211n54
   reciprocal, 108
   reform, 77–80
   rules, 69–73, 157
   struggle over, 172–74, *173*
   Subao case in, 173–74
   subprefect, 72–73, 77
   Ying Baoshi and, 161
mixed courts
   collaboration with, 172
   defined, 225n27
   in Egypt, 153–54
   Ocean incident and, 165
Möller, Eric, 14
Möller, Nils, 3–4, 14, 185
Mongols, 17–19, 21, 176
Montigny, Charles de, 64
Mori Arinori, 119, 126
Moss, Michael, 92
most-favored-nation treatment, 61, 101–4, 157, 216n87
Movement for People's Freedom and Rights, 150, 152, 155, 158
Mo Xiangzhi, 142–43
Mujangga, Grand Councilor, 56, 64
Municipal Jail, 174
Mutsu Munemitsu, 159–60
Mutual Security Assistance Pact, 183

Nagasaki
   Affair of 1883, 127–35
   Chinese in, 85, 95–97, 110, 113, 115–17, 125–41
   Dutch in, 85–87
   Incident of 1886, 135–41, *136*, *139*
   jurisdiction in, 91–92
   Land Regulations, 96
   Magistrate, 32
   police, 110, 127–30, 136–37, 140
   Wu A'er case in, 115
Namamugi incident, 93
Napier, William, 48

National Diet, 159
Nationalists, Chinese, 178
nation-state, Westphalian, 182
Neo-Confucianism, 18, 30
Nepaul, 167, 172
Netherlands, Japan and, 85–87
Niu Chunbin, 117
Norman, Arthur, 127
Normanton incident, 158–59, 170–71
Norway. *See* Sweden-Norway

Ōba Osamu, 87
occupational caste, 176
Ocean incident, 164–66
Ōkubo Toshimichi, 152
Ōkuma Shigenobu, 159
Omoto Jūtarō, 144–45
opium
   addiction, 48
   China and, 48, 53–54, 120–22
   Japan against, 120–22, 126–27
   in Nagasaki Affair of 1883, 128–29
   Russia and, 120
   U.S. and, 53–54
Opium War
   First, 48–51
   jurisdiction and, 48–51
   outbreak of, 87
   Second, 58, 140
Ōtsu incident, 159
Ottoman Empire, 12
outer lords, 30

Papua New Guinea, 8–9
Parkes, Harry, 33, 97, 117, 150
   Bankoku shimbun and, 158
   Mixed Court and, 56–59, 66–67, 96
People's Republic of China, 179, 182–83, 203n158
Perry, Matthew, 88–89
personal jurisdiction
   in China, 12
   defined, 9
   in Japan, 12, 130
Peru, 156–57
pluralism. *See* legal pluralism
police, Nagasaki, 110, 127–30, 136–37, 140
Portuguese, in Macau, 41–42, 204n29
Pottinger, Henry, 50–51
Prebble, F. N., 73–74

preliminary inquest, 133–34
Prussian constitution, 36
public debate, over extraterritoriality, 150–52
Pumpelly, Raphael, 164, 215n41

Qianlong policy, 41–42
Qing Empire. *See also* Zongli Yamen
    Code of, 16, 18–19, 40–41, 47, 59, 62, 72, 134, 162, 206n50
    commercial treaties with, 4
    corruption of, 11
    emigration and, 87
    foreigners in, 40–43, 46–55
    Inner Asian frontier of, 43–45
    judicial subprefect established in, 22–27
    Khoqand settlement of, 45–46, 205n41
    legal order of, 15–20, 36–39, 47, 59–60
    legal pluralism in, 15–20, 38–39, 149–50, 198n25
    Manchus under, 20–22, 24–29
    sinicization and, 18, 28
    subjecthood in, 15–20
    terminology, 111
    treaty draft by, 101–4
    treaty revision in, 149–78
    as unitary state, 17
Qishan, 57
Qiying, 11, 54, 60

reform
    attempts, 152–55
    Chefoo Convention and, 77–80
    legal, 174–76
Regina vs. George, 73–77
regulations of amity, 104
Republican revolution, 176–78
revision, treaty
    Britain and, 159–60
    by China, 160–78
    He Ruzhang and, 163
    Inoue Kaoru and, 154–55, *156*, 158
    legal reform and, 174–76
    in Meiji Japan, 93–94, 149–78
    by Mutsu Munemitsu, 159–60
    public debate over, 150–52
    in Qing Empire, 149–78
    reform attempts, 152–55
    Republican revolution and, 176–78
    Sino-Japanese Treaty of Tianjin and, 181
    struggle over Mixed Court and, 172–74, *173*

Terajima Munenori and, 154, 158
of Treaties of Tianjin, 49, 61–62
of unequal treaties, 160, 218n125
Zongli Yamen and, 130, 153, 161
Richardson, C. L., 93
Roches, Léon, 32–33
Romanov Empire, 43–45
rules, Mixed Court, 69–73, 157
Rules and Regulations for the Peace, Order, and Good Government of British Subjects within the Dominions of the Tycoon of Japan and, 92–93
Russia
    Alexander II of, 157
    China and, 43–45, 60, 204n29
    equal treaties of, 60
    Japan and, 174
    opium and, 120
    revolutions of 1917, 177–78
    Romanov Empire of, 43–45

Sacred Edict, 16, 22
Saigō Takamori, 35
Saitō Chikudō, 88
samurai
    in Movement for People's Freedom and Rights, 150
    privilege of, 34–35
Satow, Ernest, 92
Scripta Sinica database, 199n41, 201n92
Second Opium War, 58, 140
Seward, George F., 81, 212n76
Shanghai. *See also* Mixed Court
    British Supreme Court in, 63–84, 105–6, 142, 165–66
    consular courts in, 6
    emergence of, 64–69
    gangster age of, 177
    Japanese in, 113–14
    jurisdiction over, 3–4
    legal system, 63, 66
    Sino-Japanese murder case in, 141–48, *146–47*
    in treaty port system, 64
Shenbao, 171–72
Shen Bingyuan, 67
Shen Guanfu, 144, *146–47*
Shen Jiaben, 175–76
Siam, extraterritoriality in, 5
Siebold incident, 86, 213n8

Sinclair, Charles A., 223n150
sinicization, 18, 28
Sino-British Treaty of Tianjin
   article 16, 59, 75, 78–79
   article 17, 166
   article 50, 79
   Japan and, 90
   new, 179
Sino-Japanese cases
   envoys and, 122–27, *123*
   Japanese jurisdiction over Chinese, 115–22
   Nagasaki Affair of 1883, 127–35
   Nagasaki Incident of 1886, 135–41, *136*, *139*
   Shanghai murder case, 141–48, *146–47*
   Wu A'er, 115, 125–26, 143
   Yokohama, 117–19
Sino-Japanese Treaty of Tianjin, 11–13, 84, 126
   article 8, 105
   article 11, 105
   article 13, 105, 124, 131, 142–44
   contradictions in, 124–25
   extraterritoriality in, 97–114, 130–32, 144–45, 180
   impermanence of, 148, 181
   implementation of, 135, 163, 181
   importance of, 181–82
   interpretation of, 135, 142
   Li Hongzhang and, 97, 99–100, 104, 107–8
   monographs, 219n159
   Qing draft, 101–4
   treaty port system and, 160
   treaty revision and, 181
   Yanagihara draft, 98–103
Sino-Japanese War, First, 149, 172, 179
Soejima Taneomi, 107–8, 157
Songyun, 46
Southeast Asia, colonies in, 163
state-building projects, 8, 29–38, 203n143
status system
   abolished, 13, 18
   foreigners and, 40–43
   groups in, 30
steamship hiring practices, 226n87
Straw Shoe Channel, 164, 226n80
Subao case, 173–74
subjecthood, in Qing Empire, 15–20
subprefect. *See* judicial subprefect
Supreme Court, British
   in Hong Kong, 68
   Ocean incident and, 165–66
   in Shanghai, 63–84, 105–6, 142, 165–66

Surprise, 164
Sweden-Norway, 3, 55, 227n114
synarchy, 27

Taiping Rebellion, 57, 65
Taiwan, 160
Takasugi Shinsaku, 97
Tang Code, 34, 40
Tang Jingxing (Tong King-sing), 165–66
Tani Kanjō, 155
tariff autonomy, 163
Tei Einei, 98, *106*, 108–9, 120
Temple, Henry John, 50
Terajima Munenori, 107, 110, 119
   opium and, 126–27
   treaty revision and, 154, 158
territorial sovereignty, 46
Tibet, 19, 37
Tientsin Massacre, 99
Tokugawa Ieyoshi, 88
Tokugawa Japan
   arrests in, 129
   commercial treaties with, 4
   feudalism in, 202n114
   jurisdiction in, 31
   legal order in, 7–8, 30–31, 37
   legal pluralism in, 29–38
   secretive criminal procedure of, 133
Tokugawa Nariaki, 89
torture, 151
treaties. *See also* treaty port system; treaty revision; unequal treaties; *specific treaties*
   commercial, 4–7, 47, 84, 161
   equal, 60, 108
   as regulations of amity, 104
Treaties of Tianjin, 71, 75, 78, 84, 90. *See also* Sino-British Treaty of Tianjin; Sino-Japanese Treaty of Tianjin
   1858–60, 55–61
   justice and, 59
   language and, 59–60, 79–80
   reciprocity and, 13
   revisions, 49, 61–62
The Treaty between Japan and England (Baba Tatsui), 151
Treaty of Guangzhou, 55
Treaty of Huangpu, 54
Treaty of Kiakhta, 43–44
Treaty of Mutual Cooperation and Security, 183
Treaty of Nanjing, 50, 55–56, 60

Treaty of Nerchinsk, 43
Treaty of Shimonoseki, 13, 114, 149, 160
Treaty of the Bogue, 52–53, 59, 131
Treaty of Wangxia, 53
treaty port system
    controversies of, 5–6
    English-language press in, 132, 222n81
    Japan and, 85, 123–24, 160, 179
    Qing legal order in, 37–38
    Shanghai in, 64
    Sino-Japanese Treaty of Tianjin and, 160
    understanding of, 11
treaty revision
    Britain and, 159–60
    by China, 160–78
    He Ruzhang and, 163
    Inoue Kaoru and, 154–55, *156*, 158
    legal reform and, 174–76
    in Meiji Japan, 93–94, 149–78
    by Mutsu Munemitsu, 159–60
    public debate over, 150–52
    in Qing Empire, 149–78
    reform attempts, 152–55
    Republican revolution and, 176–78
    Sino-Japanese Treaty of Tianjin and, 181
    struggle over Mixed Court and, 172–74, *173*
    Terajima Munenori and, 154, 158
    of Treaties of Tianjin, 49, 61–62
    of unequal treaties, 160, 218n125
    Zongli Yamen and, 130, 153, 161
Tsuda Mamichi, 103, 106, *106*, 151
Tsuruhara Sadayoshi, 144
Tu Zongying, 98–99

unequal treaties, 5, 148, 182–83
    extraterritoriality codified in, 39–52
    foreigners' status and, 40–43
    mass popular politics and, 151
    revised, 160, 218n125
    United States (U.S.)
    China and, 53–54, 56, 65, 71–72, 174
    Chinese exclusion acts of, 174
    commercial treaties with, 4
    Japan and, 88–90, 183
    opium and, 53–54

Victoria (queen), 10, 160
Villiers, George, 76
Vyse, F. Howard, 153

Wade, Thomas, 59, 75–76, 78

Wainewright, Robert Earnest, 165–66, 172
Wakabayashi, Bob, 89
Wang Aran, 73–74
Wang Fa, 135
Wang Tao, 11, 161
Wan Nien Ching (*Wannian qing*) incident, 167, 168–69, 170–71, 227n112
Wei Pengcheng, 128
Wei Xiangshu, 23
Wei Yi'ao, 128
Wellington Koo, V.K., 42, 45, 205n37
Wenxiang, 10, 61, 99
Westphalian nation-state, 182
Wheaton, Henry, 93–94, 103, 109
William II, 88
Winchester, Charles A., 98
World War I, 177
Wu A'er, 115, 125–26, 143
Wu Tingfang
    against extraterritoriality, 161–62
    legal reform by, 175
    Republican revolution and, 177
Wu Xu, 67, 97

Xinjiang, 19
Xu Chengzu, 134, 137–40
Xu Chunfu, 141–42
Xue Huan, 97

Yafu, 117–18
Yamada Akiyoshi, 108–9
Yanagihara Sakimitsu, 108–9, 118
    in Date delegation, 106, *106*
    treaty draft by, 98–103
Yang Naiwu case, 171
Yang Shu, 137
Yangtze River, 164
Ye Mingchen, 56
Ying Baoshi, 69, 97–98, 101–4, 161
Yinghan, 99–100
Yinghe, 27
Yokohama
    forgery case, 117–19
    María Luz at, 156–58
    Normanton incident and, 159
    opium in, 121–22
Yoshinobu, 32–33
Yuan dynasty, 17
Yuan Shuxun, 144
Yu Qiong, 110, 115, 134

Zaifeng, 176
Zeng Guofan, 98–101, 124, 164
Zhang Binglin, 173–74
Zhang Deyi, 203n140
Zhang Jixin, 27
Zhang Sigui, 109, 122
Zheng Renrui, 117
Zheng Xiaoxu, 113, 219n155
Zheng Yongning. *See* Tei Einei

Zhu Xi, 117–20
Zhu Yuanzhang, 17–18
Zongli Yamen, 70, 81–82, 94, 97
    Alcock Convention negotiated by, 99
    George's execution and, 106
    lawyers and, 170
    treaty revision and, 130, 153, 161
    Zhu Xi and, 119–20
Zou Rong, 173–74

Mary, Millie, & Morgan

knitted dolls & clothes

by Susan B. Anderson

quince&co.

Quince & Company, Inc
quinceandco.com

Copyright © 2015 Susan B. Anderson

Photographs © 2015 Quince & Company, Inc

All rights reserved. No part of this book may be reproduced, in any form or by any means, without prior permission of the copyright holders. For personal use only.

Printed in the United States by Franklin Printing, powered by wind.